Native American Herbalist's Bible
15 Books in 1

The Complete Guide with 500+ Herbal Medicines & Plant Remedies. Build Your Apothecary Table And Improve Your Health.

By Drina Kaulja

Table of Content

- Table of Content ... 2
- BOOK 1 The Native American HerbalApothecary ... 2
- Introduction to Native's ... 3
  - Medicinal Art ... 3
  - Native People Were Skilled Hunters, Artisans and Warriors,But their Talents Did Not Stop There. ... 5
- Plants & Herbs ProcurementMethods ... 8
  - Wildcrafting: ... 8
  - Benefits of wildcrafting ... 8
  - How to select sites ... 9
- BOOK 2 ... 13
- The Native American Herbal Remedies ... 13
- The Secrets of Native American's ... 14
- Herbal Remedies ... 14
  - The Medicine Wheel and the Four Directions ... 16
- Book 3 Native AmericanPlants ... 18
- Native Plants ... 19
  - Agave (or Mescal) ... 19
  - Alder ... 21
  - Aloe ... 23
  - Amaranth ... 25
  - Balsam Fir ... 27
  - Bearberry ... 28
  - Black Haw ... 30
  - Blueberry ... 31
  - Cascara Sagrada (Buckthorn) ... 33
  - Cranberry ... 34
  - Devil's Club ... 36

- Elderberry ... 37
- Ginseng ... 39
- Hawthorn ... 41
- Honeysuckle ... 43
- Juniper ... 44
- Lady's Slipper ... 46
- Wild American Licorice ... 47

Book 4 ... 49

Native Plants ... 50

- Maple ... 50
- Oak ... 51
- Oregon Grape ... 53
- Plantain ... 54
- Prickly Pear ... 55
- Purslane ... 56
- Red Root ... 57
- Slippery Elm ... 59
- Usnea ... 60
- White Poplar ... 61
- Willow ... 62
- Yew ... 63
- Yucca ... 64

BOOK 5 ... 66

The Native American Herbal Apothecary Ancient Traditions, Secrets and Modern Uses ... 66

- Angelica ... 69
- Wild Anise ... 71
- Balsam Root ... 72
- Black Cohosh ... 73
- Bloodroot ... 75
- Boneset ... 76
- California Poppy ... 77

Centaury 78

Catnip 79

Cattail 80

Chamomile 81

Corn 83

Dandelion 84

Echinacea 86

BOOK 6 88

The Native American HerbalApothecary Ancient Traditions, Secrets and Modern Uses Part II 88

Feverfew 89

Wild Ginger 91

Goldenrod 92

Goldenseal 93

Gravel Root 95

Heal-All 96

Horsetail 97

Lemon Balm 98

Mayapple 100

Milkweed 101

Mullein 103

Nettle 104

Oregon Grape 107

Osha Root 108

Pasque Flower 110

Passionflower 111

Peppermint 113

Evening Primrose 114

Red Clover 116

Sage Shrub 117

Saint John's Wort 118

Senega Snakeroot 120

Valerian 121

Watercress 123

Witch Hazel 124

Wormwood 126

Yarrow 128

Yellow Dock 130

Zizia Aurea 131

BOOK 7 133

The Curative Properties of Herbs 133

Properties of Herbs 134

Definitions 134

PHYTOCHEMICALS 137

Alkaloids 137

Anthocyanidins 137

Chlorophyll 138

Diterpenes 138

Eleutherosides 138

Enzymes 138

Essential Fatty Acids 138

Flavonglycosides 139

Gingerols 139

Ginkolic Acid 139

Glycyrrhizins 139

Hesperidin 139

Hypericin 139

Isothiocyanates 139

Lactones 139

Lipoic Acid 139

Phenolic Acids 140

Phthalides 140

Polyacetylenes 140

Proanthocyanins 140

Quercetin 140

Rosemarinic Acid 140

Salin 140

Salin, or salicin, is found in white willow bark. It fights inflammation, relieves pain and fever, and fights the influenza virus. 140

Saponins 140

Silymarin 140

Tannins 141

Terpenes 141

Triterpenoids 141

BOOK 8 142

The Native American Ancient Remedies 142

Introduction 143

Plants and Uses 144

SomeSelected Plants and Their Uses by Native Americans 144

Blackberries 145

Cattail 145

Chamomile 145

Clover of the Red 146

Claw of the Devil 146

Feverfew (The Leaf) 146

Garlic (Root Cloves) 146

Ginger (The Root) 146

Goldenseal 147

Goldenseal 147

Ginger of the Wild 147

Greenbriar 147

Honeysuckle 147

Hummingbird Blossom 147

- Lavender 148
- Licorice 148
- Mint 148
- Mullein 148
- Prickly Pear 148
- Rosemary 148
- Rose of the Wild 148
- Rosy Periwinkle 148
- Sage 149
- Salix (Willow) 149
- Saint John's Wort 149
- Slippery Elm 149
- Sumac 149
- Uva Ursi 149
- Valerian (The Root) 149
- Yew 150

Five Essential Methods to Start with Herbal Preparations 151

- Making Teas, Infusions and Decoctions 151
- How to Prepare Herbal Teas 151
- How to Prepare Infusions 151
- An Example of a Hot Infusion 151
- How to Prepare Decoctions 152
- Tincturing Herbs 152
- How to Make a Medicinal Syrup 154
- How to Make Oleolites (Oil Infusions) for Ointments and Salves 154
- Benefits of Oleolite: 155

BOOK 9 156

Ancient Traditions and Secrets of Herbal Medicine 156

HOW TO CHOOSE THE RIGHT OIL TO PREPARE AN OIL INFUSION: THE MOST USED OILS 157

- How to Make Ointments and Salves 157

- Using Whole Herbs 159
- Ancient Remedies 160
  - Skin and Gum 160
  - Abscesses Remedies 160
  - Herbal Mouthwash 160
  - Antioxidant Tea 160
  - Happy Memory Tea 160
  - Allergies Relief Remedies 160
  - Nettle Tea 161
  - Anemia Remedies 161
  - Arthritis Remedies 161
  - Bedtime Tea 162
  - ARTHRITIS OINTMENT 162
  - Asthma Remedies 163
  - Goodbreath Tea 163
  - Bedsores Remedies 163
  - Bite Remedies 163
  - TOPICAL WASH FOR BITES 163
  - SKIN SOOTHING OINTMENT 163
  - Remedies for Bronchitis and ThroatInflamation 164
  - THROAT-SOOTHING TEA 165
  - BRONCHITIS TEA 165
  - Sunburn Remedies 165
  - SOOTHING BURN SALVE 165
  - IMMUNITY BOOSTER 166
  - Canker Sores Remedies 166
  - Cold Sores Remedies 167
  - COLD SORE BALM 167
  - IMMUNITY BOOSTER 167
  - Constipation Remedies 168
  - BOWEL-SOOTHING TEA 168

DIGESTIVE TEA	168
BOWEL-HYDRATING INFUSION	168
Colds and Cough Remedies	168
LUMBEE COUGH AND COLD FORMULA	169
COUGH SYRUP	169
FLOWER TEA	169
COUGH AND COLD INFUSION	169
Cramps Remedies	169
MUSCLE RUB	170
MUSCLE CRAMP TEA	170
Diarrhea Remedies	171
ASTRINGENT TEA	171
TEA	171
Fatigue Remedies	171
REVITALIZING TEA	172
UPLIFTING INFUSION	172
Fever Remedies	172
REVITALIZING TEA	172
Headache Remedies	173
Reflux/Heartburn Remedies	173
Hypertension Remedies	174
HEALTHY HEART HERBAL TEA	174
Indigestion/Dyspepsia Remedies	174
CARMINATIVE TINCTURE	175
DIGESTIVE TEA	175
Insomnia Remedies	175
Menstrual Cycle Irregularities and DisturbsRemedies	176
Nausea and Vomiting Remedies	176
Rash Remedies	177
Sinusitis Remedies	177
Sore Throat Remedies	178

- Sprains and Strains Remedies 179
- Stress 179
- Wounds Remedies 180

BOOK 10 185

The Native American Ancient Remedies 185

Ancient Traditions and Secrets of Herbal Medicine 185

Ancient Uses and Preparations of Plants and Herbs in Native American's Traditions 186

- Angelica 187
- Balsam Root 188
- Bearberry 189
- Bearberry can be taken internally as a tea: 189
- Black Berries 189
- Black Cohosh 190
- Bloodroot 191
- Boneset 192
- Black Cherry 192
- California Poppy 194
- Catnip 195
- Cat's Claw 196
- Cattail 196
- Centaury 198
- Centaury tea Cold extract: 198
- Chamomile 199
- Chokecherry 200
- Corn 201
- Dandelion 202
- Dogwood 203
- Echinacea 204
- Elderflower 205
- Wild Ginger 206
- Ginseng 206

Goldenrod 206

Goldenseal 207

Gooseberry 209

BOOK 11 210

The Native American Ancient Remedies 210

Ancient Traditions and Secrets of Herbal Medicine Part II 210

Gravel Root 211

Hawthorn 211

Heal-All 211

Horsetail 212

Hops 213

Indian Tobacco 213

Juniper 214

Lavander 215

Licorice 217

Lemon Balm 218

Magnolia 219

Mayapple 219

Maple 219

Marshmallow 221

Milkweed 223

Mullein 223

Nettle 224

Oak 225

Oats 225

Oregon Grape 226

Osha Root 227

Pasque Flower 227

Passionflower 228

Peppermint 229

Persimmon 231

Pine	231
Plantain	233
Evening Primrose	234
Prickly Pear Cactus	234
Purslane	235
Raspberry	236
Rabbit Tobacco	237
Ragleaf Bahia	237
Red Clover	238
Rosemary	238
Cooking Uses	239
Rosemary tea	239
Sage Shrub	240
St. John's Wort	241
Sassafras	243
Squaw Weed	244
Saw Palmetto	244
Seneca Snakeroot	245
Skullcap	245
Slippery Elm	247
Spruce	248
Stoneseed	248
Valerian	249
Violet	249
Watercress	250
Witch Hazel	251
White Pine	252
Wormwood	254
Yarrow	255
Yellow Dock	256
Yew	257

    Zizia Aurea 257

Book 12 258

The Native American Ancient Remedies 258

Some Other Specific Remedies 258

Handed Down by the Natives 259

    (Native American Apache Blessing) 259

    Analgesic Tea 259

    Warming Compress for Back Pain 259

    Soothing Back Pain Tea 260

    Tummy Tea 260

    Anti-stress Tonic Tea 260

    Aches and Pain Blend 261

    Cough Formula 261

    Burns Healing Internal Formula 262

BOOK 13 263

The Native American Practices 263

    Sacred Rituals and Ceremonies to be connected with Nature and all its Elements and Creatures 263

Chapter 1 : Native American Rituals and Ceremonies 264

    The Life Vision 264

    Lakota Worldview and Spirituality 267

    The Ceremonies 269

    The Sweat Lodge 269

    Yuwipi - The Rite of the Sacred Stone 271

    Hanblecheya – Vision Quest 272

    The Sacred Pipe 273

    Native Dances 273

    Associative dances 274

    Fantasy Dance 275

    Ghost Dance - A Promise of Fulfillment 275

    Snake Dance 275

- Rain Dance 276
- Stomp Dance 277
- Sun Dance 277
- Apache Sun Dance 278
- War Dance 278
- Pumpkin Dance 279
- Grass Dance 279
- Hoop Dance 280
- The Medicine Wheel for Self-understanding 281

BOOK 14 283
The Native American Practices Part II 283
- Sacred Rituals and Ceremonies to be connected with Nature and all its Elements and Creatures 283
- Connection with Cardinal Points 284
- Connection to the West Force 285
- Connection to the East Force 285
- Connection to the South Force 286
- The Four Forces and Colors 287
- Force of the North 288
- Force of the West 288
- Force of the East 288
- Force of the south 288
- Wakan Tanka 289
- The Four Elements 289
- Air Earth Fire 289
- Every Element is Spirit 290
- The Animal Totems 290
- Connection with the Air Element 293
- Connection with the Earth Element 295
- Connection with the Center 297
- Connection with the Fire Element 298

- Connection with the Water Element 299
- Connecting with the Inner Center 299

BOOK 15 301
Native American Remedies 301
Common Diseases and Herbal Solutions 301
Entering the Realm of Herbal Remedies 302
- Abscess and Gingivitis 303
- Aging 304
- Allergies 305
- Anemia 306
- Arthritis 306
- Herbal Allies for Arthritis 307
- Asthma 308
- Bedsores 308
- Bites and Stings 309
- Bronchitis 311
- Burns and Sunburns 311
- Herbal Allies for Burns and Sunburns 312
- Canker Sores 313
- Cold Sores 313
- Constipation 314
- Colds 316
- Cramps 316
- Diarrhea 317
- Fatigue 318
- Headache 319
- Reflux/Heartburn 320
- Hypertension 320
- Indigestion/Dyspepsia 321
- Insomnia 322
- Menstrual Cycle Irregularities 324

Nausea and Vomiting ... 324
Herbal Allies for Nausea and Vomiting ... 325
Rash ... 325
Sinusitis ... 327
Sore Throat ... 327
Herbal Allies for Sore Throat ... 328
Sprains and Strains ... 328
Stress ... 329
Herbal Allies for Stress ... 330

CONCLUSION ... 333

© Copyright 2022 by Drina Kaulja - All rights reserved.

The following Book is reproduced below with the goal of providing information that is as accurate andreliable as possible. Regardless, purchasing this Book can be seen as consent to the fact that both the publisher and the author of this book are in no way experts on the topics discussed within and that any recommendations or suggestions that are made herein are for entertainment purposes only.

Professionals should be consulted as needed prior to undertaking any of the action endorsed herein. This declaration is deemed fair and valid by both the American Bar Association and the Committee of Publishers Association and is legally binding throughout the United States. Furthermore, the transmission, duplication, or reproduction of any of the following work including specific information will be considered an illegal act irrespective of if it is done electronically or in print. This extends to creating a secondary or tertiary copy of the work or a recorded copy and is only allowed with the express written consent from thePublisher. All additional right reserved. The information in the following pages is broadly considered a truthful and accurate account of facts and as such, any inattention, use, or misuse of the information in question by the reader will render any resulting actions solely under their purview. There are no scenarios in which the publisher or the original author of this work can be in any fashion deemed liable for any hardship or damages that may befall them after undertaking information described herein. Additionally, the information in the following pages is intended only for informational purposes and should thus be thought of as universal. As befitting its nature, it is presented without assurance regarding its prolonged validity or interim quality. Trademarks that are mentioned are done without written consent and can in no way be considered an endorsement from the trademark holder.

BOOK 1
The Native American HerbalApothecary

Introduction to Native's

Medicinal Art

The underlying principle of all Native American medicinal, physical, and spiritual care is harmony between people and the environment. For them, thephysical, mental, emotional, cultural, and environmental components all played a role in the well-being of the individual and the community as a whole.

The connection with Nature and the relationship with Mother Earth were thefundamental principles of Native's culture. They believed that balance, necessary for healthy living, was the result of harmony between oneself andthe world. In recent years, even science has recognized this condition as the foundation for our mental and physical well-being.

Native people lived a life of natural interdependence in the forests, plains, and coastal regions. Depending on the area, Indians used wild plant species as food. According to the seasons, game was used as food, to make clothing,tools, and decorations.

They held in the highest consideration all the elements that made up their world, including animals, the botanical and mineral kingdom, and the weather. They treated every being with reverence, honoring with ceremoniesand rituals even the wild animals they hunted for food and clothing.

It was their way of expressing appreciation for the kindness of the Great Spirit, who was responsible for all living things. For them, disharmony withMother Nature would have terrible repercussions.

An Indian who gathered herbs or hunted animals would sing songs or prayersand give tobacco offerings to the spirits of the animals or plants, as a sign of recognition and gratitude, the lack of which would cause sickness and misfortune.

This mystical approach to nature and the environment seems alien andforgotten in the modern Western approach.

However, in recent years the ancient wisdom and holistic worldview is beingrediscovered and reawakened.

The traditions and wellness values of Native American tribes are linked totheir medicine.

Although some of these traditions exist today in some tribes, this book is primarily articulated on historical sources versus current traditions. In many Native American tribes, health care has historically focused on the principle of harmony in every area of life. Illnesses were considered as the result of inconsistency in one or more areas of existence. For Native people, consequently, disease could have concomitant natural as well as spiritual causes, and their medicinal treatments were intended to address both.

The tradition of Native American medicine dates back thousands of years, but their rituals were passed down orally, as most tribes never produced a written language.

Before Europeans began gathering on the American mainland in the 16th century, no outsider had ever been able to discover these customs.

The first written record of the herbs that Native Americans used and how they were used dates back to the first contact between Europeans and the tribes, who inhabited the east coast of North America.

Unfortunately, there are no written records of herbal use prior to that time that document exactly when and how they began healing with herbs.

In addition, most Native of the time had no desire to share their knowledge, which was considered sacred, with foreigners outside the tribe.

The adaptable and variable existence of Native American herbalism meant that no encyclopaedic medicinal work could be published. The currently available records of Native American medicinal art represent but a small portion of Native American Medicine as a whole.

However, these instances can be observed to recognize folk patterns and customs and experience their principles in one's own life.

There are still more than two hundred botanicals in use in pharmaceuticals initially discovered and produced by Native Americans. Their herbs have been widely marketed as supplements and remedies.

Today, many over-the-counter medicines are synthetic duplicates of natural herbal compounds, or made from naturally grown herbs. Progress in medical research have had an enormous effect on our lives, for better or worse.

Modern drugs are expensive, not only economically but especially in terms of long-term well-being. If the body is made dependent on the use of drugs, without action being taken to restore its balance, a gradual process of deterioration and worsening of health is set in motion.

Taking an antibiotic, which destroys the bacteria responsible for the disease, is a rational short-term solution, but it is a lost cause in the long run, as the body is constantly exposed to an infinite number of bacteria.

Antibiotics are only a temporary protection, although they are very useful to fight certain infections. They do not help the body to improve its defenses and avoid new pathogens.

According to the Natives, the best solutions were those that allowed the body to heal itself in addition to immediate assistance. They also contemplated the spiritual aspect of healing that strengthened the body as well as the mind and emotions through meditation, imagination and a series of healing rituals, making recovery much easier. Today, these principles are observed and recognized by a growing number of practitioners.

The recent increase in "alternative" methods of healing and the use of meditation harkens back to Native American wisdom, although it took hundreds of years for it to be rediscovered and integrated. Herbs and other "natural" medicines, imagination, meditation and body practices.

Native People Were Skilled Hunters, Artisans and Warriors, But their Talents Did Not Stop There.

Native Americans were well known among early settlers for their supposedly impressive healing abilities, but historians have documented little of these accounts, perhaps due to ethnic biases and relying on the assumption that the "savages" were Native Americans. However, accounts of Native American medical abilities began to circulate orally and were reported in colonial diaries and journals. While it is true that Native people were skilled hunters, tool makers, and warriors, their talents were greater than that.

Until recently, there was no mention of their remarkable abilities as healers. Native Americans were well known among early settlers for their supposedly impressive healing abilities, but historians have documented little of these accounts, perhaps due to ethnic biases and the assumption that "savages" were Native Americans. However, accounts of Native American medical abilities began to circulate orally and were reported in colonial diaries and journals.

When Western colonialism brought Americans of European descent into contact with new environments and the resulting injuries and diseases in the 1800s, indigenous tribes often provided settlers with the medicinal herbs that were necessary for their survival.

The writings of all of our great explorers, surgeons, and naturalists, such as Leonard Mc Phail & William Bartram, Meriwether Lewis & William Clark, include references to American Indians' knowledge and use of these plants to treat wounds and diseases.

During the Civil War, for example, the leaves and bark of white oak (Quercus alba), local plants such as dogwood (Cornus spp.), sassafras (Sassafras albidum), ptarmigan (Mitchella repens), and Liriodendron tulipifera (tulip trees) equipped field surgeons with a repertoire of medicines for treating wounded soldiers.

The Indians had no difficulty in choosing the most suitable plant for the plant cure, or the time when it should be harvested to be most effective.

They knew how to treat ailments of both physical, surgical and spiritual nature, with skills that surpassed modern medical teachings.

They used steam baths for many ailments.

They used sweat lodges to purify themselves and remove toxicities. The rootsof herbs were pounded finely and used as a poultice for cuts and sprains.Coca leaves were used to relieve pain.

The Indian art of healing was ceremonial in nature. Dances, chants andcelebrations were conducted to heal the patient according to symptomatologyand disease condition.

Plants growing wild in fields and forests were used for food and medicinal purposes as well as for dyes, textiles and to make baskets, brushes, ropes and decorations.

Herbs were also used in sacred ceremonies, for purification and to activate vision.

Listed in this book are the herbs that historically have been used the most to treat the ailments under consideration.

In discovering the healing herbs used by Native Americans, one must beaware of their spiritual beliefs, which are closely intertwined with and interpenetrate the daily life of a Native American.

Their medicine is the combined healing of body, mind, heart and spirit. For Native peoples, the word medicine not only describes a preparation such as acapsule, pill or surgery, it refers primarily to the greater "power" from whichthe cure is derived.

For the purification of body, mind, and spirit, herbs were often burned insmudges, bundles of herbs that are burned like incense.

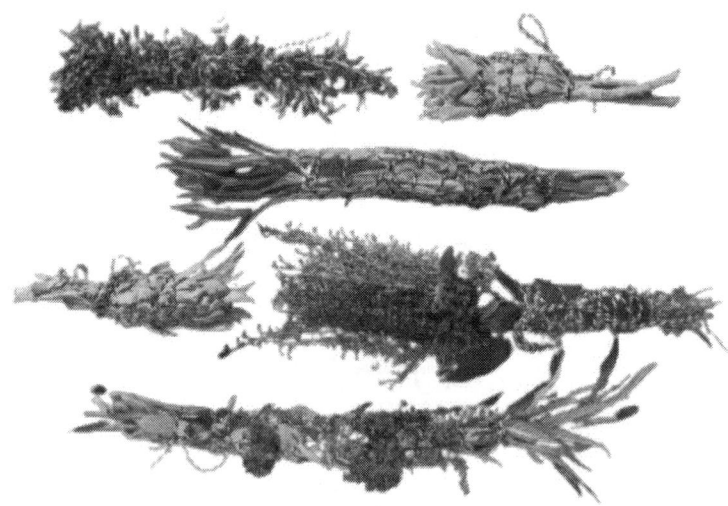

Some of the most popular herbs used to honor the spirits and elements were aromatics, including white sage, copal incense, cedar, juniper, mesquite, pine,and red willow, Herbs were also smoked for pleasure, as well as to combat respiratory ailments.

Some herbs used for these purposes include angelica, bearberry, farfara, dogwood, deer tongue, mullein, sumac, valerian and yerba sante.

As mentioned before, herbs are used in sweat lodges or in the form of enemas to detoxify and cleanse the body.

Plants & Herbs Procurement Methods

Wildcrafting:

Herbalism, also called phytotherapy, refers to the use of plants and plant extracts in medicinal practice and natural remedies. In this chapter, we look at the methods of wildcrafting, cultivation and storage of herbs for herbalism.

Wildcrafting is the ancient art of collecting wild plants and herbs in natural, unspoiled territories. It is necessary to be sure that you are allowed to collect the species you wish to select and to observe the normal safety precautions.

When collecting, it is necessary to take care of taking only what is needed, leave the beauty as you find it (leave no trace) and make a bid before you go, avoiding waste, respecting Nature and its laws.

A conscious and reverent approach is needed by entering the plant world to obtain drugs.

It can take months or even years to get what you see when you walk into the plant environment.

There is a world of complex interrelationships that we do not easily recognize if we have been disconnected from it for too long.

Wild herbs can be used for a variety of herbal remedies, including tinctures, salves, herbal ointments and infusions, and by acting judiciously, you can enjoy all the benefits of wildcrafted herbal medicines without upsetting the environment.

Benefits of wildcrafting

Wild plants grown in richer soils and in relatively untouched meadows and forests, are more powerful and nutrient- rich than cultivated plants.

Commercial agriculture, for economic and production purposes, has caused soil depletion by feeding plants with isolated nutrients, and pollution, with the use of pesticides and herbicides.

For this reason, wildcrafted herbs retain many more properties than mass- produced herbs. In addition, wildcrafting is a perfect activity to relax and be outdoor in contact with Nature, and share pleasant moments with others.

There are many easy herbal remedies that can be made from wild plants

Wild herbs can be used for:

- Experiment and enjoy nature.
- Eat healthily
- Eliminate dependence on harmful substances Stay healthy
- Create products for personal and environmental care

How to select sites

A reckless wildcrafter can seriously alter an habitat if he doesn't take care of vulnerable ecosystems.

To obtain a permission to free use for a low fee: On Bureau of LandManagement.

Both BLM and Forest Service will warn you that you may not harvest in or near campgrounds or picnic areas; on some trails less than 200 feet away andon the sides of the road lane.

Wildcrafting Equipment:

A few essentials that can really simplify the activity:

Something to carry the harvest. For a short trip, a basket will do just fine, andfor longer ones, large paper bags. Avoid plastic because the herbs can deteriorate quickly in the heat.

Something for slicing, digging and cutting, depending on what you want toharvest.

- A vegetable brush is useful for cleaning roots
- A paintbrush if you're picking mushrooms, to clean the dirt off them A trowel, for digging and collecting roots
- A good knife for cutting roots or bark
- Kitchen shears or some scissors for cutting greenery or flowers (a knife with a smooth blade and a serrated blade is especially recommended)

Recommendations:

The plants growing near you, in the grounds or gardens near your home, haveall the healing power available. Awesome, isn't it? You are part of the same ecosystem in the same area. You share the same water and the same environment.

You belong to the same habitat. Start interacting with the land you live on bystarting with the popular plants you find next to you.

Year after year, you will see and collect the same species from the same area. Your awareness of the medicinal importance of these plants will expand each year. You can learn many details about them. Your ability to connect with them will also grow. In every plant community from which the plant population comes, there live plants from our ancestors. On this planet, they have seen the dawn of humanity. It is important to know them, preserve them and honor them.

In accordance with Native principles, they should be left undisturbed, celebrated with tobacco and smudges, songs and prayers. To encounter themrepresents the connection with the archetype of their kind and has a great power.

Some plants and herbs should be completely avoided because they are at riskof extinction due to overharvesting and habitat destruction. Especially woodland plants, require healthy forests to grow and cannot be cultivated.

However, there are many herbs with similar qualities, so there is no need to harvest or buy these endangered plants. You can learn more about at-risk grasses and those that should be avoided on the United Plant Savers website,unitedplantsavers.org.

Never collect an endangered species.

Consult your local herbarium or botanical garden for a list of these plants.You can also contact the American Herbalist Guild for a national list.

Identify before harvest. Use identification keys and samples

Ask permission and say thank you, acknowledge connection to life Do not harvest mature, seed-producing plants (the progenitor plants)

When in doubt, do not collect more than ten percent of whole plants and native roots, and thirty percent of naturalized plant species or native leaves and flowers. Harvest only from abundant stands, with care taken to ensure the maintenance and well-being of plant communities.

Suggested Times for Harvesting:

- Aerial or above ground parts: Mornings between 6 a.m. and 10 a.m. If picking the leaves, many are best just before flowering. Harvest most flowers as soon as they begin to bloom. The traditional moon phase for harvesting aerial parts is near or during the full moon.
- Roots: harvest early in the morning if possible
- Biennials: traditionally in the new moon phase, harvest in the fall of the first year or spring of the second year.
- Bark: harvest in the spring or fall. The traditional phase for barks is the three-quarter waning moon.
- Seeds and fruits: Harvest when ripe, with some exceptions such as citrus fruit.

Tips for Growing:

There are several techniques and tricks for growing and caring for plants and herbs, to benefit production and crop yields, as well as the ecosystem, including wildlife.

These include thinning, top pinching, root separation, and protecting a wide variety of grandmother plants to seed and protect young plants.

Seeds should be replanted or dispersed if roots are collected and holes created by digging should be filled, and vegetation and soil should be added around cleared areas. It may be helpful to collect dried foliage from surrounding plants and scatter it around.

Do not pull roots while harvesting leaves. Root yield, as well as foliage, for some species can be improved by flower pruning.

Check always the cycles of growth, to measure the effects on the environment. The vegetal population should not grow less then 30% a year, otherwise it can be considered a degenerative process.

Drying:

Drying preserves the quality of herbs by reducing the moisture content, which inhibits the growth of microorganisms and chemical alterations during dried storage.

Some plants dry better in the sun, but most should be dried in shady, well-ventilated areas, avoiding placing them on metal screens and printed paper.

Avoid washing the flowers and aerial parts of plants, possibly shake them to remove unwanted residue.

Where quantities are sufficient, tie in bundles with a diameter of 1,5 inches or less at the base of the stems. Removing the lowest leaves, you can tie 4 or 5 branches together, securing them with a string.

Then hang them upside down and place them in a warm, dark area for a period of two to four weeks, possibly protected by a paper bag, checking periodically until the herbs are dry.

For barks, if possible, remove the outer bark and retain the inner bark.

Roots should be brushed by hand, or cleaned with a pressure hose. Wide, heavy roots without aromatic properties should be cut lengthwise.

Storage:

When you are going to store dried herbs, it is important to make sure they are completely dry first. The universalstandard for storing any herbal product is the earthenware jar.

Whether it is dried herbs, tinctures, ointments, elixirs, it is advisable to store in an airtight, dark jar. there are all sizes of them, easily available and inexpensive. Glass jars of dark color, such as amber or cobalt, prevents light from influencing the quality of the product being stored. These containers aremore expensive and, keep in mind that clear glass is fine as long as it is not indirect sunlight.

If they are stored in glass with an airtight lid, you can expect dried herbs to last 1 to 5 years, and tinctures could last up to 10 years. Oils and salves havea shorter shelf life because oils go rancid - and may only last 6 months to 1 year.

Lotions have the shortest shelf life, because the mixed oily and watery parts, are a breeding ground for mold growth, in a short time. Lotions may only last1 to 3 months, but you can extend their life by refrigerating them or adding natural preservatives.

The best way to tell if dried herbs or herbal products are still good is to checktheir smell, color and taste. This is true if they are wild herbs or fresh herbs collected from your garden and then dried for later use.

Make sure they are completely dried and free of moisture. A good indicator isthat they crumble easily by rubbing them between your fingers. Multiple factors determine how long herbs will remain vibrant, vibrant and fresh.

These include harvest date, cleanliness, type of herb and quality of storage environment. To preserve aromatic properties and other important constituents, keep dried herbs and plants at a medium, constant temperatureby storing them in food-grade plastic bags, glass jars, or fiber containers suitable for long term retention of plants texture and properties.

Label containers with collection location and dates.

Uncut and whole herbs will keep longer.

BOOK 2
The Native American Herbal Remedies

The Secrets of Native American's

Herbal Remedies

American Indians held the knowledge of the use and benefits of plants with such sacredness, that sharing was only allowed between different tribes.

Historians argue that the awareness of herbal medicine has been preserved in tradition because it includes natural healing secrets for common diseases currently treated with synthetic drugs by medical science.

Europeans had always been impressed by the rugged resilience of the natives. They were strong, brave and healthy, and for most tribes, physically beautiful. Scientific and archaeological studies show, in most cases, that they had no problems of bone or joint dysfunction, nor tuberculosis.

Herbalism was traditionally taught in tribes since ancient times, and has been passed down by indigenous cultures for many centuries, both in the Americas and elsewhere in the world.

In parallel with modern traditional pharmacology, herbal medicine is returning widely to use, and herbal connoisseurs are guiding others through the magic and practicality of their knowledge and use.

The secrets of these spiritual cures were eventually discovered, and scientists began to study the characteristics of these plants to fully understand their uses and healing properties.

You have surely heard of some of them before, and in this book you will discover their fascinating world and how to use them.

You need to know how to handle herbs before you use them. And, of course, the ones you intend to use must be accessible near where you live. An effective way to consume these medicinal plants is to buy ready-made preparations.

Natives had an empirical experience of medicinal herbs.

The shape, consistence, color, smell and taste of a plant determined its application. For example, the shape of plants was associated with the organ to be treated by analogy, they considered red plants good for blood, with yellow ones they treated jaundice. Plants that resembled the liver were used to treat liver problems. This philosophy of using similar shapes and colors is called the "doctrine of signatures" and is found in the traditional healing art of manycultures. This doctrine holds that the physical appearance of a plant can reveal its therapeutic benefits.

Although there is a wealth of herbal knowledge present in American Indian culture, they were not and are not inclined to share their herbal secrets. Somebelieved that the power of their healing systems could be weakened by sharing them with people outside the clan, who might misrepresent the techniques. Many of the sacred songs and healing rituals were passed down during vision quests or initiations into secret societies; so, naturally, Native Americans do not feel comfortable sharing this sacred and sensitive information with those who might distort, alter, or abuse it, especially havinghad to endure much to obtain and retain the knowledge.

From another perspective, however, sharing Native American healing secrets is a way to keep them alive and pass on the tradition.

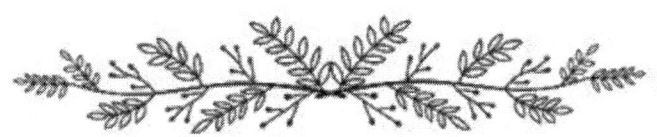

This text is meant to be a way to honor and celebrate the greatness of Native herbal medicine traditions and to share this information with you so that you can learn about them and integrate theminto your life and in your heart with gratitude and great benefit.

The relationship with plants and herbs represents only one part of the overall Native American philosophy of life and health.

At the heart of the Native American tradition is the connection to the GreatSpirit, the Creator, the higher power and its Presence in the phenomenal world.

Each tribe or nation has its own definition for this Great Spirit. The Lakota identify it as Wakan Tanka, the Arapaho call it "Man on High," the Crows refer to it as "First Creator," the Pawnees refer to it as "Ti-rá-wa," and to theSioux it is "The Great Spirit" or "Mystery."

Nearly all Native American cultures hold an animist view, and consider everyelement, animal, creature, plant, rock, tree, mountain to be a physical expression of a soul. Therefore, Nature must be treated with respect and honored.

The elements, the directions, the animals, the plants, the stones... everything in nature is a gift from the Great Spirit. According to American Indians, when properly cared for and respected, Nature and its manifestations sustain andgive health to human beings.

This principle makes humans responsible for caring for and respecting nature and the universe with awareness. All beings are part of the Whole, lovingly shaped by the Creator.

For them, Medicine is not just the treatment of a symptom or disease.

The shaman is a healer and a spiritual guide, capable of traveling betweenearthly and subtle worlds and dimensions, whose activity is ritual and ceremonial as well as factual.

The ceremony has a common denominator in all cultures of all times: it is aprocess in which the human capacity to feel and live the dimension of the sacred is celebrated and expressed.

One communicates with Earth, Water, Air, Fire and the Creator, what onefeels and thinks through specific actions, movements and intentions, and celebrates the connection between human beings, the spirit world, and thedifferent elements of the Earth.

Indigenous cultures were aware that forgetting their place in the tapestry oflife, and dichonnecting from the dimension of the sacred, was a cause of sickness of body and mind.

The Hopi, living in the longest inhabited settlements in North America, wear ceremonial masks and perform community rituals to restore connection to theEarth. This connection must be frequently re-experienced and nurtured, even in ritual form. For Native tribes, celebrations and ceremonial acts are a way to strengthen and renew this connection.

The Medicine Wheel and the Four Directions

The Medicine Wheel can be called a Circle of Knowledge that reconstitutesthe whole and empowers an individual's life." Also called the Sacred Circle,the Medicine Wheel represents the circle of all life.

Through the symbolism of the Wheel it is possible to get in touch and understand oneself and the world, according to the fundamental principle ofthe natives: "As it is inside, so it is outside". It acts as a mirror, in fact, looking at it, you can see a reflection of the universe and the Great Mystery,the Universal Principle that creates everything that exists.

In the wheel of medicine one can see the interdependence of all things,discovering the relationship that exists with everything and therefor deepening the comprehension of everything and of oneself.

The Wheel is a physical, mental, spiritual and emotional tool that allows the person to connect with the Earth and the Natural Energies that exert an actionon human's life.

The Native American sees the universe as a continuous change whose essence is not material but mental and spiritual. Everything that exists has its own reason and everything that exists is has an intelligent energy, kept together by a harmonious synchronization, everything is connected by vibrations of light, color, sound for this reason when a medicine man builds a Circle containing any representation of physical objects, forces and energy, inreality he builds a functional symbolic model of the way of operating of the Universal Mind, and therefore of the human mind.

The one and the other are not only similar, but integrated. Totems serve as connectors between different levels of consciousness: human, animal, vegetable, mineral. There is a network that allows the exchange of information between all life forms. Totems play the role of symbolic sensors by tapping into that network. So we have animal, mineral and vegetal totems.

The medicine wheel is usually represented by a structure consisting of simplestone circles arranged in a pattern on the ground.

In the past, when people encountered a sacred place on Earth, they often builta circle of stones to indicate it.

Later, more stones would be added to the circle, rising up as walls and defining the sacred space more clearly. From these structures, churches andshrines were erected by some cultures, adding the roof covering.

As Black Elk said, "This wheel exists in all things."

Even within each of us, the medicine wheel exists as our inner council.

A human cannot be in relationship with all life if the life within is in disorderand disharmony. It is important to understand how the medicine wheel workswithin us and work to establish harmony in all its parts. From this starting point you can then move outward by expanding your awareness in ever-widening outer circles, eventually encompassing the entire universe.

The Native Healers:

Usually native healers also called shamans were elderly people with greatknowledge of the animal and plant world, able to handle every element provided by nature for the treatment of the most common symptoms.

They had to understand the personal inclinations of the subject they had to heal, well aware that the mind was one with the sick body and that there wasvery often to be sought the predominant cause of an organic disorder.

Finally, they were in direct contact with the spirit world, from which they drew inspiration to heal every problem. Even though this aspect can make someone smile, it must be remembered that Indian society was deeply imbued with an animistic conception of life, for which the relationship withthe divinities was at the basis of every event.

Beyond every belief and perplexity, for Native Americans prevention and therapy were very important, with positive effects that are even today mostlyastounding.

Book 3
Native American Plants

Native Plants

Agave (or Mescal)

Apache Name: Astaneh

Century plant (Agave americana), blue agave (A. tequilana), and others

Habitat: Extreme southwestern United States—dry areas of California, Arizona, Nevada, and Mexico; Central and South America. Agaves are found on coarse soils below 5,000 feet elevation.

Description: Grayish-green desert plant to 10' with long, swordlike, succulent leaves. Produces flowers on a central fruiting spike. Also known as American century plant, because people came to believe that the plant blooms only once every 100 years. This isn't actually true: the plant booms once in 10 to 20 years. After sending up its flower, the mother plant dies.

Medicinal Parts: The leaf and the juice.

Effects: anti-inflammatory, diuretic.

Taste: sweet

Solvent: Water, alcohol.

Traditional uses: Most parts of the agave were edible, including the leaves, flower stalks, flowers, and seeds. Flower stalks were harvested in the spring and summer. The leaves from November to May.

Agave harvesting was in many tribes the preserve of men because it required a lot of strength. The leaves were harvested by pulling the entire plant out of the ground. Both the leaves and the stalks were roasted in large pits to be eaten or pounded into cakes and dried in the sun for later consumption.

The flowers of the agave were boiled to remove the bitterness and could be eaten immediately or dried in the sun. If not harvested, the flowers produced seeds that were collected and ground into flour. Some groups of Apache Indians extracted the juice from the young flower stalks to make an intoxicating drink known as Pulque. (Distilled, Pulque is the main ingredient in tequila).

Agave fibers were used to make bows, brushes, cradles, nets, shoes, skirts, mats, ropes, baskets and traps. The leaves were soaked and pounded to release the fibers, which were dried and separated by combing. Agave water (juice, sap) was used for his anti-inflammatory and diuretic effect. The fresh juice raises metabolism and increases transpiration.

The sap is used to heal wounds thanks to its cicatrizing properties.

Modern uses: Leaf wastes are used as a basic component for steroid drugs. Agave roots are used for soap production. Grating them, pressing them and mixing the mixture with water makes soap that can be used for laundry, dishes and shampoo.

The coarse fiber of the leaves is used to make ropes and fibers. The sap is still used today as an emollient and laxative.

Agave nectar is high in fructose and is processed into low glycemic index

sugar or liquid sweetener.

Food use: Native groups such as the Pima, Papago (Tohono O'odham), and Cahuilla Indian tribes collect and dry agave flowers, grind them into flour, and use it to make tortillas.

The Navajos used the cooked and dried agave heads as a thickener for soups.

The Papago people also ate these flower stalks as a green vegetable, while several Native American groups cooked or roasted the agave roots and hearts to make traditional sweets and breads.

Agave hearts can be roasted and eaten. Cooking and crushing the heart is also a method of juice extraction, which is used for tequila.

WARNING: Livestock can become fatally ill from eating agave leaves, something they avoid except in cases of severe drought or when there is noother forage available. In some parts of Mexico, indigenous people would catch fish by putting agave (A. lechuguilla) leaves in a stream. In this way the fish were intoxicated, became paralyzed and floated to the surface, making it easy to catch. The fish caught in this way posed no danger of intoxication, because the juice of Agave lechuguilla is not toxic to humans.

Alder

Betulaceae *(Alnus rubra)*

Habitat: Species ranges from California to Alaska east to Idaho. Alders are commonly found near streams, rivers, and wetlands. In Colorado the primaryspecies is Alnus tenuifolia and is common in the foothills to subalpine areas.In the Pacific Northwest of North America, the white Alder (*Alnus rhombifolia*) unlike other northwest alders, has an affinity for warm, dry climates, where it grows along watercourses

The largest species are red alder (*A. rubra*) on the west coast of North America, and black alder *A. glutinosa*), both reaching over 30 m (98.42 ft).By contrast, the widespread *green alder* is rarely more than a 5-metre-tall (16-foot) shrub.

Bark smooth and gray when young, coarse and whitish gray when mature. A.rubra bark turns red to orange when exposed to moisture. Leaves are bright green, oval, coarsely toothed and pointed. Male flowers clustered in long, hanging catkins; female seed capsule is ovoid cone. Seed nuts small, slightlywinged, flat.

Medicinal Part: The bark.

Effects: Tonic, Astringent, Purgative.

Solvent: Boiling water.

Traditional uses: Natives used the wood to make utensils and bowls, ate the inner bark in the spring, and considered it the only wood suitable for smokingsalmon.

The tree was used as an important source of natural dyes in both Europe andNorth America: red and orange from the bark, brown from the twigs, and green from the catkins. The floors of sweat-lodges were often covered with alder leaves.

Alder ashes were used as a paste to clean teeth.

Spring catkins were pulped and eaten as a purgative (to help move the bowels). The bark was mixed with other plants in a decoction and used as a tonic. The female catkins were used in decoction to treat gonorrhea. A poultice of leaves was applied to wounds and skin infections. The infusion ofleaves was a wash that relieved itching and inflammation from insect bites and hives from poisonous plants. The infusion of bark was also used to washsores, cuts and wounds.

Modern Uses: This is still an important plant in sweat lodge ceremonies. Black alder, A. glutinosa, is endemic to the northern hemisphere and is usedin Russia and Eastern European countries as a gargle to relieve sore throats and reduce fever. Research suggests that betulin and lupeol from alder may inhibit tumor growth.

Dose and usage: The bark is rich in tannin and can be used (internally) for diarrhea, gum inflammation and sore throats; and (externally) as a wash for wounds, hives, swellings and sprains. Bark tea has a shrinking, clotting and antiseptic effect and is therefore suitable for treating wounds. The best times to harvest bark are spring and fall. The bark is best used fresh or recently harvested. Make a concentrated decoction for internal use, lighter for externaluse.

Food use: Members of this genus provide a generous resource of firewood inthe Northwest for savory barbecue cooking.

To smoke meat with alder, soak the wood chips overnight in water, thenplace the moist chips on coals or charcoal to smoke meat.

The bark and wood chips are preferred over mesquite for smoking fish, especially salmon. The sweet inner bark is scraped in the early spring andeaten fresh, raw, or combined with flour to make cakes.

Aloe

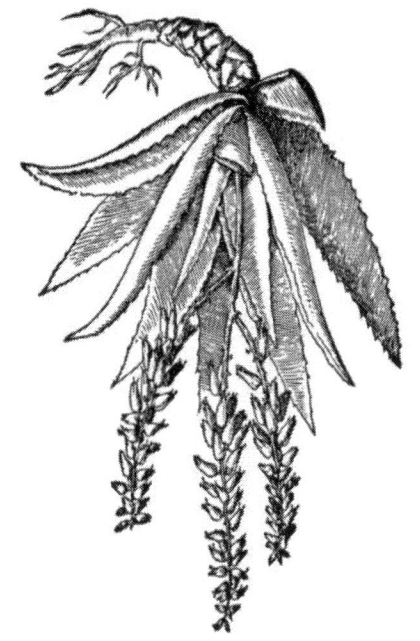

Liliacee (Aloe vera)

Habitat: Aloe vera, a semi-tropical succulent plant, is native to Africa and grows wild in Florida, U.S.A., in USDA zones 10 and 11. In the southern United States, it can withstand the outdoors year-round. In northern climates, it should be moved indoors when the first cold weather arrives. Aloe vera is found in hot, desert climates and in sandy, grainy soils. In warm climates, plant aloe vera in full sun or light shade. In cold climates, it needs full sun. It tolerates drought well and should be watered infrequently, once every two weeks.

Aloe thrives in warm regions and grows wild in Florida, U.S.A.

Description: Leaves are fleshy and elongated, green or olive in color, fairlypointed, blunt or spiny, sometimes spotted.

It has short stems with a basal rosette of leaves.

Tubular flowers (red, orange or yellow) grow at the apex of a stem in simple or branched clusters.

These characteristics change slightly in different varieties. Aloe bainesii grows to heights of 65 feet and is 5 feet wide at the base. The "aloe americana" is not an Aloe, but Agave americana.

Flavor: Bitter

Medicinal Parts: The juice of the leaves, a translucent gel of whitish-greencolor.

Powder: bright yellow.

Solvent: Water

Effects: Tonic, laxative, emmenagogue, healing, soothing, anthelmintic, detoxifying, disinfectant

Traditional Uses: Native Americans called Aloe Vera "the wand of heaven", the "plant of burns", the "plant of medicine" and the "plant of mystery" and jealously guarded their knowledge of its uses. Aloe Vera is one of the most remarkable medicinal plants nature has to offer, having a purifying effect on the tissues of the stomach, liver, spleen, kidneys and bladder, including bloodand lymphatic fluids. It's a wonderful disinfectant that dries moisture and resists bacteria, fungi and viruses.

They are very healing and soothing to all tissues. Aloe should not be used during pregnancy, or if you suffer from hemorrhoids, because it irritates thelower intestines.

It is used in cases of amenorrhea, constipation, irritable colon, dyspepsia, skinlesions, liver disease.

Modern uses: Research has shown that the Aloe Vera plant contains 20 different kinds of minerals, 12 types of vitamins, 18 amino acids and a variety of other enzymes and components that enhance its medicinal power.

Benefits of aloe vera when used internally:

- Detoxification
- Strengthens the immune system Treats infections
- Enriches the body with minerals, vitamins and enzymes
- Improves oxygenation of blood, tissues and organs Protects the kidneys
- Treats inflammation of the oral cavity Lowers cholesterol and triglycerides Stabilizes blood sugar
- Treats ulcers, irritable bowel syndrome, Crohn's disease and celiac disease
- Heals the digestive system

Benefits of aloe vera when used externally:

- Relieves itching from insect bites and rashes
- Works a immediate first aid when treating wounds (also works well for pets instead of chemical creams because animals tend to lick their wounds)
- Removes skin pigmentation and blemishes Helps heal herpes
- Helps heal dermatitis
- Improves skin health, moisturizes, heals acne and prevents wrinkles Treats burns, scalds, scars and cuts
- Stimulates hair growth by rubbing it on the scalp Helps warts heal more quickly

WARNING: Do not give in cases of degeneration of the liver and gallbladder. As a rule, it is safe to use

Aloe as it is established by FolkMedicine, but in all complicated cases it is recommended to follow theadvice of medical or trained practitioners

Amaranth

Amaranthaceae: Redroot amaranth

(Amaranthus Retroflexus), red amaranth *(A. cruentus),* and others

Habitat: Widely cultivated in Mexico and South America. Numerous speciesgrowing on waste ground across the nation along the edges of prairies, margins of fields.

Description: Amaranth plants are typically annuals or short-lived perennials.The stems are often reddish in color and sometimes have spines; they have simple, alternately arranged leaves and often have a pinkish taproot.

Plants can be monoecious (flowers of both sexes are on the same individual)or dioecious (each individual produces flowers of only one sex). The small flowers typically have colorful bracts and are arranged in dense, showy inflorescences; a single plant can produce hundreds or thousands of seeds, borne individually in dry capsule-like fruits. The purple of the leaves and flowers is given by anthocyanin pigments.

Several species of amaranth have been used as food by Native Americans and pre-Columbian civilizations since prehistoric times.

Medicinal Parts: Flowers and leaves. Edible seeds and shoots.

Effects: Astringent.

Solvent: Water.

Food use: Amaranth seeds have been a Native American food for thousands of years. The Apaches and Navajos used amaranth to make flour for bread, while the Aztecs and later the Tarahumara (Rarámuri) of what is now Mexico made pinole - made of toasted amaranth mixed with sugar, spices and water and eaten as a hot cereal or base for desserts. Amaranth flour, mixed with cornmeal, was also made into dumplings, and the seeds were popped like popcorn.

The traditional Mexican dessert alegría (which means "joy" in Spanish) made with popped amaranth seeds mixed with honey and chocolate, sometimes with the addition of pumpkin or sunflower seeds, is made for the Day of the Dead and other celebrations.

The origins of the recipe go back to the Mayans and Aztecs. Amaranth again became an important food for the descendants of the Maya, who cultivated it and obtained products from the seeds.

Leaves are also edible, and they are an excellent source of vitamin C and vitamin A, they can be consumed fresh in salads or steamed. Young leaves are a great source of vitamin C and vitamin A, and can be eaten fresh in salads or steamed and served as a cooked vegetable. The roots can be eaten cooked as an addition to soups.

Amaranth, so rich in nutrients, can help reduce malnutrition rates wherever it is grown. Easy to grow and rich in nutrients, amaranth is likely to be an important food in a future influenced by climate change.

Traditional Uses: Native Americans considered it a sacred ritual plant, mixed and eaten with green corn in ceremonies.

The astringent leaves were used to treat an overly heavy menstrual cycle, and the infusion was taken to treat hoarseness.

Pioneers and herbalists reported the herb as astringent and useful for treating inflammation of the mouth and throat, as well as therapy for diarrhea and ulcers.

Notes: Excellent as pink coloring. Excellent bird food.

Balsam Fir

Pinaceae

(*Abies balsamea*)

Habitat: North American fir, native to most of eastern and central Canada, and the northeastern United States (Minnesota east to Maine, and south in the Appalachian Mountains to West Virginia)

Description: Small to medium-size evergreen tree typically 14–20 metres (46–66 ft) tall, occasionally reaching a height of 27 metres (89 ft). The narrow conic crown consists of dense, dark-green leaves. At higher altitudes this tree is spreading, low. Smooth barked; bark has numerous resin pockets. Flat needles to 1¼" in length with white stripes beneath, more thickly rounded at the base. Cones purplish to green, to 4" in length, scaly, twice as long as broad.

Medicinal parts: Resin, root, needles and bark

Effects: Analgesic, antiseptic, balsamic

Food: The needle infusion relaxing and laxative.

Traditional uses: The resin was used by Native Americans to treat burns, wounds and bruises to soothe sores, scratches, insect bites, stings. Tea made from the needles was used to treat upper respiratory problems: asthma, bronchitis and colds.

The natives stuffed the leaves into pillows as a general cure.

In sweat lodges, resin was poured with water onto hot stones to inhale the balsamic vapor.

Branches were steamed to treat arthritis (rheumatism).

Decoction of bark induced sweating and was used to treat acute infections.

Many tribes, including the Algonquin, Woodlands Cree, Iroquois, Menominee, Micmac, Ojibwa, and Potawatomi treat colds with an infusion made from the sap or bark. The Ojibwa also inhale smoke from needles to treat colds. The Chippewa inhale the steam created by the fusion of balsamicgum to relieve headaches, while the Iroquois used the steam emanating froma decoction of branches to relieve rheumatism and as an aid to childbirth.

Modern uses: the resin obtained from the bark is an ingredient of many ointments and lotions, as an antiseptic, and of ointments and creams used to treat hemorrhoids. To treat diarrhea and cough, mixtures containing resin areproduced.

Dosage and use: To make a tea, pour teaspoon of bark in two cups of waterin a pot and bring to a boil. Boil for thirty minutes and strain. Take one- quarter cup daily.

Bearberry

Ericaceae (Arctostaphylos uva-ursi L. Spreng)

Habitat: Northern United States from East to West, and Canada in relativelydry areas, at the base of pines, tamarack, and juniper.

Description: The name "bearberry" for the plant derives from the edible fruitwhich is a favorite food of bears. The fruit are edible and are sometimes harvested as food for humans. The leaves of the plant are used in herbal medicine.

Trailing shrub, low lying, prostrate and mat forming. Leaves are dark, evergreen, leathery, smooth edged, obovate or spatula shaped, less than ¾" wide. Alpine variety of bearberry has larger leaves. The fruit is a dry red berry. Also called kinnikinnick or uva-ursi.

Medicinal parts: The leaves. **Effects**: Astringent, Diuretic, Tonic. **Solvents**: Alcohol, water.

Food use: Berries are dry and unflavored, so they were traditionally cooked with animal fat or mixed with fish eggs (such as salmon) and stronger-flavored foods. Berries can be dried and then ground into a flour.

Many Native Americans boiled the berries with roots and vegetables to make a soup.

Traditional Uses: The whole plant was soaked in water and mixed with goose, duck, bear or mountain goat fat. Then cooked glue from the hoof of an animal, horse or deer, was mixed with the fat. The resulting ointment was used on sores, children's scalps and rashes. To treat canker sores and sore gums, a mouthwash made with an infusion of aerial parts in water was used. Dried leaves and stems were ground and used as a poultice on wounds. The infusion of leaves, berries and stems was taken orally as a diuretic, to clean kidneys and bladder disorders.

The berries were eaten or infused with the whole plant for colds. Kwakiutl peoples smoked the leaves for their narcotic effect.

Native Americans used bearberry leaves with tobacco and other herbs in religious ceremonies, either as a smudge (type of incense) or smoked in a sacred pipe that carried the smoker's prayers to the Great Spirit. Pioneers used the leaf infusion as a diuretic, astringent and tonic.

Modern uses: Modern Uses: Approved by the European Commission to treat urinary tract infections. It is commercially available dried, powdered in capsules, and as whole leaves for infusion. Numerous homeopathic preparations exist. Hot tea is astringent, antibacterial and diuretic. tea for internal and external use is considered antimicrobial and anti-inflammatory.

Dosage and Use: Orally as follows: soak the leaves in enough alcohol or brandy to cover, for a week or more. Place 1 teaspoon of soaked leaves in 1 cup of boiling or cold water and drink 2 to 3 cups daily. Can be taken orally as follows: soak leaves in enough alcohol or brandy to cover, for a week or more. Put 1 teaspoon of soaked leaves in 1 cup of boiling, or cold, water and drink 2-3 cups daily.

Amount of tincture to be poured into water, 10-25 drops in a cup three or more times a day, depending on symptoms.

The tea can be made without the brandy or alcohol, if desired, by steeping the leaves in boiling water only.

WARNING: *Do not use during pregnancy or while nursing.*

Avoid eating acidic foods when using the tea to treat urogenital and biliary tract diseases. Prolonged use of uva-ursi may damage the liver and inflame and irritate the bladder and kidneys. Its use is not recommended for children, and it should not be used if you have high blood pressure.

(**Notes**: Berries used for grayish-brown dye.

Native Americans used an application of crushed berries to waterproof baskets.

Several herbal formulas for horses incorporate bearberry, for joint-rebuilding and protecting supplements, and fertility boosters.)

Black Haw

Viburnum prunifolium, (N.O.:Caprifoliaceae)

Habitat: Black haw is found in most of the North American states, more abundantly from New York to Florida.

Description: It's an erect bushy shrub or tree from 10-25 ft. tall, 10 in. of trunk diameter. The bark is irregular, transversely curved and greyish brown, or where the outer bark has scaled off brownish-red; inner surface reddish brown.

The root bark is cinnamon in color and tastes bitter and astringent. The deep-green leaves are broadly elliptical or obovate, finely and sharply toothed, the under-surface smooth, 1-3 in. long. The flowers bloom from May to June in small white clusters 2-4 in. across and 3-5 lobes in each flower. The fruit known as Black haw is edible, but to some unbearably sweet. They are shiny black; cadet blue on red stems.

Medicinal parts: Root bark (preferred), bark of stems and branches.

Solvents: Water, alcohol.

Effects: Diuretic, Tonic, Antispasmodic, Nervine, Astringent.

Traditional Uses: The Cherokee had several uses for the plant. They took an infusion of it to prevent recurrent spasms, used the root bark as a diaphoretic and a tonic, and took a compound infusion of it for fever, smallpox and ague. They also used an infusion of the bark as a wash for a sore tongue.

The Lenape combine the root bark with leaves of other plants and use it to strengthen female generative organs. The Mi'kmaq take an infusion of the plant before and during parturition.

Black haw is an almost infallible remedy to risk of abortion. The preparationfor this purpose should be anticipated two or three weeks before the expectedreoccurrence of the misfortune and continued for about two weeks after any disturbance. If there are no more symptoms during the last weeks, discontinue until after delivery.

A decoction of this plant will generally alleviate chills and fever and usuallygives speedy relief in palpitation of the heart and is a valuable agent in diarrhea and dysentery. Notice that the herbs that have healing qualities on the stomach and intestinal tract are also effective for symptoms in the mouthand throat.

Modern uses: The most common use of black haw is as an antispasmodic formenstrual pain. To relax the uterus and relieve menstrual cramping, the most commonly recommended dose is 5 mL (1tsp) of the tincture in water, taken three to five times daily as needed. Black haw is sometimes used to prevent chronic miscarriage. It has been similarly utilized for the condition of irritableuterus occurring in late **pregnancy**. The reported nerve-calming effect of black haw may be useful in addition to its pasmolytic properties.

Dose: 1 oz. to 1 pint of boiling water taken in tablespoonful amounts three or four times a day; 1 teaspoonful of the tincture, three or four times a day. As a tea and decoction it is used for painful menstruation, excessive menstrual bleeding, cramps and hysteria. Sometimes associated with and used as a hearttonic, to improve blood circulation, kidney and bladder. Bark decoction for cramps. Berries for ulcers. Leaves as tea and decoction.

Blueberry

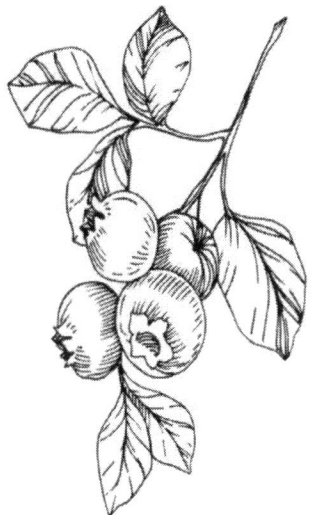

Ericaceae (Vaccinium spp.)

Habitat: Northern tier states from coast to coast. Wetlands, lowlands, and highlands, including eastern and western mountains. One of the principle species is V. myrtillus, known simply as Bilberry, which is found in acid soil,in forests, heaths, rocky barrens, bog and tundra.

Description: Deciduous shrub from 1' to 15' tall. Sharp-edged green branches. Leaves alternate, ovate and oblong, finely serrated. Flowers greenish tinged with pink, ¼" long, containing eight to ten stamens shorter than the styles. Globular fruit blue black, often frosted, with numerous seeds dispersed through the purple pulp. There are numerous species that vary significantly. The terms "blueberry" and "bilberry" may be used interchangeably.

Medicinal parts: Leaves and berries.

Solvents: alcohol and boiling water.

Effects: Diuretic, Refrigerant, Astringent.

Food use: This highly nutritious fruit may be eaten fresh, dried, stewed, or as a jam or marmalade.

Leaves can be made into tea.

We have energy bars; the Iroquois, and other Native American tribes, had pemmican. This highenergy food was a mixture of meat (often buffalo or fish), nuts and seeds, animal fat, and berries or other types of fruit. They called these pemmican cakes, and they were a way to preserve food for winter and provide portable nutrition for hunting and other trips. Blueberries and other fruits were first dried like raisins, then added to the cakes. Our modern high-energy trail bars are really just a version of those early pemmican cakes — minus the meat and animal fat — usually with oats or other grains added.

Traditional uses: Native Americans used a decoction of fresh or dried berries to treat diarrhea. The Iroquois used a whole aerial part decoction as a topical application to dermatitis. Bog blueberry (V. uliginosum) leaves were infused in water and sugar and taken as a tonic by women after childbirth.

Blueberries are a good source of vitamin C and have a folk use to prevent scurvy. Dried pulverized leaves were infused and taken for nausea.

Other Native American uses may be found Native American Ethnobotany. Pioneers used the leaves in decoction for treating diabetes. Berry tea was taken to treat mouth sores and inflammations.

Modern uses: The use of the fresh and dried fruits and leaves is approved by the European Commission for the treatment of diarrhea and inflammation of the pharynx and mouth. The fruit is considered an antioxidant and capillary protector that can improve circulation.

It is antiatherosclerotic, antiplatelet, antiglaucoma and may provide protection from vision disorders. Research suggests it may prevent varicose veins. Blueberry induces the release of dopamine. It is used as additional nutritional support for Alzheimer's disease.

The rich purple-blue color of blueberries is a sign of their high levels of anthocyanins: powerful antioxidants that are important for vascular health, especially in the eyes. Medical research has shown that the anthocyanins found in blueberries are good allies in treating macular degeneration.

Dose and usage: Decoction of leaves is indicated in case of diarrhea. To prepare the decoction, put a teaspoon of leaves in 1 cup of boiling water. With a mixture of equal parts of blueberry leaves, thyme and strawberry leaves, it is possible to prepare an excellent infusion. In case of intestinal discomfort, gas or diarrhea, consume a handful of fresh blueberries daily.

For the tincture: Put two or three handfuls of Blueberry in a bottle and pour a good royal brandy over it. Secure with a good cork or stopper. The longer the steeping time is, the more potent the medicine of this berry spirit will be. Violent, continuous diarrhea accompanied by pain is stopped by taking 1 tablespoon of blueberry brandy in 1/4 quart of water; repeat every 8 to 10 hours. Dry The berries can be dried with a food drier and stored in the freezer for consumption in winter.

(**Notes**: This attractive, deep-rooted, spreading plant is a colorful addition to your garden and provides edible seeds for baked goods. In California it is illegal to pick this plant, as it is the state flower. In addition to being a key provider for wildlife, California poppy is frequently included in wildflower seed mixes used for restoration and roadside plantings in California, where the poppies are helpful in managing soil erosion.9

Cascara Sagrada (Buckthorn)

Rhamnaceae (Rhamnus cathartic L.; R. purshiana)

Habitat: R. purshiana is widespread in the foothills of British Columbia, Idaho, Washington, Montana, and Oregon. R. Cathartica is found in the dunes of Lake Michigan and other lake dune areas.

Description: Shrub or small tree 4' to 20' tall. Highly branched, thornless, densely leafed. When adult, has gray-brown bark with gray-white lenticels. Leaves are thin, elliptical or oval, hairy on the veins, 2" long. Greenish-whiteflowers are numerous and grow in axillary cymes. The flowers are very smalland have five petals. The mature fruit is red or purple-black with two or threeseeds. R. purshiana (cascara buckthorn) is taller, at 30", with leaves that have twenty to twenty-four veins with white clustered flowers.

Medicinal part: The bark and root.

Effects: Laxative

Solvents: Diluted alcohol, boiling water.

Traditional Uses: Native Americans used the infusion of the bark as a purgative, laxative and vermifuge tea. An infusion of the twigs and fruit wasused as an emetic.

Modern Uses: Cascara is a laxative that can be taken in the form of powdered bark, root decoction or tincture. R. purshiana bark extract is alaxative approved by the European Commission for the treatment of constipation.

Dosage and Use: Bark should be harvested in spring and early summer whenit is easily detached from the wood. The bark should then be stored for a minimum of one year (up to 3) to allow its more bitter components to decompose: dry in the shade.

WARNING: The drug should never be used to clear intestinal obstructions. Bark infusion is considered a cleansing tonic, but chronicand continuous use may be carcinogenic. Use only under prescription. Berries are not edible.

Cranberry

Ericaceae (Vaccinium oxycoccus L.)

Habitat: This particular species grows in the northern areas of the United States, particularly in Canada, where, thanks to the heterogeneous but alwaysrather cold climate, it finds its ideal habitat in humid and swampy environments, such as the banks of rivers and streams.

Description: Dwarf evergreen shrub 5" to 15" inches tall, more like a lowliana that makes its way through bogs on slender stems. Bark hairy to smooth, brown to black in color.

Flowers are pink, solitary or in pairs, with petals sharply bent back like shooting stars. Fruit color varies from pink to red, depending on ripeness.Small berries are juicy and very tart.

Medicinal part: Berries, bark.

Effects: Antispasmodic, Nervous, Tonic, Astringent, Diuretic.

Solvents: Water, diluted alcohol

Traditional Uses: Berries and berry juice were used as a therapy for urinarytract infections. The juice was also used to treat bladder infections and to prevent urinary stones. It contains vitamin C and prevents scurvy.

Many tribes used the fruit as food.

First Nations such as the Mohawk and Inuit, in present-day Canada, also usedit as medicine; they made a poultice of the fruit to relieve sore eyes and dranktea made from cranberries to treat urinary tract infections.

Its astringent properties helped reduce swelling and tighten and tone irritated mucous membranes, both internally and externally; this cured a range of conditions, from infected wounds to ulcers. Women made a tea from the barkto relieve discomfort during their menstrual cycles.

Modern Uses: One study showed that drinking the juice can prevent E. colifrom adhering to the linings of the intestines, bladder and urinary tract, thuspreventing the bacteria from multiplying and inducing disease. In another study, 16 ounces of blueberry juice was shown to be 73% effective against urinary tract infections.

There is evidence that using concentrated juice (no added sugar) withantibiotics can help suppress urinary tract infections.

To determine how much cranberry or cranberry extract you need to treatbladder infections and stones, consult a holistic doctor.

Devil's Club

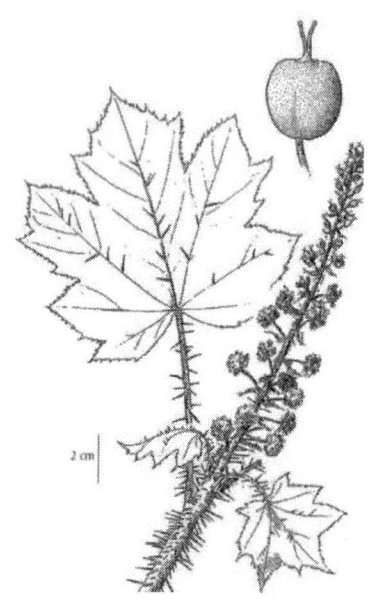

Aralioideae (Oplopanax horridus)

Habitat: Commonly found in moist wooded areas, especially in well-drained areas or along stream banks. Widespread in low to mid-elevation areas, sometimes growing in subalpine forests and at forest edges in the north.

Prefers dark and moist oldgrowth forest, shady areas with nitrogen-rich soils. Devil's club grows primarily in the northwest States.

Description: Devil's club is a member of the ginseng family. Also known as devil's walking stick or Alaskan ginseng, it's a large shrub native to the Pacific Northwest. The stems grow from 6 inches to 12 feet tall and are usually an inch or less in diameter. They possess needle-like spines that literally cover most of the outside of the stem. It resembles a cane with thousands of steel needles protruding from the stem.

The plant grows upright until its height becomes too much for the root and then it falls, new roots forming along its length. The reclining stem remains perhaps five inches above the forest floor. The wood has a sweet smell. The berries are bright red, flattened.

Medicinal part: The bark of the root, less often the whole stem.

Effects: Hypoglycemic, Tonic

Solvents: Boiling water, alcohol.

Traditional Uses: Native Americans burned the plant, then mixed the ashes with grease to make a black face paint that they believed providing the warrior supernatural power. Bella

Coola Indians used thorny sticks for protection.

For hunting, the natives sprinkled their bodies with a decoction of the plant's bark to eliminate human scent.

Modern uses: Devil's club is often used to treat inflammatory conditions. It provides relief for symptoms of arthritis, deep tissue pain, tendinitis, sore muscles, joint pain and various skin conditions like eczema and psoriasis. In addition, the leaves contain several antioxidant compounds, which can neutralize the harmful effects of free radicals.

Some studies show that devil's club can help block the growth of certain type of fungi and bacteria.

Although studies in humans are limited, test tube studies suggest that Devil's club may help block the growth of some types of cancer cells.

Studies in humans are still needed to determine if and how the plant affects cancer cells when used as a supplement.

Elderberry

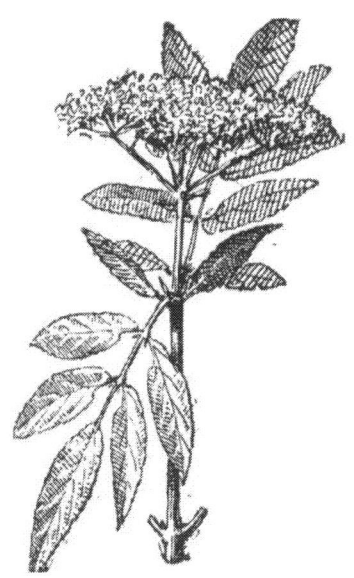

Adoxaceae (Sambucus racemosa L.; S. cerulea; S. nigra L.; S. canadensis L.)

Habitat: Nationwide, typically in wetlands, along streams in the plains and mountains of the West. S. canadensis is typically found in wet groves, along the edges of streams, rivers, and lakes in the eastern states and southeastern Canada.

Description: Elderberry is a tall shrub that forms bushes, up to 4-5 m tall, with an expanded, dense, globular crown; the trunk is erect and branched from below, is sinuous and often forked, has large branches with gray bark and an arching, drooping habit. The section of the branches of the trunk is characteristic because it has the central pith white, soft and elastic.

The leaves are opposite, with 5-7 oval serrated segments, 20-30 cm long, with toothed margin, and evident secondary veins. The leaves are equipped with stipules (appendages present at the base of the leaf stalk), and if crumpled they give off a strong characteristic odor, not very pleasant.

The flowers are small, organized in umbrella inflorescences up to 20 cm big; at first erect, then recumbent; they have a short and bell-shaped calyx, corolla composed by 5 ivory petals, sometimes reddish, oval shaped.

Fruits are small globular drupes, green at first, then blackish-purple, shiny and juicy when ripe, containing 2-5 oval and brown seeds; they are grouped in pendulous grapes on reddish peduncles.

Medicinal Parts: The roots, inner bark, leaves, and berries are all recognized as a natural medicinal treatment.

Solvent: Water.

Effects: Emetic, Cathartic;

Flowers: Diaphoretic, Diuretic, Alterative, Emollient, Gentle stimulant.

Traditional Uses: Infusion of flowers was used to lower fever and soothe irritations; Elderberry tea was administered to treat flu, colds, allergies, sinusitis, asthma, bronchitis, to support cardiac functions, and against arthritis. Native Americans scraped off the bark and used the infused root as an emetic and laxative. The berry infusion was used to treat rheumatism. The infusion of flowers was given to children with colic. Infused leaves were used as a wash for sores.

Modern uses: Standardized extractions are approved by the European Commission for the treatment of coughs, bronchitis, fever and colds.

The therapeutic dose of the flowers is reported to be 1 to 3 teaspoons of dried elder flowers in 1 cup of boiling water. Over-the-counter elderberry extracts indicate the recommended dosage on the bottle. Flower and berry extracts are used to treat acute infections such as colds and flu.

Dose and usage: The inner, green bark and the leaves, as an expressed juice in doses of one-half to one fluid ounce, is considered reliably effective as an emetic.

Lower doses will encourage gastric and fluid secretions. Because the bark is so strong, it is advisable to become informed in the use of the plant before using it too freely.

Generally, the flowers and berries are most often used in conventional herbal practice. The flowers are excellent for upper respiratory inflammations such as colds, flu, and hay fever. The flower tincture (one to three times a day) will help clear mucous conditions in the upper respiratory tract, reduce inflammation, and help healing. The flowers, when steeped as a hot tea (cup of hot water to two teaspoons of the fresh or dried flowers), are considered to be a general stimulant for the body.

When prepared in cold water (same proportions) they are felt to be a good laxative and effective diuretic. The berries are also often used for their laxative properties, primarily through taking a glass of the expressed juice, diluted with hot water twice a day. The flowers and leaves are often used insalves for wounds to soften the skin and help in general healing.

WARNING: The leaves, bark, root, and unripe berries of Sambucus species may cause cyanide poisoning. The western variety, S. racemosa, with red berries, may be more toxic than the blue and black berries of thevarieties S. cerulea, S. canadensis, and S. nigra. Avoid eating red elderberries—the fresh berry juice has caused illness.

(**Notes**: Elderberry (fruit) may be dried in a food dryer, then frozen and usedin cooking throughout the cold months for disease prevention. Flowers may be gathered in June, dried, and made into tea. Be sure to cut away the stems before eating the flowers and remove the stems from berries too.)

Ginseng

Araliaceae (Panaxginseng C; P. quinquefolius L.; Panax trifolius L.)

Habitat: Needs shading forest with mature canopy and well-drained soil.Cultivated from coast to coast, found wild in the Northwest and eastern forested areas.

Description: Perennial to 3' in height, with a smooth round stem. Three to five leaves in terminal whorls with three to five palmate leaflets. Greenish- yellow flowers give rise to a pea-sized, rounded, glossy seed. Seeds in a cluster on a central stalk separate from leaves. Dwarf variety (dwarf ginseng,Panax trifolius) similar but smaller, to 8" to 9" tall.

Medicinal Part: The dried root.

Solvent: Water.

Effects: Stimulant, Tonic, Demulcent, Stomachic, Nervine, Aphrodisiac.

Traditional uses: Before colonization, various Native American peoples used ginseng medicinally. The Ojibwe Midewiwin, spiritual leaders skilled in medicine, used the root for digestive problems and to relieve pain. The

Muscogee people used a ginseng tea to treat fever and respiratory ailments, and they made a poultice with the root to stop bleeding.

The Meskwaki people of the Great Lakes region used it both as an aphrodisiac and as a "universal remedy for children and adults," writes Daniel Moerman in Native American Medicinal Plants. The Native Americans also used the root as a ceremonial fetish to keep ghosts away. The decoction made from fresh or dried roots reduced fever and induced sweating.

Modern uses: The root is considered a panacea in China and Korea as a tonic and an adaptogen — that means, it helps to adapt to stressful conditions. It is used to potentiate normal function of the adrenal gland. Ginseng root has stimulant and aphrodisiac properties that enhances the immune response and may improve cerebral circulation and function as well as regulating blood pressure and blood sugar. In Traditional Chinese Medicine terms, it helps stimulating primordial energy (increases libido). It is a tonic for the spleen and lungs.

Chinese, Russian, Korean, and European studies suggest that ginseng enhances production of interferon. It is considered an ergogenic aid and may improve endurance. It is reported to regulate plasma glucose. Other research focuses on its anticancer and antitumor activity against leukemia and lymphoma. Ginseng's antimicrobial and antifungal activity has been demonstrated by clinical trials. Root preparations balances blood pressure.

Ginseng an immune-system stimulant to help resist infection.

Preliminary studies suggest it may increase mental acuity, and it has an estrogen-like effect on women.

Asian ginseng (P. ginseng) is considered warming and stimulating.

Other studies have shown its ability to protect against diseases caused by radiation and other physical, chemical and biological stresses, thus supporting its anti-stress applications.

It is considered by many to be a natural panacea. Korean red ginseng (different preparation of P. ginseng) warms more than Asian white.

American ginseng (P. quinquefolius) cools, moistens, and soothes. American ginseng is considered a better tonic than Asian ginseng, at least in the eyes of Asian practitioners.

Dose and use: Korean ginseng is usually made in a powdered form from the dried root and taken by mouth as a supplement. Although a tincture (a liquid preparation made with alcohol) and a tea form are available, most clinical research studies are based on the use of powdered ginseng as a supplement. Ginseng should be stored at room temperature and kept dry, away from heat.

To make a tea, take 3 oz. of powder (Ginseng 6-7 years old), add 1 oz. of honey, 60 drops of wintergreen, and blend.

Use 1 tea- spoonful to 1 cup of boiling water, let it stay a little short of theboiling point for 5 min., drink hot before each meal. To make tea from thedried leaves, steep as you would for ordinary teas. Excellent for nervous indigestion.

You can also put a 60 to 100 gram root (cut to size) in 1 liter of liquor (vodkaor rum) for two weeks. Drink judiciously for its physiological effects.

Powdered herb can be purchased; use 1 teaspoon of powder in 1 cup of hotwater twice a day.

WARNING: Always use under the supervision of a therapist. The intake of more than 3 grams of ginseng daily may cause diarrhea, anxiety, dermatitis and insomnia. Mild side effects reported include headaches and rashes.

Ginseng can enhance the effects of caffeine. Large doses can cause hypertension, asthma-like symptoms, heart palpitations, and in some cases,dysmenorrhea and other menstrual problems.

Avoid in cases of diabetes, fever, emphysema, hypertension, arrhythmia,upper respiratory infections, asthma and bronchitis.

Chinese practitioners caution against using ginseng in cases of colds (thisis in contrast to its proven benefits fighting reinfection of a cold), pneumonia and other lung infections. Do not use during therapy with steroids for internal use. Avoid during pregnancy and lactation.

(**Note:** Ginseng is becoming rare in the wild due to overharvesting.)

Hawthorn

Rosaceae (Crataegus spp.: C. laevigata; C. monogyna Jacquin Emend.; C. oxyacantha C.

douglasii Lindl; C. macrosperma Ashe)

Habitat: Hawthorn species are found nationwide. C. macrosperma: UnitedStates east of the prairie. They grow in large, dense bushes. They are generally found in woodlands, on moist, fine textured soils and are commonly used as hedges. In North America, hawthorn (Crataegus mollis)fossils from the middle Miocene Epoch (15 million years ago) were discovered in the mid-1900's by a geological survey in the southern Black Hills of South Dakota

Description: Common hawthorn typically grows 3 to 6 feet (10 to 20') inheight. Branches are spiny. Branching is alternating.

Leaves are pedunculate, broadly ovate and pinnate. The lobes are rounded, with entire margins but toothed at the end; the veins are finely hairy. Its bladeis dull on top and bluish-green underneath. Flowers are small and white, with5 calyx lobes, broadly triangular, blunt, curved and finely hairy. Flowering typically occurs in June. Flowers produce a red, egg-shaped drupe.

Fruits are rounded, oblong or pear-shaped, relatively small (the size of a large cultivated blueberry) and, depending on the species, range in color fromyellow-orange to red, scarlet, blue or black. The flesh is floury and dry, similar to the rosehip fruit.

Food: The fruit is edible, and despite its floury texture, it is worth eating forits characteristics that make it a valuable heart ally. It can be dried and consumed in the form of a decoction or infusion as a healthy drink. Berries are harvested in August and soaked in boiling water for thirty seconds and then cut in half, seeds are removed and dried in a food drier.

Traditional Uses: Native Americans chewed the leaves and applied the chewed mashed potato to sores and wounds as a poultice. The herbal art of the Okanagan-Colville Nation was practiced burning the thorn to the patient'sskin, similar to burning incense (moxibustion) on Chinese acupuncture points. A decoction of new sprouts was used as a mouthwash to treat canker sores, and sprout infusion to treat diarrhea in children.

In addition to promoting heart health, hawthorn has a long history of use for emotional well-being. The Celts believed that hawthorn could heal a broken heart. Edward Bach, an English physician and surgeon, developed flower essences - a natural preparation made by macerating flowers in water and preserving them with brandy - to treat the symptoms of emotional imbalance.Hawthorn flowers, in particular, were indicated for the emotions of the heart.

Modern Uses: Most studies have been conducted on C. laevigata leaves, fruits, flowers, and new terminal growth. Hawthorn is said to improve and protect cardiac and vascular function by dilating coronary blood vessels andinitiating regeneration of heart muscle. The extract can be antianginal and improve Buerger's disease (paresthesia of the foot or single toe, an arterial spasm). It is also used to treat tachycardia. Hawthorn is considered hypocholesterolemic and hypotensive. The anthocyanidins and proanthocyanidin fraction are said to be synergistic with vitamin C.

The standardized extract improves exercise tolerance in cardiac patients. Other studies suggest that the extract may relieve leg pain caused by partiallyoccluded arteries.

In Chinese medicine, the dried fruit is used in decoction to treat irritable bowel and gallbladder problems. The berry is considered antibacterial forshingella species (dysentery). A decoction of the dried fruit is consideredanti-diarrheal and useful in treating dyspepsia. Hawthorn extract has the ability to lower blood pressure in diabetics.

WARNING: Not recommended during pregnancy and lactation.

(**Note:** Some herbs with circulation-boosting properties, in addition to hawthorn, include garlic, ginger, ginkgo biloba extract, and cayenne. The bitter bioflavonoids in the infused flowers, leaves and fruit have hypotensiveand anti-anginal actions.)

Honeysuckle

Caprifoliaceae (Lonicera japonica Thunb)

Habitat: Native to northern latitudes in North America and Eurasia. **Description**: Caprifoliaceae (Lonicera japonica Thunb)

Habitat: It grows at the edges of wooded areas, along trails and stream edges. Several species of honeysuckle have become invasive when introduced outside their native range. Approximately 180 species ofhoneysuckle have been identified.

Description: Shrubby or climbing vine with elegant, trumpet-shaped, whiteto off-white flowers, other species red. Leaves green, glabrous, oblong to 2"long. Fruit is a black, spherical berry.

Traditional Uses: The American species, L. dioioa, L. canadensis Bartr. ex Marsh, were all used by Native Americans: Floral tea used to treat dysentery,acute infections such as flu, colds, laryngitis, enteritis.

Tea is antimicrobial, also applied externally as a wash for edema, furuncles, scabies. Also used by natives as a blood detoxifier. These traditional uses aredue to the antimicrobial properties of the bark infusion for the treatment of syphilis, gonorrhea and urinary infections.

Modern uses: Honeysuckle is used for digestive disorders including pain andinflammation of the small intestine (enteritis) and dysentery; for upper respiratory tract infections including colds, influenza, swine flu, and pneumonia. Also used for urinary disorders and diabetes. Honeysuckle is sometimes applied to the skin for inflammation and itching, and to kill germs.

WARNING: Contact with hops and its pollen may cause allergic reactions. Fertilizers and pesticides have been eliminated as the cause; theeventually dermatitis is caused by the plant.

Juniper

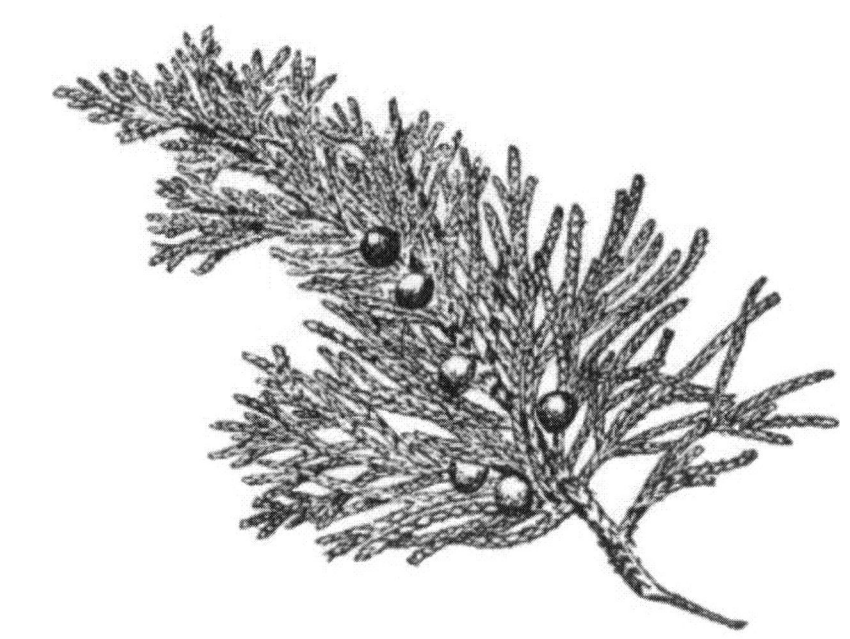

Cupressaceae (Juniperus communis L.;Juniperus osteosperma [Torr.] Little)

Habitat: J. communis is a gymnosperm and, as such, is a plant with few water requirements, so it is easy to find it in places not easily populated by other plants. It is found throughout the nation, J. osteosperma is found in thedry upland areas of the Southwest and Wyoming.

Description: A plant with needle-like leaves and reproductive structures similar to fleshy fruits called galbules or more properly called cuddles typical of the Juniperus genus only.

The habit can be arboreal or creeping depending on the type of habitat where the plant lives: a creeping habit will be easy to find where impetuous winds act (on Mediterranean or Alpine rocky promontories where the plant can grow), excellent example of plasticity of the phenotype in relation to environmental conditions.

Evergreen tree or shrub; often grows in colonies. with pointed, stiff, lightgreen leaves; whorls of three spreading from branches.

Buds are covered with scale-like needles. Fruits are edible, hard, blue berries with one or more seeds and a pungent, aromatic odor and flavor. Male flowers are catkin-like with numerous stamens in three segmented whorls; female flowers are green and oval.

Medicinal part: The ripe dried berries. **Effects:** Diuretic, Stimulant, Carminative.**Solvents:** Boiling water, alcohol.

Food use: Dried berries are used to flavor game and poultry. They can be ground and added to bean soups and in meat stews.

A hot drink can be made from the berries. Gin, vodka, schnapps and aquavitare flavored with juniper berries. Do not exaggerate in the consumption: large quantities of berries can be toxic (like large quantities of pepper and salt), therefore they must be used in small quantities for flavoring.

Traditional Uses: The diluted essential oil is applied on the skin to clean the skin tissue deeply. It was used to relieve PMS and dysmenorrhea.

Infusion: 1 teaspoon of berries in 1 cup of water boiled for 3 minutes and left to infuse until cool. The berry is considered an antiseptic, diuretic, tonic and digestive aid. It is strongly antiseptic for urinary tract problems and gallbladder disorders, but is contraindicated in the presence of kidney disease.

Modern Uses: Approved by Commission E for the treatment of dyspepsia. One-tenth of a milliliter of essential oil used to treat dyspepsia. The berry is diuretic, so the extract is diuretic.

The extract of the berry is used in Europe to treat arthritis and gout. Juniper oil is successfully used as a diuretic and may be useful as a supplemental therapy for diabetes.

WARNING: Use juniper sparingly, it may cause allergic reactions. Avoid during pregnancy: it may induce uterine contractions. It may increase menstrual bleeding. Do not use in case of kidney infection or disease. Do not use the essential oil internally without guidance from a licensed holistic healthcare therapist.

(**Notes**: You can easily cultivate Juniper in your garden and wild varieties, especially western ones, produce fruit in abundance.)

Lady's Slipper

Cypripedioideae (Cypripedium acaule Aiton)

Habitat: Lady's slippers are some of the most beloved orchids in North America. They're found in every U.S. state and Canadian province exceptthree (Nevada, Hawaii and Florida). The continent's 12 species display awesome colors and patterns occasionally open wetlands. More prolific in the northeastern states and southern Ontario. Grows in profusion along the north shore of Lake Superior.

Description: Perennial. Leaves lilylike, basal, stalkless, broadly lance shaped, to 10" in length, bright green above and pale underneath. Horizontal rhizome gives rise to orchidlike, slippershaped flower, typically pink, rarelywhite. Fruit capsule brown.

Medicinal Part: The root.

Solvents: Boiling water, diluted alcohol.

Effects: Calming, Soothing, Nervine, Tonic.

Traditional uses: Native Americans used it to lower fevers, cure headaches and relieve menstrual cramps and birth pains. The most popular species was the yellow lady's slipper, Cypripedium parviflorum, favored by the Cherokeein Georgia to the Ojibwe in Canada. The Menominee of Wisconsin and the Penobscot of the Northeast also used the pink variety.

But the orchid's most important quality was its soothing property. The horizontal rhizome (root) contains the active principle. It is styptic and astringent, considered a superior nervine (calming) and for that reason overharvested in the wild. The rhizome was used in decoction or tincture and considered by Native Americans as a panacea for nervousness, cramps, flu, hysteria, menstrual problems, spasms, and inflammations.

The rhizome is harvested in autumn and used fresh or dried. Following the Doctrine of Signatures, this plant was once considered one of nature's aphrodisiacs because of the flower's shape.

Modern uses: This plant has been overharvested and is now protected. Its chemical constituents are still used to treat anxiety and insomnia.

WARNING: Contact with pink lady's slipper may cause contact dermatitis.

Wild American Licorice

Fabaceae (Glycyrrhiza lepidota [Nutt.] Pursh)

Habitat: This North American Licorice grows in full sun and average to moist soil, in open fields, prairies, roadsides, and disturbed areas. Ranges over the entire West and prairie states, with some extension into the Northeast.

Found along irrigation ditches and slow-moving streams. Often quite prolific.

Description: American licorice is a native, perennial, leguminous, Member of the pea family, that grows from 1 to 4 feet (0.3-1.2 m) tall. It may form colonies by adventitious shoots from roots and deep-seated rhizomes.

Rhizomes are many-branched and may grow up to several feet long. In addition to rhizomes, American licorice has an extensive system of deep, fleshy roots. It grows in large colonies formed and connected by creeping rootstalks.

The leaves are made up of many smaller leaves along the leaf stalk (typical pea family) and are odd numbered, eleven to seventeen in number, with a single leaf at the tip. The plant stands 1,5 feet to 3 feet in height and has white to yellow-green, clover-like blossoms. The seed pods of the plant are numerous and are a dark rusty brown. The burr-covered seed pods make this plant easily identifiable. The roots are the medicinal part of the plant and they are easy to harvest, growing fairly shallowly beneath the soil.

Taste: The American licorice is not sweet as is the European licorice. It tastes much more "pea-like."

Medicinal Part: The dried root.

Effects: Demulcent, Expectorant, Laxative, Pectoral.

Solvent: Water, sparingly in alcohol

Food use: Warriors and hunters chewed the root as a sialagogue (produces saliva) to increase running endurance.

Traditional uses: Native Americans used the root extensively as an herbal remedy for common diseases like fever, stomach-ache, toothache, ear infection and sore throat. The Dakotas steeped the licorice leaves in boiling water to make a topical medicine for earache The Cheyenne drank medicinaltea made from the peeled, dry roots of the plant for diarrhea and upset stomach. The Lakotas used the root as a medicine for flu. Blackfoot made a tea from roots to treat coughs, sore throat, and chest pain. They also applied foliage and wet, smashed roots to swollen joints.

Modern uses: Used as a flavoring agent. Holistic practitioners use the herbto treat ulcers, strengthen the immune system, reduce physical and mental stress.

Dosage and Use: Decoction: 1 pound of licorice root boiled in 3 pints ofwater, reduced by boiling. Consume 1 teaspoon three times daily.

Herbal tea: 1 teaspoon of dried root in 1 cup of boiling waterChewed root is indicated in case of low blood pressure.

Tincture of red root, mixed in equal parts with echinacea is an anti-influenzaremedy.

WARNING: Go gently. Glycyrrhizin in root raises blood pressure

Book 4
Native AmericanPlants Part II

Native Plants

Maple

Aceraceae (Acer spp.; A. saccharum; A. rubrum; A. macrophyllum; A. nigrum)

Description: Sugar maple, (Acer saccharum), also called hard maple or rock maple, large tree in the soapberry family (Sapindaceae). The sugar maple tree may grow to a height of 130 feet. It has a dense large rounded crown of leaves, which turn various shades of gold to scarlet in fall. Its three- to five- lobed leaves appear after the greenish yellow flowers of spring. Different species range from 30' to 150' tall. Smooth bark when young, furrowed with age. All maples bear pairs of winged seeds, called samaras or keys. Common species include sugar maple (A. saccharum); red maple (A. rubrum); bigleaf or Oregon maple (A. macrophyllum); and black maple (A. nigrum).

Habitat: Found in a variety of soil types. Widely diverse species throughout the United States and southern Canada. Wet and dry woodlands. Red and sugar maples are generally found east of the Mississippi; bigleaf maple is native to the northwest. Black maple overlaps the sugar maple range in the eastern United States, but is somewhat restricted to the upper Midwest.

Medicinal parts: The inner bark and leaves.

Solvent: Water.

Effects: Astringent, blood tonic, diuretic, expectorant, liver tonic

Food: The sap contains a large percentage of sugar. It is used as a refreshing drink, or concentrated into a syrup by boiling water. The syrup is used as a sweetener on many foods. Sap can be collected in late winter or early spring, flowing best on a warm, sunny day after a frost. Trees on southern slopes in sandy soils give the best yields. Yields of 40 to 100 gallons per tree can be obtained.

The best sap production comes from continental climate areas with cold winters. Sap contains 2 - 6% sugar, so about 32 liters are needed to make one liter of maple syrup. Self-seeded seedlings, harvested in early spring, are consumed fresh or dried for later use. Seeds - cooked. The wings are removed and the seeds boiled and eaten hot. The seed is about 6 mm long and is produced in small clusters. Inner bark - cooked. It is dried, ground into a powder and then used as a thickener in soups, etc., or mixed with cereal when making bread. Maple sugar and maple syrup from winter and spring sap are what these trees are all about.

Traditional Uses: Maple syrup is a glucose-rich sugar substitute with the addition of many minerals, a more nutritious sweetener than refined white sugar. Fresh unfinished sap is considered a mineral-rich tonic. The Iroquois composed the leaves in water and drank the drug as a blood purifier. The infusion of the bark was used as an antiseptic eye drop. And the inner bark was decocted as a cough remedy and expectorant.

Modern Uses: Maple syrup is touted as a good source of minerals, but there are no proven pharmaceutical uses yet. Maple syrup has been used to flavor and sweeten cough syrups and has less sugar than honey

Maple sap also contains polyphenols as well as a phytohormone known as abscisic acid, useful in helping the pancreas in its insulin production.

Oak

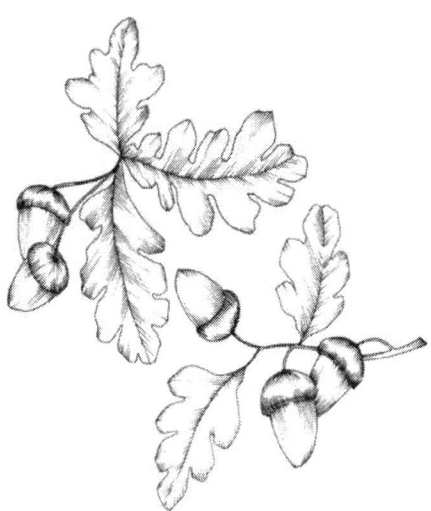

Fagaceae (Quercus spp.)

Habitat: Molte specie a livello nazionale, in aree boschive, e ai bordi di strade.

Descrizione: Many species nationwide, in wooded areas, and on roadsides.

Description: The best way to learn how to identify oaks is to visit an arboretum. Acorns vary in size and taste. The leaves are lobed, cut, pointed, or rounded, depending on the species.

The fruit is a nut called an acorn or oak nut borne in a cup-like structure known as a cupule; each acorn contains one seed (rarely two or three) and takes 6-18 months to mature, depending on their species; the fruit is a nutcalled an acorn or oak nut, contained in a cup-like structure known as a cupule; each acorn contains one seed (rarely two or three) and takes 6-18 months to mature, depending on the species.

Acorns vary in size and taste. Leaves are lobed, cut, pointed, or rounded, depending on species; fruit is a nut called an acorn or oak nut, contained in acuped structure known as a dome; each acorn contains one seed (rarely twoor three) and takes 6-18 months to mature, depending on species.

Effects: Astringent, Antiseptic, Antidiarrheal

Medicinal Parts: Bark and galls of oak, which contain most of the tannins. White oak bark is dried and used in medicinal preparations. Oak bark is alsorich in tannin and is used by tanners to tan hides. Acorns are used to make flour or roasted for acorn coffee.

Food use: In general, acorns from oaks that have rounded leaf lobes are lessbitter than acorns from oak species with pointed leaf lobes. White oak, scruboak, swamp oak, and chestnut oak are good examples of sweet acorns from the eastern United States. Chinquapin oak or yellow chestnut oak also has bittersweet acorns.

Traditional uses: Native Americans used to sun-dry and pound the pulp ofthe acorn as food, to make it more palatable. The bark of the white oak (Q. alba) has antiseptic and astringent properties due to the presence of tannins.

Native Americans drank a tea made from the bark to treat canker sores, and applied it as a poultice to burns and superficial wounds. Dried and pulverizedbark was sprinkled on an infant's navel to heal the wound caused by the removal of the umbilical cord. Chinquapin oak bark (Q. muehlenbergii) was used as a decoction by people in the Delaware and Ontario nations to stop nausea and vomit.

Most species of oak bark were boiled and the decoction taken internally for dysentery and diarrhea. Tannin-rich oak bark decoction was used externallyto treat inflammation, sores, hemorrhoids, sore muscles and joint problems. Red oak bark (Q. rubra) decoction was used to stop diarrhea; the effectiveness of this remedy was again due to tannins. Pine oak bark (Q. palustrus) decoction was used for dysentery and joint edema. The inner barkwas heated with water by dipping a hot stone into a gourd or leather pouch, and the tea thus prepared was taken to relieve intestinal pain.

Indian tribes would let the acorn flour soak in a dark, damp place and thenuse the mold to apply to sores and other skin conditions.

Modern Uses: Oak bark extract, typically from Q. robur or Q. petraea, is approved by the European Commission for the treatment of bronchitis, coughs, diarrhea, mouth and throat sores, and skin inflammation. The chemicals in oak bark have been tested as a cancer therapy.

Dose and use: A decoction is made from 1 oz. of bark in 1 quart of water, boiled to 1 pint, and taken as a gargle for sore throats. The infusion is often used as a mouthwash for gum inflammation, and to soothe skin abrasions, burns, bleeding wounds, diarrhea, dysentery, and hemorrhoids. One teaspoon of bark powder in one cup of water is boiled for fifteen minutes and applied to the affected area.

(**Note:** Acorns can be softened by soaking overnight in cool water. Native Americans would shell, break or crush acorns, then put them in a leather bag and soak them in a stream for a day or two to remove the bitter tannins.

Finely chop the pulp of the acorns and then dry them, to mitigate the bitter taste.)

Oregon Grape

Berberidaceae (Mahonia aquifolium [Pursh] Nutt.; M. nervosa [Pursh] Nutt.)

Habitat: Oregon Grape is native to the Pacific Northwest, from British Columbia to northern California. It is found primarily in rocky woodlands and coniferous forests. It grows best in moist soils sheltered from cold winds. Excessive exposure to sunlight can lead to foliage scorch. Optimal growth occurs in partially shaded, moist areas with good drainage. On the UVic campus, it is found in Bower Creek, Haro Woods, Garry Oak Meadows, Cunningham Woods, South Woods and Mystic Vale. Mystic Vale is the location I chose to manage and harvest Oregon Grape.

Description: M. aquifolium: This is an evergreen shrub up to 6' tall with a gray colored stem. It has needle-shaped, glossy leaves; pinnate, with pointed edges. The flower is small and bright yellow. Fruits are deep blue, waxy berries. The peeled roots are bright yellow inside due to the presence of the alkaloid berberine.

M. nervosa is a smaller species, with rosette of compound leaves in a spiral up to 3' high, berries on central spikes.

Food use: The tart berries of M. aquifolium are eaten in late summer in theNorthwest. Native Americans crushed the berries and dried them for later use. They can be boiled to make jam, with honey or sugar added to mitigatethe sour taste.

The Carrier Indians of the Northwest ate the boiled leaves. Berries can bepounded into paste, as an ingredient in pies and dried for winter.

Traditional Uses: Native Americans believed the berries were slightly emetic. Decoction of stems was used by the Sanpoils as an antiemetic. Thesetwo species of bitter herbs were used to treat liver and gallbladder disorders. The infusion of the bark was used by Native Americans as an eye drop.

Decoction from the inner bark (berberine) stimulates the liver and gallbladder, has detoxifying and cholagogue effects. Apparently, the decoction from the bark and root was used externally to treat staph infections.The Blackfoot used the decoction to stop bleeding. They also used the roots in decoction for stomachaches.

Modern Uses: Ointments made from M. aquifolium extracts are commercially available for the treatment of dry skin and psoriasis.

WARNING: Do not use during pregnancy or while nursing.

(**Notes**: Boiling the shredded bark and roots of both species produces a brightyellow natural dye. The berries are birds food. Oregon Grape is an ingredientin a training mix and a supplement for the nervous system of horses.)

Plantain

Plantaginaceae (Plantago lanceolata; P.*major; P. maritima)*

Habitat: These plants grow on open ground, at the margins of fields along roadsides, and in lawns. Plantago maritima, is found in the upper tidal zoneand particularly abundant in the

Pacific Northwest. Several varieties are found across the United States.

Description: The difference between the various species is in the leaves: P. major's leaves are broad and ovate, and P. lanceolata's leaves are narrow and lances-haped. Plantago maritima leaves are narrow and linear. The green flowers of all three species grow on terminal spikes.

Medicinal Part: The whole plant. **Effects**: Astringent, Diuretic, Antiseptic. **Solvent**: Water.

Food use: Whole leaves can be eaten into salads or cooked with nettles, dandelions and watercress. The fruit is sweet and excellent fried.

Traditional uses: Native Americans chewed the leaves, mixing in saliva to provide an antiseptic and immunestimulating poultice that was applied to wounds, cuts and scrapes.

Plantain is antihemorrhagic, it stops blood flow. Lotions and ointments are used to treat hemorrhoids, skin fistulae, and ulcers.

The plantain tea has diuretic, decongestant and expectorant properties. Maybe helpful in diarrhea, dysentery, irritable bowel syndrome, laryngitis, and urinary tract inflammation.

Modern uses: Modern Uses: The extract of the fresh plant is antibacterial and is used to treat colds, relieve symptoms of bronchitis and cough, and can reduce fever.

The european commission also approves the use of the plant to treat inflammation of the pharynx and mouth and skin. For the preparation of the herbal tea: 3 to 6 grams of fresh whole plant (aerial parts and flowers) added to 1 cup of boiling water. Strain and drink 3 times daily.

Prickly Pear

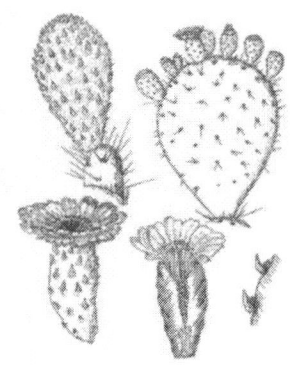

Cactaceae *(Opuntia* spp.*)*

Habitat: Like most cactus species, prickly pears are native only to the Americas.

Found in abundance in Mexico, in the United States, and Caribbean Islands. Dominant in the desert of Southwest.

Various species found in dry, sometimes sandy areas and limestone hills, along roadsides in eastern Colorado, much of Wyoming, Utah, and other dry areas of western states.

Description: Cactus with large oval pads (4" to 10") and spiny leaves of various sizes. Yellow flowers. Fruits typically white, red or purple, 2" long and 34" wide.

Food Use: The pads the flowers and the fruits are edible. Most edible species have flat joints between the pads. The plump pads and flowers can be cooked over hot coals and roasted, to burn off the coils and cook the inside. The inner core is eaten after they are cooled and peeled. The fruit is great peeled, sliced and flavored with cayenne pepper.

A jelly is extracted from the red, ripe fruit. Pima Indians eat the boiled unripe green fruit.

The pads are mixed with water, sugar and yeast and fermented to make an alcoholic beverage.

Traditional uses: The flowers, which have astringent properties, are used as a poultice on wounds, as is the ash from the stem.

Polyacantha (prickly pear of the plains), was used to treat diarrhea. Tea made from the flowers cures stomach ailments, diarrhea and irritable bowel syndrome. The Pima also used edible pads against gastrointestinal disorders. They are burned to remove the thorns, then cut in half and the moist inner part is applied to clean and heal wounds, infections, bites and stings.

Modern Uses: In Mexico and the American Southwest, the prickly pear is still used according to traditional methods. The inner pulp of the pad is a surfactant, drawing serum from the wound site, disinfecting and healing it.

The prickly pear cactus (nopal fruit) contains twenty-four of the known betalains, which are powerful anti-inflammatory agents. The juice extracted from the fruit is anti-inflammatory and hypoglycemic.

Purslane

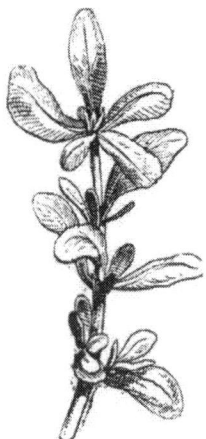

Portulacaceae (Portulaca oleracea)

Habitat: Found nationwide, Common purslane habitats include gardens, cultivated or fallow land, rocky bluffs, cracks in city pavement, and waste areas with barren soil.

Description: Purslane is a common garden climbing plant. Fleshy, succulent annual groundcover. Featuring reddish branching stems and 1" long, thick, fleshy, smooth, shiny leaves that are oval or teardrop-shaped.

Flowers are small, varying in color depending on the species. Flowering: from June to November.

Food use: It can be eaten fresh, in salads, or cooked and added to soups. It is a valuable source of omega-3 essential fatty acids.

Native Americans ate the leaves both raw and cooked. Purslane can be dried and stored as a winter food.

Traditional Uses: Used as a poultice and skin lotion. The whole plant in decoction was used to treat worms. The juice of the whole plant was considered a tonic and detoxifier. Infusion of the leaf stalks was used as an anti-diarrheal. The whole plant was pounded and applied as a poultice on burns and bruises. The decoction of the whole plant was considered an antiseptic wash.

Modern Uses: The omega-3 essential fatty acids in purslane help prevent inflammatory conditions. There are commercial skin lotions made from the plant extract.

Note: May be a good fodder for wildlife and domestic animals, source of essential fatty acids.

Red Root

Rhamnaceae (Ceanothus spp.)

Habitat: This plant is native in Canada to Manitoba, south to Nebraska, Texas and South Carolina. Profusely distributed throughout the Rocky Mountains from British Columbia south through Colorado, the Cascades of Oregon and California, and the Coastal Ranges of California. Common on dry plains, prairies, on sandy and rocky soils, in forest clearings or lakeshores.

Description: There are about 35 species native to North America. In California, red root grows often as small trees. In Colorado, the common species is most often encountered as a scruffy, semi-thorny ground cover spreading over fairly good sized areas.

The seed pods are a bright dark red color, similar to the dye you get from the roots.

They are small, about half the size of a pea, and triangular.

Before the pods form, clusters of small, fragrant flowers arise on the branches, which can be white, pink, lilac or purple depending on the variety. The stems have many sharp spines.

The outer bark of the root is a dark color tending to black, which contains a bright red inner bark. The bright red is proportional to the potency of the plant.

Root harvesting periods are spring and fall, when the reddish color is most pronounced. When the root core has a slight pinkish tinge, it is more potent. This tinge can extend to the entire root.

The root is very woody and should be cut fresh into pieces about 2 inches in size. When completely dry the root is very hard and is very difficult to cut.

Medicinal part: the root.

Effects: Expectorant, Sedative, Antispasmodic. Astringent

Solvent: Boiling water.

Traditional uses: Catawba people used it as a medicine to treat inflammations of the oral cavity.

Modern Uses: The root contains a large amount of prussic acid. It helps the lymphatic system process waste cells very quickly and increases the number of lifocyte-T cells. It is used as an adjuvant for the immune system.

Slippery Elm

Ulmaceae (*Ulmus rubra*)

Habitat: in fiels and forests of North America, expecially at east of theMissouri River.

Description: Slippery Elm is a medium-sized deciduous tree that commonlygrows to 39-62 ft.. Its red-brown wood gives the tree the common name "redelm."

It has brown or reddish hairy buds and red, slimy inner bark. The broad oblong to obovate leaves are 4-8 in long, rough on top and velvety underneath, with coarse margins. Leaves are often red at birth, turning dark green in summer and then dull yellow in fall.Flowers are produced before theleaves in early spring, usually in tight clusters of 10-20. The reddish-brown fruit is a winged, orbicular to obovate samara with a single central seed.

Effects: Demulcent, emollient, expectorant, diuretic, astringent

Medicinal Part: The inner and outer bark

Solvents: Water, dilute alcohol.

Traditional uses: Native Americans used the bark of slippery elm in their pharmacopoeia (Moerman, 1998). The bark infusion was used to treat gastritis and ulcers. The bark extract of this tree has antioxidant and emollientproperties. For external use it was used on burns, wounds and to treat gout, rheumatism and arthritis.

The outer bark was used to induce abortions.

Modern Uses: Slippery elm became a commonly marketed bark in the U.S.herbal market. It is still used by holistic medicine practitioners to treat colds, sore throats and bronchitis. Ointments and salves are made from the outer bark. The inner bark is dried and pulverized, diluted in water and drunk to treat gastric ulcers, duodenal ulcers and colitis.

Dosage and Usage: Decoction: Mix 1 part of powder with 8 parts of water (initially mix the powder with a small amount of cold water to ensure mixing.

Usnea

Parmeliaceae (*Usn a*)

Habitat: Forests of the Pacific Northwest and in the broader north temperateclimate zone of the West; grows in moist and damp habitats.

Description: Parasitic epiphyte, a tree lichen, a fungus living symbiotically with an algae. There are numerous hairlike parasitic organisms hanging fromconifers.

Usnea is light graygreen and best identified by teasing apart the outer mycelia sheath of its skin to expose a tough white central core or cord, threadlike and supple. Other clinging lichens do not have this white centralcore. Also called old man's beard.

Habitat: Forests of the Pacific Northwest and in the broader north temperateclimate zone of the West; worldwide in moist and damp habitats.

Medicinal Part: The whole plant.

Solvent: Water.

Effects: Carminative, Mucilaginous, Demulcent, Antiseptic.

Traditional uses: Native Americans moistened the crushed plant and appliedit as a poultice over boils and wounds. In Traditional Chinese Medicine it is used to treat tuberculosis.

In Europe and Asia, it was used for thousands of years as an anti-infective.

Modern uses: Commission E–approved for mouth inflammations and inflammations of the pharynx. Widely used by naturopaths to treat acute bacterial and fungal infections. Scientific studies report that the extract is effective against gram-positive bacteria (pneumococcus and streptococcus). Antiviral effects have been shown in vitro. Where available, the drug is produced in the form of lozenges. Usnea species contain antioxidants as tested in vitro.

Dose and usage: Powdered or whole it can be applied to skin infections withexcellent results. Tinctured in alcohol, eaten whole, or infused as a tea, it canbe taken for internal problems from tuberculosis to acute bacterial infections. As a douche it can be used to treat trichomonas and yeast infections.

Herbalists generally use Usnea clinically for fungus infections, acute bacterial infection, lupus, trichomonas, mastitis, varicose and tropic ulcers, second- and third-degree burns, plastic surgery, athlete's foot, ringworm, urinary tract infections, colds, flu, bronchitis, pleurisy, pneumonia, tuberculosis, sinus infections, staphylococcus, dysentery, and streptococcus.

(**Notes**: Campers used the lichen as stuffing material for mattresses, pillows,as a soft bedding under sleeping bag. Moerman reports that the Nitinaht women used usnea as sanitary napkins and as diaper material for babies (Moerman, 1998).)

White Poplar

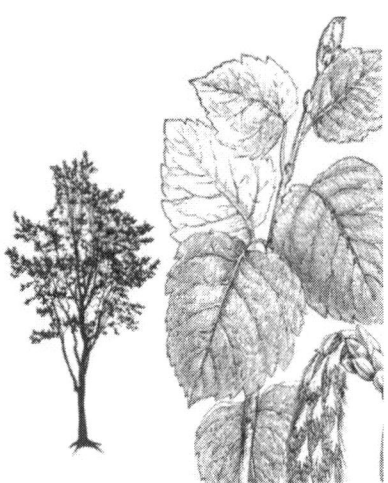

Salicaceae (Populus alba)

Habitat: commonly called silver poplar, it is most widely escaped in the eastern United States and Canada. White poplar populations occur in opendisturbed sites, grasslands, early-seral forests, and floodplain woodlands.

Description: Most have ovate leaves on long petioles. The flowers are drooping catkins. Poplar (P. deltoides) when mature has thick, furrowed bark. Aspen (P. tremuloides) has greenish-white bark. Balsam poplar (P. balsamifera) has broad, heart-shaped leaves edged with fine teeth; leaf stalks are slightly flattened to rounded.

Medicinal parts: Leaves, bark, buds.

Solvent: Boiling water

Effects: Tonic, diuretic, stimulant, febrifuge.

Food use: The inner bark is eaten raw. The shoots, leaf buds and catkins areeaten boiled. It has a high Vitamin C content.

Traditional uses: Native Americans considered balsam poplar an excellentmedicinal remedy for many ailments: the decoction of the inner bark was used as a tonic, as a detoxifier to purify the body in case of acute infectionsand as a cure for colds.

Modern uses: Leaf bud extract is approved by the European Commission to treat hemorrhoids, wounds and burns.

It has antibacterial and antiphlogistic (relieves inflammation) properties. Salicin from the bark and leaves is analgesic. The bark and leaves are antispasmodic and used in arthritis, rheumatism and urinary disorders resulting from prostatic hypertrophy.

WARNING: Do not use poplar if you are allergic to aspirin or othersalicylates.

Willow

Salicaceae (Salix: S. alba L.; S. nigra)

Habitat: Widespread throughout the nation, especially north of the Arctic. Grows in swampy areas, along mountain streams and rivers on the banks oflakes.

Description: 10' to over 100' tree or shrub with fine-toothed lanceolate leaves; has yellow male flowers and green female flowers in the form of catkins. White willow (S. alba), sometimes called weeping willow, has drooping branches. Black willow (S. nigra) is upright, large with droopingbranches. Both prefer moist soil.

Medicinal part: The bark.

Solvent: Boiling water.

Effects: Tonic, Astringent, Cleansing.

Traditional Uses: Native Americans used the bark of young branches indecoction form to treat tendinitis, arthritis, headaches and bursitis.

An infusion of the stem and leaves releases salicin, a natural active ingredient that is synthesized in the form of aspirin.

It strengthens the immune system, but has side effects and can aggravateulcers and cause intestinal bleeding.

The branches were used by natives to build sweat lodges.

Modern Uses: The extraction, though little used from the tree, is approved by Commission E for the treatment of pain and rheumatism. It should not beused by people allergic to salicylates.

WARNING: Recent evidence shows that willow can concentrate cadmium, a toxic metal, in its tissues. All willow species are known to concentrate this metal when it is available in the soil. Prefer to use aspirinfor its therapeutic effects.

Yew

Rhamnaceae (Taxus brevifolia)

Habitat: Grows in moist, shady areas from northern California, Oregon andWashington through Idaho and Montana north to British Columbia and Alberta.

Description: Evergreen shrub or small tree up to 50' tall. Purple-red to red-brown bark. Falling branches with needles, in opposite rows. Produces small pine cones and scarlet, berry-like fruits with fleshy cup around a single seed.

Traditional Uses: Cowlitz Native Americans used the boiled needles of the American yew (T. brevifolia) as a poultice on wounds and to relieve pain.

Decoctions of the bark were used to treat stomach aches. Women of the Okanagan and other Northwest Coast tribes ingested yew berries as a method of contraception.

Modern Uses: The toxic drug taxin (paclitaxel) from American yew is used to treat cancer. It prevents cell multiplication and may prove to be an effective therapy for leukemia and cervical, ovarian and breast cancer.

WARNING: Both species can induce abortion. All parts of the plant are toxic. Unless guided by an expert, avoid eating any part of this plant.

(**Notes:** Many North American tribes considered the yew tree a sacred tree symbolizing protection, strength and virility.)

The wood was used for various ceremonial objects, including spirit poles, shaman rattles, drums, and other devotional items.

In Europe, the yew tree has also long been considered sacred. For the Celts, the European species of yew, T. baccata, was one of the nine sacred woods, which was burned in ritual fires.

Yucca

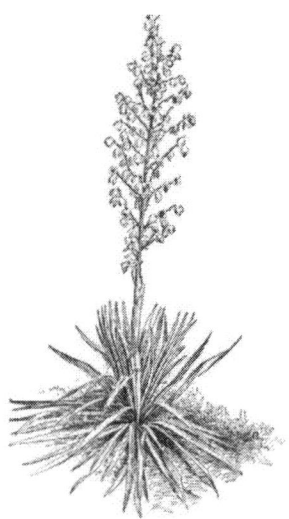

Agavaceae (Yucca spp.: Y. filamentosa L.; *Y. glauca*; *Yucca baccata*)

Habitat: Native to tropical climate regions, Mexico, California coastal hills, sandy soils, deserts.

Description: Medium to large 2' to 20' perennials often in colonies. Long, fibrous, stiff, sword-like leaves radiating from basal rosettes. White or cream-colored, cup- or bell-shaped flowers, borne on tall, woody spikes that extend well above the leaves. Flowering from May to July. Also called Adam's needle, Spanish bayonet or Joshua tree.

Food: The white flowers are edible, can be cooked fresh in omelets or omelets, or eaten raw in salads. The fruits of these plants are also edible.

Y. baccata has large succulent fruits that are not very tasty but rich inflavonoids.

Traditional Uses: Traditionally the decoction of the root was used to repair damaged hair. The infusion made from the shredded root was taken for internal use to relieve headaches. Yucca root extract is a surfactant useful as anatural soap.

The root is a male warrior plant and was used in cleansing rituals to rid thebody of negative energies and evil spirits. Y. baccata root was taken to facilitate childbirth; they supposed that the bitter saponins stimulated contractions.

Modern uses: The extract of the root and leaf (steroidal saponins) of Adam'sneedle (Y. filamentosa) is still used to treat liver and gallbladder disorders.

WARNING: Excessive intake of steroidal saponins can cause side effectssuch as stomach upset and nausea.

BOOK 5
The Native American HerbalApothecary Ancient Traditions, Secrets and Modern Uses

Welcome to the world of NativeAmerican medicinal and sacredherbs.

This volume is dedicated to the knowledge of the herbs and their characteristics, as well as their therapeutic use, according to the Native traditions, by whom the vegetable kingdom is considered asa source of life and healing.

In the tabs you will find uses andproperties of

numerous herbs, to have a deeper understanding of their potential anduse.

For the natives, plants and herbs had the role of teachers and helpersto which even modern man can resort to obtain physical and spiritual healing, with love and respect for nature.

Angelica

Apiaceae (Angelica atropurpurea)

Description: Biennial herb; height up to 9'. The stem is purple and erect. The large compound leaves are divided into three or five leaflets with hollow petioles, elongated oval in shape, about three to four inches long. The upper leaves are surrounded by a sheath when they emerge, which remains around the base of the petioles.

The flowers are greenish-white and grow in umbrella-like clusters. It has a peculiar smell slightly similar to celery, especially the root, but also seeds and leaves. After harvesting, the inside of the cut root, gives a slippery sensation to the touch, resembling soap.

Habitat: Eastern North America, Newfoundland to Ontario and Minnesota, south to Delaware, Illinois and Iowa, east of the Mississippi River. It grows along streams and rivers in wet lowlands.

Medicinal Parts: Root, aerial parts and seed.

Solvent: Boiling water

Effects: Carminative, expectorant, diuretic, emmenagogue, aromatic, stimulant, diaphoretic, expectorant.

Traditional uses: More than eighteen American Indian tribes used Angelica species for medicine.

Native Americans used A. atropurpurea root decoctions to treat chills, fevers, rheumatism and flatulence and as a gargle for sore throats. The root was smashed and applied externally as a poultice to relieve pain. It was often used in sweat-lodge ceremonies for treating hypothermia, arthritis, headaches and frostbite.

The Creek Indians chewed the root and drank the juice or smoked it dry with tobacco to treat stomach disorders.

The Iroquois used Angelica infusions in steam baths to treat headaches and frostbite. The root poultices were applied to broken bones, and angelica tea served as a topical treatment for ulcers.

Angelica was also widely used for purification, added to sacred pipes and burned in healing ceremonies.

Modern uses: It has similar properties of Angelica archangelica, though it is less aromatic. A tea from the leaves is used to improve the digestion. It is also used in the treatment of colds and rheumatism. To improve the effects, seeds and roots can also be used.

Angelica is used by herbalists as a normalizer; to stimulate delayed menstruation; for cramps (reproductive or intestinal); to normalize digestion and relieve flatulence; as an expectorant during coughs and colds; as a diaphoretic and diuretic to cure urinary tract infections. It is a urinary antiseptic. It has effect in relieving joint inflammations.

The part used is primarily the root, though the seeds work very well for stomach disorders.

In Europe stems and leaves are used candied as a dessert and to some extent in the liquor industry as a flavoring.

To make a tea, pour one cup of boiling water over two teaspoons of crushed angelica seeds. Let steep for thirty minutes. Strain. Take two tablespoons up to four times a day. If using angelica root, place two teaspoons of dried angelica root in a pan with three cups of water. Bring to a boil, then reduce heat and simmer until the liquid is reduced to one and a half cups. Remove from the heat and strain. Take a quarter cup up to four times daily.

Angelica's root can be eaten in its raw, whole form, by simply carrying a portion of the root and nibbling at it from time to time. Generally, the root is used as a tincture, thirty to sixty drops up to four times a day. The seeds can be tinctured also (ten to thirty drops up to four times a day), or several seeds can be taken in raw form and chewed.

(**Notes:** Angelica roots are used as a flavoring agent for gin, vodka, cooked fish, and jams.

Angelica is pollinated by bees, flies, and beetles. The fruit is crushed and decocted as a wash to kill head lice. Oil from the root attracts fruit flies.)

WARNING: Angelica can be confused with water hemlock, which is quite poisonous. One must be sure of the correct identification and be able to tell them apart.

Wild Anise

Apiaceae (Myrrhis odorata)

Description: Commonly called sweet cicely, il grows to less than 3'. Broken root smells like anise seed.

The leaves are shiny green and bright; flowers are small and white, in umbels, and appear in late spring to early summer. Odor and taste are sweet. .Leaves smell like lovage and taste like anise. Fruit is pyramid shaped, compressed at sides and brown to glossy black, plus or minus an 1" in length.Fernlike leaves are covered underneath with hairlike soft bristles, leaves deeply cleft.

Habitat: Forests throughout entire United States except extremes of desert,mountains. Shade preferring.

Food uses: Leaves and root edible, but looks like poison hemlock. Be careful. Use root to spice cooked greens and baked goods. Leaves can be added to salads. Cooked root can be eaten cold or pickled; try it in salads andsoups.

Traditional uses: Traditionally used as expectorant to treat asthma and other breathing difficulties. Wild Anise was also used as a blood purifier.

Effects: Root tea is expectorant, decongestant, and a digestive regulator.

Modern uses: It is still considered effective in treating anemia, probably dueto iron in root. As a food additive or spice, the cooked root acts as a carminative.

Dose and usage: Pick leaves for salads. Use root for food and medicine.Anethole, a volatile oil, imparts the aniselike flavor.

Preparation: Root is infused in water as a tea. Keep pot or cup covered so as not to lose essential oils. Keeping macerated root in stoppered bottle of water may yield more of the aromatic, volatile oils.

WARNING: Wild Anise is a hemlock lookalike but much smaller even when mature.

Balsam Root

Asteraceae (Balsamorhiza sagittata)

Description: Balsam Root plant in the sunflower tribe of the aster family known by the common name arrowleaf balsamroot. B. sagittata grows in clamps, 1' to 2' in height.

The basal leaves are hairy and rough to touch, petioled, and arrow shaped, from 8" to 12" in length. Flowers are yellow and long stalked. Up to 22 yellow rays encircle the yellow disc of florets.

Habitat: Dry or well-drained sunny slopes. Foothills and higher elevation of the Rockies from Colorado north to Canada and west to British Columbia.

This plant is widespread in the Bitterroots and other Idaho wilderness areas and on the south-facing slopes of Rainbow Lake, Absaroka/Beartooth Wilderness.

Medicinal parts: The whole plant.

Effects: Antiseptic, antibacterial.

Food uses: The young leaves, shoots and young stems are edible. They can be eaten raw or steamed. Peeled roots are also edible, but are bitter unless cooked slowly and long enough to break down the indigestible polysaccharide (inulin). The roots can be dried after cooking, then reconstituted in boiling water. The seeds are consumed whole or made into flour.

The Nez Perce roasted and ground the seeds, and formed balls by adding fat.

Traditional Uses: Native Americans used the wet leaves as a dressing for wounds and as a poultice for burns. The sticky sap sealed wounds and was considered antiseptic and antifungal. The decoction of leaves, stems and roots was drunk against colds and stomach aches.

The root contains inulin that can stimulate the immune system, providing protection from acute illnesses such as colds and flu. The chewed root was used as a poultice on sores, wounds and burns. The root was also used to treat gonorrhea and syphilis.

In the sweat lodge, the smoke and steam of the balsam root is employed to relieve headaches. It is considered a warrior plant, and in smudging ceremonies it is a disinfectant and is inhaled for body aches and pains.

Black Cohosh

Ranuculaceae (Actaea racemosa)

Description: Black Cohosh is a large perennial herb (*Cimicifuga racemosa* synonym *Actaea racemosa* that has ternately compound leaves and clusters of small white flowers. Flower raceme drooping, with three to eight petals. Sepals enclose flower bud.

Perennial to 5½' in height. Rhizome is blackish, knotty, tough.

Habitat: native to moist woodlands of the eastern and northern United States and southern Canada. Primarily east of the plains in forests.

Medicinal Part: Root.

Solvent: Boiling water enhances the properties of the root but dissolves partially; alcohol dissolves wholly.

Effects: Alterative, diuretic, expectorant, diaphoretic, anti-spasmodic, sedative (arterial and nervous), cardiac stimulant, emmenagogue.

Traditional uses: Pulverized roots in hot bathwater were used as a soak to alleviate arthritis pain. An alcohol infusion of the root was used to treat rheumatism. The infused root was taken to treat coughs and was said to be cathartic and stimulating, a tonic and blood purifier.

Infusions were also used to induce abortions, stimulate menstruation, and promote lactation. Externally, the bruised root was used by natives as an antidote for snakebites, which was applied to the wound, and the juice, in very small amounts, was taken orally.

Modern Uses: The plant extract is approved by Commission E for premenstrual syndrome and menopausal disorders. Commercial preparations are used to treat conditions of the female genital system including menstrual pain, uterine spasms (cramps), hot flashes, menopause, and vaginal atrophy. The estrogenic effect reduces luteinizing hormone levels.

A recent study of the use of Remifemin, a proprietary extraction of black cohosh, significantly reduced hot flashes and mild mood disturbances in a test group of 304 postmenopausal women. The results of the study confirmed the efficacy and tolerability of an isopropanolic extract of black cohosh.

A study showed increased bone formation in postmenopausal women. Holistic health practitioners still use the plant to treat fever, arthritis, and insomnia.

Dose and Uses : The tincture should be made from the fresh root, or recently dried; 2 ounces to 1 pint of alcohol (96 per cent proof) taken 5-15 drops four times a day.

As a tea 1 teaspoon of cut root in 1 cup of boiling water three times a day, or 15-30 drops of tincture added to 1 cup of water, sweetened with honey.

WARNING: Before using this herb for menopausal symptoms, dysmenorrhea, hormone replacement therapy, consult a licensed holistic health-care practitioner. Avoid completely if you are lactating or pregnant.

(**Notes**: The United Kingdom health-care products regulatory agency (MHRA) and the European Medicines Agency (EMEA) have warned patients to stop using black cohosh if they develop signs suggestive of liver toxicity (blood in urine, tiredness, loss of appetite, yellowing of skin or eyes, stomach pain, nausea, vomiting, or dark urine).

Black cohosh is used in a proprietary horse product called Fertility Boost.)

Bloodroot

Papavaraceae (Sanguinaria canadensis)

Habitat: Eastern forests south to Florida, west to Minnesota, and north to Manitoba. Rich, damp forests, along forest trails.

Description: Perennial herb up to 7" tall with a thick, curved rhizome that exudes a red liquid when cut; small roots are reddish. Also known as red raccoon or Indian red paint.

The flower is solitary with eight to twelve white petals and bright yellow stamens (male reproductive structures) in the center; flowering is short-lived, early spring. The 2-inch flower is borne on an 8-inch reddish stem. A large veined leaf wraps around the flower stalk. Leaves grayish-green, covered with down, clustered; growing in a basal rosette, 5 to 9 lobed, with prominent veins. Also known as red raccoon or Indian red paint.

Medicinal parts: The root

Solvents: Water, alcohol.

Effects: Expectorant, anesthetic, antimicrobial.

Traditional uses: The extract of this toxic plant is antispasmodic and warming. Native

Americans discovered that the herb induced vomiting. It issaid that the root juice was used to treat warts. Reports describe that the useof the red exudate of the bloodroot, when diluted with water and applied to the skin, was an effective mosquito repellent.

May be, the popular red skin of Native Americans, as defined by invadingEuropeans, was actually bloodroot applied as a mosquito repellent.

Modern Uses : Research shows that sanguinarine and chelerythrine found inbloodroot have anticancer properties. It is still used topically as an anti- inflammatory. Sanguinarine, although toxic, has low oral toxicity and is antiseptic. Small amounts of it are used in a name-brand mouthwash and toothpaste.

Boneset

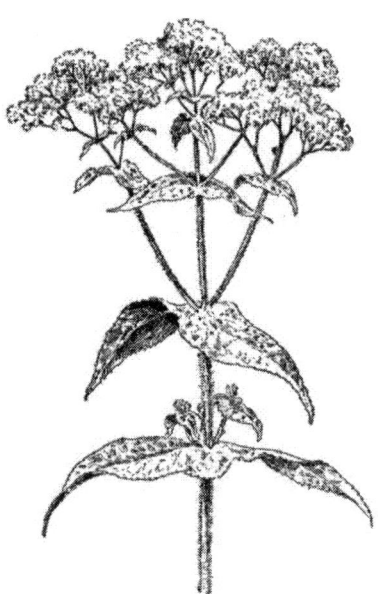

Asteraceae(Eupatorium perfoliatum L.)

Description: Boneset is a perennial herb, wich grows up to 5'. The roots are horizontal and hairy. Stems and leaves are also hairy and rough. Paired leaves, united basally, up to 7" long, are "perforated" by the erect stems. Theyare lance-shaped, with a thin tip. The stem appears to grow through the fused leaf. The small white flowers form a large convex head at the top of the plant.The fruit is tufted.

Habitat: Woodlands and wetlands, moist prairies and swamps of the easternUnited States.

Medicinal Parts: Leaves and whole aerial parts.

Solvents: water and alcohol

Effects: Laxative, diaphoretic, tonic, febrifuge.

Traditional uses: The tea of leaves was considered immunostimulant and were used to treat colds, flu, pneumonia, malaria, arthritis, joint pains and gout and to induce sweating. Poultice of the whole aerial parts was applied to relieve edema and swelling.

This Native American panacea was also put as a poultice on bone fractures. The infusion of the aerial parts was used as a gargle to treat sore throats and for its cathartic and emetic properties. Other uses included the treatment of hemorrhoids, stomach pain and headaches as well as for the treatment of urinary problems.

Modern Uses: Homeopaths use a microdose to treat colds, flu and fevers. The dried and pulverized aerial parts of the herb infused in water are immunostimulant and are taken to fight colds, infections, flu and other acuteinfections.

Dosage and use: Infusion: 1-2 teaspoons of herb per cup of water; duringfevers 1 cup of hot infusion every half an hour.

WARNING: Don't use Boneset without the consultation of a licensed holistic health-care practitioner. Small doses of the herb are laxative and diuretic. Larger doses may induce catharsis and vomiting. Pyrrolizidine alkaloids present in this plant make it potentially dangerous to consume inany form, as these alkaloids have a liver-destroying capacity. Never use boneset without the consultation of a licensed holistic health-care practitioner.

California Poppy

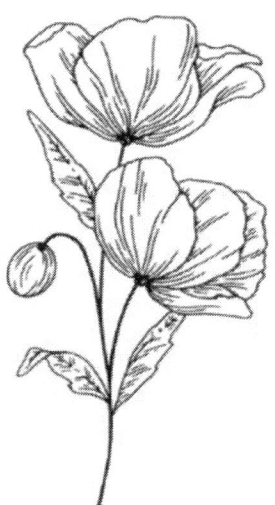

Papaveraceae (Eschscholzia californica)

Description: Annual plants with gray-green foliage. Four-petaled flowers, borne on 8- to 12-inch-long stems, are usually yellow, orange or cream. Hasfew leaves, tapered and pointed, feathery or fern-like. The cup- or bowl- shaped seed receptacle contains several chambers filled with small seeds.

Habitat: California, Columbia. Open areas, dry soils, roadsides. Grown in gardens nationwide.

Traditional Uses: Infusion of aerial parts as a sedative to induce sleep. It was used to calm anxiety and nervousness and as an antispasmodic. It is considered warming and diuretic and has an analgesic effect. Native Americans used the milky sap from the leaves as an analgesic to relieve toothaches. The Ohlone crushed the seeds and combined them with bear fat as a tonic lotion for hair.

Members of the Costanoan tribe brewed a strong flower tea as a rinse to remove lice from the hair. Tribes in the Mendocino area would extract juice from the roots to treat a variety of ailments, from headaches to stomachaches to toothaches. Nursing mothers washed their breasts with juice from the root to stop the flow of milk when it was time to wean their babies; Pomo women made a poultice or strong tea from the crushed seeds and applied it to their breasts for the same purpose.

However, several tribes believed the plant to be poisonous and avoided its use.

The Yaqui Indians scattered California poppy flowers at processions and during special ceremonies, a tradition later adopted by the Gileño and Pima tribes of the Southwest, who scattered the flowers at Easter just outside the church entrance and in front of processions.

Women of the Cahuilla Indian tribe applied pollen as eye shadow and body color on special occasions.

Modern uses: Californidine, an alkaloid in the plant, is used as a sleep aid and sedative by a few qualified holistic medicine practitioners. These qualities have been proven in animal studies only. Homeopathic preparations are used to treat insomnia and used under professional supervision.

WARNING: Not to be used during pregnancy.

(**Notes:** This attractive, deep-rooted, spreading plant is a colorful addition to your garden and provides edible seeds for baked goods. In California it is illegal to pick this plant. California poppy is a key provider for wildlife and is frequently included in wildflower seed mixes used for restoration and roadside plantings in California, to manage soil erosion.)

Centaury

Gentianaceae (Centaurium Erytraea)

Common names: pink rose, sour clover, sour bloom.

Description: This is an upright biennial herb with numerous species and colors. It reaches a half meter in height. It has a small basal rosette screwed to an erect, leafy stem. The triangular leaves are arranged oppositely along the stem and the inflorescences grow parallel to it. Each inflorescence can contain many flowers. The tiny flower is pink or lavender, flat-faced with yellow anthers. The fruit is a cylindrical capsule. It blooms from June through September. At night, the flowers close. The American variety is known to be superior to the European variety.

Habitat: This plant is common and endemic to most of the United States. In many environments, centaurea can grow in moist soils, ditches, tall grass, andprairies

Solvents: Water

Medicinal Part: Whole herb

Effects: Tonic, diaphoretic, febrifuge

Uses: Ancient great American antidote, bitter tonic, prevention against all periodic febrile disorders, dyspepsia and convalescence from fever, tightening the stomach and aiding digestion. Help for both joint andrheumatic pains.

Modern uses : The following is a home treatment for expelling worms and recovering menstrual secretions, preparing a warm infusion: of the powder, 1/2-1 gram; of the extract, 2-6 grams.

One teaspoon to 1 cup of boiling water, one dry leaf dissolved. This potent and bitter herb, is a pleasant accompaniment to all herbal teas. You can mixCentaury with other herbs for flavor, such as anise, ginger, cardamom, peppermint, fennel and others.

Catnip

Lamiaceae (Nepeta cataria)

Description: Catnip is a perennial that grows up to 3.5' and blooms from latespring to autumn. The square stems are erect and branched. Leaves are grayish green, ovate and serrated with a gray underside. Leaf petiole to 1.5" long. Flower spike has a large cluster of individual flowers attached with short pedicles. The small, bilabiate flowers of N. cataria are fragrant and are either pink in color or white with fine spots of pale purple.

Habitat: Across North America, border to border, coast to coast: In gardens, along roadsides, and over waste ground. Tolerates well-drained, dry areas.

Solvents: Diluted alcohol, boiling water.

Medicinal Part: The Whole herb.

Effects: Carminative, Stimulant, Tonic, Diaphoretic, Emmenagogue, Antispasmodic

Traditional Uses: The aerial parts (mainly the leaves) of the plant when infused are a bitter antispasmodic, astringent and refreshing. Herbal teas of catnip leaves and flowers have a mild sedative effect. It is useful in digestivetract disorders, such as flatulence.

It can calm menstrual cramps by slightly stimulating menstruation. Herbal teastimulates sweating, thus lowering fever in acute infections, and like many herbal teas it is a light diuretic.

Modern Uses: Naturopaths use it to treat colic and stomach upset in children. Catnip can be used externally as a tincture for relief of rheumatic and arthriticjoint pain. The tea is also used to stimulate the gallbladder, and is a purifying herb for the urinary system.

Naturopaths combine catnip leaves with elder flowers to treat acute infections. Another combination as a sleep aid is catnip, valerian root andhops. This mixture is also used to reduce stress and as a relaxant.

WARNING: Avoid during pregnancy.

(**Notes:** Actinidin, an iridoid glycoside, is the chemical in the plant that attracts cats. The drug of choice for cats: for felines it is stimulating, but for humans it has a calming effect. The tea is prepared by cold infusing the freshherb to maintain its properties.)

Cattail

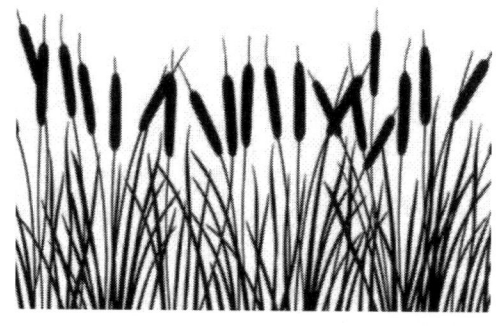

Typhaceae (Typha latifolia; T. angustifolia)

Description: Upright perennial herb to 8' tall emerging from creeping rhizomes. The long leaves are tapered with smooth margins and are somewhat spongy. Small unisexual hotdog-like flowers grow in the spring, on a dense cylindrical spike, with the male flowers positioned above the female flowers. After releasing their pollen, the male flowers wilt and fall off. When mature, the spike disintegrates into cottony masses of tiny seeds that scatter in the wind. Cattails grow in large stands and colonize easily. Two species are broadleaf cattails (Typha latifolia) and narrowleaf cattails (Typha angustifolia).

Habitat: Nationwide on moist, rich soils, edges of lakes and streams, marshes, shallow ponds.

Traditional Uses: Native North Americans have used cattail leaves for morethan 12,000 years for weaving. Cattails have also been a food dish since at least 800 AD.

The Blackfeet and Paiute tribes of the North and early settlers roasted the seeds and dried the roots, then ground them into flour to make cakes, bread, and porridge. Other indigenous groups, such as the Yuma, mixed pollen withwater and kneaded it to make cakes, which they baked.

The hearts of the young spring shoots were eaten as cooked vegetables, andthe heads of the still-green flowers were boiled and eaten as corn on the cobis now eaten.

Modern use: Cattail roots are rich in polysaccharides. Burnt, leaf ash helpsseal and keep wounds clean.

(**Note:** Cattail pollen is very flammable and has a tendency to burst when ignited; in fact, it has been a component for fireworks for at least 200 years.In the mid-1800s, miners and settlers discovered that they could tie ripe brown cattail heads to sticks, dip them in oil or beeswax, and use them as slow-burning flashlights. This practice was later replaced by safer alternatives.

Today, enthusiasts of primitive survival skills mix cattail fluff with oil orbeeswax to shape a rustic, but useful, type of candle 0lighting.)

Chamomile

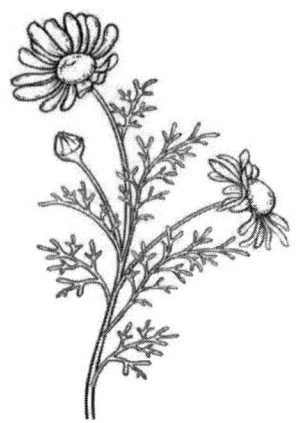

Asteraceae (Matricaria chamomilla; Matricaria recutita)

Description: It has a branched, erect, smooth stem that grows to a height of 6-23.5 in. The leaves are long and narrow, bipinnate or tripinnate. The flowers that bloom in early to mid-summer are paniculate and very aromatic. The white ray florets are provided with a ligule, while the disc florets are yellow. The hollow receptacle is swollen and scale-free. This property distinguishes German chamomile from corn chamomile (Anthemis arvensis), which has a receptacle with scales. The flowers contain a blue essential oil, which gives the characteristic aroma and properties.

This characteristic color of the oil, due to the chamazulene contained in it, explains why the plant is also known by the common name blue chamomile. Unlike the domestic cultivated herb, wild chamomile has a small yellow flower without the white rays (petals) of chamomile. It is prostrate and spreading, heavily branched. The rayless flowers are conspicuous and smell like pineapple.

Habitat: Widespread throughout the United States, along roadsides, trails, wastelands, the especially along trails and roads in the northwest and mountainous areas.

Medicinal Parts: Aerial parts

Solvents: Water and alcohol.

Effects: Antispasmodic, digestive, sedative, carminative, diaphoretic, emmenagogue

Food uses: Tea, fresh flowers preferred to dried ones. Fresh pineapple herb is more potent than chamomile. Leaves edible but bitter. Native Americans pulverized the dried plant and mixed it with meat and berries as a preservative.

Traditional Uses: Native Americans used the herb mainly to relieve stomach pain. It is considered a feminine plant, applied wet to the rocks in the sweat lodge as an aromatic calming agent that invites a good mood. Infusion of the herb used to relieve menstrual cramps stress tension.

Modern uses: Chamomile is widely used topically to treat skin inflammations, abrasions, eczema and itching and to treat inflammations associated with hemorrhoids. One study suggests azullene in chamomile maystimulate liver regeneration. Commercial preparations in lotions and ointments used as antiseptic treatment of sore gums, wounds and other inflammations. Infusions and teas are worldwide known and prepared to helpgood sleep and relaxation.

WARNING: Like many herbs, although antiallergic for some, chamomilemay be allergenic to others, even anaphylactic to a few. If allergic to ragweed, avoid using this plant externally or internally. Reports say a few people get skin rashes and allergic stomachaches from drinking or applying chamomile-containing products and cosmetics.

(**Note:** A pineapple weed or chamomile bath is a great skin emollient and moisturizer. Inhaling the steam can relieve sinusitis. In a pot, mix ¼ cup offresh flowers in 1 quart of boiling water.)

Lay a towel over your head, lower your head over the water and inhale.Washing your hair with the infusion improves its texture and shine.

Corn

Gramineae(Stigmata Maydis)

Description: Maize is a member of the Gramineae family, the genus Zea andthe species Mays. Its scientific name is Zea Mays. Common Indian corn is generally believed to be native to the New World, where it was grown beforeChristopher Columbus discovered America. Columbus brought it to Spain and many mistakenly thought it was brought from Asia. The leafy stem of theplant produces pollen inflorescences and separate ovuliferous inflorescences called spikes that produce grains, which are fruits. The active ingredient is maizene acid.

Solvents: Water, diluted alcohol. **Medicinal parts:** The green pistils. **Effects:** Diuretic, emollient

Traditional uses: Corn was an important crop for Native Americans. Consumed at almost every meal, it was one of the main foods of the Indians. It was often dried for later consumption. The dried corn was then soaked in water until the kernels opened. These were drained and fried over a fire.

American Indians also ground corn into flour with mortars and pestles made of rock or wood. Cornmeal was then used for cornbread, corn syrup or pudding. Often the flour was mixed with beans to make succotash or to thicken other foods. Known and yet not recognized by most for its medicinal properties.

Herbalists and naturopaths use corn silk when dangerous dust deposits are present in the urine and to remove the cause of discomfort in cystic irritation due to the accumulation of phosphates and uric acid. Stigmata Maydis helps in inflammation of the urethra, bladder and kidney, which is the cause of local and general malfunction of the body due to uric acid retention.

Uses and doses: Tincture of Corn silk (Stigmata Maydis) 15-30 drops, tincture of Agrimony (Agrimonia eupatoria) 10-30 drops, in water between meals and at bedtime. For more severe urinary disorders combine 4 ounces of corn silk, 2 ounces of dandelion root (Leontodon taraxacum), 1 ounce of golden seal (Hydrastis canadensis) _ Infuse 1 teaspoonful in 1 cup of boiling water. Take every three to four hours or as needed. Sweeten with honey to taste. Golden seal (Hydrastis canadensis)_ Soak 1 teaspoon to 1 cup boiling water. Take every three to four hours or as needed. Sweeten with honey to taste.

Dandelion

Asteraceae (Taraxacum officinale)

Description: Perennial herb with a basal whorl of toothed leaves and yellow composite flower with numerous rays. The taproot is deep and bitter. At the end of flowering, the dandelion flower head dries out. The dried petals and stamens fall off, the bracts curve, and the parachute ball opens to form a complete sphere. When development is complete, the mature seeds are attached to fluffy white "parachutes" that easily detach from the seed head and drift with the wind, dispersing.

Habitat: Common in meadows, along trails and in fallow land in temperate regions throughout the world.

Food: Steamed or boiled or eaten fresh in salads, it is a source of vitamins and minerals. Tea is rich in minerals from the roots and leaves. Simmer freshchopped roots for the stomach. Fresh leaves are great cooked and dressed with olive oil and lemon juice. As the season progresses and they grow, the bitterness of the leaves increases.

Medicinal part: Root and leaves

Solvents: Boiling water, alcohol.

Effects: Diuretic, digestive, detoxifying, depurative, carminative.

Traditional Uses: Native Americans applied the steamed leaves as a poulticeto relieve stomach upset. The green parts were used as a tonic to purify the blood. Root decoction was also used as a mild laxative and for dyspepsia.

Root decoction is a tonic that cleanses the liver and aids in digestion and blood cleansing. It is also diuretic and traditionally used to treat premenstrualsyndrome. It has a mild laxative effect and can relieve gallbladder and liver disorders.

Modern Uses: Dandelion is a stimulant, diuretic and mildly laxative tonicwith blood sugar and cholesterol regulating abilities. The bitter taste of dandelion stimulates appetite and digestion. It stimulates the production ofhydrochloric acid in the stomach, promoting the decomposition and absorption of calcium, and also stimulates the production of bile.

Uses and doses: of the tincture 5-40 drops. For infusions, fill a cup with the green leaves, add boiling water, let infuse 1 hour or more. Drink when cold, three or four times a day. Or add 1 teaspoon of cut or powdered root to 1 cupof boiling water and let infuse for 1 hour. Drink cold three times a day.

(**Notes:** Eight plants are enough to provide a good amount of edible leaves for two people. You can eat the leaves and make root tea throughout the year. In southern latitudes the plant is available in the garden year-round, in cold areas it should be kept under cover. The flower petals are edible and cangarnish salads and other foods as desired.)

Echinacea

Asteraceae (Echinacea purpurea; *E. angustafolia*)

Description: Upright 3' tall perennial whose solitary purple flowers are up to 3" large with flat, umbrella-like rays. The bracts are stiff and pointed. Leaves are large, opposite or alternate, with rough surface and smooth margins. The root, cut into slices shows a yellow center speckled with black, covered with a thin bark-like skin.

Habitat: Found in the eastern and central United States, in meadows and prairies, at the edge of fields and parks. It grows in Arkansas, Montana, Kansas, Wyoming, New Mexico, Texas, Nebraska, and sporadically in Colorado.

Medicinal parts: Root, leaves and flowers.

Solvent: Alcohol.

Effects: Diaphoretic, antiviral, immunostimulant

Traditional Uses: Root and flowers were used as a cure for snakebites and the decoction of root to treat sore throats. Crushed plant was applied to wounds and as a remedy in case of infections. Chewed root was kept on the

diseased tooth to treat infection. Bear-with-White-Paw, a Lakota healer, used echinacea as one of his main medicines. He used it for tonsillitis, intestinal pain, and toothache.

Modern Uses: Preparations of roots, leaves, and flowers are used to treat colds, flu, coughs, fevers, bronchitis, urinary infections, inflammation of the mouth and pharynx, to boost immunity, and to treat wounds and burns.

Clinical research from 2015 reports that a concentrated herbal and root extract of Echinacea is as effective as a synthetic antiviral drug when administered at the onset of symptoms.

Echinacea aerial parts and root extracts improve immunity in several ways. Also used for skin diseases, fungal infections (both candida and listeria) slow-healing wounds, furuncles, upper respiratory tract infections, sinusitis. For external use, for acne treatment. Root oil inhibited leukemia cells in in vitro and in vivo studies.

WARNING: A study done on 412 pregnant Canadian women (206 of whom took Echinacea during pregnancy) showed malformations of babies to be equivalent between the control group and the test population, but spontaneous abortions were twice as frequent in the Echinacea group, including 13 spontaneous abortions (Chow, Johns, and Mill, 2006). As with all herbal remedies, consult your doctor before using Echinacea while pregnant. The herb should be avoided in case of allergies to the aster-daisy family and also in case of autoimmune disease.

Dose and usage: You can prepare a tincture of E. purpurea flowers as a gargle for mouth and tongue ulcers and as prevention for colds and the flu. Echinacea salve is extremely effective in speeding tissue repair. Torn ligaments respond well to echinacea and it is also of great use to heal connective tissue.

In combination with St. John's wort as a salve, surgical and other wounds canbe reduced noticeably. Echinacea is also of great help in strep infections, particularly strep throat, taken as tincture by oral intake.

The herb anaesthetizes affected throat tissue and helps alleviate symptomsbut it acts also directly against the infection itself. Commercial extracts are available in solid and liquid standardized form with recommended dosage.

(**Note**: Echinacea flower is particularly attractive to butterflies and bees. Many herbalists use Echinacea products to treat acute infections in pets.)

BOOK 6
The Native American HerbalApothecary Ancient Traditions, Secrets and Modern Uses Part II

Feverfew

Asteraceae (Tanacetum parthenium)

Common names: Feather few, Featherfoil, Midsummer Daisy, Santa Maria

Habitat : The plant is native to Europe but widespread in the U.S. Widespread throughout the eastern states, from Texas to New England, inopen prairies in dry forest clearings. Usually grown in gardens.

Description: The plant is a perennial herbaceous plant which spreads rapidlyby seed and covers a vast area after few years; it grows in small bushes up to 28 in height, with light green-yellowish, serrated-edge alternate leaves leaves,with a pungent aroma, flowering in June and July. The numerous daisy-like flowers reach up to 20 millimeters in diameter, and occur in lax corymbs. Theouter ray florets have white ligules and the inner florets are yellow and tubular, like chamomile. The tapering base, with dark brown bark, is rich ininuline. The yellowish, porous wood, with its sialagogue influence, has a distinct odour and a sweetish taste, very pungent, acrid, and tingling.

It is said that bees hate this plant very much.

Medicinal part: The intire herb.

Solvents: alcohol (partial solvent), hot water.

Effects: Aperient, stimulant, vermifuge, carminative, tonic, emmenagogue

Traditional uses: American parthenium has a long history of use for fever, migraine, menstrual irregularities, psoriasis, arthritis, asthma, allergies, dyspepsia including indigestion and flatulence, as a general intestinal stimulant and tonic, and to expel worms and intestinal parasites.

The Quapaw Indians used its pounded leaves as a poultice for burns andmade a compound to cure horses.

Modern Uses : Experimental studies have confirmed that feverfew has activity similar to common nonsteroidal anti-inflammatory drugs, such as aspirin. Parthenium extracts have been shown to inhibit the synthesis of compounds that promote inflammation (including leukotrienes, inflammatoryprostaglandins, thromboxanes, lactones, and tanetine, a lipophilic flavonol).

Parthenium has also been shown to have immunostimulant and antimicrobialactivity in addition to its broad anti-inflammatory properties.

The use of feverfew in the prevention and treatment of migraine is iscurrently confirmed by scientific documentation.

Dose: The following preparation is a remedy for fevers as Dr. Clymer, interacting with the curing agents of nature

- Feverfew (Chrysanthemum parthenium) tincture, 10–30 drops
- Coneflower (Echinacea Angustifolia) tincture, 10-20 drops
- Cayenne pepper tincture, 10–20 drops

The dose of feverfew alone: 10-30 drops every 2-3 hours in the water. One teaspoonful to one cup of boiling water steeped for 1/2 hour should be used as a tea: two cups a day in small mouthful amounts.

(**Note:** Hot compressed leaves are helpful for the discomfort of congestion or inflammation of the lungs, stomach, and abdomen.)

Wild Ginger

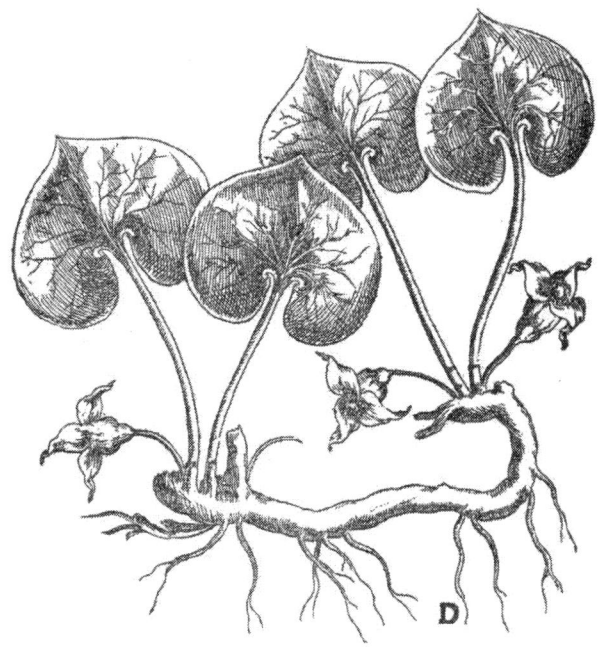

Aristolochiaceae (Asarum canadense)

Description: Low-lying colonial perennial herb with an aromatic root, smellslike ginger; two dark-green, heart-shaped leaves. Note the hairy stem and leaves. A primitive red flower emerges under the leaves in May in Michigan. The plant grows from an adventitious rhizome and is spreading.

Habitat: Various species grow across the entire United States, except extreme desert, southern California, and lower Florida. Found on rich soil inmoist woods as a ground cover in shady areas.

Food: For the daring gourmet, try boiling the root until tender and thensimmer in maple syrup.

The result is an unusual candy treat. Taste the leaves. Crushed root added tosalad dressings. When dried and grated it is an adequate substitute for Asianginger.

Medicinal Part: The root.

Solvent: Boiling water.

Effects: Stimulant, Carminative, Tonic, Diaphoretic, Diuretic.

Traditional uses: Root traditionally used to treat colds and cough; antisepticand tonic. Also used in compounding traditional medicine to treat scarlet fever, nervousness, sore throat, vomiting, headaches, and earaches as well asthma and convulsions—considered a heal-all.

Modern uses: The stimulating root considered an appetite enhancer. Herbalists use the root in tincture to dilate peripheral blood vessels, but this is unproven without double-blind, placebo controlled studies.

Goldenrod

Asteraceae (Solidago canadensis; Solidago *spp.*)

Description: Perennial with numerous species. S. canadensis the most common eastern species, and has a smooth stem at the base, but hairy just below flower branches. Sharp-toothed leaves are plentiful, lance-shaped with three veins. Golden flowers line up atop stem, in a broad, branched spire or triangular cluster (panicle). Plant found most often in colonies. Flowers July through September.

Habitat: Nationwide fields, meadows, roadsides, railroad right of ways, vacant lots, edges of fields.

Medical Parts: The leaves and tops.

Solvent: Water.

Effects: Aromatic, Carminative, Stimulant, Astringent, Diaphoretic.

Food: Seeds, shoots, and leaves edible. Flowers made into a mild tea or used as a garnish on salads and other cold or hot dishes.

Traditional uses: First, goldenrod is not the weed that causes autumn allergies—that's ragweed—but informants say goldenrod floral tea (fresh or dried) may protect a person from allergens (hypoallergenic). Dried leaves and flowers can be applied to wounds (styptic). Traditional herbalists and pioneers used the tea to ward off acute infections like colds and flu or bronchitis, as it induces the production of mucus. Diuretic whole-plant tea is a kidney tonic. The aerial parts infused were used to treat snakebite.

Modern uses: Commission E–approved for kidney and bladder stones as well as urinary tract infections. Plants gathered when in flower and then driedare used in Europe as a relaxant (spasmolytic) and anti-inflammatory. The drug is prepared with 6–12 grams dried aerial parts in infusion. People with kidney and bladder problems should only use the herb under medical supervision. Whole-plant tea is a kidney tonic (diuretic) and may relieve nephritis (NIH) (GRIN). According to the PDR for Herbal Medicines, fourth edition (2007), the herb "has a weak potential for sensitization (can cause allergies)." Plant drug rarely causes allergic reaction.

Dose and use: 1 teaspoonful of the leaves to 1 cupful of boiling water.

Externally: The Indians used the solution from boiled leaves as an external lotion for wounds and ulcers, sprinkling the affected parts with the powdered leaves as a protective dressing. The same was used for saddle sores on horses,The Spanish Americans used the fresh plant mixed with soap for a plaster to bind on sore throats. Missouri golden rod (S. missouriensis), recognized by its unusually long stemmed and fluted leaves, was eaten as salad greens.

(**Notes**: A colorful garden addition. Also, the whole plant may be infused andused as a yellow dye.)

Goldenseal

Ranunculaceae (Hydrastis canadensis)

Description: Perennial to 11" in height. Bright yellow (golden) rhizome. Two ribbed leaves up to 7" wide; lower is typically smaller, sessile; upper leaf on a long petiole, with seven lobes, finely serrated. Solitary flower, found on an erect stem, with three small greenish white petals that disappear quickly. Fruit scarlet, with one or two black glossy seeds. Grows in dense colonies.

Habitat: Eastern United States. Forest dweller; wet, well-drained soil; in spreading colonies on banks in woods. Often found growing near ginseng. Cultivated nationwide.

Solvents: Alcohol, Water

Effects: antibacterial and anti-inflammatory, antidiarrheal, appetizing, antiseptic

Traditional uses: Cherokees used root decoction as a tonic and wash for wounds, inflammations and infections. An aqueous decoction of the root was filtered through animal skin or cloth and applied as eyewash. Decoction was also used for earaches.

Goldenseal was also used as an appetite stimulant and to treat dyspepsia. Air-dried rhizomes and root were used to treat diarrhea. The dried root was chewed to treat cough.

The root macerated in whiskey was taken as heart tonic. The root extract has traditionally been used to treat numerous diseases, including tuberculosis, scrofula, liver and gallbladder problems.

Modern Uses: Standardized extracts from the air-dried rhizomes and root are administered with water or in capsules to stimulate the secretion of bile or hydrochloric acid and to promote peristalsis. The drug has mild antibiotic and antineoplastic (anticancer) activity.

For internal use, it can stimulate the immune response by increasing white blood cells in case of deficiency, according to traditional Chinese medicine. It is stimulating and depurative of the liver. It is used as a therapy for upper respiratory tract infections. Some holistic practitioners still recommend it today as a topical eye drop. Clinical studies have shown it to be effective against infectious diarrhea. The root paste is applied externally to treat wounds and fungal infections. The bitter taste of Goldenseal can stimulate the appetite.

WARNING: Goldenseal may interfere with some medications. Avoid during pregnancy and lactation, Goldenseal has uterine-stimulating activity due to alkaloids and insufficient data on breast milk alkaloid rates. Goldenseal is extremely bitter and may be rejected for that reason by some. At recommended dosages, it is not toxic, however, large dose of the active chemicals in goldenseal—berberine and hydrastine—may be fatal.

Excessive dosage may cause stomach upset, nervousness, and/or depression, hypertension, involuntary reflex action, respiratory failure, convulsions, paralysis, and death.

The herb may inhibit the activity of heparin, as reported for the isolated alkaloid berberine.

(**Notes**: Goldenseal is scarce in the wild due to overharvesting. Many botanical gardens exhibit goldenseal, and the plant is widely cultivated in the United States and Canada. Furthermore, there are safer efficacious herbs for the same ailments, as Echinacea, Astragalus or Siberian ginseng.

Goldenseal is one of several natural products as herbal supplement to rebuild nerves in horses. It is also used in training mixes, wound treatment, and fertility-enhancing formulas for horses.)

Gravel Root

Asteraceae (Etrochium purpureum)

Identification: Perennials to 5' tall in the northern range, and up to 10' in the southern states. It grows from a rhizome on a stout stem, topped with flower heads that are domed to flat topped. Flowers are pink to purple and tubular- shaped disks. Leaves are lance shaped and in whorls, up to seven in a whorl, each leaf toothed, rough and hairy to the touch.

Habitat: Primarily eastern United States and eastern Canada. Marsh, wetlands, seeps, lakesides on damp ground.

Solvent: Boiling water.

Effects: Diuretic, antimicrobial, tonic, laxative

Food: Not generally edible. Some American Indian tribes used the root ash as a spice or as a salt substitute and aerial parts and roots as a medicinal tea to treat infections and colds.

Traditional uses: Native Americans used it as a revitalizing tonic, to relieve
constipation and as a diuretic to treat kidney stones and other urinary tract problems. It was used by Cherokees to treat rheumatism and arthritis and as a diuretic.

An infusion of the root is said to be a laxative. Potawatomi used fresh leaves as a wound poultice. Navajos used the root as antidote to poisoning.

Infusion was used as a wash on infections to cleanse and promote healing. The root of E. purpureum was used by the Meskwakis as an aphrodisiac and they sucked the root while courting a man or woman.

Medicinal Part: The whole plant, especially the leaves.

Modern uses: Naturopaths suggest hot infusions of the aerial to treat colds, fever, and arthritis.

WARNING: Avoid during pregnancy and lactation.

(**Notes**: Joe Pye, spelled historically Jopi, was a Native American healer whointroduced the plant to the colonists to treat typhus fever caused by the Rickettsia bacteria. When carrying the E. maculatum species, Cherokees andother tribes used the hollow stems like straws. This plant is a striking latesummer bloomer worth adding to your wildflower garden.)

Heal-All

Lamiaceae (Prunella vulgaris)

Description: Prunella vulgaris is an edible perennial 2.0-11.8 in tall, with square stems that are erect when young and then with growth, creeping, self-rooting, and reddish.

Leaves are lanceolate, serrated and reddish at the tip, and grow in oppositepairs along the square stem.

It has blue to purple flower bracts clustered in a whorl at the end of the square stem. The flowers are double-lipped and tubular. The upper lip is a blue to purple cap, and the lower lip is often white; it has three lobes, with thecentral lobe being larger and fringed upward. Flowers bloom at different times depending on climate and other conditions, but mostly in summer (Juneto August in the U.S.).

Effects: anti-viral, anti-bacterial, immunostimulating, antioxidant, hepatoprotector, anti-hyperglycemia and antifungal, anti-inflammatory

Habitat: Nationwide. Fallow lands, meadows, forest and field margins,wetlands.

Traditional Uses: the Cherokee ate the small leaves cooked. The ThompsonFirst People drank a cold infusion of the aerial parts. Leaves and flowers canbe eaten in salads.

Heal all was used in traditional Chinese medicine as hepatoprotector. The whole plant was used in infusion to stimulate the liver and gallbladder. It isconsidered alterative, wich means capable of produce effects on chronic diseases.

Modern Uses: Heal-all is still used internally by natural medicine therapists to treat hypermenorrhea and externally to treat burns, cuts and sores. The infusion of the whole plant is used for gargling for mouth and throat ulcers.

Dose and uses: a remedy for diarrhea and to enhance gynecological health isthe heal-all tea, made with 1 teaspoon of the dried whole aerial parts per 1 cup of water.

Extracts of the herb are components of a toothpaste to treat gingivitis.

Horsetail

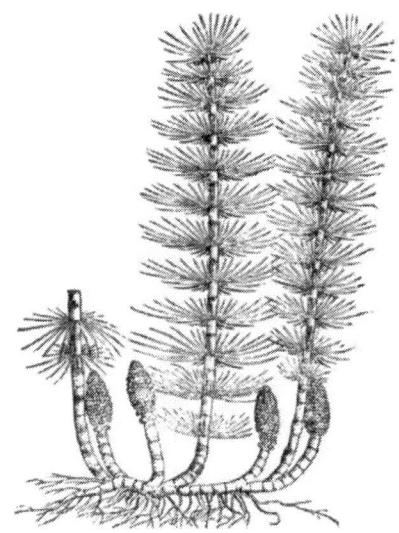

Equisetaceae(Equisetum hyemale)

Description: They are "living fossils" in fact they are the only living ones ofthe entire Equisetidae subclass that dominated the undergrowth in the late Paleozoic era. The most recurring biological form is rhizomatous geophyte (G rhiz), they are herbaceous perennials 3' or 5' tall, that carry their buds underground. During the adverse season they do not have aerial organs and the buds are located in underground organs called. Appears in the spring as anaked segmented stem with a dry-tipped sporangium. Later the sterile-stage stem arises, with many long needlelike branches arranged in whorls up the stem. Also known as scouring rush or equisetum.

Habitat: Nationwide. Around swamps, bogs, marshes, streams, lakes, rivers.

Medicinal parts: Leaves and root.

Solvent: Water, alcohol

Effects: Anodyne, demulcent, astringent. antihemorrhagic, healing, hemostatic, diuretic, antituberculous and remineralizing.

Traditional Uses: This is one of the most widely used herbs by ancient peoples. The Blackfoot and Mexican Americans use the dried aerial parts of horsetail in an infusion or decoction to treat cystitis. The equisetonin and bioflavonoids in the plant may explain its diuretic effect. Native Americans used a poultice of the stem to treat armpit and groin rashes. The Cherokee used an infusion of aerial parts to treat their horses' coughs. An infusion of the plant was used to treat sores, wounds, and back pain. Native Americans of the Northwest eat the young shoots as a tonic and to purify tonic blood.

Native Americans in the Southwest eat the roots. The Meskwaki fed the plant to wild geese and claimed it fattened them within weeks.

Modern Uses: Approved by the European Commission to aid in the healing of wounds and burns and for internal use for urinary tract infections and kidney and bladder stones. The herb has a high silica content.

WARNING: An overdose of the herb may be toxic. Use only under the supervision of a qualified holistic practitioner.

(**Notes:** Ingestion of horsetail by grazing animals has caused weight loss, weakness, ataxia, fever, and other symptoms.)

Lemon Balm

Lamiaceae (Melissa officinalis)

Description: Herbaceous plant, perennial, with lignified horizontal rhizome, up to 3" tall, caulis erect, quadrangular, branched, tomentose. Leaves petiolate, decussate opposite, oval rhomboidal, cordate at base with crenate margin, glossy on upper page and with coating and secretory hairs. Flowers are small, white, bilabiate arranged on inflorescences (whorls) briefly stalkedat the upper leaf axils. Calyx persistent, tubular campanulate divided into twolips. Corolla tube-shaped with two unequal lips: the upper straight bifid, the lower is trifid; 4 stamens. Flowering from July to September.

Fruit: tetrachenio of brown color and elongated oval shape. Aggressive garden herb. The whole plant emanates a pleasant lemon smell and has aslightly bitter taste. Also called balm melissa.

Habitat: Garden plant that escapes from garden to garden; It is cultivated allover the world. It lives in the shade of farmyards, in woods and uncultivatedplaces up to 1000 m.

Medicinal Part: The aerial parts.

Solvents: Boiling water, alcohol.

Effects: aromatic, sedative, nervine, carminative, diaphoretic, febrifuge,antidepressant, mild analgesic, antispasmodic.

Traditional uses: A Cherokee elder called the balm "bee," or wa du li si. The herb is used for ointments; the leaves to make cold drinks or hot tea. It is used to relieve the painful symptoms of menstruation, cramps, headaches and/or anxiety. It was also used in one of several formulas to calm a person's spirit when they seemed to be "acting strangely". Phytochemicals in lemon balm may relax muscles in the autonomic system of the digestive tract and uterus.

Modern uses: Lemon balm is used to improve digestive processes, regulatebowel motility and reduce abdominal swelling, promote relaxation and goodmood.

Internally it can be taken alone or in association with other plants having a similar action - such as lavender, passion flower, chamomile - in the form of infusion or mother tincture or by using a lemon balm supplement. The benefits of the plant can also be enjoyed by using its essential oil and hydrolate, both for internal and external use. Lemon balm is considered a saferemedy with negligible side effects.

Taken internally, high dosages and for long periods should be avoided, especially in people suffering from hypothyroidism because, as we have seenin the use of lemon balm and thyroid, this plant can reduce the production of thyroid hormones. Flowers and leaf may be eaten in salads, desserts, toppings, or cooked with vegetables. A cold infusion made with other mints is excellent. Stuff a jar with all kinds of mint leaves and lemon balm leaves. Commission E–approved for insomnia and anxiety.

German studies suggest that citral and citronellal in lemon balm relax thecentral nervous system. Polyphenolic compounds are antiviral, used specifically on herpes simplex (cold sores).

WARNING: ***Avoid when pregnant or lactating, as it is considered a*** *uterine stimulant. Lemon balm may inhibit thyroid function. Naturopathsuse it to treat overactive thyroid.*

Mayapple

Berberidaceae (Podophyllum peltatum)

Description: Perennial herbaceous 12 to 18 inchestall. Its dark green, umbrella-like leaves, nearly to 10" diameter, have five to seven lobes. The cup-shaped flower, with six to nine white petals, is 1 to 2 inches across and appears from April to June. The fruit is an edible yellow berry that is sometimes used in jams or beverages. Fruit ripens from mid- to late summer;the unripened fruit is toxic. Also known as American mandrake.

Habitat: Extensive ground cover in eastern forests, rich woods.

Medicinal Parts: Root and resin

Solvent: Boiling water and alcohol.

Effects: Cathartic, Purgative, Cholagogue, Alterative.

Food use: Native Americans dried the fruit as fruit cakes that were later reconstituted in water and used as a marmalade.

Traditional uses: Minute doses of mayapple were used by Native Americansto treat a variety of illnesses. The roots were used by them as a purgative, emetic, "liver cleanser", and worm expellent. Roots were also used for jaundice, hepatitis, fevers and syphilis. It treated verruca. It is a powerful laxative. Root powder was applied externally on difficult-to-heal sores. Fresh juice from the root (approximately 1 drop) was put in the ear to improve hearing. It seems that a potent mayapple extract was used by Native Americans to commit suicide. In the mid-twentieth century, mayapple resin was injected as a treatment in venereal warts.

Modern uses: P. peltatum is approved by Commission E for the treatment of warts, particularly genital warts. The root extract contains an agent from which synthetic etoposide, a treatment for lung and testicular cancer, was formulated. The roots and leaves are poisonous, and handling the roots can cause allergic dermatitis. Himalayan pineapple (P.

emodi) is richest in the toxic drug podophyllotoxin.

WARNING: The roots and leaves are poisonous, and handling the rootsmay cause allergic dermatitis. Use under medical supervision.

The active ingredient can be absorbed through the skin. It is allergenic, toxic and antimitotic.

(**Notes:** the Menominees used an infusion of Mayapple to kill potato bugs.Corn seeds and corn roots were soaked in a pineapple decoction to preventfungus and other pests.

To make a garden insecticide: Mix about 8 ounces of fresh root in 2 quarts ofwater, then strain the mixture through cheesecloth or panty hose into a gardensprayer.)

Milkweed

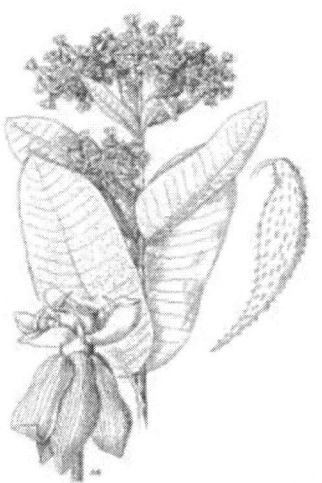

Asclepiadaceae (Asclepias speciosa)

Description: Perennial herbaceous to 4' tall with numerous species. Most have a milky juice, flowers with five joined petals, pod-like fruits, and usually tufted seeds. The highly fragrant, nectariferous flowers vary from white through pinkish and purplish and occur in umbellate cymes. The maleand female parts of each flower are joined into a single structure, and the flowers are typically arranged in clusters. Pollen is typically clustered in bundles called pollen, the pairs of which are connected by a ball of yarn-liketissue that forms from the stigma of the pistil. The 3 main species of milkweed used in herbal medicine: the common milkweed, *Asclepias speciosa*, *Asclepias asperula* and *Asclepias tuberosa*. They have specific properties but also have certain similarities in their effects on the body.

Habitat: Field and road edges, wastelands, meadows, desert and gardens. Various species found nationwide. Common Asclepias speciosa grows throughout the west. Inmortal grows primarily in the Southwest Desert andextends into western Nebraska and Arkansas.

Effects : Potentially poisonous and cardio-toxic, but also cardiotonic, diuretic

Traditional Uses: Native Americans pounded or cut the roots and dried them to make decoctions with a mild cardio-stimulating effect. Many tribes chewed the root to treat sore throats and rashes. They also believed the plant to enhance the production of breast milk because of the milky white sap, according to analogy as indicated by the doctrine of signatures. The latex of the leaves was applied on warts and, it seems, on cancerous tumors.

Another traditional recipe prepared by the Native an infusion to induce sterility : about one cup of dried and crushed milkweed, mixed with three dried rhizomes of Arisaema (jack-in-the-pulpit) and water. The mixture was steeped in a skin or gourd for 20-30 minutes and swallowed one cup per hour.

A poultice of all Milkweed varieties were used by them to heal wounds. The white sap was applied on stings of insects and poisonous spiders, ringworm, snakebites and various skin problems. The root infusion was drunk to treat kidney disorders and the leaf infusion was used to relieve gastric disorders. The decoction of boiled root was also used externally for edema and ringworm.

Modern uses: Homeopathic preparations are used to treat many ailments including edema, dropsy, dysmenorrhea. The variety Asclepias curassavica, from China is used to lower fever and improve blood circulation. The whole plant is dried and used in decoction as a cardiotonic. Other Chinese formulations are used for tonsillitis, pneumonia, bronchitis, urethritis, externally for wounds. According to herbalist Michael Moore, the dried gum can be chewed in small portions to treat dry coughs, as an expectorant; the bitterness stimulates saliva flow, a potential sialogogue.

WARNING: Only A. syriaca. is edible; other species can be toxic. Do not harvest unless you are an expert. Root decoction may be emetic; may stimulate the heart; and milky sap may cause allergic reactions.

Food use: Native Americans ate the sprouts of Asclepias syriaca and made a flour from the seeds. To cook them, they can be boiled and then sautéed with oil.

The flower buds are cooked if harvested unopened. Recipe for flower buds and seeds : Boil water, let pods steep for five minutes, then strain. Repeat, pour a second amount of boiling water over the flower buds, after a few minutes drain again and then sauté in olive oil or butter. The flowers can be dried and added to soups and stews. They can be cut, sweetened and made into jam.

Dosage and Use: Milkweed is a plant with many advantages. Sprouts can be harvested from 4 to eight 8's tall and cooked. The water in which milkweed is cooked should be changed once or twice as the milky sap contains cardiac glycosides and is quite bitter.

The root, when taken as a medicine, is primarily useful for the lungs. It fluidizes bronchial mucus, facilitates expectoration, so it is useful in treating asthma, cold and flu symptoms, bronchitis, pleurisy, and in chronic conditions such as emphysema and cystic fibrosis. The herb also acts well as a diuretic and increases sweating. Too much can cause nausea and vomiting.

The recommended starting dose is 15 drops of tincture three to four times a day. Dosage may be increased if nausea is not experienced.

(**Notes:** Resin can be collected from leaves and stems. Cut and harvest, working downward from the top of the plant. Collected resin should be allowed to dry in a glass or stainless steel collection dish to prevent oxidation. Stir occasionally until completely dry.

This process will not kill the plant if ample growth is left for it to survive. Strong, fibrous stems can be used to make strings.

The plants are decorative in the garden. They attract bees, butterflies (monarch, fritillary) and hummingbirds.)

Mullein

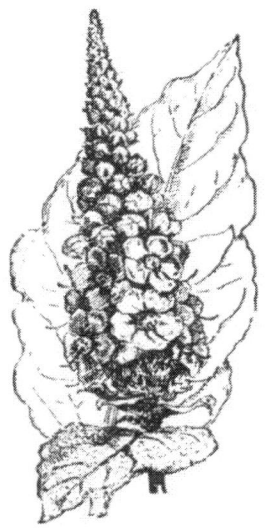

Scrophularaceae (Verbascum thapsis)

Description: They are biennial or perennial plants, rarely annuals, that grow from 1.6 to 9.8 feet tall. Plants initially emerge with a dense rosette of leaves at ground level, and then develop a tall flowering stem. Biennial plants form the rosette the first year and the stem the following season. The hairy or smooth leaves depending on the species have a spiral arrangement, the flowers have five symmetrical petals; petal colors in different species include yellow (most common), orange, red, purple, blue or white. The fruit is a capsule containing many small seeds.

Habitat: Found on fallow land, along roadsides, fields, in mountainous areas across the nation.

Medicinal parts: Leaves and flowers

Solvent: Boiling water.

Effects: Demulcent, diuretic, anodine, antispasmodic, astringent

Traditional Uses: Native Americans made a necklace from the roots for children to wear to reduce teething discomfort.

Decoction of leaves was used for colds, and a poultice of crushed raw leaveswas used to treat wounds and painful swellings.

Tea for affections of the upper respiratory tract, coughs, congestion and infections, bronchitis and tracheitis, to thin mucus. Often mixed with other expectorants: for example, thyme (Thymus vulgaris) and farfara (Tussilago farfara). Used to treat bronchitis and tracheitis. Mucilaginous leaves are alsorubbed on rashes. Dried leaves were smoked to stop hiccups and as an expectorant

Modern Uses: Approved by Commission E for bronchitis and cough.

Dose: Antispasmodic tea. Pour one cup of boiling water over 1 tablespoon ofdried, crushed or powdered leaves. Drink at room temperature.

(**Notes:** Protect any mullein preparation from heat and light. Add one or twoof these plants to your garden: just transplant a first year's growth, a basal rosette of leaves. It will flower the following year.

For insect and spider bites, make an infusion of fresh flowers in olive oil. Pack flowers into a small jar and cover with olive oil. Let infuse for at least 3days. Apply warm oil over bite, sting or inflammation every hour for 12 hours.)

Nettle

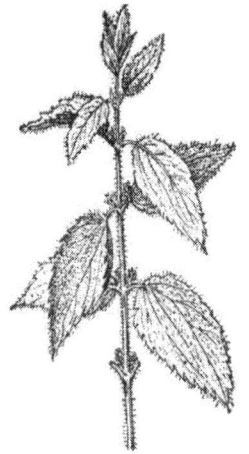

Urticaceae (Urtica dioica L.)

Description: Herbaceous perennial, deciduous, up to 5' tall. It has an erect, sparsely branched, densely hairy stem, striated and, at the top, grooved with aquadrangular section.

The plant also spreads due to the vigorous creeping, heavily branched rhizome from which new plants grow. The leaves are large, ovate and opposite, lanceolate, serrated and acuminate, dark green on the upper side, lighter and more hairy on the underside. The lamina is up to twice as long asthe petiole.

Nettle is a dioecious herb: female and male flowers arise from separate plants. The female flowers are gathered in long, drooping spikes, while the male flowers are gathered in upright spikes. Both have four tepals enclosingthe four stamens (in male flowers) or the ovary (in female flowers).

An oval achene develops from the female flowers, with a tuft of hairs at theapex.

Habitat: Nationwide, edges of fields, streams, rivers, roadsides, in wet andmarshy areas, wastelands.

Medicinal Parts: The roots and leaves.

Solvent: Water

Effects: Diuretic, astringent, tonic, expectorant, antihemmoragic

Food use: Nettle contains a significant amount of minerals, such as calcium, iron and potassium, vitamins (vitamin A, vitamin C), proteins and amino acids, making it a food with high nutritional value. Eating nettles can improve the color, texture, luster and health of hair and skin. Young shoots infall and spring are harvested and steamed or sautéed. Older nettles, hardenedin summer, can be simmered with other herbs - to make a vegetable stock or soup base. Boil for twenty-five minutes, then strain. Use the vegetable broth in your recipes.

Traditional uses: Native peoples enjoyed a strong relationship with the stinging nettle plant since long time. They have used it as medicine for centuries. The Hesquiaht and Miwok used the plant to relieve conditions suchas arthritis, muscle and joint pain, by whipping fresh nettle stems over affected areas of the body. The serum (serotonin, isthamine, acetylcholine, acetic acid, butyric acid, leukotriene and formic acid) contained in the leaves,in contact with the skin caused temporary burning and blistering, but it also increased blood circulation in the muscles and joints.

The Cherokee made a tea from nettles and drank it as a tonic for the stomach.The Cree Indians considered nettles an important herb for women during childbirth. Nettles have also been used for generations to treat allergies. The infusion of the aerial parts has expectorant qualities ; effective for asthma andcoughs.

Nettle tincture is used to treat colds, flu, pneumonia and bronchitis. The aerialparts can be infused as a tea and used for urinary tract infections, kidney and bladder stones, and rheumatism. Tincture of the root is used for irritable bladder and prostate disorders.

Many tribes, including the Winnebago, Omaha, Menominee, and many others, wove clothing from nettle. Several tribes used it as a material for constructing their fishing nets. The list of native uses for nettle is extensive, however. It was food, medicine, clothing, and used in ceremonial practices. Many tribes made a tonic nettle infusion in the spring to cleanse the blood and liver. Pregnant women also routinely used the plant to prevent internal bleeding, relieve labor pains, and strengthen both the uterus and fetus (Schneider, 2004). The antihemorrhagic properties made it popular for woundcare, which was treated with dried and pulverized nettle.

Nettles have been also used for generations to treat allergies. The infusion of the aerial parts has expectorant qualities having been used for asthma and cough.

There are also many documented ceremonial uses of stinging nettle. Nevada tribes burned nettle leaves in sweat lodges to treat flu and pneumonia.

Kawaiisu walked barefoot through fields of nettle to prepare themselves to step into the dream world and stimulate powerful healing through dreams.

Modern uses: U. dioica and other Urtica species have been used against arthritis since Ancient Egypt. Modern studies prove the effectiveness of the medicinal use of U. dioica and U. urens against arthritis, rheumatism, allergic rhinitis, urinary tract infections, cardiovascular problems.

Approved by Commission-E for the treatment of benign prostatic hyperplasia (BPH), in combination with saw palmetto to treat prostate enlargement symptoms (Blumenthal, et. al., 2000).

In Russia, the roots are tinctured for hepatitis and gallbladder inflammation. In Germany, as in the US, nettle root extract is approved for the treatment of prostate problems.

A randomized study of arthritis sufferers suggests that stinging nettle extract, when accompanied by a lowered dose of the anti-inflammatory drug diclofenac, improved or enhanced the efficacy of the prescription drug.

Dose and usage: A nettle tonic is strong but gentle in action. It's a wholebody tonic, because it supports the functions and health of the entire system. It's been used in many ways, from stimulating good digestion, to alleviating allergies through its antihistaminic action. It constitutes remedies for respiratory and skin conditions and to nourish the blood. Mostly the aerial parts are used, but a tea or tincture made from the roots and taken internally can support men's prostate health.

(**Note:** Nettle grows easily in a garden and provides edible leaves. Harvest the newly growing leaves at the top of the stem so that two new shoots can grow.

Nettle juice mixed with seeds of is a good tonic for pet hair care.)

Oregon Grape

Berberidaceae (Mahonia aquifolium)

Common Names: Holly-leaved barberry, Oregon grape holly, MountainGrape, Oregon barberry, Blue Barberry, Mahonia.

Description : Oregon Grape is a flowering plant, used as medicinal herb, much before the arrival of settlers. It is an evergreen shrub 3 ft to 10 ft tall by5 ft wide, with pinnate leaves composed of spiny leaflets, and dense clusters of yellow flowers arising in early spring, followed by dark bluish blackberries. Today, it is used as a substitution for Goldenseal, with similar antimicrobial properties.

Habitat : Oregon Grape is native on the Pacific Coast from British Columbiato Northern California. It also grows in the Eastern United States, mostly in the Great Lakes Region, often occurring in the understory of Douglas fir forests (although other forest types contain the species) and in brushlands in the Cascades, Rockies, and northern Sierras.

It can easily grow in shade under large trees, also tolerant of moist but not wet conditions. It can grow in full sun, but needs shade in hot climates, andmore regular water. A beautiful, bird-friendly addition to the garden.

Medicinal part: The roots (golden yellow) and the fruits

Traditional Uses: Indigenous tribes of America used the Oregon grape for several illnesses, including cold, flu, fever, jaundice, arthritis, diarrhoea, hepatitis, syphilis, stomach disturbs, skin conditions and much more. The plant has also been used by indigenous tribes for indigestion and to stimulateappetite.

Native Americans used the yellow roots or bark to make a dye for coloringbaskets, wool or porcupine quills ; it is still used today as a natural dye forwool. They ate the fruit fresh or dried in small quantities and made into preserves or jellies.

Modern uses: Herbalists use Oregon grape to successfully stimulate liver activity and to improve digestive health. In patients with insulin intolerance, it reduces glycaemic rate.

It has cholesterol-lowering properties as well.

Oregon Grape is considered to have antifungal and antibacterial effects due to its alkaloid content. Alkaloids counteract different kinds of infections. It has been used to relieve problems such as diarrhoea and yeast infection. Oregon grape is often known to reduce the skin cells overproduction in case of psoriasis and to alleviate skin inflammation.

Dosage : tea is prepared by boiling 3 to 7 grams of chopped roots a cup of water (250 milliliters) for 15 minutes, then let it cool and filter the mixture

Herbalists suggest not to drink more than three cups (750 ml) of tea per day. As a tincture, an alcohol-based herbal mixture, ingested 3 times a day in doses of 1/2 - 3/4 teaspoon (3 milliliters). A special blend of 10 percent Oregon grape bark extract cream as a topical psoriasis cream, applied to the infected region of the skin two to three times daily for at least two months.

WARNING: Some medications may interact with Oregon grapes by limiting the body's ability to break down certain liver medications.

Examples of drugs with which Oregon grapes should not be combined: Cyclosporine (Neoral, Sandimmune)' Doxycycline, Tetracycline. Any medication that is modified by the liver.

Osha Root

Apiaceae/Umbelliferae (*Ligusticum porteri*)

Description: Oshá has the typical appearance of members of the carrot family (apiaceae), with parsley-like leaves, reddish at the base, and double umbels of white flowers. The fibrous roots have a dark brown, wrinkled outer skin, internally they are yellowish-white with a pleasant pungent fragrance.

Oshá roots are surrounded by a layer of hairy leaf material. If ingested fresh, they can cause blisters to the mouth and mucous membranes in humans. Dry roots, on the other hand, do not have the same astringent and inflammatory effect. The roots of older plants are much stronger and more bitter than those of younger plants. Oshá plants tend to form circular colonies with crowns of roots growing from a central root, and can become very large

Habitat: Osha is an upland plant, found primarily in deep, fertile, moist soils., along forest edges and cliffs of the Colorado Columbine and Aspen Bluehills Rocky Mountains. In areas of New Mexico, Colorado, and Utah, oshá reaches a height of 6-7 feet.

Taste: Bitter, spicy, woodsy

Medicinal part: **Root**

Effects: antiviral, antibacterial, antifungal and antiinflammatory, aromatic, immune stimulant, diaphoretic, expectorant, circulatory stimulant

Solvents: Alcohol, Water

Traditional uses: This aromatic root also called Bear root or Snakeroot, was traditionally administered topically to disinfect wounds. Native Americans used oshà root to treat fever, cough and sore throat, gastrointestinal problems and wounds.

In Mexico, the Tarahumara tribe used L. porteri during ritual ceremonies for protection against negative energies and spirits; pieces of the root are burned on the hot rocks during sweatlodge ceremonies as part of Native American smudging. The Zuni people chewed it during healing rituals.

Modern uses: Today, osha root is most commonly used as a tea, tincture, or decongestant.

Osha root extract can fight oxidative stress due to its powerful antioxidant effects, and boost the immune system.

Warning: Avoid oshà during pregnancy and lactation. Ingesting osha could start menstruation in pregnant women and cause miscarriage. Effects during breastfeeding are unknown, so it's recommended to avoid osha completely.

(**Note:** The osha is a plant valued by bears.)

Pasque Flower

Ranunculaceae (*Pulsitilla spp.*)

Description: This herbaceous perennial plant has upright rhizomes, as food-storage organs. Its leaves and stems are long, soft, silvergrey and hairy. The 33 species of the plant have similar features: finely dissected leaves, hairy stems, and bell shaped flowers with sepals. The biggest difference is height;the varieties range from 3" to 9". Seed heads are plumed. The lilac Pasqueflower (*Pulsitilla patens*) is covered with a soft hairy down, and produces only one or two flowers.

Medicinal Parts: Flower and aerial parts

Effects: Tonic, sedative, nervine

Habitat: Found in the prairie and mountain meadows. Pictured specimenfrom the Cloud Peak Wilderness, Bighorn Mountains, Wyoming.

Traditional uses: Blackfoot use dit to induce uterine contractions leading to abortion. Also believed to speed difficult childbirth. The Dakotas call it hokshi-chekpa wahcha, twin flower. The Lakotas call it hoksi' cekpa, child's navel.

Blackfeet call it napi, old man.

Omaha and Ponca call it te-zhinga-makan, little buffalo medicine. It was one of the sacred power medicines of the Omahas and Poncas. Among these two tribes, the right to use the pasque flower was limited to the medicine men.

Modern uses: Used as a homeopathic preparation or in combination with others, for a variety of ailments to include colds, coughs, and digestive problems. The essence of the Pasque flower is used in aromatherapy to relieve shyness.

WARNING: *Not edible, highly toxic. May slow heart and cause cardiac arrest.*

Passionflower

Passifloraceae (Passiflora incarnata)

Description: There are numerous varieties, all similar Passionflower is a perennial herbaceous plant, climbing and branching, which has a robust and woody stem that can reach 35' in length. Bark is longitudinal and striated.

Leaves are alternate, with petioles, serrated with fine hair on both the top and bottom. Leaf blades have bumps called floral nectaries. Flowers are single, hermaphrodite, mandala-shaped, with ray-like, showy petals, up to 5" wide.

Habitat: Climbers of open areas and the forest edge. Most species are tropical or subtropical, native to the southeastern United States, Argentina and Brazil but can grow in temperate climates. With a worldwide distribution, many species are found in seven climate zones. It is found wildin the southeastern United States.

Medicinal parts: Flowers and aerial parts

Solvent: Diluted alcohol.

Effects: Anodyne, sedative, diuretic, antispasmodic.

Food use: Tea of leaves and flowers has mild sedative properties. Fresh fruit can be eaten raw or squeezed. Mexicans mix it with cornmeal of other grainas soup. Native Americans eat the leaves generally boiled and pan-fried in vegetable oil or animal fat.

Traditional Uses: Fresh or dried aerial parts or whole dried herb, infused asa mild sedative, to treat nervousness and insomnia, and in many tribes as a blood purifier. The antispasmodic effect of the infusion is supportive of the gastrointestinal system in cases of pain and cramps from nervous stress. Thenatives used the infusion of the crushed root to treat earache. L The poulticeobtained from the crushed root was applied on inflamed bruises, boils and cuts. Water from the plant root was mixed with lye-treated corn and used to wean babies. Pioneers used the whole plant with Epsom salts as a sedative bath. Tea of roots and aerial parts to treat hemorrhoids.

Modern Uses: As above. In animal studies, the infusion has been reported tobe sedative, antispasmodic. Approved by Commission E for the treatment of nervousness and insomnia. Use as an antidepressant and for the treatment of somatization disorder is unproven.

(**Note:** The Doctrine of Signatures suggests that this sensual-looking plant isan aphrodisiac. Passionflower contains harmala betacarboline alkaloids, which have antidepressant properties. Usually the flower has only traces of the chemicals, but the leaves and roots of some species have been used to enhance the effects of psychotropic drugs.

The extract is used to calm stressed cats, and has been used as a mild sedativefor horses.)

Peppermint

Lamiaceae (Mentha piperita)

Description: The common characteristics of the many varieties include: square, erect stem, leaves almost always aromatic when crushed, aggressive and spreading. Species vary in height from 8" to 30" tall. Root is a spreading rhizome. Leaves are lance shaped, elongated to ovate to roundish, normally serrated. Flowers in dense whorls culminating in a spike of flowers or in clusters at the axil of the leaves. Flower colors vary by species: white, purple, blue. A common species is peppermint (Mentha piperita).

Habitat: Nationwide. M. piperita is usually found near water, shorelines, stream banks and dunes in the Great Lakes and along mountain passes in moist meadows.

Medicinal Parts: Leaves and stems.

Solvent: Water, alcohol

Effects: Aromatic, stimulant, stomachic, carminative.

Food use: Peppermint is used in teas, salads and cold drinks and to flavor hot and cold dishes. Romans such as Pliny the Elder used mint to flavor wines and sauces.

Traditional uses: Native Americans used it to soothe cramps and tummy aches even in children.

This herb has long been known for its calming effects on stomach pain and soothing of the digestive system.

Modern Uses: Approved by Commission E for the treatment of dyspepsia, gallbladder and liver problems. Peppermint oil is approved for colds, coughs, bronchitis, fever, inflammation of the mouth and larynx, infection prevention, dyspepsia. Recent studies in Europe suggest it may be a treatment for irritablebowel syndrome. The tea and oil have an antispasmodic effect on the digestive system.

Peppermint is also used to treat gastrointestinal disturbs as colic, cramping and flatulence. It can help relieve diarrhea, spastic colon and constipation. Headaches due to digestive weakness can be relieved by taking peppermint.In aromatherapy the essential oil is used to treat headaches and respiratory infections, smeared on the chest. Capsules are used for irritable bowel syndrome and to relieve colonic spasms.

WARNING: In too high a concentration, mint oils are irritating to theskin. Be careful. Peppermint is contraindicated for ulcers, gastritis andgastric reflux because it relaxes the esophageal sphincter, allowing stomach acid to go up into the esophagus.

(**Note:** Peppermint, spearmint, mountain mint and other mints have edible flowers and leaves that can be used in salads and desserts. Historically, mintwas sprinkled on floors to release the house of insects and rodents.)

Evening Primrose

Onagraceae (Oenothera biennis)

Description: This biennial reaches 3' or more in height and has turnip-likeroots.

The first year it develops a basal rosette of leaves without flowers; the secondyear it blooms erect and showy, and in the fall it produces large fruit capsules full of seeds. Leaves are oblong, lanceolate, pointed and toothed.

Fragrant yellow trumpet-shaped flowers, 1" long, open in the evening. Fruits are linear-oblong, 4-sided, downy, containing dark gray or black seeds with sharp edges.

Habitat: Nationwide, grows in gardens, along roadsides, on fallow land, fields and prairies

Food use: Root is edible, best when young. New leaves from the first or second year are edible raw and sautéed. Older leaves are tough and should be cooked.

Effects : antiallergic, cholesterol-lowering, analgesic, anti-inflammatory, soothing, pain relieving.

Traditional Uses: Native Americans made a hot root poultice to treat hemorrhoids. The roots were chewed to increase strength and stamina. The whole plant was crushed and used as a poultice on bruises and sores.

Modern Uses: The seed oil is used to treat essential fatty acid deficiency and to lower cholesterol. The cholesterol-lowering effect was successful in a double-blind crossover study conducted in 1994 (Guivernau, Meza, Barja, et al.). Seed extract is said to dilate coronary arteries and clear arterial blockages.

The oil may provide relief from symptoms of premenstrual syndrome (PMS). Also used as a treatment for recurrent breast cysts (Ooman, 1998). The essential fatty acids and amino acids in the seeds are considered effective in treating mild depression. Evening primrose oil (EPO) has been used successfully with a vitamin B6 therapy to treat breast pain. The oil is considered anticoagulant, demulcent, and anti-inflammatory.

One study showed that in women who had recurrent breast cysts, treatment with evening primrose oil resulted in a lower rate of recurrence than placebo. Another study suggests that the plant may reverse neurological damage in diabetic patients.

WARNING: In excessive doses E.Primerose may cause headache, diarrhea, indigestion, and nausea. Avoid in cases of schizophrenia and epileptogenic drugs: phenothiazines. No scientific evidences during pregnancy and lactation.

(**Notes:** Evening primrose oil is high in GLA, a naturally occurring nutrient also found in breast milk. This widely used nutritional supplement has been marketed for over thirty years.

Seeds are fine additions to bird feeders; finches, sparrows, and numerous other birds will be attracted.

Omega 6 essential fatty acids from Evening Primrose are a constituent in skincare products.)

Red Clover

Fabaceae (Trifolium pratense)

Description: A perennial herbaceous, with 3 leaves with a distinct V markingon each leaflet. Leaflets are ovated and fine toothed. Flowers tint: pink to red,dome shaped or rounded in a dense cluster. Grows to 12" to 18" tall.

Habitat: Nationwidw, on full sunny fields, roadsides, waste ground, alongand abandoned railroads.

Medicinal part: flower and leaves.

Solvent: Boiling water.

Effects: Alterative, antispasmodic, expectorant

Traditional uses: Red clover was introduced to the Americas from Europe and was widely used by native peoples. The leaves and flowers were used asan infusion (tea) for whooping cough, a general remedy for cancer, menopause, and as a "blood medicine" to purify the blood. An ointment wasmade from it for poisonous bites. Tribes in California and Arizona cooked and ate it. Floral tea traditionally used as a panacea, a cure-all. Decoction or tea used as an external wash on burns, wounds, and insect bites. Floral tea also used as an antispasmodic and mild sedative. Isoflavone estrogen-like compounds in clover are used to treat menopausal problems.

Modern uses: Red clover is still used to treat menopausal symptoms and it may improve circulation and blood flow in the heart. Standardized extracts are used, and should only be used under the supervision of a licensed health-care practitioner. The drug may increase bleeding and has also other side effects.

WARNING: Because of potential increased bleeding time from cloverchemistry, floral teas should be used sparingly or not at all, unless supervised by a holistic health-care professional.

Sage Shrub

Asteraceae (Artemisia tridentata)

Description: Sage, Salvia Officinalis, is an evergreen aromatic plant, with oval lanceolate leaves and very decorative blue-purple flowers, which can reach up to 7' tall. It has thick and oblong leaves, with very intense fragrance, silvery-green colored and covered with hairs. Its fruits are formed at the base of the flowers and contain the tiny dark brown seeds.

Yellow and brownish flowers form spreading, long, narrow clusters. Bloom in July to October.

Habitat: Dry areas of Wyoming, Washington, Montana, Texas, New

Mexico, California, Idaho, Oregon, Colorado, and other areas in the West.

Effects: carminative, antispasmodic, antiseptic, astringent and antisudoric, wound healing, depurative

Food use: The seeds, raw or dried, are added in some liquors as a flavoring, and are made into ground flour as a survival food. The leaves can be fried or added as a flavoring to many recipes.

Traditional Uses: This powerful sacred and warrior plant is rubbed on the body and fumigated to rid the person of evil spirits and negative energies.

Tea made from the leaves helps cure infections, soothe stomach aches, ease childbirth and soothe eye inflammation. Leaves soaked in water are applied as a poultice on wounds and as an antirheumatic.

The infusion was used to treat sore throats, coughs, colds and bronchitis. A decoction or infusion was used as a wash for sores, cuts and pimples. The aromatic decoction of the smoking herb was inhaled for respiratory ailmentsand headaches. This panacea was also drunk to regularize bowel functions. Native Americans also rubbed the herb on their bodies to conceal human scent while hunting.

Modern Uses: Still very popular and important in Native American religious rituals, including smudging, sweat lodge, and as a disinfectant. Gram-positivebacteria are sensitive to A. tridentata oil.

(**Note:** Add this herb to your hot bath or sweat lodge for a fragrant, disinfecting, and relaxing cleanse. The sage bush is often the only source of firewood in the desert. As a moth and flea repellent, decoction of the herb was also applied to the hair and wounds of pets in addition to other repellentherbs.)

Saint John's Wort

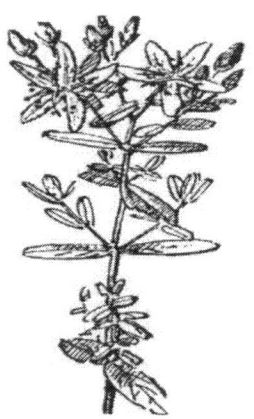

Hyperacaceae (Hypericum perforatum L.)

Description: Almost woody erect stem; may grow to 4' in height. Semi- evergreen perennial medicinal plant; the name Hypericum Perforatum derivesfrom the fact that the leaflets, in backlight, appear pitted, effect due to translucent glands also present in sepals and petals. The plant is glabrous, with an erect stem crossed by two longitudinal stripes in relief. Leaves are black spotted on the margins, with glandular structures containing hypericin (a red colored oil), these glandular structures are present especially in petals. Leaves are oblong opposite. The golden yellow flowers have 5 delicate petalsand are gathered in corymbs and flourish in june and july.

Habitat: Nationwide. Roadsides, waste grounds, fields, prairies, streambanks, riverbanks, full sun. There are numerous garden varieties.

Effects : anti-inflammatory, antibacterial, antiviral, antidiarrheal, astringent, cicatrizant, antidepressive, anti-oxidant

Traditional uses: Native American used Saint John's Wort to heal wounds,as cicatrizant and for its antibiotic properties. They also chewed the root of indigenous species of Saint John's Wort for internal use in the treatment of severe physical wasting and fever, for external use for snakebites.

Crushed leaves and flowers were stuffed in nose to stem nosebleed. In addition, oil infusion of the aerial parts were used to treat bruises, burns, and ulcers (FRICHSENBROWN, 1989). The whole-plant decoction was used to induce abortions by stimulating menstruation.

St. John's wort was a plant already known to ancient Greeks and Romans. Its medicinal properties were described by Dioscorides and Galen. Dioscorides recommended it for sciatica and as a remedy for burns.

He also recommended the decoction of its seeds for malaria. Galen instead believed it was an effective amulet against spells and apparitions. Even Pliny the Elder, in the first century, described its use with wine against the bite of snakes and in particular to treat burns.

In the Middle Ages St. John's wort was gathered in bunches and burnt in houses in order to keep demons and evil spirits away from people and houses: St. John's wort was popularly known as "fuga daemonorum".

Modern uses: Appreciated for its numerous effects on injured and irritated skin, St. John's Wort oil is widely used in phytotherapy for the treatment of various skin disorders.

Oil and Essential Oil: a bit of clarity

The wording "St. John's wort oil" could generate confusion, since from the plant it is also possible to obtain an essential oil and a fixed oil. However, when we talk about St. John's wort oil we commonly refer to the oleolyte obtained by maceration in vegetable oil of the flowers and aerial parts of the plant.

Thanks to its multiple properties, St. John's Wort oil is particularly indicated in case of dry and reddened skin, sunburns, minor burns and small burns.

Moreover, St. John's wort oil can be useful to promote the healing of small wounds and sores.

By internal use, as tincture, it slows down the reabsorption of neurotransmitters (serotonin, dopamine, noradrenaline) at the level of the central nervous system; without negative effects on wakefulness, attention and memory, it does not alter sleep phases and does not cause any dependence.

Several studies in Europe show the benefit of this herb to treat mild depression. A standardized extract of 0.3 percent hypericin, 300 milligrams three times a day, was found comparable in antidepressant effect to a drug standard of imipramine.

A recent study suggests a 5 percent hyperforin extract of the plant showed a slight increase in cognitive function. Other trials suggest that the drug may combat fatigue, relieve anxiety, improve sleep, help with weight loss, and attenuate menopausal symptoms.

Infusion of flowers and leaves is used externally as a cooling, wound-healing antiseptic treatment. It is antiviral and anti-inflammatory and helps healing when used externally as a poultice or wash for infections, burns, bruises, sprains, tendonitis, sprains, neuralgia, or cramps.

WARNING: Don't use Saint John's Wort to treat severe depression or bipolar depression. Its use may lower activity of simultaneously administered drugs, including nonsedating antihistamines, oral contraceptives, certain antiretrovirals, antiepileptics, calcium channel blockers, cyclosporine, some chemotherapeutics, antibiotics, and select antifungals. At high doses it causes photosensitization, so it is not recommended to undergo sun exposure and UV rays after intake of highdosages of dry extract titrated in hypericin or isolated hypericin.

It is not recommended the contemporary use with SSRI antidepressants, because of the possible effects of addition and therefore toxic dose overcoming. It is also contraindicated in pediatric age and adolescence, during pregnancy and lactation. Side effects include gastrointestinal irritation, restlessness, and mild allergic reactions. It appears to be synergistic with serotonin reuptake inhibitors, thereby increasing serotoninlevels. Recent evidence suggests the chronic long-term use (abuse) of Saint-John's-wort is undesirable and may have negative health consequences.

Purchase products only after consultation with a health-care professional.

Senega Snakeroot

Polygalaceae (Polygala senega)

Description: This indigenous plant is a small perennial herb, native to the eastern regions of North America, with a tortuous root, little branched, alternate and lanceolate leaves, greenish flowers in terminal bunches. 8-14in. high, occasionally tinged with red. Blooms in May and June. The new, small white flower consists of five sepals, three petals and small, bicellular,two-valved acpsulas. The English name is Milkwort.

Habitat: Most species are sub- tropical but nearly 200 are North American.

P. senega, known as Mountain Flax or Senega snakeroot, grows from New Brunswick to Alberta and southward to Georgia and Arkansas, in part shade,sun; sandy or rocky soil, open woods, prairies, stream banks

Effects: expectorant, antispasmodic, stimulating, diuretic

Medicinal Part: The root.

Solvents: Water, dilute alcohol.

Traditional uses: At the beginning of the eighteenth-century Dr. John Tennent, a Scottish physician living in Pennsylvania, was introduced to theuse of the root by the Seneca Indians for curing rattlesnake-bite.

The Ojibwa call Seneca snakeroot *bi'jikiwuk'* which literally means "buffalomedicine". They usually combined Seneca snakeroot with other herbs, to prepare their principal war medicine called *bi'jikiwuk*. Seneca snakeroot is considered to be the principal herb, without which the preparation would notbe efficacious. It was said to make men strong and to be a powerful healing medicine. Ojibwa warriors used to chew it and spray it from the lips on theirbody and equipment. The herb was considered to be effective in counteracting negative influences. It was taken four times daily all throughout life and was considered to increase vitality and personal power.

Modern uses: It is useful in fighting cold and flu, pleurisy, chronic catarrh, asthma and cough. It is also used as an anti-inflammatory in rheumatism andas a cataplasm for swellings.

The roots of this plant are used in herbal medicine as they have stimulating,diuretic and expectorant properties.

Valerian

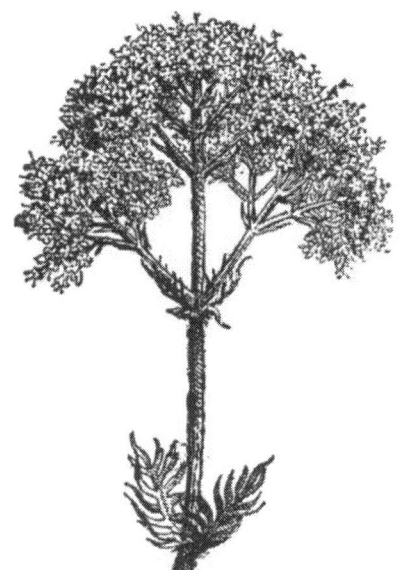

Valerianaceae (Valeriana sitchensis; V. officinalis)

Description: Herbaceous and perennial plant, with short stoloniferous rhizome, erect stem and furrowed on the surface by grooves, fibrous roots giving off an unpleasant and penetrating smell; in optimal conditions it canreach heights of about 24".

The leaves are opposite and without stipules, with petiole only in the lower ones (the upper ones are sessile); all of them are compound and imparipinnate, made up of 11-19 leaflets with entire or toothed lamina and ofa beautiful intense green color.

The flowers, slightly perfumed, form a corymb; they are hermaphrodite, withreduced calyx and 5-petaled corolla, tubular and light pink in color; the androecium is composed of 3 stamens, the gynoecium of a tri-carpellar pistilwith inferior and unilocular ovary. Flowering in April-June and pollination isentomogamous (by Insects). The fruit is a striated achene provided with feathery bristles deriving from the modification that the small teeth of the calyx undergo with the maturation.

Habitat: Montane plant, typically found on north-facing slopes. It prefers cool, moist environments and grows at the edge of woods and shady meadows, in alpine meadows and along trails in the Olympics, Cascades,North Cascades, Mount Rainier, and Mount Baker, especially along Heliotrope Trail.

Medicinal Part: The root.

Solvent: Water.

Effects: Antispasmodic, sedative, tonic, nervine

Traditional uses: All parts of the plant (leaves, flowers, stems, seeds, androots) have been used for their sedative and mild psychoactive effects.

Indians of northern Mexico commonly used Valerian as a painkiller and mildsedative in the same manner as opium. V. sitchensis roots were decocted in water to treat pain, colds, and diarrhea. A cataplasm of the root was used to treat cuts, skin inflammation, wounds and bruises.

Modern uses: In phytotherapy, the Valerian's tincture is used, sometimes combined with other sedative herbs, such as lemon balm or hops, to facilitatesleep without the typical effects of hypnotics and without causing mental heaviness at the wake up. A few people still use V. sitchensis in the traditional way. Herbalists use it also as a nerve tonic. Is best combined with Skull cap, Blue vervain, and Mistletoe, Gentian and Peppermint. The effect of valerian on gamma amino butyric acid (GABA) may reduce blood pressure.

Watercress

Brassicaceae (Nasturtium officinale L.)

Description: Watercress is a perennial herb, smooth and shiny in appearance, known since ancient times as "the salad that heals";

The stems of the watercress are hollow and angular, weak and often creeping, easily emitting roots in the lower part; when erect their height can reach 14".

The leaves, alternating along the stem, are undivided or tripartite in the lowerpart of the stem, while they become imparipinnate, that is, composed of leaflets of oval shape and slightly waxy texture, opposite along a central rib and a larger, almost round terminal leaf, in the upper part of the same. Leaf margins may be entire or toothed. The small white flowers, grouped in modest corymbs, consist of four petals and bloom between April and August depending on location.

Habitat: Nationwide in temperate areas; Grows near ditches and streams orotherwise in moist wooded areas.

Medicinal Parts: Leaves, root.

Solvent: Water.

Effects: Tonic, stimulant, blood purifying, anti-oxidant, anti-inflammatory, diuretic

Food: It is recognized as a food with great nutritional properties, full of vitamins, especially vitamin K, vitamin A, C, riboflavin, vitamin B6, calcium, manganese and folic acid. It has a low content in carbohydrates, proteins, fats and dietary fibers, has an excellent taste and is extremely versatile; in order to preserve its nutritive properties, it is recommended to eatit raw, however it is also generally used for soups or combined to beef.

Traditional uses: Native Americans ate it raw or cooked. It has a peppery spicy flavor and sometimes is used in salads or as a garnish. Mexicans consider this plant as a spring tonic, dampened and then grilled over charcoal.

Hippocrates described watercress as a heart tonic, expectorant and digestive.It is good for coughs, colds, and bronchitis and it relieves gas, fluid retentionand has cleaning action on kidneys and bladder.

Modern uses: It is rich in mineral salts and vitamin A, B C, E, PP, iron, iodine, phosphorus, therefore a good tonic, also used against rickets, but it isalso good for bronchi, helps to fight anemia, it is also effective in case of diabetes, obesity, in the treatment of acne and urinary tract infections.

Excellent depurative and also diuretic

Excellent as a restorative, antianemic,(its juice by centrifuging its plantproves useful). Always to be consumed in moderation.

Fresh watercress juice is also used externally to treat skin diseases, eczemaand eruptions.

(**Notes**: Watercress attracts snails, insect larvae, and frogs.)

Witch Hazel

Hamamelidaceae (Hamamelis virginiana)

Description: With Hazel is a plant with a shrubby habit, which can reach aheight 10'.

The leaves, deciduous, are brownish green, yellowish in autumn; they are oval or obovate, alternate, glabrous, with a short and robust petiole; the margin is irregularly indented and the apex is briefly acuminate and obtuse. From the median vein depart, from two sides, 5-6 straight or slightly curved secondary veins, which reach the margin and are strongly raised on the lowerpage.

The flowers, which usually bloom in September and October, are grouped intwo or three in axillary glomerules, and have four sepals and four yellow petals, each flower has four stamens and two styles.

Fruits are woody, two-lodge capsules, 3/4" long, which open when ripe,releasing one or two dark, shiny seeds.

Habitat: Typically east of the Mississippi River. Coastal forests ;along trails,specifically Grand Mere State Park, Stevensville, Michigan.

Medicinal Part: The bark and the leaves

Solvent: Boiling water and alcohol.

Effects: Stimulant, Expectorant, Diuretic, Antiseptic, Disinfectant.

Traditional uses: The healing properties of Hamamelis decoction were known to Native Americans, who used it to treat wounds. In the nineteenth century, the distillate obtained from the leaves was used by European settlersagainst sunburns and eye irritations after long exposure to light. Witch hazel was used by the Cherokee, Chippewa, Iroquois, Mohegan, Menominee, and Potawatomi peoples living in the range of the plant east of the Mississippi.

They used the leaf tea internally for coughs, asthma, colds, sore throats, dysentery, and diarrhea, and externally to treat muscle aches, wounds, burns,and many skin conditions.

Also twigs and inner bark are still used in infusion to treat colds, pain, sores,fevers, sore throat, and tuberculosis. Sprouts in decoction were used as a blood purifier and tonic. Root and twig decoctions were considered a heal-allfor just about any ailment : bruises, edema, cholera, and arthritis.

Modern uses: Witch Hazel is used in herbal medicine for the preparation of fluid extracts and ointments with decongestant, astringent and hemostatic properties, used in the treatment of hemorrhoids, varices, phlebitis and ocularinflammation. In cosmetics it is used for emollient lotions for dry skin.

Distilled witch hazel water contains no tannins but is still astringent and isused as a gargle for sore throat and sore gums.

(**Notes:** Witch hazel twigs have traditionally been used to create wands for dowsers, those who search for places where water exists underground beforedigging a well. Early Americans called this practice "water witchcraft," because witch hazel was one of the branches selected, although willow and peach branches were also sometimes used.

A flexible Y- or L-shaped twig was held in front of a person as they slowlymoved through the area where groundwater was sought. If the twig tilted downward or contracted, then that movement was thought to indicate the presence of water below the surface.)

Wormwood

Asteraceae (Artemisia campestris)

Description: There are numerous varieties of Artemisia worldwide. It is a biennial or a shortlived perennial. The branches, ascending, generally have anarching habit. For each plant the number of stems varies from 1 to 5.

The plant is woody at the base, with overwintering buds placed at a heightfrom the ground between 2 and 30 cm with a shrubby appearance.

The herbaceous portions dry up every year, with only the woody parts remaining alive. It is a basically glabrous plant with a strong aromatic odor.

They also lack latex (like other Asteraceae), however, they contain etherealoils sesquiterpene lactones. The roots are secondary from taproot and the underground part is taprooted.

The leaves, mostly basal and with petiole, are tomentose (white - pubescent)or viscous and gray-green and thin. First-year leaves are a basal rosette, each leaf up to 4" long and 3" wide.

Second-year leaves have a green undersurface and whitish-green top. On the mature plant, leaves get smaller and deeply cut or linear toward the top of theplant. Leaves are hairy at first and become smooth as they mature. The petiole at the base is enlarged into two leaflets similar to auricles. The segments of the lamina are thin, linear, narrowly oblong laciniae with a sharpapex. The flowers are actinomorphic, tetracyclic and pentamerous and unitedin inflorescences.

The inflorescences are relatively bare and terminal and are formed by small lateral racemes (2nd - 3rd order branches), at the axil of short bracts, composed of small pedunculated, pyriform and pendulous flower heads. Thestructure of the flower heads is typical of the Asteraceae.

Each flower head can contain 20-50 external female flowers and 12-30 internal male flowers. The length of the peduncle is 1 - 2 mm and the size ofthe flower heads is 1.5 - 3 mm wide and 2 - 3 mm long. Anthesis is betweenAugust and October. Fruits are oblong-lanceolate, compressed cypselae (achenes), 0.8 - 1 mm long, glabrous, brownish and with absent pappus.

Habitat: most common in the eastern and central United States and is occasional in the West . It occurs as far north as New Brunswick and Saskatchewan and as far south as Florida and Texas. In Michigan, found inGreat Lakes dunes area ; on dry roadsides, hills, and other dry, sandy areas.

Medicinal Parts: The tops and leaves.

Solvents: Diluted alcohol, water.

Effects: Tonic, febrifuge, narcotic, stomachic, stimulant, anthelmintic,shingle, crevices.

Food use: Not edible. Tea of leaves is often used to treat indigestion. Absinthe from other Artemisia species is used to flavor vermouth and otherspirits, to include the cordial absinthe.

Traditional uses: Tewa nation people chewed and swallowed juice to relievegas and upset stomach. Leaf infusion also used to treat fever and chills.

The green plant is cut and gathered together in a bundle and wrapped with small string and allowed to dry. The end is lit and used as a "smudge wand"in ceremonial smudging. The plant is also used, dry or moistened, in the sweat lodge. The plant is placed on the hot stones in the center of the lodge and the resulting vapor inhaled.

Modern uses: Wormwood has many applications in non-Western medicinal practices, including Traditional Chinese medicine. Wormwood oil contains the chemical thujone, which excites the central nervous system. Thujone and artemisinin are anthelmintic, that is, they kill intestinal worms and other parasites. In Europe wormwood is used as a stomach bitters and after-dinner drinks, such as vermouth or absinthe. Artimisinin, a synthetic derivative fromsweet wormwood (Artemisia annua) is used to control malaria and other parasites. A recent clinical trial showed artimisin 97 % effective against noncomplicated cases of malaria.

Dose and usage: A rounded teaspoon of the dried plant in a cup of hot water,allowed to steep for fifteen minutes, is useful to promote sweating in feverishstates or to increase scanty menstruation.

Wormwood tea, though bitter, is a good remedy for stomach indigestion. Ithas also been traditionally used, as its name suggests, in cases of intestinal worms.

Michael Moore suggests two cups a day for at least two weeks, making sure its use is constant.

WARNING: Avoid during pregnancy and breast-feeding. Thujone in large amounts blocks gamma amino butyric acid, which can lead to seizures and even death. Artemisia chemistry is toxic in large enough dose, and the amount of Artemisia extract used in alcoholic drinks is government controlled.

(**Note:** Wormwood extracts are used to treat worm infestations in domestic animals.)

Yarrow

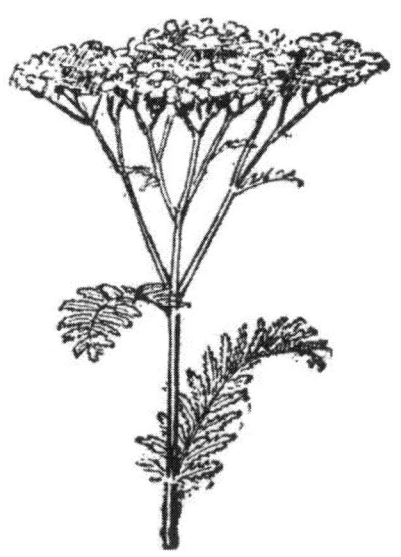

Asteraceae (Achillea millefolium)

Description: Yarrow is a plant belonging to the family of Asteraceae, herbaceous, perennial and aromatic with branched and creeping rhizome and straight stem at the top of which corymbs carry several heads of white or pink scented flowers. The underground part (hypogeal) of the stem has horizontal rhizomes, whose ends can eventually germinate into an aerial part with leaves and flowers, and hypogeal stolons. The aerial part epigeo is striated, hairy, and erect in a tomentose and branched way up to 50 - 100 cm high with soft feather-like leaves to 3' to 4' in height. Fragrant.

White flowers in flat clusters, flowers have five petal-like rays.

Habitat: Distibuted along roadsides, fields, yards, gardens, mountain slopes, streams, edges of woods nationwide, prevalent in montane areas.

Medicinal Part: Aerial parts and root

Solvents: Water, alcohol

Effects: Astringent, alterative, diuretic, tonic, carminative, emmenagogue

Traditional uses: Native American uses: Yarrow is of the most important herbs used by Native Americans.

Whole plant (aerial parts) was infused and used to treat acute infections: colds, fever, flu, cough and as a diuretic.

Infusion of the whole plant was used as a wash d for bites, stings and snakebites.

Root decoction may be used as a wash for pimples.

Leaves are infused and consumed as tea to induce sleep, as an antidiarrhoic, to reduce fever, and as a poison ivy treatment.

Fresh or dried leaves are used as a poultice on wounds, or nipple abscesses. Dried, crushed and snorted leaves are inhaled against headaches, put in the nasal cavities they also stop nasal bleeding.

Bella Coola chewed the leaves and applied them as a poultice to treat burns and boils, used leaves and flowers in decoction for headaches or chest pains, and poultices of flowers (chewed) to reduce edema.

Finally, leaves mixed with animal fat were used as a poultice on the chest and back to treat bronchitis.

Modern uses: The dried flowers are used for antispasmodic (relaxing baths), astringent, healing and anti-inflammatory properties. It can be used instead of chamomile as it contains azulene and in digestive disorders. It is also prepared as an oleolite.

Approved by Commission-E to treat lack of appetite, liver and gallbladder ailments, indigestion, and intestinal pains.

Infusion of the aerial parts is used as a carminative, digestive, tonic, and emmenagogue. Wound healing is facilitated by an infusion in distilled water and application as a wash to the wound.

Dose and usage: Prepared as a hot tea, yarrow stimulates perspiration. The tincture is effective to settle the stomach, and it is more effective in combination with other herbs such as mint). It stimulates digestion and tones the stomach. As such it is useful in cases of hiatal hernia The herb is traditionally used to aid the body in case of fevers. It has a mild hypotensive action (more effective used in conjunction with passion flower for this purpose). The fresh leaves are an excellent remedy for bleeding; placed to small cuts they stimulate coagulation. The tea or tincture is also excellent for decreasing menstruation in case of excessive flow.

WARNING: Drinking the tea and applying the herb has induced photosensitivity, sensitivity to light. The tea may also contain a small amount of thujone, a liver toxin.

(**Notes**: Yarrow is used to flavor gin and other liquors. A smudge of leaves and stems acts as a mosquito repellent.)

Yellow Dock

Poligonacee (Rumex crispus)

Description: Perennial, highly weedy plant, 1,3 ft to 3,2 ft tall; cespitose appearance; erect stem; fleshy/woody taproot that can sink deep into the soilup to 2,6 ft; basal leaves with medium-long, flattened petiole, lanceolate rosette with acute apex; stem leaves are small with reduced petiole; hermaphrodite flowers. Hermaphrodite flowers appear in late spring, united in green-reddish racemes emerging from the upper leaf axils and forming a dense and long panicle; fruit achene subovoidal with acute base and apex, enclosed by three internal tepals of the flower. Pollination occurs by anemophilous way. It blooms from June to July.

Habitat: Nationwide in a wide variety of habitats, including disturbed soil, waste areas, roadsides, fields/meadows, coasts and forest edges.

Taste: The root is scarcely aromatic, but has astringent, bitter taste.

Medicinal Part: The root.

Solvents: Water, alcohol.

Effects: Alterative, astringent, antioxidant, tonic, laxative, antianaemic, immunostimulant.

Food use: Seeds may be gathered and eaten. Young leaves may be steamed, sautéed, or stir-fried. Inner pulp of flowering stem is also eaten cooked.

Squeeze pulp from outher skin to reduce bitterness.

Traditional uses: Most Native American tribes applied a poultice of the rootto the skin to treat arthritis. Cherokee used the root juice for treating diarrhea. One unusual use was rubbing the throat with a crushed leaf to treat sore throat. Cooked seeds were eaten to diarrhea. Dried and powdered root was applied to wounds to stop bleeding. Pioneers considered the plant an excellent blood purifier, a spring tonic for every ailment.

Modern uses: Yellow Dock is one of the best sources of plant iron (it concentrates iron from the earth and combines it with the vitamins and minerals needed to absorb it). This makes it an excellent herb for treating mild cases of anemia. Naturopaths recommend it during pregnancy, without the resulting constipation from taking elemental iron supplements. The bitter taste of the root and the leaves stimulates digestion, the production of saliva, digestive enzymes and bile in readiness to transform and absorb the food. A necessary part of a healthy digestive process, bile acids are particularly usefulin helping to break down fats in the liver. The herb has also a gentle, natural laxative action, encouraging regular bowel emptying.

Whole plant in decoction eliminates toxins from body and fights constipation.It can be applied topically to alleviate swelling, rashes, sores, fungal infections, insect bites, acne and in case of chronic skin problems like eczema. Sometimes combined with dandelion root to treat skin problems.

Yellow Dock Root Tincture can be added to water or fruit juice and takenwhen required. Traditionally Taken: 2-3ml taken 2-3 times per day, or as directed by a Herbal Practitioner.

WARNING: Because of the high tannin content and oxalic acid content, leaves should be eaten in small quantities. These chemicals may strain thekidneys and may negatively affect bone density when eaten in excess.

Zizia Aurea

Apiaceae *(Zizia Aurea* Apiaceae)

Description: The Golden Zizia, or Golden Alexander, is a native, perennial forb to 1 – 2 feet tall perennial, but can sometimes grow taller. The leaves cangrow up to 3+1/4 in length and 2 in width, attached to the stems alternately.

Each leaf is compound and uneven, with usually lanceolate or ovate leaflets with serrated edges. The root system is made up of a dense group of coarse fibrous roots.

It blooms from May to June, with yellow, flat-umbrella flowers. Each flower has five sepals, five petals and five stamens and produces a single oblong fruit 0.12 to 0.16 in long that contains two seeds. In the fall both the leaves and the fruit turn purple.

Habitat: Golden Alexander is native to the United States and Canada ; grows in various habitats, well-drained soils in full sun to part shade, moist black soil prairies, in moist to mesic woodlands, savannas, thickets, limestone glades and bluffs, woodland areas, abandoned fields, and wet meadows. It can tolerate dry summers. Widely distributed from Quebec to Saskatoon, Montana and south to Florida and Texas.

Medicinal parts: Flowers, leaves, and root.

Effects: Febrifuge, anesthetic, root is vulnerary and hypnotic

Solvents: Water

Food use: The flowers can be used in salads, and the green stems can be cooked.

Traditional uses: Native Americans used the pulverized root to treat severe pains. A tea made from the leaves and flowers was drunk to sooth "female disorders"; poulticed root was applied on inflammations and sores.

Dose and usage: A tea made from the root is febrifuge.

WARNING: The root may be slightly toxic. Seek a specialist advise for usage.

BOOK 7
The Curative Properties of Herbs

Properties of Herbs

Indigenous people had a deep knowledge of the effects of the herbs they used and of their healing properties, even though they did not know their organoleptic characteristics. For example, they used herbal teas made from rosehip, pine and echinacea to treat colds or flu, without knowing that the active ingredients contained were vitamin C and bioflavonoids.

By now, science has identified most of the healing substances and properties contained in herbs, including vitamins, minerals, enzymes and phytochemicals.

Listed below are the terms concerning the organoleptic properties of plants and herbs, with their meanings.

Definitions

ALTERATIVE: herbs that gradually restore the proper function of the body and increase health and vitality, without any immediate perception of this healthful alteration. Such as stinging nettle (*urtica diocia*), yellow dock (*rumex crispus*), dandelion (*taraxacum off. radix*).

ANODYNE: pain-relieving. Such as *Valeriana off.* (Valerian) and *Atropa belladonna* (Deadly Nightshade)

ANTHELMINTIC: antiparasitic herbs or preparations that expel parasitic destroy or expel worms from the digestive system. The term is synonymous with vermifuge and antiparasitic. Such as *Artemisia absinthium* (Wormwood).

APERIENT: mild laxative. Such as *Juniperus communis* (Juniper).

AROMATIC: a spicy stimulant with a strong and often pleasant odour. Such as *Pimpinella anisum* (Aniseed) and *Melissa officinalis* (Lemon Balm).

ASTRINGENT: causing the tightening of skin, mucosae, and other exposed body tissues. Such as *Rubus idaeus* (Red Raspberry) and *Quercus sp* (White/Red Oak).

ANTIBILIOUS: preparations that counter disorders of the liver.

ANTIEMETIC: to stop vomiting. Such as *Chionanthus virginicus* (Fringetree)

ANTILEPTIC : anticonvulsant, soothing.

ANTIPERIODIC: preparations preventing the recurrence of certain symptoms.

ANTIRHEUMATIC: herbs or preparations used in the treatment of inflammatory arthritis, rheumatoid arthritis, and others. Such as *Sambucus nigra/canadensis* (Black Elderberry) and dandelion (*taraxacum off. radix*).

ANTISCORBUTIC: to cure or prevent scurvy.

ANTISEPTIC: antimicrobial herbs or preparations to reduce the possibility of infection, sepsis, or putrefaction. Such as *Hamamelis virginiana* (Witch Hazel), *Capsella bursa-pastoris*

(Shepherd's Purse), and *Quercus alba* (White Oak).

ANTISPASMODIC: to prevent or soothe spasms or craps of themuscles. Such as *Viburnum prunifolium* (Black Haw) and *Passiflora incarnata* (Passionflower).

CARMINATIVE: herbs and preparations rich in volatile oils, thatincrease the peristalsis of the gastric and intestinal mucosae and relieve cramping by expelling gases. Such as *Pimpinella anisum* (Anise).

CATHARTIC: to accelerate defecation. Such as *Juglans nigra* (BlackWalnut) and *Podophyllum peltatum* (May Apple).

CEPHALIC: related to the treatment of headaches.

CHOLAGOGUE: to stimulate the flow of bile from the liver. Such as *Hydrastis canadensis* (Goldenseal)

CONDIMENT: to improve the flavour of foods.

Demulcent: herbs rich in mucilage that can soothe and protect irritated or inflamed internal tissue. Such as *Althea off.* (Marshmallow leaf or root) and *Glycyrrhiza glabra* (Licorice).

DEOBSTRUENT: to clear or open the natural ducts of the fluids andsecretions of the body; see aperient.

DEPURATIVE: detoxifying; see alterative.

DETERGENT: cleansing herbs that contain saponins. Such as *AgaveAmericana* (Agave).

DIAPHORETIC: to stimulate perspiration and the production ofsweat. Such as Eupatorium perfoliatum (Boneset) and *Sambucus niger* (Elderberry).

DIURETIC: to increase the secretion and flow of urine. Stimulating diuretics such as *Arctostaphylos uva-ursi* (Bearberry) and *Juniperus communis* (Juniper) either irritate the kidneys or increase the flowof blood (caffeine) to the kidneys to increase the flow of urine. Osmotic diuretics such as *Agropyron repens* (Couch Grass) and *Althea officinalis* (Marshmallow) works as unmetabolized polysaccharides change the osmoticpull of the kidneys and increase the flow of water.

EMETIC: herbs that induce vomiting; first aid treatment for poisoning.Such as Lobelia (*Lobelia inflata*) and Ipecac (*Cephaelis ipecacuahana*)

EMMENAGOGUE: to stimulate and increase menstrual flow and function. Such as Achillea millefolium (Yarrow), Actaea racemosa (Black Cohosh), and Caulophyllum thalictroides (Blue Cohosh).

EMOLLIENT: softens and soothes the skin. Such as *Plantagomajor/lanceolata* (Plantain) and *Aloe barbadensis* (Aloe).

EXPECTORANT: herbs that help the body to remove excess mucousfrom the lungs, or more generally a tonic for the respiratory system.

Stimulating expectorants such as *Inula helenium* (Elecampane), *Glycyrrhiza glabra* (Licorice), and *Sanguinaria canadensis* (Bloodroot) work as chemical irritants to the mucosae of the bronchiole forcing the expulsion of the congested material.

Soothing or Relaxing expectorants such as *Tussilago farfara* (Coltsfoot) and *Verbascum thapsus* (Mullein) soothe bronchial spasms and loosen mucous secretion.

FEBRIFUGE: Abates and reduces fevers. Such as *Sambucus nigra* (Elderberry) and *Filipendula ulmaria* (Meadowsweet).

HEPATIC: herbs or preparations that aid the work of the liver. Such as *Taraxacum officinalis* (Dandelion root) and *Silybum marianum* (Milk thistle).

LAXATIVE: to promote bowel movements. Stimulating laxatives such as *Cassia angustifolia* (Senna), *Rheum palmatum* (Turkey Rhubarb), and *Rhamnus purshiana* (Cascara) contain anthraquinones which stimulate the contractions of the muscle wall of the large intestine. Osmotic laxatives such as *Althea off.* (Marshmallow) bulk up the colon by drawing water and softening the stool.

MUCILAGINOUS: soothe and protect irritated tissues in the body. Such as *Althea off.* (Marshmallow), *Plantago lanceolata* (plantain), and *Verbascum Thapsus* (Mullein).

NERVINE: a remedy that has a beneficial effect on the nervous system, either relaxant, stimulant, or tonic. Such as *Hypericum perforatum* (St. John's wort), *Humulus lupulus* (Hops), and *Lavendula off.* (Lavender).

REFRIGERANT: cooling. Such as *Borago off.* (Borage).

RUBIFACIENT: to increase capillary circulation and produce redness of the skin. Such as *Bryonia alba/diocia* (White Bryony).

Sedative: to reduce stress and aid sleep. Such as *Gelsemium sempervirens* (Yellow Jasmine), *Piscidia erythrina* (Jamaican Dogwood) and *Eschscholzia california* (California Poppy).

SIALOGOGUE: to increase the secretion of saliva. Such as *Rheum palmatum* (Turkey Rhubarb).

STYPTIC: capable to stop bleeding when it is applied to a wound.

TONIC: invigorating and strengthening.

VERMIFUGE: that destroys or expels parasitic worms

PHYTOCHEMICALS

Phytochemicals are the chemicals found naturally in plants ("Phyto" means plant). These plant nutrients can be extracted from herbs and plants.

Some phytochemicals are effective antioxidants and anti-cancer; others lower cholesterol, decrease plaque in the arteries, stimulate immune system function or enzyme production. Below are some of the phytochemicals found in many of the herbs used by American Indians over the centuries.

Alkaloids

Alkaloids are basic, naturally occurring organic compounds found in several plants, including goldenseal (*Hydrastis Canadensis*). Alkaloid content in plants is usually in small percentages and is inhomogeneous in plant tissues.

Depending on the type of plant, the highest concentration is contained in the leaves. They prevent yeast overgrowth in the body, support the immune system and help keeping healthy levels of bacteria in the gastrointestinal and urinary tracts.

Anthocyanidins

Anthocyanidins are a class of phytochemicals found in blueberries, blackcurrants and raspberries.

They reduce free radicals (a byproduct of metabolic reactions in the body that can lead to degenerative diseases such as cardiovascular disease and cancer); reduce plaque formation in blood vessels, aiding circulation and reducing therisk of cardiovascular disease; inhibit edema (swelling due to fluid accumulation); fight inflammation; and improve vision.

Chlorophyll

Chlorophyll is a pigment found naturally in all green plants and a few other organisms. It absorbs sunlight and allows for photosynthesis. It has a similarstructure to our hemoglobin, which is why it is also known as plant blood. Itis useful for the intestines, especially for balancing the bacterial flora.

Chlorophyll helps our organism to eliminate toxins and promote purification,as it acts against free radicals, and has anti-aging properties.

It improves circulation and for this reason it is considered a good help to prevent varicose veins, it also stimulates metabolism and helps our body tobetter use energy and resist stress. It fights bacteria, helps in healing burns and wounds and fights cancer. It is also an excellent source of vitamin K.

Diterpenes

Diterpenes are found in many herbs, including rosemary. They are powerfulantioxidants, an anti-cancer agent, and liver detoxifiers.

Eleutherosides

Eleutherosides are found in Siberian ginseng. They increase stamina, stimulate appetite and enhance physical and mental vigor. They stimulatemetabolism, the immune system and the central nervous system. They arealso helpful in combating some of the problems of menopause, including irregular cycles and hot flashes.

Enzymes

Enzymes are present in all herbs that have not been exposed to high temperatures or to alcohol during preparation. The presence of enzymes isessential in order to activate the phytochemicals and other nutrients in theherbs.

Enzymes also are very important for improving the absorption, action, and bioavailability of these herbs in the body. If enzymes have been destroyed during the processing of the herbal preparation, it is important to take enzymesupplements in addition to the herbs. Enzyme supplements should contain a combination of proteases (enzymes that work on proteins), lipases (break up fats), and amylases (break up carbohydrates).

Essential Fatty Acids

Essential fatty acids, namely omega-3 and omega-6 fatty acids, are fats thatare essential to good health but cannot be made by the body. They maintain the integrity of cell membranes and of myelin sheaths (the protective covering of nerve fibers). They stimulate the production of prostaglandins (hormonelike substances that mediate metabolism, smooth-muscle activity, and nerve transmission, among other functions), lower blood cholesterol levels, and strengthen immunity. They can be found in many herbs, including saw palmetto.

Flavonglycosides

Flavonglycosides are potent antioxidants (fighters of free radicals). They also dilate blood vessels, improving blood flow; improve mental clarity; improve vision and hearing; and help alleviate depression. They are found in Ginkgo biloba.

Gingerols

Gingerols are antioxidants and improve digestion of proteins and fats. They also soothe the stomach and fight liver toxicity and inflammation. They are the active constituents of ginger.

Ginkolic Acid

Ginkolic acid, found in Ginkgo biloba, is yet another antioxidant. It improves circulation and mental clarity, treats depression, and fights cancer.

Glycyrrhizins

Glycyrrhizins, the protective phytochemicals found in licorice, have antiviral, anti-inflammatory, and skin-protective properties. They also inhibit tumor formation.

Hesperidin

Hesperidin, found in milk thistle seeds, is an antioxidant that protects capillaries and strengthens cell membranes. It works well against liver disease and protects against ultraviolet rays.

Hypericin

Hypericin is the active component of St. John's wort. It helps improve mood, possibly by regulating neurotransmitters in the brain.

Isothiocyanates

Isothiocyanates are found in horseradish. They induce the production of protective enzymes and inhibit DNA damage, thereby reducing the risk for breast cancer.

Lactones

Lactones, found in kava kava root, protect the body against cancer by eliminating carcinogens.

Lipoic Acid

Lipoic acid, found in many plant foods, is a potent antioxidant that eliminates heavy metals from the body, protects against cancer and heart disease, normalizes blood-sugar levels, and slows aging. Lipoic acid is a key factor in energy production.

Phenolic Acids

Phenolic acids are antioxidants that inhibit the formation of nitrosamines (cancer-causing agents). They are found in berries, parsley, and all floweringplants.

Phthalides

Phthalides, found in parsley, detoxify carcinogens, and stimulate theproduction of beneficial enzymes.

Polyacetylenes

Polyacetylenes also are found in parsley. They regulate the production ofprostaglandins and protect against carcinogens.

Proanthocyanins

Proanthocyanins, found in elderberry and bilberry, are another class of antioxidants. They protect against cancer, high blood-cholesterol levels, andthe influenza virus. They also strengthen blood-vessel walls.

Quercetin

Quercetin is a flavonoid that is widely distributed in the plant kingdom. (Flavonoids are naturally occurring antioxidants found in many fruits, vegetables, and other plants.) Quercetin has antihistamine, anti-inflammatory,and anticancer properties. It also stabilizes cell membranes and reduces capillary fragility.

Rosemarinic Acid

Rosemarinic acid is the active constituent of rosemary. It fights nausea,intestinal gas, and indigestion. It is also effective against headaches.

Salin

Salin, or salicin, is found in white willow bark. It fights inflammation, relieves pain and fever, and fights the influenza virus.

Saponins

Saponins, found in ginseng root, licorice, black cohosh, yucca, and many other herbs, fight cancer formation, enhance wound healing, and reduce cholesterol levels. They have antiinflammatory, antibacterial, and antifungalproperties.

Silymarin

Silymarin is the active constituent of milk thistle. It is an antioxidant andprotects the liver.

Tannins

Tannins are widely distributed in plants. They are antioxidants that have antiviral properties and strengthen capillaries. They protect against cancer, heart disease, and asthma.

Terpenes

Terpenes (the common name for monoterpenes) are antioxidants found in Ginkgo biloba.

Triterpenoids

Triterpenoids prevent dental decay and fight ulcers, cancer, and liver toxicity. They are found in licorice root and gotu kola.

BOOK 8
The Native American Ancient Remedies

Introduction

For thousands of years Native Americans have used herbs not only to heal the body, but also to purify the spirit. In particular, oral traditions have shown that Native Americans had learned the healing powers of herbs by observing the behavior of sick animals that, in order to heal, ate them.

Among the most used natural remedies there was tobacco, smoked pure and used for healings, rituals and ceremonies, together with sage, which was known to solve problems of the stomach, colon, kidneys, liver, lungs, skin and to protect from evil spirits.

The knowledge of herbs by Native Americans was mixed with beliefs of their magical properties, and their ancient tradition is still used today for therapeutic purposes of great effectiveness.

Such as American ginseng, useful for common colds, black wild cherry and hops, natural painkillers, willow, able to eliminate fever.

The list of curative herbs of the Native American population is very vast and includes species that nowadays are not used because of their contraindications, whereas there are some whose use in modern herbalism is still very actual. These medicines were usually administered as tisanes or compresses either ingested or applied externally. Sometimes the plants were eaten as food or were added to water or food. In some cases a paste or ointment was applied to heal wounds.

In the list below you will find a brief resume of the most common herbs used by native tribes, and you will discover how to prepare the various traditional remedies and recipes that you can try according to your needs. Enjoy experiPenting!

Plants and Uses

Common name (Latin name)	Family	Native American tribes	Native American indications	Current Effects
Echinacea (Echinacea purpurea, Echinacea angustifolia, Echinacea pallida)	Asteraceae	Cheyenne, Choctaw, Dakota, Delaware, Fox Kiowa, Montana, Omaha Pawnee, Ponca, Sioux, Winnebago	Relief from pain, fever, cough and sore throat, smallpox, mumps, measles, rheumatism and arthritis; antidote for poisons	Immune stimulating
Ginseng (Panax quinquefolius)	Araliaceae	Cherokee, Creek, Delaware Fox, Houma, Iroquois, Mohegan Pawnee, Penobscot, Potawatomi	Tonic, expectorant. fevers, tuberculosis, asthma, and rheumatism	Cardiovascular health and cholesterol lowering; tonic
Garlic (Allium sativum)	Liliaceae	Cherokee	for scurvy, asthma, and prevention of worms	Cardiovascular health and cholesterol lowering, stimulant, expectorant, mild cathartic

SomeSelected Plants and Their Uses by Native Americans

Common name (Latin name)	Family	Native American tribes	Native American indications	Current Effects
Goldenseal (Hydrastis canadensis)	Ranunculaceae	Cherokee, Iroquois, Micmac	for fever, whooping cough, and pneumonia	Immune function, tonic
Evening primrose (Oenothera biennis)	Onagraceae	Cherokee, Iroquois, Ojibwa, Potawatomi	For premenstrual and menstrual pain, obesity, intestinal pains	Antioxidant, pain reliever
Cranberry (Vaccinium macrocarpon)	Ericaceae	Algonquin, Chippewa and Cree	For pleurisy, fever, stomach cramps, and a slew of childbirth-related injuries	antioxidant, blood purifier, immune function, tonic

Native Americans are known for their medicinal plant knowledge. They have a philosophical and spiritual viewpoint on existence, and in order to live healthy and happy, a person has to follow a respectful, harmonious, and balanced way of living. They thought that disorders were life lessons. Several modern treatments and medications are based on the Native American understanding of the many plants and herbs they have used for centuries.

In order to protect the plants from over-harvesting, the medicine men used to collect every third plant they encountered. Below, a list of the plants mostly used by Native Americans during their everyday lives:

Blackberries

The Cherokee used this herb to heal stomach conditions. They used blackberry to cure diarrhea and soothe sore tissues and joints (tea).

Combined with honey or maple syrup, blackberry root can create an all-natural cough remedy and sore throats treatment. To soothe gum infections, they sucked the leaves. This plant is also helpful to strengthen the whole immune system.

Cattail

This is one of the most common medicinal plants used by indigenous people for food and also as defensive medicine. It helps to recover from illness, as it is a food that is easily digestible. Native North Americans have used cattail leaves for more than 12,000 years for weaving. The Blackfeet and Paiute tribes of the North and early settlers roasted the seeds and dried the roots, then ground them into flour to make cakes, bread, and porridge. Other indigenous groups, such as the Yuma, mixed pollen with water and kneaded it to make cakes, which they baked. The hearts of the young spring shoots were eaten as cooked vegetables, and the heads of the still-green flowers were boiled and eaten as corn on the cob is now eaten.

Chamomile

Native Americans used the herb mainly to relieve stomach pain. It is considered a feminine plant, applied wet to the rocks in the sweat lodge as an aromatic calming agent that invites a good mood. Infusion of the herb used to relieve menstrual cramps stress tension.

In the United States, chamomile is widely used for anxiety and relaxation as an anxiolytic and sedative, considered by few to be a cure-all. In Europe, it is used for wound healing and to minimize swelling and inflammation. Few trials have investigated how well it operates for any disease. Chamomile is used or used as a compress as tea. Sleepiness triggered by drugs or other herbs or supplements can increase. Chamomile may interfere with the way the body uses other medications, allowing the amount of medication to be too big in certain persons.

Speak, as for any medicinal plant, with the healthcare provider before taking it.

Clover of the Red

This herb has also been used by healers to cure asthma & respiratory issues. The new studies have shown that red clover helps prevent heart risk by increasing breathing and reducing cholesterol.

Claw of the Devil

It was used by the American Indians to treat various ailments, from treating fever to calming skin conditions, enhancing metabolism, and controlling arthritis, whereas a toxic plant may be suggested by the name. While a concoction made from the plant's roots prevents stiffness and helps with sores, joint disease, gout, back pain, headache, and arthritis, the effects of diabetes may be reduced through tea. Notice that although medical treatmentis not accessible, knowledge is the only doctor that will save you.

Feverfew (The Leaf)

The Quapaw Indians used its pounded leaves as a poultice for burns andmade a compound to cure horses.

Historically, Feverfew has been used as a cure for fever. In order to treat arthritis and alleviate migraines, it is still commonly used. Any evidence hasindicated that migraines can be avoided with any feverfew preparedness.

Among the adverse effects are oral ulcers and abdominal pain. People who suddenly avoid taking feverfew for migraines can have their headaches returned. It cannot be used with nonsteroidal anti-inflammatory drugs since these drugs can impact how well feverfew performs.

Garlic (Root Cloves)

For cholesterol levels & control of blood pressure, garlic is used. It has antimicrobial effects. Reports from minor, short-term, & badly defined trials suggest that slight decreases may be induced by total & LDL cholesterol. The German research results on garlic's cholesterollowering influence have been distorted, however, with a positive result, the FDA says. The possible role of garlic in cancer prevention is currently being studied by researchers. The FDA considers garlic to be safe. It should not be mixed with warfarin, since large amounts of garlic can induce clotting. Big doses must not be administered until oral surgery or surgery for the same reason.

Ginger (The Root)

Ginger is used to pain and motion sickness relief. The study indicates that ginger could decrease pain caused by pregnancy and chemotherapy. Surgeryand motion-induced nausea are implicated in these areas under review. Gas,bloating, heartburn, and nausea are among the side effects identified.

Goldenseal

Cherokees used root decoction as a tonic and wash for wounds, inflammations and infections. An aqueous decoction of the root was filteredthrough animal skin or cloth and applied as eyewash. Decoction was also used for earaches. Goldenseal was also used as an appetite stimulant and to treat dyspepsia. Air-dried rhizomes and root were used to treat diarrhea. Thedried root was chewed to treat cough.

The root macerated in whiskey was taken as heart tonic. The root extract has traditionally been used to treat numerous diseases, including tuberculosis, scrofula, liver and gallbladder problems.

Goldenseal

It is used in the treatment of eye and skin diarrhea & itching and as an antiseptic. It is also an unproven treatment for colds. In Goldenseal, berberine, an herbal alkaloid with a long history of medicinal use in bothAyurvedic and Chinese medicine, is contained.

The efficacy of Goldenseal for diarrhea has been proven by research. But it'snot allowed because it could be unsafe in broad quantities. Skin, mouth, stomach, & gastric pain may be enticing. It is not recommended, even because of the plant's endangered species status.

Ginger of the Wild

Root traditionally used to treat colds and cough; antiseptic and tonic. Also used in compounding traditional medicine to treat scarlet fever, nervousness,sore throat, vomiting, headaches, and earaches as well as asthma and convulsions—considered a heal-all.

To treat earaches & ear infections, this herb is used by healers. They alsofound a gentle tea for the rootstock to stimulate the digestive system & reduce bloating and it also aids in bronchial diseases and exhaustion.

Greenbriar

To purify blood or to relieve joint pain, this root tea has been used. A salve combined with hog lard from leaves and bark was generated by some healers,which was applied to mild sores, scalds, & burns.

Honeysuckle

Native Americans used this plant as a natural medicine to treat asthma, but ithas many medical applications, including hepatitis, rheumatoid arthritis, andmumps. It helps in upper respiratory tract infections, such as pneumonia, as well.

Hummingbird Blossom

The American Indians used this herb, also known as the buck brush, in orderto treat mouth and throat issues, as well as cysts, fibroid tumors, & inflammation. It may be turned into a potion to help in treating wounds, sores, & injuries. A diuretic that increases kidney function may be developed using the roots of such an herb. The early colonists used this unusual plant as a substitute for black tea. The new studies have also shown that The Buck Brush is helpful in controlling the lymph stream's elevated blood pressure & blockages.

Lavender

This herb has been used by healers as a medication for fatigue, anxiety, tension, headaches, and exhaustion. In the essential oil, antiseptic & anti-inflammatory properties are found. Infusions can be used to soothe insectbites and burns.

Licorice

This root is commonly used for flavoring candies, foods, and beverages. Butit has also been used by healers to treat stomach disorders, bronchitis, food poisoning, and chronic fatigue.

Mint

The Cherokee used to create a mint tea to help an irritated stomach and treatdigestive problems. A salve was made from its leaves to treat sore skin and rashes.

Mullein

It was a tobacco-like plant and was mainly used for the treatment of respiratory disorders. Native Americans made concoctions from the roots inorder to alleviate swelling in the joints, paws, or feet.

Prickly Pear

This plant is used both as a diet and as a medicine. Native Americans produced a poultice from developed sheets as an antiseptic & for treating burns, boils, and wounds. Tea was developed to treat the infections of urineand to improve the immune system.

The study further shows that cholesterol can be decreased and heart failureand diet-related diabetes can be avoided.

Rosemary

Native American tribes considered this herb sacred. They used it mostly as ananalgesic for relieving sore muscles. This herb improves concentration, relieves muscle pain and spasms, indigestion, and stimulates the circulatory and nervous systems and the immune system.

Rose of the Wild

This herb was used as a preventive and a remedy for mild common cold by Native Americans. For the bladder & kidneys, the tea stimulates and is a milddiuretic. For a sore throat, a petal injection was used.

Rosy Periwinkle

Both parts of the plant are venomous. In Rosy periwinkle, there are many compounds of therapeutic potential, two of which, vincristine & vinblastine, are important drugs in the treatment of leukemia and certain other cancers.

Sage

Sage is commonly used as a seasoning, but it was a sacred plant for many indigenous populations as it was thought to have strong purifying energies & to cleanse the body of toxic energy. To tackle medical conditions such as abdominal cramps, spasms, fractures, wounds, colds, and influenza, it has been used as a remedy.

Salix (Willow)

Both the Greeks and American Indians valued Willow bark as pain relief and among the first therapeutic substances to be collected from plants in 1852 was the active ingredient of the herb, salicin. It proved to be a successful painreliever, yet weakened the stomach sufficiently to form a drug that is now manufactured as aspirin, which is identical and safer.

Saint John's Wort

Saint John's Wort is deemed an antidepressant. The latest studies have not shown that depression has more than a tiny effect. Further testing is needed to determine the right dose. A side effect is an exposure to light, but this is often found in people consuming large doses of the medication.

St. John's Wort can cause a dangerous association with other commonly used drugs. Please contact the healthcare practitioner prior to eating this plant.

Slippery Elm

The Native Americans made bowstrings, yarn, fabric, and rope using the inner bark. Tea was developed to soothe toothaches, nasal irritations, skin issues, intestinal pain, sore throats, and even leaf and bark spider bites.

Sumac

In various herbal remedies, this plant may be used, but this is one of the few plants used as remedy for eye problems. A sumac decoction was used as a gargle to cure sore throats or taken as a diarrhea remedy. Teas and potions made from leaves and berries were prepared to soothe symptoms of poisoning (poison ivy) and to relieve fever.

Uva Ursi

It is also known as Bearberry & Bear grape, due to the affection of the bear for this plant's fruits. Native Americans used this herb mainly to treat bladder & urinary tract diseases.

Valerian (The Root)

For sleeplessness treatment and anxiety relief, Valerian is included. Research suggests that valerian can be a helpful sleep aid, but there have been no well-designed research to support the claims. Valerian is used as a flavoring for root beer as well as other foods in the United States. Speak, as for any medicinal plant, with the medical professional before taking it.

Yew

The Pacific yew from North America (Northwest) was used by Native Americans to treat skin cancer. Clinical study has shown that Taxol, a medicine that has become an effective treatment for cancer of the breast, ovary & cervix, is included. Fortunately, English yews were found to have acertain compound that could be turned into Taxol in their leaves, and pharmaceutical companies are collecting yew hedge clippings for this purpose.

Five Essential Methods to Start with Herbal Preparations

Making Teas, Infusions and Decoctions

Herbal teas, infusions and decoctions are very diluted herbal beverages. Ideal to be enjoyed hot, they are a panacea with the arrival of the first cold weather. These herbal products are made from water and officinal plants.

Thanks to the solvent effect of hot or cold water, the beneficial substances present in herbal ingredients are extracted. Once prepared, they can be sweetened with sugar or honey. The mix of herbs useful for the preparation of these beverages can be easily bought in herbalist shops.

How to Prepare Herbal Teas

We talk about herbal teas to indicate drinks obtained from a mix of officinal herbs and therefore having beneficial properties. Herbal teas can be of many types according to the effect they allow to obtain. There are draining ones, which contrast the effects of water retention, the ideal ones to be included by following a diet regimen.

Herbal teas are distinguished in infusions, decoctions or macerates according to the method of extraction of plant drugs. The choice depends on the result you want and the type of plant ingredient used.

Glass or earthenware vessels are best for making infusions and decoctions. Quart or pint canning jars are very good as they will not break from heat, and the screw cap keeps the nutrients from floating away in the steam.

How to Prepare Infusions

One of the possible ways of preparing herbal teas is by making infusions. The infusion method consists in pouring boiling water directly on the plants already chopped up or dried. The preparation must rest for at least 5-10 minutes.

Once this time has passed, the beverage has to be consumed immediately because it is not suitable for being kept. This method of extraction is generally useful to use the most delicate parts of the plant, such as flowers and leaves.

An Example of a Hot Infusion

This infusion is used for its general nutritive properties, especially for women in menopause.

1. Mix together one pound each of dried, cut, and sifted nettles, oat-straw, red clover, alfalfa, horsetail, and spearmint.
2. Put one cup of the mixture in a quart container, fill with hot water and screw on the lid. Leave overnight. In the morning strain the mixture to remove all the herbs and drink the mixture throughout the next two days.

3. Do not keep infusions longer than two days

In general, use the following guidelines to make infusions with hot water:

Leaves: one ounce per quart of water, four hours in hot water, tightlycovered. Tougher leaves require longer steeping.

Flowers: one ounce per quart of water, two hours in hot water. More fragileflowers require less time.

Seeds: one ounce per pint of water, thirty minutes in hot water. More fragrantseeds such as fennel need less time (fifteen minutes), rose hips longer (three to four hours).

Barks and roots: one ounce per pint of water, eight hours in hot water.Though some barks such as slippery elm need less (one to two hours).

Cold infusions are preferable for herbs, which perform differently in cold andhot water.

Yarrow, for instance, can be quite bitter when prepared in hot water but is notbitter when prepared in cold water. The aromatic components of yarrow, and their corresponding antispasmodic properties, are soluble in cold water while the bitter components of the herb are not.

Cold infusions are prepared as hot infusions but each herb will need to beimmersed a period of time specific to itself.

Decoctions, prepared with boiling water, can be much more potent than infusions. The general method is to take one ounce of herb in three cups ofwater and boil steadily until the liquid is reduced by half.

Use only a stainless steel or glass container, never aluminum. The dosagescan range from a tablespoon to a cup depending on the plant used.

Decoctions should be kept only a maximum of two days, refrigerated.

How to Prepare Decoctions

The preparation of decoction by means requires putting in cold water the parts of the plant you want to use. Generally these are the hardest and mostconsistent ones, such as barks, roots, seeds, or leaves and flowers. The mixture is brought to boiling point. The time required is variable and dependson the hardness and consistency of the parts of the plant used. Usually it takesfrom 3 to 10 minutes at most.

After a rest of 10-15 minutes, with the pot covered, it can be filtered. In orderto do this it is necessary to use a special strainer with narrow meshes in ordernot to let the whole plant parts pass through.

Tincturing Herbs

Tinctures are concentrated extracts made from medicinal herbs and alcohol. They are suitable methods to extract from herbs the beneficial substances contained in them, so that they can be preserved for a long time. Among the advantages of the use of herbal tinctures there are the ability of the same to bequickly absorbed by the body and to retain for a long time the volatile and semi-volatile components present in the herbs without them undergoing the alterations that could occur due to heat, for example during drying.

Let's follow step by step the procedure for the preparation of an herbaltincture

First and foremost, it is necessary to purchase quality food grade alcohol. Vodka is one of the best solutions in this regard, as it has no color and its smell and taste are not annoying. Vodka can be substituted by brandy, rum or whiskey. In any case it must be 40% alcohol minimum, in order to preserve the herbs in the best way.

- Choose a suitable container. It should be made of glass or ceramic. Plastic and metal containers should be avoided. For its preservation the best solution is represented by dark glass bottles, with a cap that keeps them tightly closed, avoiding air infiltrations, but
- Making them easy to use. Every container must be well cleaned and sterilized before use.
- The preparation of the tincture begins with the choice of the herbs. The amount of herbs and alcohol to use varies depending on whether you are in the presence of fresh herbs, powdered herbs or dried herbs. In the case of fresh plants, quantity must be used to fill the chosen container, which will be filled with alcohol until the herbs are completely covered. 113 grams of powdered herbs for every 473 milliliters of alcohol. In case of dried herbs, 198 grams per liter of alcohol.
- Now, the container must be well sealed with its lid and placed in a dark and cool place where it will rest for a period ranging from 8 to 30 days according to the preparation. Its content should be shaken from time to time. Label the container with a date, in order to count the days the herbs are in the alcohol.
- A good resting time for herbal tinctures is 2 weeks. It can be adjusted according to experience or according to the specific recipe. After the resting period, tinctures must be filtered, preferably through a thin cotton cloth.
- Transfer the liquid into the small dark glass bottle specially prepared to contain the tincture. It could be useful to use a funnel to facilitate the operation. Close and label the bottle indicating the date of bottling of the tincture.
- Conservation and use. A tincture can have a shelf life of up to five years, as alcohol is a natural preservative. To use a tincture, follow the advices of an expert, such as an herbalist, in order to avoid overdoses and wrong uses.

Generally, dried plants are tinctured at a five-to-one ratio; that is, five partsliquid to one part dried herb.

For example, osha root contains 30% water by weight. If you have ten ouncesof powdered osha root you would add to it fifty ounces of liquid, 35 ounces of 95% alcohol and 15 ounces water.

Dried herbs are generally powdered as finely as possible, often in a blender. It is best to store them whole until they are needed. Again, the tincture is left for two weeks and then decanted, and the liquid squeezed out of the herbal material.

With fresh plants you can generally get out about as much as you put in. With dried material, especially roots, you get out as much as you can.

Amber jars are quite useful for tincture storage as they protect the integrity of the tincture from the chemical breakdown that can occur from sunlight. So protected, the tinctures can last many years.

Herbal tinctures can then be combined together (though a certain few do not combine well) for dispensing. Because of their long keeping quality and ease of dispensing many herbalists prefer tinctures.

How to Make a Medicinal Syrup

The easiest way to turn any plain syrup into an epicurean feast.

- 1 cup (225 g) water
- 1/2 ounce (about 2 cups, 250 ml) fresh herb leaf or flower, or 1/2 ounce (about 1/2 cup) (50 ml) herb root or bark (reduce by half if using dried herbs)
- 1 cup (250 ml) honey,
- Maple syrup, rice syrup or other sweet syrup

1. Bring water to a boil.
2. Remove from heat and add herb leaf or flower. (If you are using root or bark, do not remove from heat, but allow to simmer over low heat until water is reduced by one-half.)
3. Let stand for about half an hour.
4. Strain out herbs, reserving liquid in a saucepan. You now have a very strong cup of tea.
5. Add honey or other syrup to the reserved liquid. Simmer over very low heat on the stove or in an electric warmer that maintains a temperature between 90° and 100°F until most of the liquid is evaporated and the liquid is close in consistency to what the syrup was originally.
6. Bottle, label, and store in a cool dark place or the refrigerator Bottle, label, and store in a cool dark place or the refrigerator

How to Make Oleolites (Oil Infusions) for Ointments and Salves

Oleolite is an oil mixed with a fresh or dried plant, that has released its properties inside.

Useful for alleviating skin issues, it's one of those products to have at hand.

Do it yourself: You don't need a specific laboratory, but a few usefulaccessories to prepare it at home.

It is enough to get:

- a jar or a glass bottle, better if darkened dried
- flowers of the plant you want to use a vegetable
- oil of your choice
1. Put the dried plant in the glass jar (about 200 grams for a medium size
2. jar or bottle).
3. Then add the vegetable oil of your choice until the quantity of dried plant is reached and cover it with just enough oil to make sure that nopart of the plant is exposed to air; be careful to not exceed with oil quantity.
4. Finally close the glass container.
5. Some oil infusion need to be covered with tinfoil in order to be kept in the dark in a cool and dry place, other like Saint John's Wort infusionsneed to stay in the sun.
6. The glass container should be gently shaken a couple of times a week and kept in these conditions for about 40 days. After 40 days, you haveto filter it.

Benefits of Oleolite:

Depending on the plant you decide to use, you will get benefits rather thanothers. Among the oleoliths that are usually prepared at home there are:

Lavender oil infusion: ideal for inflammation of any nature, such as fever, colds, headaches, tension and fatigue. Also useful in case of allergies and tofight bacteria. Lavender is a plant with high antiseptic properties. It is indicated for vaginal problems and counteracts inflammation from fissures and hemorrhoids. Also useful in case of insect bites.

Calendula oil infusion: indicated in case of spasms or burns or skin lesions, itis refreshing and soothing. It is an excellent emollient that can also be used for internal use, as it scours the walls of the intestine.

Arnica oil infusion: very useful in case of muscle and joint pain and in caseof bruises.

BOOK 9
Ancient Traditions and Secrets of Herbal Medicine

HOW TO CHOOSE THE RIGHT OIL TO PREPARE AN OIL INFUSION: THE MOST USED OILS

OLIVE OIL: rich in vitamin E, helps to preserve the oil infusion correctly and for a long time, has an emollient and moisturizing action.

SWEET ALMOND OIL: very nourishing, leaves the skin very moisturized and elastic, prevents the formation of stretch marks. It does not last long and should be used within short periods.

RICE OIL: nourishes the skin, leaving it elastic. Soothes redness.

SUNFLOWER OIL: excellent for dry and cracked skin because it is rich in vitamin E.

Other types of oil may be used as well, as long as they are suitable to be ingested if you want to use the oleolite for internal use as well.

How to Make Ointments and Salves

Ointments are preparations for external use with a semi-solid consistency, formulated to be applied on healthy or diseased skin or on mucous membranes, in order to produce a local medicinal action, to convey the transdermal penetration of active principles or simply to produce an emollient and protective action.

Ointments are not defined by the official pharmacopoeia and - included in the wider category of semi-solid preparations for skin application - are divided in ointments and creams, according to the physical system they are made of.

Ointments: they are anhydrous or almost anhydrous preparations (that is with low water content and very rich in fat), made of a base poor in water and rich in fatty and resinous substances.

The peculiarity of the ointments is to have a considerable content of fatty substances; for this characteristic, they are indicated in the treatment of dry, squamous dermatitis and hyperkeratosis (in general in all cases of marked skin dryness, while they are contraindicated in the presence of significant skin inflammations, especially in acute phase).

They are not absorbed by the skin, but they form a superficial layer on the skin, which is difficult to spread and particularly greasy; consequently, due to its occlusive and "barrier" properties, this layer of fat has an advantageous long-lasting emollient effect, with reduction of TEWL. Being waterless, ointments generally keep very well, making the use of preservatives unnecessary.

Creams and salves : they are emulsions formed by two phases - fat (O) and aqueous (A) - one of which prevails over the other (in O/A, the most common, the aqueous phase prevails and for this reason they are defined hydrophilic; in A/O, the fat phase prevails and for this reason they aredefined hydrophobic or lipophilic, getting closer to ointments).

They are generally used as a carrier for medicines, because especially theO/A emulsions are easily absorbed by the skin; the fatty ones, on the other hand, are rather unctuous to the touch and are mainly used in products whose functionality is linked to the permanence on the skin surface, such as protective cosmetics for the sun, massage creams and those with barriereffect. As they contain water, creams need preservatives.

Note: Commonly, the ointment is often considered as an ointment or as a lipophilic cream O/A; not surprisingly, it is generically described as a "fat cream".

In their simplest formulation, ointments consist of a simple base (such as Vaseline, animal fat or beeswax) in which one or more active ingredients are dissolved.

Among the most common lipophilic or oily excipients contained in the bases of ointments are Vaseline, cocoa butter, beeswax, animal fat (pork or porkfat, cod liver oil or shark oil, spermaceti...), almond oil, olive oil, sunflower seed oil, argan oil, jojoba oil; among the hydrophilic excipients, lanolinstands out. Clearly, the typical excipients of popular medicine (such as animal fats), although they are easy to find, have some negative aspects rather limiting, such as bad smell, easy rancidity, so the poor shelf life, and excessive oiliness.

Generally, the oily bases (for ointments or salves intended as "fatty creams") are prepared by melting the lipidic bases placing them in a pot, gently heated in bain-marie; it can be used exclusively a lipidic or waxy solid or semisolid substance (lanolin, chicken or pig fat, beeswax etc.), or mix it with a part of oil (mostly used are olive and sweet almonds).

Once the oily base is melted, add the vegetable extracts and mix everything for some minutes, while continuing to heat over low heat. It is filtered with a cloth or a gauze, allowing the melted liquid to come out, which once solidified in jars will have a semi-solid or solid consistency.

Creams need a more articulated and complex preparation in order to avoid theseparation of the two phases (watery and oily). Basically, it is like preparing amayonnaise, therefore the use of an immersion blender can be of help.

Emulsifiers are used to prevent the separation of the two phases. Besides the fat part it is therefore necessary to add a certain percentage of water and an aqueous base (such as glycerine).

A recipe for an A/O cream foresees the melting of about 150 grams of pure beeswax placed in a glass jar heated in bain-marie, then, by stirring vigorously, 70 g of glycerine and 80 ml of water are added; at this point addalso the vegetable extracts, stirring and then let it simmer for some ten minutes (always using the bain-marie); the whole will be then filtered with a gauze and stirred until it will be cooled and will be thickened as a cream.

Pour into a jar and mix with the help of a spatula: first put a little bit of creamaround the edge, then fill the center of the container. "Leaner" preparations are often more problematic and require the addition of specific emulsifiers such as glyceryl-stearate.

Basic recipe for 50 g of ointment:

- 8 g of beeswax
- 40 ml of vegetable oil or oleolite (oil infusion)
- 15 drops maximum of essential oils

Procedure: Melt the wax with the vegetable oil over very low heat in double boiler. In the cooling phase add the essential oils. The properties of the ointment depend on the oil infusion used and the essences you add.

Oleoliths are obtained from the maceration of the plant in oil instead of distillation with alcohol. Some medicinal plants such as arnica, helichrysum and marigold are not well suited for distillation. In the recipe they replace the basic vegetable oil or complement it.

In the case of plants that are suitable to distillation, it's great to use essential oils. When the ointment is obtained, pour it before cooling (still liquid) into white or brown glass jars. Stir from time to time with a small spoon until completely cooled to avoid the formation of a crust on the surface. Finally label it.

Using Whole Herbs

The same herbs used in the wound salve are excellent when applied directly on a wound. They are pulverized as finely as possible, mixed together, and lightly sprinkled over the wound. The fine powder helps reduce the friction against the wound that sometimes occurs with a larger grind.

Many herbs can be eaten as needed. Osha for example can be used for sore throats and upper respiratory infections of both viral and bacterial origin. Sometimes a combination of whole herbs and herbal tinctures is useful and more effective.

Ancient Remedies

Skin and Gum Abscesses Remedies

Topical Wash for Skin and Gum Abscesses

- 1 to 2 teaspoons Barberries
- 1 tablespoon White oak bark
- 1 teaspoon Echinacea root
- 1 teaspoon granulated Oregon grape root
- 2 cups boiling wate

Pour the boiling water over the herbs, in a glass container. Soak for 3 or 4 hours. Strain and use 2 or 3 times a day as a wash. To treat gum abscess, hold the liquid in the mouth for at least 5 minutes before spitting it out.

Herbal Mouthwash

- 4 fluid ounces water
- 1 teaspoon of sea salt
- 2 teaspoons aloe gel
- 1 fluid ounce tincture of uva-ursi
- 1 fluid ounce tincture of yarrow
- ½ fluid ounce tincture of calendula
- ½ fluid ounce tincture of plantain
- ¼ fluid ounce tincture of Echinacea
- ¼ fluid ounce tincture of meadowsweet

Combine all the ingredients in a jar with a lid. Cover the jar and shake well. Use this mouthwash twice a day.

Antiaging Remedies

Antioxidant Tea

- 5 drops cayenne tincture
- 15 drops goldenseal tincture
- 10 drops ginger root tincture
- ½ cup slippery elm tea
- 1 cup warm water

Combine all ingredients. Take 2 to 3 tablespoons 3 times per day

Happy Memory Tea

- ½ cup Ginkgo Biloba tea
- ½ cup Ginseng tea

Combine the ingredients. Take one-third of a cup three times daily. Ginkgo isknown to improve memory, while ginseng boost energy levels and stabilizes blood pressure.

Allergies Relief Remedies

Allergies Relief Tea

Makes about 3 to 4 cups dried herb mix (enough for 18 to 22 quarts of tea)

Nettle and goldenrod contain the antioxidant quercetin, which stabilizes mast cells and prevents the release of histamine. Meanwhile, mullein supports the mucous membranes in the lungs and sinuses, reducing phlegm and mucus and quelling cough. Calendula and licorice improve liver function. You can also add some honey to your tea, especially raw, local honey! Unfiltered honey helps reduce allergic response.

- 1 cup dried nettle leaf (see Tips)
- 1 cup dried goldenrod leaf and flower
- ½ cup dried mullein leaf
- ½ cup dried calendula flower
- 2 to 4 tablespoons dried licorice root

1. In a medium bowl, mix together all the herbs, including the marshmallow (if using, for a dry constitution). Store in an airtight container.
2. Make a long infusion: Prepare a kettle of boiling water. Measure 2 to 3 tablespoons of herbs per quart of water and place in a mason jar or French press. Pour in the boiling water, cover, and steep for 8 hours, or overnight.
3. Drink a quart or more every day, especially in the month before and during your personal peak allergy season. The earlier you start, the less you'll suffer.

TIP: Omit the nettle leaf and increase the goldenrod if you take blood-thinning pharmaceuticals.

Flower decoction

- 1 teaspoon oxeye daisy leaves
- 1 teaspoon pearly everlasting flowers
- 1 teaspoon yerba sante leaves
- 3 cups boiling water

1. Combine the herbs in a glass container and cover with the water; steep for 30 minutes; strain.
2. To use, take one-half to one cup every six hours.

Nettle Tea

- 2 tablespoons nettle leaves
- teaspoon Oregon grape root cups
- boiling water

1. Combine all the herbs in a glass container and cover with the water; steep for 30 minutes; strain.
2. Take one-quarter cup three times a day.

Anemia Remedies

Anti-Anemic Tea

- 2 teaspoons barberry root
- 2 teaspoons Oregon grape root

1. Combine the herbs in a glass container. Cover with the water
2. Soak overnight. Strain. Take up to one-half cup three times daily.

Arthritis Remedies

Quick Analgesic Tea

- 25 drops black cohosh tincture
- 90 drops wild cherry bark tincture 90 drops mullein tincture
- cup warm water

1. Combine the herbs in a glass container and cover with water. Take 1/3 of the mixture 3 times daily

Bedtime Tea

- teaspoon black cohosh root
- teaspoon chamomile flowers
- teaspoon cascara sagrada bark cups
- water

1. Combine the above herbs in a glass container; cover with the water; stir thoroughly to combine.
2. Place 1½ teaspoons of the mixture in one cup boiling water; steep for 10 minutes; strain.
3. Take one cup in the evening, just before going to bed

ARTHRITIS OINTMENT

Ingredients for about 150 g of ointment
110 g jojoba oil;

- 30 g of organic beeswax;
- 24 drops of lavender essential oil;
- 12 drops of ginger essential oil;
- ½ teaspoon of cayenne pepper;
- 6 Tbsp. devils claw infused oil

You will also need:

- a precision scale;
- a heat-resistant Pyrex glass container;
- a small saucepan that is not too tall and can hold the Pyrex for bain-marie cooking;
- a glass or sturdy plastic jar with a cap; a steel spoon for stirring (optional).

1. Before proceeding to the preparation of the recipe is good to sterilize the Pyrex in which we will dissolve the ingredients. Boil it in a large container, with enough water to cover it completely, for about ten minutes. Turn off the fire and when the water has cooled down enough, remove the Pyrex and let it dry.
2. Take the saucepan large enough to hold the Pyrex container and put water in it so that they can dissolve the oils. Be careful that the water does not escape during boiling.
3. Place the beeswax and vegetable oil in the Pyrex along with the turmeric and pepper, then place the container inside the pot with water for the water bath. Turn the heat on to a moderate flame so that it doesn't boil too hard.
4. Melt the beeswax and stir gently (I use the handle of a steel spoon. I avoid wooden tools in this case because it is a porous material that absorbs and may not be perfectly clean).
5. When the wax has melted completely, remove the Pyrex from the saucepan with the help of a potholder and add the essential oils. Stir so that it all comes together. Then pour the ointment while still warm into the jar.
6. Close tightly with the cap and let the jar rest in a "safe" place, that cannot be reached by children or pets, until the ointment has solidified (I usually let a couple of days pass to be sure that it has solidified perfectly) and at that point it will be ready to use.
7. If properly stored (away from heat and light and tightly closed) the ointment will keep for several months

Asthma Remedies

Asthma Relief Tea

- teaspoon elecampane root teaspoons horehound herb
- teaspoon blue vervain leaves
- 2 cups water

1. Combine the herbs in a pan and cover with water.
2. Bring to a boil; reduce heat and simmer for about 20 minutes; strain and cool.
3. Drink up to two cups a day, a mouthful at a time.

Goodbreath Tea

- 2 teaspoons powdered Indian root
- 2 teaspoons granulated echinacea root
- 2 teaspoons elecampane root
- teaspoon horsetail cups water

1. Combine the herbs in a pan and cover with the water.
2. Soak for several hours, then strain. Take one-half cup two times daily.

Bedsores Remedies

TOPICAL WASH FOR BEDSORES

- 2 teaspoons marigold flowers
- teaspoon granulated echinacea root
- tablespoon white oak bark
- cups water

1. Combine the herbs in a glass container and cover with the water; soak overnight; strain.
2. Use as a wash periodically throughout the day.

Bite Remedies

BITE RELIEF SPRAY

Makes 8 fluid ounces

If you regularly walk through clouds of mosquitoes or black flies or live in anarea infested with chiggers, you'll want this cooling, itch-relieving spray stocked for when you come inside.

- 4 fluid ounces nonalcoholic witch hazel extract or apple cider vinegar
- 2 fluid ounces tincture of rose fluid
- ounce tincture of self-heal fluid
- ounce tincture of yarrow

1. In a bottle with a fine-mist sprayer top, combine all the ingredients.
2. Cap the bottle and label it.
3. Liberally spray wherever you've been bitten

TOPICAL WASH FOR BITES

- 2 teaspoons comfrey leaves
- 2 tablespoons marshmallow leaves
- tablespoon dried yarrow
- cup boiling water

1. Combine the herbs in a nonmetallic container and cover with boilingwater.
2. Steep for 15 to 30 minutes; strain.
3. Use as a topical wash.

SKIN SOOTHING OINTMENT

- Ingredients (for about 150 g of ointment) 80 g jojoba oil;
- 20 g calendula infused oil 24 g of organic beeswax;
- 12 drops of chamomile essential oil;
- 12 drops of rose essential oil;

- 20g aloe gel

You will also need:

- a precision scale;
- a heat-resistant Pyrex glass container;
- a small saucepan that is not too tall and can hold the Pyrex for bain-marie cooking;
- a glass or sturdy plastic jar with a cap;
- a steel spoon for stirring (optional).

1. Before proceeding to the preparation of the recipe is good to sterilize the Pyrex in which we will dissolve the ingredients. Boil it in a large container, with enough water to cover it completely, for about ten minutes. Turn off the fire and when the water has cooled down enough, remove the Pyrex and let it dry.
2. Take the saucepan large enough to hold the Pyrex container and put water in it so that they can dissolve the oils. Be careful that the water does not escape during boiling.
3. Place the beeswax and vegetable oil in the Pyrex along with the turmeric and pepper, then place the container inside the pot with water for the water bath. Turn the heat on to a moderate flame so that it doesn't boil too hard.
4. Melt the beeswax and stir gently (I use the handle of a steel spoon. Iavoid wooden tools in this case because it is a porous material that absorbs and may not be perfectly clean).
5. When the wax has melted completely, remove the Pyrex from the saucepan with the help of a potholder and add the essential oils and aloe gel. Stir so that it all comes together. Then pour the ointment whilestill warm into the jar.
6. Close tightly with the cap and let the jar rest in a "safe" place, that cannot be reached by children or pets, until the ointment has solidified (I usually let a couple of days pass to be sure that it has solidified perfectly) and at that point it will be ready to use.
7. If properly stored (away from heat and light and tightly closed) theointment will keep for several months

Remedies for Bronchitis and ThroatInflamation

FIRE CIDER

Makes about 1 quart

Traditional fire cider recipes are blends of pungent and aromatic stimulating expectorants that will heat you up and help you get the gunk out. In this version, we sneak in some immune stimulants and a good source of vitamin

C. Do not consume this if you take pharmaceutical blood thinners.

- whole head garlic, cloves peeled and chopped (2-inch) piece fresh ginger, chopped
- ¼ cup dried pine needles
- ¼ cup dried sage leaf
- ¼ cup dried thyme leaf
- ¼ cup dried elderberry
- ¼ cup dried rose hips
- tablespoons dried elecampane root tablespoons dried angelica root quart apple cider vinegar
- Honey or water, for sweetening or diluting (optional)

1. In a quart-size mason jar, combine the garlic, ginger, and remaining herbs
2. Fill the jar with the vinegar. Cover the jar with a plastic lid, or place a sheet of wax paper under the jar lid before you screw down the ring. (The coating on the bottom of metal mason jar lids corrodes when exposed to vinegar.)
3. Let the herbs macerate in the vinegar for 2 weeks or longer.
4. Strain, bottle, and label the finished fire cider. If the vinegar is too heating to be comfortable on your stomach, add some honey (up to one-fourth the total volume), or dilute your dose with water.
5. Take a shot (about ½ fluid ounce) at the first sign of mucus buildup in
6. the lungs, and every couple hours thereafter until symptoms resolve.

THROAT-SOOTHING TEA

- 2 teaspoons black cohosh root
- 2 teaspoons powdered Indian root
- 2 teaspoons chamomile flower
- 2 cups water Honey, to taste

1. Combine the above herbs in a pan; cover with the water.
2. Bring to a boil; reduce heat and simmer for 30 minutes; strain.
3. Add honey if desired. Take one tablespoon in two cups of water several times a day

BRONCHITIS TEA

- to 2 slices of fresh ginger root
- teaspoon pearly everlasting flowers or leaves
- 1 teaspoon redroot
- 1 cup boiling water

1. Combine the above herbs; steep in the boiling water for 30 thirty minutes; strain.
2. Take one-half cup of the tea, three times daily.

Sunburn Remedies

SUNBURN SPRAY

Makes 8 fluid ounces

A few spritzes refresh the skin reduce inflammation. quart boiling water

- tablespoon dried peppermint leaf
- 1 tablespoon dried plantain leaf
- 1 tablespoon dried self-heal leaf and flower
- 1 tablespoon dried linden leaf and flower
- 4 fluid ounces rose water

1. Make a hot infusion: In a mason jar, combine the peppermint, plantain, self-heal, and linden.
2. Pour in the boiling water, cover, and steep for 20 minutes.
3. Move the jar to the refrigerator until it's cold.
4. Strain out 4 fluid ounces of the infusion and transfer to an 8-ounce bottle with a fine-mist sprayer top. Use the remaining infusion for compresses or a cooling drink. It will keep, refrigerated, for 3 days.
5. Add the rose water to the spray bottle. Cap the bottle and label it.
6. Apply copiously and frequently. Keep the spray refrigerated when not in use

SOOTHING BURN SALVE

- Ingredients (for about 190 g of salve) 60 g jojoba oil;

- 20 g calendula infused oil 30 g of organic beeswax;
- 40 g of Saint John's Wort infused oil; 40g aloe gel
- 12 drops chamomile essential oil You

will also need

- a precision scale;
- a heat-resistant Pyrex glass container;
- a small saucepan that is not too tall and can hold the Pyrex for bain-marie cooking;
- a glass or sturdy plastic jar with a cap; a steel spoon for stirring (optional).:

1. Before proceeding to the preparation of the recipe is good to sterilize thePyrex in which we will dissolve the ingredients. Boil it in a large container, with enough water to cover it completely, for about ten minutes. Turn off the fire and when the water has cooled down enough, remove the Pyrex and let it dry.
2. Take the saucepan large enough to hold the Pyrex container and put water in it so that they can dissolve the oils. Be careful that the water does not escape during boiling.
3. Place the beeswax and vegetable oil in the Pyrex along with the turmericand pepper, then place the container inside the pot with water for the water bath. Turn the heat on to a moderate flame so that it doesn't boil too hard.
4. Melt the beeswax and stir gently (I use the handle of a steel spoon. Iavoid wooden tools in this case because it is a porous material that absorbs and may not be perfectly clean).
5. When the wax has melted completely, remove the Pyrex from the saucepan with the help of a potholder and add the essential oils and aloe gel. Stir so that it all comes together. Then pour the ointment whilestill warm into the jar.
6. Close tightly with the cap and let the jar rest in a "safe" place, that cannot be reached by children or pets, until the ointment has solidified (I usually let a couple of days pass to be sure that it has solidified perfectly) and at that point it will be ready to use.
7. If properly stored (away from heat and light and tightly closed) theointment will keep for several months

IMMUNITY BOOSTER

- 30 drops echinacea tincture
- 20 drops wild indigo root tincture 1 cup warm water

1. Combine the above herbs in the warm water.
2. Take up to five times a day.
3. A burn can weaken the body, leaving you vulnerable to illness and infection. Use this tea to strengthen immunity.

Canker Sores Remedies

ANTI-INFLAMMATORY MOUTHWASH

- ½ cup barberry tea
- ½ cup white oak tea
- ½ cup echinacea tea
- ½ cup Oregon grape root tea

1. Combine the above ingredients in a glass container with a lid.
2. Use three times a day as a mouthwash. Be

sure to swish the liquid around in your mouth for several minutes.

Cold Sores Remedies

COLD SORE WRAP

Makes 5 cups dried herb mix (about 50 applications)

This direct application stimulates local immunity and improves tissue quality so your body has the best chance to suppress the virus.

- cup dried calendula flower cup dried plantain leaf
- 1 cup dried chamomile flower
- 1 cup dried linden leaf and flower
- ½ cup dried self-heal leaf and flower
- ½ cup dried St. John's wort leaf and flower

1. In a large bowl, mix together all the herbs. Store in an airtight container.
2. Make a hot infusion: Prepare a kettle of boiling water. Measure 2 to 3 tablespoons of herbs per quart of water and place in a mason jar or French press.
3. Pour in the boiling water, cover, and steep for 20 minutes. (Meanwhile, fill a hot water bottle.)
4. Soak a cloth in the warm tea, holding it by a dry spot and letting it cool in the air until hot but comfortable to the touch.
5. Lie down and place the wet cloth over the affected area. Cover with a dry cloth and lay the hot water bottle on top. Get comfortable and let it soak in for 10 to 20 minutes. Repeat 2 to 3 times per day

VARIATION: You can also perform a steam using these herbs as they're infusing. Simply make a blanket tent, position your face over the steaming pot, and steam yourself with these herbs for a few minutes before you sit with the compress.

COLD SORE BALM

Makes 5 ounces (about a 3-month supply)

This gentle salve is very soothing to irritated cold sores and helps reduce inflammation while making your body's environment less hospitable to the virus.

- fluid ounce calendula-infused oil fluid ounce plantain-infused oil
- ½ fluid ounce self-heal–infused oil
- ½ fluid ounce chamomile-infused oil
- ½ fluid ounce St. John's wort–infused oil
- ½ fluid ounce thyme-infused oil
- 1 ounce beeswax, plus more as needed

1. Make a salve as usual (see here for complete instructions). Make it nice and soft if you'll keep it in little jars; make it slightly firmer if you're using lip balm tubes.
2. Apply liberally to the affected area 3 to 5 times daily.

IMMUNITY BOOSTER

Often canker sores appear in conjunction with a lowering of immune defenses.

- 30 drops echinacea tincture
- 20 drops wild indigo root tincture cup
- warm water

1. Combine the above herbs in the warm water.

2. Take up to five times a day.

Constipation Remedies

BOWEL-STIMULATING TINCTURE

Makes 4 fluid ounces (30 to 60 doses)

- These bitters and carminatives will spur the bowels to movement by stimulating bile flow and intestinal peristalsis.
- 1½ fluid ounces dandelion root tincture 1½ fluid ounces St. John's wort tincture
- ½ fluid ounce angelica root tincture
- ½ fluid ounce ginger tincture

In a small bottle, combine the tinctures. Cap the bottle and label it. Take 2 to 4 drops every 20 minutes until relief occurs

BOWEL-SOOTHING TEA

- One large handful of boneset flowers
- One large handful of dandelion flowers
- 4 ounces cascara bark
- 2 quarts

1. Combine the above herbs in a pan and cover with two quarts of water; bring to a boil; boil until the mixture reduces to one quart; strain.
2. Take one cup before breakfast and one at bedtime. You may want to add honey to sweeten.

DIGESTIVE TEA

- 2 teaspoons cascara sagrada
- 3 to 4 slices ginger root
- 1/2 teaspoon cayenne
- teaspoon Oregon grape root cups boiling water

1. Combine the above herbs in a pan and cover with two cups of boilingwater
2. Steep for 30 to 45 minutes, cool, and strain.
3. Take one tablespoon at a time, up to two cups per day.

BOWEL-HYDRATING INFUSION

Makes 2½ cups dried herb mix (enough for 14 to 18 quarts of tea)cup dried linden leaf and flower

- ¼ cup dried lemon balm
- ¼ cup dried licorice root
- ¼ cup dried mallow leaves and flowers

1. In a medium bowl, mix together all the herbs. Store in an airtightcontainer.
2. Make a cold infusion: Measure 2 to 4 tablespoons of herbs per quart ofwater and place in a mason jar or French press.

Pour in cold or room-temperature water and steep for 4 to 8 hours beforestraining.

Colds and Cough Remedies

LAKOTA COUGH AND COLD FORMULA

- teaspoon goldenseal root teaspoon mullein leaves
- 1 teaspoon osha root
- 1 teaspoon pleurisy root
- 1 teaspoon yerba mansa root
- teaspoons yerba sante leaves
- 2 cups boiling water

1. Combine the above herbs and cover with the boiling water; steep for 30 minutes,

cool, and strain.
2. Take two tablespoons at a time, as needed, up to two cups a day.

LUMBEE COUGH AND COLD FORMULA

- 3 teaspoons goldenrod leaves
- 4 teaspoons horehound leaves
- 2 teaspoons white pine inner bark
- 4 cups boiling water

1. Combine the above herbs in a cheesecloth; tie closed with a string.
2. Place the bag in the boiling water; boil for 15 minutes; cool; remove the bundle.
3. Take half a cup of the hot mixture at a time, as needed, up to two cups a day.

COUGH SYRUP

- cup of mullein tea
- 1 pound honey

1. Combine the above ingredients in a pan and heat until the honey is liquid.
2. Remove from heat, cool, and pour into a glass container. Take a tablespoon at a time, as needed.

FLOWER TEA

- teaspoon elder flowers
- teaspoon yarrow flowers cup
- boiling water

1. Combine the herbs in a nonmetallic container and cover with one cup of boiling water; steep for 20 minutes and strain.
2. Drink hot every two hours, as needed.

COUGH AND COLD INFUSION

- 2 slices fresh ginger
- 2 teaspoons pleurisy root cup
- boiling water
- teaspoon honey

1. Combine the herbs in a glass container; pour one cup of boiling water over the herbs; steep for 30 minutes, cool, and strain.
2. Take a tablespoon at a time, up to two cups a day. This tea is good for bronchial congestion.

Cramps Remedies

WARMING OINTMENT

- Ingredients (for about 150 g of ointment) 30 gr Saint John's infused oil
- 30 g jojoba oil
- 30 g devil's claw infused oil
- 30 g of organic beeswax;
- 12 drops of lavender essential oil;
- 12 drops of ginger essential oil;
- 8 drops of mint essential oil;
- ½ teaspoon of cayenne pepper.
- 8 gr. devil's claw tincture

You will also need:

- a precision scale;
- a heat-resistant Pyrex glass container;
- a small saucepan that is not too tall and can hold the Pyrex for bain-marie cooking;
- a glass or sturdy plastic jar with a cap; a steel spoon for stirring (optional).

1. Before proceeding to the preparation of the recipe is good to sterilize the Pyrex in which we will dissolve the ingredients. Boil it in a large container, with enough water to cover it completely, for about ten

minutes.
2. Turn off the fire and when the water has cooled down enough, remove the Pyrex and let it dry.
3. Take the saucepan large enough to hold the Pyrex container and put water in it so that they can dissolve the oils. Be careful that the water does not escape during boiling.
4. Place the beeswax and vegetable oil in the Pyrex along with the turmeric and pepper, then place the container inside the pot with water for the water bath. Turn the heat on to a moderate flame so that it doesn't boil too hard.
5. Melt the beeswax and stir gently
6. When the wax has melted completely, remove the Pyrex from the saucepan with the help of a potholder and add the essential oils. Stir so that it all comes together. Then pour the ointment while still warm into the jar.
7. Close tightly with the cap and let the jar rest in a "safe" place, that cannot be reached by children or pets, until the ointment has solidified (I usually let a couple of days pass to be sure that it has solidified perfectly) and at that point it will be ready to use.
8. If properly stored (away from heat and light and tightly closed) the ointment will keep for several months!

MUSCLE RUB

Ingredients for 8 fluid ounces (30-day supply)

These warming herbs increase local circulation, simultaneously reducing inflammation and soothing tension. If, after applications, you're still in a lot of pain when it's time to go to bed, take 1 to 2 drops of wild lettuce tincture for further relief.

- 2 fluid ounces ginger-infused oil
- 2 fluid ounces goldenrod-infused oil
- 2 fluid ounces tincture of ginger
- 2 fluid ounces tincture of meadowsweet
- 80 drops peppermint essential oil

1. In a small bottle, combine the infused oils, tinctures, and essential oil(s). Cap the bottle and label it, including Shake well before each use.
2. Hold your palm over the bottle's mouth and tilt to deposit a small amount in your palm. Rub between your hands to warm the treatment, and apply to the painful joints.
3. Massage the liniment into the joints until your hands no longer feel oily. Really work the liniment into the tissue.
4. Repeat the application 3 to 5 times per day.

MUSCLE CRAMP TEA

- 2 teaspoons black cohosh root
- tablespoon ginseng root
- cups water

1. Combine the above herbs in a pan and cover with two cups of water; bring to a boil;
2. Reduce heat and simmer for 30 minutes, cool, and strain.
3. Take two to three tablespoons up to six times a day.

Diarrhea Remedies

IROQUOIS TEA

- 2 teaspoons raspberry leaves
- 2 teaspoons strawberry leaves
- 2 tablespoons yarrow
- 2 teaspoons yellow dock root
- 2 cups boiling water

1. Combine the herbs in a glass container; pour the boiling water over the herbs; steep for 30 minutes; cool and strain.
2. Take up to one cup a day. The Iroquois made a similar tea to treat bloody diarrhea.

ASTRINGENT TEA

The tannins in these herbs help bind lax tissues back together so fluids stay where they belong and barriers keep their integrity. Drink a quart of tea over the course of the day.

- 1½ cups dried self-heal leaf and flower
- ½ cup dried meadowsweet flower
- ¼ cup rose petals

1. In a medium bowl, mix together all the herbs. Store in an airtight container.
2. Make a hot infusion: Prepare a kettle of boiling water.
3. Measure 2 to 3 tablespoons of herbs per quart of water and place in a mason jar
4. Pour in the boiling water, cover, and steep for 20 minutes or until cool enough to drink.

TINCTURE VARIATION: If you prefer, make a tincture blend using the same proportions:

Combine 1½ fluid ounces tincture of self-heal, ½ fluid ounce tincture of meadowsweet, and ¼ fluid ounce tincture of rose petal. Take 1 to 6 drops every 20 minutes until relief occurs.

TEA
QUICK AND EASY DIARRHEA

- tablespoons agrimony leaves
- 3 tablespoons plantain leaves
- 2 tablespoons self-heal
- cups water

1. Combine the herbs in a pan; cover with the water; bring to a boil;
2. Reduce heat and simmer for 30 minutes; cool and strain.
3. Drink as needed, up to one cup a day

Fatigue Remedies

ENERGY TEA

- teaspoon Ginkgo biloba leaves

teaspoon dried Mirabilis root
- 1 teaspoon Pulsatilla herb
- 1 teaspoon dried ginseng root
- 1 teaspoon Gotu kola leaves
- 1 teaspoon St. John's Wort leaves
- 4 cups boiling water

1. Combine the herbs in a glass container; Cover with boiling water;
2. Steep for 30 minutes. Strain.

REVITALIZING TEA

- 2 cups boiling water Honey (to taste)
- teaspoon strawberry leaves teaspoon blackberry leaves
- 1 teaspoon raspberry leaves

1. Combine the above herbs in a glass container; cover with the boiling water; steep for 10 minutes; strain.
2. Sweeten with honey if desired.

UPLIFTING INFUSION

- 55 gr of Ginseng roots
- 40 gr of Licorice roots
- 5 gr of Peppermint leaves
- liter of water

You may also choose to add a few drops of Rosehip extract, containing vitamin C, which is a perfect tonic to fight fatigue.

1. Mix all the ingredients. Boil 40 grams of the mixed mixture in water, then strain into a cup and consume.
2. It is advisable to take the energizing herbal tea as soon as you wake up, in order to find the right charge to face the day

Fever Remedies

IMMUNITY BOOSTER TEA

- teaspoon Echinacea root teaspoon Balsam root
- 1 teaspoon White willow root
- 1 teaspoon Centaury
- 4 cups water

1. Combine the roots in a pan and cover with the water.
2. Bring to a boil; reduce heat and simmer for 30 minutes; cool and strain.
3. Take half a cup, up to four times a day.

FEVER RELIEF TEA

- 2 teaspoons peppermint leaves
- teaspoon angelica root
- teaspoon ground ivy leaves
- 1 teaspoon barberry berries
- teaspoons Blue Vervain leaves
- tablespoon dried yarrow
- 1 teaspoon catnip leaves
- 1 cup boiling water

1. Combine the above herbs.
2. Place one tablespoon of the mixture in a cup;
3. Pour the boiling water over the herbs; Steep for 30 minutes; Strain. Take 1 cup a day

REVITALIZING TEA

- teaspoon Ginkgo Biloba leaves
- teaspoon Echinacea
- 1 teaspoon Pulsatilla herb
- 1 teaspoon dried ginseng root
- 1 teaspoon Gotu kola leaves
- 1 teaspoon St. John's Wort leaves
- 5 cups boiling water

1. Combine the above herbs in a glass container; cover with the boiling water; steep for 30 minutes;
2. Strain. Take as needed.

Headache Remedies

HEADACHE RELIEF HERBAL TEA

- teaspoon catnip leaves
- teaspoons feverfew leaves1 to 2 cups boiling water

1. Combine the catnip and the feverfew in a glass container.
2. Pour one to two cups of boiling water over the herbs; steep for 30 minutes; strain.
3. Take up to one cup a day, a tablespoon at a time.

RELAXING TEA

- teaspoon chamomile teaspoon marigold
- 1 teaspoon valerian
- Honey (to taste) cups
- water

1. Combine the above herbs in a glass container;
2. Cover with the boiling water; steep for 30 minutes; strain.

SOOTHING HEADACHE TEA

- teaspoon catnip leaves
- teaspoons feverfew leaves1 to 2 cups boiling water

1. Combine the catnip and the feverfew in a glass container.
2. Pour one to two cups of boiling water over the herbs; steep for 30 minutes; strain.
3. Take up to one cup a day, a tablespoon at a time.

Reflux/Heartburn Remedies

SOOTHING HEARTBURN TEA

- teaspoon catnip leaves
- teaspoon oxeye daisy herb cup
- boiling water

1. Combine the herbs in a non-metallic container and cover with the boiling water;
2. Steep for 30 minutes; strain.
3. Take a tablespoon at a time, as needed.

STOMACH CARE TINCTURE

Makes 3½ fluid ounces (30 to 60 doses)

To restore normal stomach acid levels and reduce the conditions for heartburn to develop, take these drops before every meal.

- fluid ounce tincture of dandelion root
- ½ fluid ounce tincture of catnip
- ½ fluid ounce tincture of chamomile
- ⅓ fluid ounce tincture of fennel
- ⅓ fluid ounce tincture of meadowsweet
- ½ fluid ounce tincture of St. John's Wort

1. In a small bottle, combine the tinctures. Cap the bottle and label it.
2. Take ½ to 1 dropperful 10 minutes before eating. Omit the St. John'sWort if you are concurrently taking pharmaceuticals.

QUICK ANTI-REFLUX TEA

- teaspoon dried angelica root
- teaspoon crushed juniper berries

cup boiling
- water

1. Combine the herbs in a nonmetallic container and cover with the boiling water;
2. Steep for 20 to 30 minutes; strain.

Hypertension Remedies

HEALTHY ARTERIES TEA

- 1 to 3 ginger slices
- 2 teaspoons Ginkgo Biloba leaves
- teaspoon Ginseng leaves
- cups boiling water

1. Combine the herbs in a nonmetallic container and cover with the boiling water.
2. Steep for 30 minutes, cool, and strain. Take up to half a cup per day.

FREE-FLOW TEA

- teaspoon Burdock root teaspoon Goldenseal root
- 1 teaspoon Cayenne
- 1 teaspoons Slippery elm bark slices Ginger root
- cups boiling water

1. Combine the above herbs in a nonmetallic container, and pour the boiling water over them.
2. Steep for 30 minutes, cool, and strain.
3. Take up to one cup a day, two tablespoons at a time.

HEALTHY HEART HERBAL TEA

- 1 teaspoons black cohosh root
- 4 teaspoons ginkgo biloba leaves
- 2 cups boiling water

1. Combine the above herbs in a nonmetallic container, and pour the boiling water over them.
2. Soak for 30 minutes, cool, and strain.
3. Take two to three tablespoons at a time, up to six times a day.

HAPPY HEART TEA

- 2 teaspoons hawthorn berries
- 4 teaspoons sage leaves and roots
- 2 cups boiling water

1. Combine the above herbs in a nonmetallic container, and pour the boiling water over them, Soak for 30 minutes, cool, and strain.

Indigestion/Dyspepsia Remedies

ENZYMES ACTIVATOR

Makes 4 fluid ounces (60 to 120 doses)

This formula stimulates all your digestive fluids—saliva, stomach acid, bile, and pancreatic enzymes to facilitate your digestion

- fluid ounce tincture of dandelion root
- fluid ounce tincture of sage
- fluid ounce tincture of catnip

- fluid ounce tincture of chamomile
1. In a small bottle, combine the tinctures.
2. Cap the bottle and label it.
3. Take 1 to 2 drops 10 minutes before eating.

CARMINATIVE TINCTURE

Makes 4 fluid ounces (60 to 120 doses)

This formula warms the body's core, stimulating your digestive organs and keeping the bowels from getting sluggish. If peppermint isn't your style, substitute angelica.

- ½ fluid ounces tincture of ginger fluid ounce tincture of fennel
- 1 fluid ounce tincture of peppermint (see headnote)
- ½ fluid ounce tincture of licorice
1. In a small bottle, combine the tinctures.
2. Cap the bottle and label it.
3. Take 1 to 2 drops after each meal, or whenever your guts feel uncomfortably stuck.

DIGESTIVE TEA

- teaspoon angelica root
- teaspoon grated ginger root
- teaspoons chamomile flowers
- teaspoons peppermint leaves cup boiling water
1. Combine the above ingredients in a container.
2. Take one tablespoon of the herb mixture and place in the boiling water; steep for 30 minutes; cool and strain.
3. Take as needed, up to two cups a day.

Insomnia Remedies

SWEET SLEEP INFUSION

- 1 teaspoons catnip leaves
- teaspoon hops
- teaspoons chamomile flower
- teaspoons passionflower cup
- boiling water
1. Combine the above herbs in a glass container; cover with the boiling water; steep for 30 minutes; cool and strain.
2. Take one hour before bedtime.

GOOD NIGHT TINCTURE

- Makes 4 fluid ounces (60 to 120 doses)
- 2 fluid ounces passionflower tincture fluid ounce valerian tincture
- ½ fluid ounce chamomile tincture
- ½ fluid ounce linden tincture
1. In a small bottle, combine the tinctures. Cap the bottle and label it.
2. One hour before bedtime, take 1 to 2 drops. 30 minutes before bedtime, take another 1 to 2 drops. At bedtime, take the final 1 to 2 drops.

RELAXING POTION

Makes 4 fluid ounces (60 to 120 doses)

This blend of relaxants and gentle sedatives doesn't force sleep but helps relieve anxiety and tension.

- fluid ounce chamomile tincture fluid once passionflower tincture
- ¾ fluid ounce valerian tincture
- ½ fluid ounce catnip tincture
- ½ fluid ounce linden tincture
- ¼ fluid ounce honey (plain or rose petal–infused)

1. In a small bottle, combine the tinctures and honey. Cap the bottle andlabel it.
2. One hour before bedtime, take 1 to 2 drops. 30 min. before bedtime, take another 1 to 2 drops. At bedtime, take the final 1 to 2 drops.

Menstrual Cycle Irregularities and DisturbsRemedies

CRAMP RELIEF INFUSION

- teaspoon St. John's Wort leaves
- teaspoon raspberry leaves
- 1 cup boiling water

Combine the herbs in a glass container and cover with the boiling water;steep for 15 minutes; strain. Drink as needed.

DYSMENORRHEA TINCTURE

- fluid ounce angelica flower tincture fluid
- ounce chamomile tincture
- 1 fluid ounce sage tincture

1. In a small bowl, mix together all the herbs. Store in an airtight container.
2. Make a hot infusion: Prepare a kettle of boiling water. Measure 2 to 3tablespoons of herbs per quart of water and place in a mason jar or French press.
3. Pour in the boiling water, cover, and steep for 20 minutes or until coolenough to drink.

CYCLE STIMULATING TEA

Makes 3 cups dried herb mix (enough for 20 to 26 quarts of tea) 1 cup dried chamomile flower

- ⅓ cup dried goldenrod leaf and flower
- ⅓ cup dried ginger
- ⅓ cup dried angelica root drop angelica tincture

1. In a small bowl, mix together all the herbs. Store in an airtight container.
2. Make a hot infusion: Prepare a kettle of boiling water. Measure 2 to 3 tablespoons of herbs per quart of water and place in a mason jar or French press. Pour in the boiling water, cover, and steep for 20 minutes or until cool enough to drink.

SOOTHING TEA

- 1 teaspoons black haw root or bark
- 2 teaspoons passionflower
- 2 cups cold water

Combine the above herbs in a pan and cover with the cold water; soak overnight; strain. Take half a cup, up to four times daily.

Nausea and Vomiting Remedies

SOOTHING INFUSION

- cup dried catnip leaf and flower cup dried chamomile flower
- ½ cup dried peppermint leaf
- ½ cup fennel seed
- ¼ cup dried ginger

1. In a medium bowl, mix together all the herbs. Store in an airtight container.
2. Make a hot infusion: Prepare a kettle of boiling water. Measure 2 to 3 tablespoons of herbs per quart of water and place in a mason jar or French press. Pour in the boiling water, cover, and steep for 20 minutes or until cool enough to drink.
3. Drink a cupful, slowly, in small sips. If the nausea is very severe, just sit for a while and inhale the scent rising off the hot tea.

GINGER TINCTURE

Makes 5 fluid ounces (60 to 120 doses)

This mixture of tinctures is one to keep in your herbal first aid kit at all times2 fluid ounces tincture of ginger

- fluid ounce tincture of catnip
- fluid ounce tincture of chamomile
- 1 fluid ounce honey

In a small bottle, combine all the ingredients.Cap the bottle and label it. Take1 to 2 droppers every 20 minutes until relief occurs.

Rash Remedies

RASH LOTION

- teaspoon comfrey root
- teaspoon white oak leaves or bark
- 1 teaspoon slippery elm bark cups water

Place the herbs in a container and cover with the water; bring to a boil andboil for 20 to 30 minutes; cool and strain.

Use as a topical wash, as needed.

SOOTHING SALVE

Makes 9 ounces (60-day supply)

Salves are emollient due to their oil and wax content, especially when they have a moisturizing oil, like olive oil, as the base. In this simple formula, theherbs' healing and anti-inflammatory effects enhance the emollient effect.

- 2 fluid ounces calendula-infused oil
- 3 fluid ounces plantain-infused oil
- 2 fluid ounces licorice-infused oil
- ounce beeswax, plus more as needed

Prepare a salve as usual. Gently apply a thin layer to the affected area atleast twice a day.

SOOTHING TEA

- teaspoon burdock root teaspoon
- Oregon grape root
- 1 teaspoon Echinacea root
- 1 teaspoon yellow dock root cups water
1. Combine the above herbs in a pan and cover with the water.
2. Bring to a boil; reduce heat and simmer for 10 to 15 minutes; cool andstrain.

Take a tablespoon at a time, up to half a cup a day.

Sinusitis Remedies

BALSAMIC STEAM BATH

Makes 2 cups dried herb mix (enough for 4 to 8 steams)1 cup dried pine needles

- ½ cup dried sage leaf
- ½ cup dried thyme leaf

- ½ gallon water
- 5 garlic cloves, chopped, per steam (optional)

1. In a small bowl, mix the pine, sage, and thyme. Store in an airtight container.
2. Make and execute an herbal steam: In a medium pot over high heat, boil the water.
3. Place the pot on a heat-proof surface, someplace where you can sit near it, and make a tent with a blanket or towel.
4. Add ¼ to ½ cup of the herb mixture to the water, along with the garlic (if using).
5. Position your face over the steam and remain there for 5 to 20 minutes. Repeat 2 to 3 times per day.

Similar microbe-clearing benefits can be gained by working with aromatic herbs as incense or a smudge stick

SINUS RELIEF INFUSION

- teaspoon Echinacea root
- teaspoon Yerba Mansa root
- 1 teaspoon goldenseal root
- 1 cup boiling water

1. Combine the above herbs. Take two teaspoons of the mixture and cover with the boiling water;
2. steep for 20 to 30 minutes; strain.

Take warm, up to one cup per day, as needed.

BREATH LIFE TEA

- teaspoon bayberry root
- teaspoon white willow bark
- cups boiling water

Combine the above herbs and cover with the boiling water; steep for 15 minutes. Take warm, up to two cups a day.

Sore Throat Remedies

THROAT SOOTHING GARGLE

- Makes 16 fluid ounces (enough for several gargles)
- 8 fluid ounces water
- 2 tablespoons dried sage leaf
- 8 fluid ounces apple cider vinegar
- 3 teaspoons salt

1. In a small pot over high heat, bring the water to a boil. Remove it from the heat and add the sage. Cover tightly and let infuse for 20 minutes.
2. Strain the liquid into a pint-size mason jar.
3. Add the vinegar and salt, cover the jar, and shake well.
4. Pour off 1 fluid ounce or so and gargle with it for 2 to 3 minutes. Rinse your mouth out with water afterward—the vinegar's acidity can wear down

THROAT SOOTHING TEA

- 1 teaspoon Canadian fleabane leaves
- 1 teaspoon slippery elm bark
- 1 teaspoon Echinacea root cups boiling water

Combine the herbs in a nonmetallic container and cover with the boiling water; steep for 20 to 30 minutes; strain.

Take up to two cups per day, warm.

IMMUNOSTIMULATING TEA

- teaspoon dried Echinacea root
- teaspoon rosehip
- 1 teaspoon sage leaves
- 1 teaspoon dried rosemary cups boiling water

1. Combine the herbs in a nonmetallic container and cover with the boiling water;
2. Steep for 20 to 30 minutes; strain. Take up one to two cups per day, warm.

Sprains and Strains Remedies

INJURY OINTMENT

- Makes about 9 ounces ointment (30-day supply) 3 fluid ounces Ginger-infused oil
- 1 fluid ounces Solomon's seal-infused oil or tincture of Solomon's seal
- fluid ounce tincture of St. John's Wort fluid ounce tincture of self-heal
- 1 fluid ounce tincture of Meadowsweet
- 1 ounce beeswax, or more as needed 40 drops peppermint essential oil

Prepare an ointment as usual. Gently apply a thin layer to the affected area at least twice a day.

PAIN RELIEF TEA

- 1 teaspoons black cohosh root
- tablespoon ginseng root
- cups water

1. Place the above herbs in a pan and cover with the water; bring to a boil; reduce heat and simmer for 30 minutes;
2. cool and strain.

Take two to three tablespoons, up to six times a day.

Stress

CALMING TEA

- teaspoon powdered ginger
- teaspoon powdered valerian root
- 1 teaspoon powdered pleurisy root
- 2 cups boiling water

Combine the above herbs in a nonmetallic container and cover with the boiling water; steep for 30 minutes; cool and strain.

Take one tablespoon at a time, as needed, up to two cups a day.

RESCUE TINCTURE

This remedy works best if you can dedicate a moment to relax. Center yourself, breathe deeply for a few breaths, take your tincture, breathe a few more times, and return to the world.

- ½ fluid ounce tincture of betony
- ½ fluid ounce tincture of catnip
- ½ fluid chamomile tincture
- ½ fluid elderflower tincture
- ½ fluid ounce rose tincture
- ¼ fluid goldenrod tincture
- ¼ fluid sage tincture
- ½ fluid ounce honey

In a small bottle, combine the tinctures and honey. Cap the bottle and label it. Take 2 to 4 drops whenever needed.

ENERGY BOOSTING TEA

If your stress manifests with a feeling of heaviness and downtrodden exhaustion, include 1 teaspoon dried goldenrod and/or sage. If it shows up as digestive upsets, include 1 teaspoon dried chamomile

- teaspoon dried linden leaf and flower teaspoon ginseng root
- ½ teaspoon elderflower
- 1 teaspoon dried St. John's Wort leaf and flower
- 1 teaspoon ginkgo Biloba leaves
- 1 teaspoon rosemary

1. In a medium bowl, mix together all the herbs. Store in an airtight container.
2. Make a hot infusion: Prepare a kettle of boiling water. Measure 2 to 3 tablespoons of herbs per quart of water and place in a mason jar or French press.
3. Pour in the boiling water, cover, and steep for 20 minutes or until cool enough to drink.

Omit the St. John's Wort if you are concurrently taking pharmaceuticals.

Wounds Remedies

WOUND WASH

Makes 3 cups dried herb mix (enough for 10 to 20 quarts of wound wash)

If you're in a hurry, a simple wash with rose water or nonalcoholic witch hazel extract is very effective during the cleaning stage. After that, transition to soaks and compresses with a formula like this. In the later stages of wound healing, you may want to add ½ cup dried marshmallow or kelp for their emollient effects.

- ½ cup dried calendula flower
- ½ cup dried plantain leaf
- ½ cup dried rose petals
- ½ cup dried goldenrod leaf and flower
- ¼ cup dried chamomile flower
- ¼ cup dried self-heal leaf and flower
- ¼ cup dried St. John's Wort leaf and flower
- ¼ cup dried yarrow leaf and flower Salt, for the infusion

1. In a medium bowl, mix together all the herbs. Store in an airtight container.
2. Make a hot infusion: Prepare a kettle of boiling water. Measure 4 to 6 tablespoons of herbs per quart of water and place in a mason jar or French press. Pour in the boiling water, cover, and steep for 20 minutes or until cool.
3. Stir in 1 teaspoon of salt for each quart of infusion you've made.
4. Soak the wounded part, or apply a compress over the affected area. Repeat as frequently as you can, at least 3 times per day.

WOUND OINTMENT

The main problem with wounds is healing, which often is not fast and painless, so it will be good to disinfect the part and protect it with a plaster, not before applying a disinfectant and healing cream, which you can prepare in a few minutes at home.

To prepare it you'll need:

- 1 tablespoons of shea butter tablespoon Beeswax
- tablespoon rose hip oil
- 1 teaspoon honey
- 5 drops essential oil of lavender, thyme or tea tree

1. To prepare the cream melt in a bain-marie, the shea butter, the beeswax, rose hip oil and honey in a container.
2. When everything is melted, let it cool and add 5 drops of your chosenessential oil to the mixture.
3. Sterilize small glass jars with their lids by boiling and dry them well with kitchen paper.
4. Place the lotion in the jar and let it cool and it will be ready to be used. Only caution, use a chopstick to take the cream, not to contaminate thecontents of the jar.
5. Apply the cream even twice a day on the wound. The injured skin tends to quickly absorb all the soothing and emollient principles of the cream.

QUICK HEALING OINTMENT

Makes 8 ounces (40-day supply)

Pine resin salve is the best choice for wounds that have closed or were neververy deep. You can work with the resin of other conifers, too. Resin can be harvested directly from the trees—you'll find whitish globs of it along the trunk where branches were lost. Leave enough on the tree to keep the woundsealed—this resin is how the tree forms a scab!

It will probably have bits of bark, dirt, insect parts, etc., stuck in it—don'tworry: you'll filter that out during processing.

After gathering resin, use a bit of oil to wash your hands6 to 8 ounces pine resin or another conifer resin

- 8 fluid ounces total calendula-infused oil, goldenrod-infused oil,
- and/or plantain- infused oil
- ounce beeswax, chopped or grated, plus more as needed

1. In a small pan over low heat, combine the resin and infused oil and heatgently, stirring frequently. The resin will soften and dissolve, infusing the oil with its virtues.
2. Pour this warm oil through a few layers of cheesecloth. Wrap the massthat remains and squeeze it to extract as much oil as possible.
3. Prepare a salve using this resin-infused oil (see here for complete instructions).
4. Apply to the wound several times a day, using fresh, neat bandages each time.

WOUND COMPRESS

- teaspoon white pine inner bark
- teaspoon wild cherry bark

- 1 teaspoon wild plum root cups
- water

1. Combine the above herbs in a pan and cover with the water.
2. Bring to a boil and boil until the bark and roots are soft. Cool and strain.
3. To use, soak a clean (preferably sterilized) cloth in the solution and apply to the affected area.

Shamanic Smudges

The smudge is a combination of herbs and flowers (single or synergy) used for the purification of our aura and the environments in which we live. All together, they possess an intense and persistent aroma that purifies the environment, bringing peace, harmony and positive vibrations, but at the same time promoting meditation and relaxation. Moreover, burning a smudge before going to sleep promotes relaxation and a pleasant restful sleep.

How to prepare a smudge?

Smudges are made from fresh, just-picked vegetable parts. Some precautions are necessary:

Do not pick leaves, flowers or branches that have fallen to the ground.

Cut twigs from 10 to 20 centimeters long;

It is also possible to use sprigs of small size, but in this case the smudge willbe small and will be, therefore, made with the parts of only one virgin (for example, sage);

The sprigs must all be placed in the same direction (i.e. top with top, andbases with bases);

A naturally occurring thread (i.e. cotton thread, twine, or wool thread) is used to tie the different plants that make up the smudge.

The twigs/plant parts are tied by going up in a spiral and making a double turn at the apices, and then going down and making a double turn at the bases. In this way, you will obtain a sort of stick that you will leave to dry ina white cotton bag and hang in a ventilated place away from sunlight.

Afterwards, it is possible to tie the twigs with a colored or white string. Themost commonly used colors are the following:

White (air) = light, purification, healing;
Red (fire) = energy, strength and power;

Blue (water) = inner balance, calm, relaxation;Green (earth) = positivity, balance, harmony

When can we create a smudge?

Smudges should be prepared in the period of July/August, when the plantsare in their "balsamic period", that is when they are at their maximum potential at the plant level. I suggest to harvest them preferably in crescent moon, in order to benefit from their positive vibrations.

Which accessories to use to perform a smudging?

Among the most used accessories, we remember the Abalone shell, the feather or the shamanic feather fan.

Which are the most known and used smudges?

Laurel: purifier par excellence, infuses wisdom, inner strength and protection; it is also the talisman par excellence against negative influences;

Mugwort: traditionally used to purify and eliminate negative energies, it is also known for its qualities of stimulating lucid dreams; consequently, many burn mugwort before bedtime;

Cedar: useful for eliminating negative energies, it is also used to bless and protect the rooms of a newly purchased home;

Juniper: used in ritual purification to invigorate the mind and body; it is an excellent tonic for the nervous system;

Lavender: with a strong relaxing and anti-stress action, it favors meditation and night rest;

Palo Santo: is a natural incense, used to purify the aura and cleanse the environment from any kind of negativity or dissonant energy, also promotes the connection with the divine;

Rosemary: is a powerful purifier, often used to purify the aura when Palo Santo or White Sage are not available; excellent for stimulating concentration and memory;

White Sage: used in shamanic and esoteric ceremonies, it is excellent for purifying environments and people, but also to re-harmonize the energies of the chakras and one's aur

Sweet grass (or "Hair of Mother Earth"): it is a sacred plant for Native Americans, which is hand-picked by the indigenous tribes of Canada; it is burned to attract positive energy, to purify one's aura and to raise one's vibrations, but it is also used for the purification of objects.

How to use the smudge correctly?

Close the windows, and turn on the stick;

Go to the places in the house where congested energies may lurk (cracks, corners, windows or doors); go around the rooms making a clockwise path (and never counter-clockwise);

Then, let the smudge fumigate in an earthenware saucer (preferably handmade) or in an Abalone shell, until it goes out on its own;

Never wet the smudge to try to extinguish it.

What crystals can we combine with shamanic incense?

Crystals are true gifts of Mother Earth, which are characterized by a specific vibrational charge. Therefore, they can be used in combination with smudges in order to perfect, for example, a purification or meditation. Among the most used crystals, we can remember:

Crystals with a protective action (or

shield/rejection of negative energies), such as Obsidian, Black Onyx, Black Tourmaline, Mahogany Obsidian, Snowflake Obsidian, Apache Tear;

Crystals to balance the heart Chakra, such as Avventurine, Rose Quartz, Jade, Lepidolite, Rhodochrosite, Malachite, Rhodonite and Unakite;

Crystals to promote meditation, such as Amethyst, Selenite, Labradorite, Hyaline Quartz and Moonstone.

.

Cautions :

To prevent the smudge from burning too quickly, we must let it burn in a stone bowl, for example in alabaster or bakelite; currently bakelite saucers can be easily found in stores and have a moderate cost;

There are 2 types of smudge, the small one and the extra-large one. Both are good and you can safely choose them according to your needs

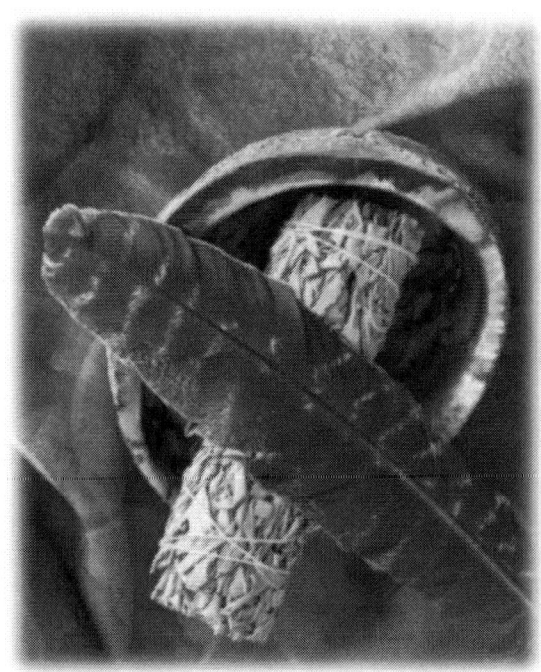

BOOK 10
The Native American AncientRemedies Ancient Traditions and Secrets ofHerbal Medicine

Ancient Uses and Preparations of Plants and Herbs in Native American's Traditions

An ancient Cherokee legend tells that the Creator gifted Mother Earth with all the animals and plants. These could communicate by speaking the common language of peace, harmony and friendship. At that time, people hunted only what they needed and did not forget to express their respect and gratitude. As the times passed, they began to multiply and plan for the future, cultivating the land and building fences and borders. Humans forced animals into smaller and smaller spaces and invented tools that gave them an unfair advantage. Soon realizing their superiority, they began to trample ants, worms and other small creatures.

At first, without thinking about it and then with contempt. They began to hunt the larger animals for meat and skins.

They also killed for fun or simply to show their superiority, forgetting that they were children of the same Creator. Only a few humans could still understand the language of nature, most babbling a language that only they understood. Alarmed, the animals gathered to decide what to do. The first who spoke was the powerful Yonah, the chief white bear who quickly decided to start a war: "Every time a human shoot one of us, we will return the favor!".

So, to fight them, some bears fashioned pieces of wood into bows and arrows. Others, sacrificed themselves by donating sinews for strings, but when they tried to use these tools they got caught in them. trees or dig through roots to find food? "This will never happen!" said the chief bear. "You won't die of hunger just to shoot arrows!

It is better to trust the natural weapons that the Creator has given us". The wise Ahwi, lady of the deer, was the second who spoke, finding an ingenious strategy for their protection and to restore the balance of nature. "Every time a hunter kills a deer without asking for forgiveness, our spirit will follow the trail of blood back to his house, paralyzing him with rheumatism".

And the fishes and the reptiles intervened: "We will appear in the dreams of those ungrateful two feet showing ourselves slimy and rotting, so they will lose the desire to eat us and will die of hunger". So, it went. Each of the creatures devised a disease of punishment, complaining about the man's cruelty and injustice. Since then, men began to get sick and only those who were still able to speak and were in harmony with Nature were spared. At that point, the plant kingdom, which was still friendly towards humans, held a new council. The old willow said: For every health in the World that an animal inflicts on man, one of us will help cure him.

From that moment the spirit of the plants agreed to speak to humans in their dreams, suggesting that any herb, shrub, as well as any other plant or tree would become a remedy.

Below, a list of the most used plants and herbs, their uses by Natives and some tips and recipes to apply them for your needs.

Just relax, tune into their energy and enjoy!

Angelica

More than eighteen American Indian tribes used Angelica species for medicine in a similar manner to that of Western medicinal use.

Native Americans used A. atropurpurea root decoctions to treat rheumatism, fevers, sore throats, and flatulence. It was often used in sweat-lodge ceremonies for treating arthritis, headaches, frostbite, and hypothermia. The root was pulverized and applied externally as a poultice to relieve pain.

The Creek Indians chewed the root and ingested the juice or smoked it dry with tobacco for stomach disorders.

Angelica infusions were used by the Iroquois in steam baths to treat headaches and frostbite. The root poultices were applied to broken bones, and the tea was applied as a topical treatment for ulcers. Angelica was also widely used for purification, smoked with sacred pipes and burned in healing rituals.

A. sinensis and A. atropurpurea are used differently in Asian and Western traditions, and there are minor chemical differences between the plants too.

The uses described below are for A. sinensis. The root, a warming tonic, is the number one female herb in traditional Chinese herbal medicine, and it is used to treat menstrual cramps and may improve menstrual flow. According to Chinese practitioners, angelica improves peripheral circulation to distal parts of body.

In particular Angelica can be used as a remedy for:

- respiratory complaints such as;
- bronchitis, asthma, pleurisy, catarrh
- colds, flu
- digestive problems; indigestion, wind and heartburn poor circulation
- rheumatic pains (external) swellings and itching (external)

Parts used: Leaves, stems, dried roots and seeds.

Infusion (tea) The fresh or dried leaves can be steeped in hot water to make Angelica tea.

Infusion (root tea)

- tsp dried Angelica root
- cup boiling water

Steep 15 to 20 min. Take 1 spoonful 3-4 times a day

Decoction: Dried roots and stems, mashed and boiled for 8-10 minutes, then strained.

External use: Add crushed leaves to a bath to relieve exhaustion andrheumatic pains.

Poultice: fresh leaves can be crushed and rubbed on skin areas for swellings,itching and rheumatism.

Infused Oil: You can make your own infused oil by adding the fresh or driedroot to your carrier oil of choice in a sealed jar. Place it in a dark, dry location and shake daily for 4 to 6 weeks to agitate the mixture. Strain, and store in a sealed jar in a cool, dark place for 4-6 months. Angelica oil is pleasantly soothing for sore muscles.

Balsam Root

Native Americans used the wet leaves as a poultice to heal wounds and burns. The goopy sap sealed wounds and was used as antiseptic. The bitter root contains inulin, that promotes healthy intestinal flora and can stimulatethe immune system, providing protection from acute illnesses such as coldsand flu. The sap is considered antibacterial and antifungal. A decoction of the leaves, stems and roots was taken for stomachaches and colds.

All parts of the plant are edible. The leaves were eaten raw, boiled or steamed. The long taproot was steamed or roasted and was often used as acoffee substitute. The seeds, were roasted and pulverized into flour.

Arrowleaf balm helped relieve the pain of burns, wounds, and bruises. The Cheyenne tribe steamed the entire plant to inhale the vapors against stomachpain and headaches.

The root was also used to treat gonorrhea and syphilis. In the sweat lodge, thesmoke and steam of the balsam root helps relieve headaches. It is considered a warrior plant, smudged as a disinfectant and inhaled for body aches. The chewed root was used as a poultice over sores, wounds, and burns.

How to make a balsam root tincture :

Clean and cut up several fresh balsam roots.

- Put them in a clean container (preferably glass)
- Use a vodka that has at least 50% alcohol content or more (also known as 100 proof), or a grain alcohol that is 95% alcohol (190 proof)
- Add the alcohol at a 2:1 ratio (i.e. 2 cups of vodka to 1 cup of fresh roots)
- If you are using dried roots, use a 5 to 1 ratio instead (i.e. 5 cups of vodka to 1 cup of dried roots)
- let your tincture sit for about two weeks. Then strain it and pour it into your preferred containers

Bearberry

Bearberry is part of the tobacco mixture smoked with the sacred pipe. This herb has mild sedative effects, and was commonly smoked during tribal councils, perhaps as a way to promote friendship and agreement among triballeaders.

Bearberry (named for the enthusiasm bears showed for this fruit) is also a powerful diuretic and antiseptic. Native Americans used it to treat stones andurinary tract infections.

Bearberry can be taken internally as a tea:

Infusion:

- one to two teaspoons of dried leaves for 10 to 15 minutes in a cup of boiled water.

You can also use bearberry as a mouthwash or antiseptic lotion by followingthe same recipe and using the liquid cooled to body temperature.

Black Berries

The Cherokee tribe used them, above all, to calm stomach problems.

An infusion from the leaves is also used by Native Americans as a tonic tostimulate the entire system. A decoction from the roots, sweetened with honey, is an expectorant syrup and useful for relieving stomachaches and sore throats.

Blackberry Leaf tea:

- ounce of the dried Blackberry leaves and root bark pint of boiling water

- Steep 10 minutes. Drink a tea cup at a time.

Use Blackberry fruit to make jellies, jams, cobblers, and in any recipe whereyou would use raspberries.

Black Cohosh

The root (rhizome) is the medicinal part. Root infusions were used to induce abortions, stimulate menstruation, and promote lactation. An alcohol infusionof the root was used to treat rheumatism. The infused root was taken to treat coughs and was said to be cathartic and stimulating, a tonic and blood purifier. Pulverized roots in hot bathwater were used as a soak to alleviate arthritis pain.

Herbalists often use alcohol to extract the healing compounds from blackcohosh, but it also performs well as a tea when steeped in boiling water.

Black Cohosh Tea:

- teaspoon ful of dried root a cup of water
- Bring to a boil, and let simmer for 15 minutes.
- Drink three times a day

Black Haw

This plant, also called "crampbark," was used by many tribes to treat the discomforts of pregnancy—a use widely recommended by herbalists today.

Native Americans used black haw for many other conditions as well. It was taken as a tea to relieve heart problems, stomach pain, and diarrhea. The leaves of the plant were chewed and applied as a paste to the skin to reduce swelling caused by infections and sprains.

The easiest, most effective way to use black haw is as a tea.

Black Haw tea:

- 1 ounce root
- a pint of cool water in a saucepan,
- Bring to a boil, and simmer for 20 to 30 minutes.
- Strain the liquid, cool, and drink as needed.

Bloodroot

Bloodroot must be used with extreme caution. It is incredibly potent and toxic in large doses. The juice can even "burn" one's skin.

Blood root is made into a very weak decoction and is then used to treat fevers and rheumatism, and to induce vomiting. It is also used as an expectorant for lung congestion. A poultice of the root is also used in the treatment of skin cancers and other skin condition.

Boneset

In the 19th century, leaf tea was considered an excellent remedy to treatfevers associated with acute infections.

Leaf tea was considered immunostimulant and used to treat colds, influenza,malaria, arthritis, painful joints, pneumonia and gout and to induce sweating.Whole aerial parts of the plant were applied as a poultice to relieve edema, swelling and tumors.

This Native American panacea applied as a poultice to treat bone fractures. The infusion of the aerial parts was ingested to purify, due to its cathartic andemetic effect. The infusion was also used as a gargle to treat sore throat.

Other uses included treating hemorrhoids, stomach pain and headaches;reducing chills and relieving urinary problems.

How to prepare an immune stimulating tea:

Mix Boneset with Cayenne Pepper:1 ounce dried boneset leaf

- ½ teaspoon cayenne pepper
- 1 quart boiling water
- honey

Put the dried boneset in a container and pour enough boiling water over it tofill the jar. Let this infusion steep for 20 minutes, strain and drink it. This remedy is very bitter tasting.

Black Cherry

Wild cherry bark is a natural substance extracted from the inner bark of the cherry (Prunus serotina) tree. Long used as an herbal remedy by Native Americans for coughs and congestion, you can now find it in syrup, capsuleand tea form.

Widely available for purchase online, wild cherry bark is sold in many healthfood stores and stores specializing in dietary supplements.

Uses:

Applied to treat colds and suppress coughs, wild cherry bark is an ingredientin some cough syrups, cough drops and capsules. Along with coughs and colds, wild cherry bark is typically considered a natural treatment for the following health conditions:

- Asthma
- Bronchitis
- Diarrhea Fever

- Gout
- Inflamed throat
- Whooping Cough

In addition, wild cherry bark is used to relieve pain and stimulate the digestive system. Some herbalists also claim that wild cherry bark can help prevent cancer.

An extract of the bark is sometimes used in hair products to aid in hair growth and to condition hair. Last but not least, as an eyewash for inflamedskin, the wild cherry bark's anti-inflammatory properties are especially effective.

Wild cherry bark has been commonly used in formula for people of all ages, often in tea or syrup for cough and upper respiratory disease, for more than 30 years.

Due to a lack of research, little is known about the safety of using wild cherry bark supplements. The compound prunasin in wild cherry bark breaks down to produce the chemicals hydrogen cyanide and benzaldehyde and could be potentially toxic if taken orally (due to the risk of cyanide poisoning, especially if taken in larger amounts or for longer periods).

While some experts suggest limiting use to no more than 10 days, you shouldtalk to your doctor before using wild cherry bark to discuss whether it is appropriate and safe for you. Pregnant and nursing women should not use wild cherry bark.

There is some concern that wild cherry bark may be harmful to people withliver or kidney disorders. Also, wild cherry bark may have sedative effects.

Keep in mind that supplements have not been tested for safety and dietarysupplements are largely unregulated.

In some cases, the product may provide doses that differ from the amount specified for each herb. In other cases, the product may be contaminated withother substances such as metals.

Black Cherry syrup preparation:

- 3 Tbsp. organic elderberries
- 2 Tbsp. organic black cherry bark
- 2 Tbsp. organic echinacea purpurea root
- 1 Tbsp. organic mullein leaf
- Tbsp. organic licorice root
- pint raw honey
- Brandy (optional preservative)

1 Mix herbs and spices together in a pot and combine with 1 quart ofwater.

2 Allow to soak for 2 to 3 hours. You may reduce soaking time, ifnecessary.

3 Heat at a low simmer until mixture has been reduced to approximatelyhalf its original volume (1 pint).

4 Remove from heat and strain out herbs.

5 Return strained liquid to pot. Add honey.

6 Gently heat mixture over low heat, just until honey warms enough so that mixture can be thoroughly stirred together.

7 Once mixed, remove from heat and allow to cool.

Optional: To help preserve and extend shelf life, measure out a quantity of brandy that is 15 to 20% of the volume of the syrup. Stir into cooled syrup.

Pour into clean bottles and store in refrigerator. Syrup will last for several weeks to several months.

California Poppy

Members of the Costanoan tribe prepared the flowers as a strong tea to rinse their hair, to kill head lice. The Ohlone people crushed the seeds and mixed them with bear fat as a hair tonic dressing. Tribes in the Mendocino area juiced the roots to treat many different ailments, from headaches to stomachaches to toothaches, and nursing mothers would wash their breasts with the root juice to help dry the flow of milk when it was time to wean their babies; Pomo women made a poultice or a strong tea from the mashed seedpods and applied it to their breasts for the same purpose.

However, several tribes believed the plant to be poisonous and avoided its use.

The Yaqui Indians scattered the flowers of California poppy (E. mexicana,

which they called hoohi e'es) ahead of processions during special ceremonial events, a tradition later adopted by the Gileño and Pima tribes of the Southwest, who would scatter the flowers at Easter time just outside the church entrance and ahead of processional walks.

Women from the Cahuilla Indian tribe applied the pollen as eye shadow, and as body paint for special occasions.

The base of the mature stem can also be consumed both raw or cooked.

It is often edible raw, fried or prepared in a soup, the tender, young flowering stem.

Pollen *is edible, raw, cooked or refined into a rich in protein additive used in the processing of bread, porridge, etc.*

Seeds *can be roasted or fried, and edible oil can be extracted from the seeds.*

How to make a tea:

You can make tea with any aerial part of the plant: leaves, stems and flowers. You can use them fresh or dried.

Stuff a tea basket with fresh leaves, pour hot water over them and let it steep a good long time, maybe 10 minutes. Put a saucer over the top of the cup to help keep the tea warm. The long soak ensures a stronger, more potent and bitter brew

Cardinal Flower

Formally, this plant is called Lobelia Cardinalis. This plant is native to the Americas, starting from southeastern Canada south through all the eastern & southwestern United States, Mexico & Central America. It usually has bright red flowers.

The root was used by Native Americans to cure bowel problems, typhoid, worms, epilepsy, cramps, and syphilis. For colds, bronchial symptoms, croup, nosebleeds, fever, headache, and rheumatism, leaf tea was used. A poultice of the roots was used on sores to heal and applied to the head to alleviate headache pain. The dried leaves were smoked by the Penobscot tribe as a replacement for tobacco. It is regarded as potentially toxic as a member of the Lobelia family, but the degree of toxicity is uncertain. It has been acknowledged that the plant's sap causes skin irritation.

The plant is potentially toxic, but the degree of toxicity is unknown. It contains the alkaloid lobeline which has a similar effect upon the nervous system as nicotine. he sap of the plant has been known to cause skin irritation.

Catnip

Aerial parts (primarily leaves) of the plant in infusion are a bitter, astringent, and cooling antispasmodic. Catnip leaf and flower teas provide a mild sedative effect. It is antiflatulent and may settle a colicky baby (check with your holistic health-care professional before using it in this manner). Also used to soothe the digestive tract.

How to make a catnip tea :

- 1 teaspoons of dried catnip leaves or flowers

- 1 cup of boiling water.
- lemon juice and honey

Stir, and let cool for several minutes.

Many people prefer a steeping time of about 10 to 15 minutes.

Cat's Claw

Officially referred to as Uncaria Tomentosa, also known as Cat's Nail. It has been used for medicinal purposes as a general health tonic, anti-inflammatory agent, contraceptive, gastrointestinal and urinary tract issues, breathing issues, diarrhea, rheumatic disorders, acne, and diabetes for more than two thousand years as a tropical vine that grows in the rainforests and jungles of South America and Asia. Current studies also indicate that it can have beneficial effects on prostate disorders, PMS, Aids, diabetes, chronic fatigue syndrome and cancer care and improve the body's immune system.

Cat's claw tea:

- 1/4 teaspoon (1 gram) of root bark
- 1 cup (250 ml) of water
- boil for ten to fifteen minutes.
- Cool, strain and drink one cup three times per day.

Cattail

Indigenous North Americans have been weaving with cattail leaves for more than 12,000 years; cattail shoots, roots and seeds were eaten, cattail leaves and stems were used to make mats and baskets, the roots and pollen were used as medicine and cattail feather was used as moccasin lining and pillow stuffing. In the southwestern tribes, it also has particular symbolism: cattail is connected with water and rain by the Pueblo tribes, and are used ceremonially in rain dances. The Mexican Kickapoos associate cattails with water serpents and make offering to the snake people before gathering cattails. The Navajo believed cattail leaves were a protective amulet against lightning. Many southwestern tribes used cattail pollen as a traditional face paint.

The Cattail is also used as a clan symbol in some Native American cultures, like Osage tribe.

Cattail is more like a prevention therapy than an active drug. Except for the seeds and the leaves, any part of the plant is edible.

For open wounds such as bruises, abrasions, and scrapes, Cattail is effective as an antiseptic. The Cattail's root may be simply cut and applied on the open wound, then tied with a rope. For this purpose, also cattail ash may be used. Simply put it into close contact with the open wound.

Health benefits of Cattail: Improves digestion, high nutritional value, skin health

Cattail is worldwide cultivated. Some of the common health benefits of cattail consumption are described in detail below:

Cattail contains immense quantities of nutrients and organic compounds that primarily promote its effectiveness to cure sores and lessen the occurrence of cicatrix. Topically, cattail jelly may be used for mosquito bites, but the flour also has an antiinflammatory ability that reduces some affected discomfort.

Hypertension

Assists adrenal glands, reducing stress levels thanks to its protein and carbohydrate content. Cattails tend to activate the metabolism and therefore lower stress.

Diabetes

Phytochemicals are necessary for insulin absorption. Daily intake of Cattail may reduce diabetes mellitus.

Atherosclerosis

Because of the presence of vitamin C, carotenoids and bioflavonoids, the intake of Cattail decreases LDL. These components ensure that complications of coronary heart disease are minimized and LDL is eliminated from the system. In addition to this, the absorption of cholesterol is also decreased.

This reduces the risk of developing atherosclerosis.

Cardiotonic and lipid-lowering effects

The composition of Cattail, reduces lipids in the body and dilates the coronary artery. It is used to treat coronary conditions like angina, hyperlipidemia, etc. It tends to decrease the accumulation of lipids on the walls of the arteries. Therefore, the occurrence of heart failure is reduced.

Antiseptic Application

Cattail is famous for its natural antiseptic quality, which has been useful to various cultures for centuries. In wounds and other parts of the body where foreign agents, bacteria or microbes can damage our system, the gelatinous compounds extracted from the young leaves are used. This gelatin is considered a powerful analgesic, both for internal use and applied externally, to relieve discomfort and inflammation.

Constant Energy Boost

Cattail is a rich source of starch and carbohydrates, so it has the potential to increase energy levels. Absorption is very slow because Cattail is composed of complex carbohydrates, which means energy levels remain stable throughout the day.

Slow Bleeding

Several parts of Cattail have coagulant properties. It can be effective for wounds but also if you suffer from excessive menstrual bleeding, reducing its severity. But for patients who still have moderately poor circulation, it's potentially harmful because it essentially slows down the blood while also stimulating the skin's clotting response.

How to eat cattail:

Several parts of the herb, including dormant sprouts on the leaves, roots and bases, ripe pollen, the stem and starchy roots, are edible.

Roots: Raw or cooked roots are edible.

They can be boiled and eaten similar to potatoes or macerated to create sweet syrup and then boiled.

Roots may also be dried or ground into a powder and subsequently used or added to cereal flours as a thickener in soups, etc., and this protein-rich powder is used to produce cookies, etc.

Sprouts: Young shoots are eaten raw or cooked during the spring.

Centaury

Great old American antidote, it is one of the best bitter tonics, highly valued by American Indians. A remedy for all diseases of the blood and liver, Centaury is also famous as a female remedy for disorders or infections due to childbirth. A vermifuge, also for liver worms.

External use:

As a lotion for all types of sores and wounds, and to disinfect mouth ulcers soothe inflamed gums, prevention against all periodic febrile disorders, dyspepsia and fever convalescence, tightening the stomach, and encouraging digestion. Help for both joint pains and rheumatic pains.

Externally it is used to treat wounds and to deter mosquitoes.

Use the infusion liberally, pouring it on wounds, and as a mouth and gum rinse.

In the kitchen, the centaury is used in salads, soups, cabbage dishes or dressings, for high-fat dishes, the herb is an interesting variety with very spicy and bitter taste.

Internal use:

The following is a domestic treatment for expelling worms and recovering menstrual secretions

Centaury tea Cold extract:

- 1/2 to 1 teaspoon centaury

- 1 cup of water

1 Let it rest for six to eight hours.

2 Remove the tea and warm it gently to serving temperature

3 Drink daily two cups in small sips before meals

Centaury is very well suited in mixed teas with such as anise, chamomile, yarrow, sage, wormwood or oregano

Warm infusion:

- 1 teaspoon of the dried herb
- 1 cup of boiling water.
- Let the mix steep for up to 10 minutes.

Dose: of a standard infusion of the whole herb, two tablespoons before meals for liver disorders

Chamomile

Native Americans used the herb in the same way, primarily for relieving stomach pain. It is considered a female plant, poured with water on hot rocks in the sweat lodge as an aromatic calming and mood tonic. Infusion of the herb used to relieve menstrual cramps and relieve cold symptoms.

Chamomile Uses

Chamomile may be used to produce tea, cream, or tablets for all sorts of other purposes. Tea can help with many diseases, primarily dealing with stomach issues. To cope with anxiety and tachycardia, it is prepared in infusion. Due to its composition, chamomile is also useful in minimizing intestinal gas and bloating. It helps relieve migraines, premenstrual syndrome and abdominal cramps.

External uses:

With chamomile is also prepared a cream that assists in problems of the scalp or skin. such as bruises, wounds and scratches.

The cream is also used to cleanse the skin, especially in cases of acne or eczema. Topically, chamomile is incredibly soothing to the skin and indicated for red, irritated skin issues. It's great in an all purpose salve, or alone.

Chamomile is also optimal in oil infusion. The oil is also wonderful rubbed into children's feet before bedtime to help them unwind and prepare for restful slumber.

This oil's sweet, comforting scent is so pleasing that you may be tempted to use it as a perfume!

How to make an oleolyte:

- Chamomile, dried or fresh
- Sunflower Oil
- Clean jar (disinfected if possible to prevent spoilage)
1. Start by finding the right sized jar, keeping in mind that you will need room to cover the chamomile by at least 1 inch, with an additional ½-1
2. ½ inches of space from the top (this allows room for the dried herb toexpand).
3. Add chamomile to clean, dry jar.
4. Pour olive oil over the chamomile, covering it by 1 inch or a little more.
5. Place jar in warm, dark place for 4-6 weeks.
6. Shake the jar when so inspired to encourage the extraction and pour positivity and good intention into the infusion. Many herbalists also singto their herbs as they shake them.
7. When it's time to decant the oil, strain through a cheesecloth, taking thetime to squeeze out every last drop you can–this is precious stuff! Pour into a clean jar/jars, label and store in a cool, dark place

Chokecherry

It is also named Western Chokecherry, Black Chokecherry, and Wild Cherry and is formally known as Prunus Virginiana. There are varieties all over the United States and Canada, with small differences between varieties, ranging from red to purple to black, including the color of the fruit. The tree has long been used as a source of food and medicine by various tribes, including the Chippewa, Miami, Mohawk, Huron, Penobscot, Delaware, Cree, Ojibwe and Iroquois. It was considered one of the most significant native drugs in early American medicine. The berries were harvested and dried, and the bark of thetree was used in the treatment of colds and coughs, smallpox, scurvy, chest and throat pain, pulmonary hemorrhage, intestinal inflammation, diarrhea, stomach cramps, cholera, digestive disorders, cancerous wounds, sores, severe burns and wounds.

Berries are edible, whereas it is necessary to pay attention to pits because in acertain dose they are poisonous.

Wild Chokecherry Syrup for Cough:

- 1 cup of chopped chokecherry twigs, leaves, or bark
- 1 pint of water

Simmer the liquid for an hour, strain it, and add 1 cup of honey to each 1 1/2cups of juice.

Cook the mixture down until it has a syrupy texture, bottle it, and sample it—when necessary—to soothe a cough.

(Note : If you use bark when making the syrup, gather it in the autumn and remove the outer layer. Dry the inner one. Avoid bark from very old or veryyoung limbs, and don't plan to keep the material very long as it deflorateswith age.)

Chokecherry Vinegar:

1 cup of honey to every two gallons of mashed fruit

1. Cover the mixture with cold water.
2. Top the container with a clean cloth and store it in a warmplace.
3. After about four weeks, skim off the top layer and add 1 cup ofgood cider vinegar
4. The ingredients should work for six months or more before youdrain off the liquid.

(Note : homemade vinegar can become much stronger than the commercial product, so it should be bottled when the flavor suitsyour taste.)

Corn

Native Americans introduced maize in the diet, and it is perhaps their greatest contribution to our modern diet. Peoples who used to cultivate maize (Olmecs and Mayas) were already able to process the cereal in order to improve its nutritional content; in particular, through the process of nixtamalization (cooking maize with lime - calcium hydroxide), natives compensated the lack of bioavailable niacin (vit.PP or B3), avoiding the onset of the famous pellagra (disease caused by nutritional deficiency of the same). However, corn is much more than a versatile and nutritious cereal. It has also been widely used for its healing powers.

Spanish explorers in the 16th century reported that Native Americans drank acorn-based drink to treat kidney and bladder problems. Historians have foundthat a corn-based drink was used to treat dysentery and indigestion, to treat kidney and bladder problems, and to increase milk production in nursing mothers.

Corn was also widely used by Native Americans to make poultices for skin incases of ulcers, burns and swelling, and corn oil was applied to relieve eczema and dry skin. Corn cobs were also used medicinally. Native Americans burned the cobs, making fumigations to relieve itching caused by insect bites and poison ivy.

Corn is multi-talented, medicinally.

For internal conditions, its silk can be used fresh or dried to make a tea. Steep two teaspoons, chopped, in a cup of boiling water.

Externally, a corn poultice can soothe minor burns and other skin irritations. To prepare the poultice, mix dried cornmeal with milk and apply the paste tothe affected areas.

Dandelion

Native Americans applied apoultice of steamed leaves to heal stomachaches. Greens are considered atonic blood purifier. Root decoction was drunk to increase lactation. And also, as mild laxative and for dyspepsia.

Liver protection

Dandelion also has beneficial effects on the liver. A study performed in liver-damaged rats showed that compounds abundant in its flavonoids could reverse liver damage and make it function at its best.

How to Eat Dandelion:

The roots can be added to soups and stews.

The young shoots can be consumed raw. They can also be cooked likeasparagus.

The berries can be consumed raw. They can also be cooked.

The tendrils can also be consumed.

It is generally used as an ingredient in soft drinks.

Dandelion Tincture :

First, gather 1 or 2 cups. Clean your roots and slice them relatively thinly. Then put them in an appropriately sized Bell or Mason jar (or whatever jar you happen to have) and cover with 100 proof vodka.

Set the jar in a cool, dark place and within 8 weeks, you'll have a very strongtincture that may be added by the dropperful to water and used as a health tonic. Add a bit of honey for flavoring.

Dogwood

This flowering tree native to the U.S. is scientifically known as Cornus Florida. Its berries, inner bark and twigs have long been used in Native American remedies with many other common names, including Cornelian Tree, American Dogwood, Boxwood, Budwood, Flowering Dogwood, Green Ozier and others. Flowering dogwoodwas used by Native Americans who applied the bark and the roots to prepare remedies against malaria, cough, pneumonia, colds, diarrhea and to boost appetite and digestion. Moreover, always in the past, from the roots was alsoextracted a red dye.

Poultices have been used externally for treating ulcers and sores. Documentsfrom the 19th century report that Native Americans in Virginia had extraordinary white teeth.

Twigs were used as chewing sticks, as toothpicks and as a toothbrush.

The Iroquois were famous for using the twigs to make a decoction for gonorrhea, and the Cherokee chewed the bark against headaches and used a decoction of the bark to treat children's problems such as worms, measles, and diarrhea. They also made poultices to treat wounds and other skin conditions. The bark was used in enemas by the Menominee, and the Arikara mixed it with bearberry to make sacred tobacco.

Echinacea

To the Indians of North America dates back the therapeutic use of one of theechinaceas, Echinacea angustifolia, in the external treatment of wounds and burns, and especially as an internal remedy for coughs, cold diseases, sore throat.

This amazing plant comes from the great prairies of North America where it is called Elk Root. Why? Legend has it that American Indians discovered the wonderful properties of echinacea while observing elks. These ones, when they were sick or perished, used to ruminate the flowers of the plant. It is testified that Cheyenne, Pawnee and Lakotah-Sioux tribes used it to fight sorethroat, cough or even used it as an analgesic. The populations of the New World, moreover, believed it had supernatural powers because it was able to contrast many snake poisons. Bear-with-White-Paw, a Lakota healer, used echinacea as one of his principal medicines. He used it for tonsillitis, pain in the bowels, and toothache.

Boiled root water was used to treat sore throats. Poultice of aerial parts and roots was applied to wounds, and as a therapy for infections. Root infusion once considered a treatment for gonorrhea. Masticated root was held on soretooth to treat infection.

***The roots** should be harvested late in the fall after several hard frosts. Theyshould be cleaned, dried for several weeks, then ground into a coarse powder for making teas.*

Echinacea Infusion:

Add one or two teaspoons of powdered herb to a cup of hot water.

Let rest for abot 10 minutes, cool, and drink as needed, up to three times aday.

The infusion can also be used externally for treating cuts, burns, and eczema or as a mouthwash to treat gum problems.

Some herbalists recommend gargling with the tea to relieve sore throats.

Echinacea Decoction:

1 gram of echinacea root per cup of water, boil for about 10 minutes. Up tothree cups daily.

Echinacea Tincture:

The "drug" (utilized part) of Echinacea Angustifolia corresponds to the root, harvested in winter, whereas for Purpurea it corresponds to the aerial part harvested in late spring. The plant is used fresh, (dried, it loses most of its properties). Mother Tincture of Echinacea is prepared with following ratio inweight-drug: solvent of 1:10 and alcoholic strength of 55% vol.

Internal use: 30-40 drops in little water three times a day between meals, to prevent flu and seasonal illnesses. To treat flu and infections: 30-40 drops, 2times a day

External use: it is advisable an ointment with 10% of echinacea mother tincture, for all skin affections. It can be gargled against sore throat andinflammations of the oropharyngeal cavity by diluting 10 drops in a littlewater.

Elderflower

In various ways, elderflower can be consumed: some of the most common arejelly, syrup, and tea. But be careful, for the flower section itself is the only edible component. Since they are poisonous, the leaves, roots, twigs and stems cannot be eaten safely.

What's used for medicinal purposes is the extract of the elderflower. Theextract should, precisely, be used as a remedy for sweating influenza, the common cold, bleeding, bronchitis, constipation.

Elderflower Tincture:

- Gather your elderflower heads (about 5, large) Snip off all green stalks and leaves.
- Place the flowers in a larger jam jar and pack as many as you can in. Cover completely with a clear alcohol (ideally minimum of 40 % proof, but the stronger alcohol the better, you can use something like vodka) and close the jar.
- Label the jar with name and date as you might forget later. Place the jar in a cold and dark cupboard and shake every week
- After about 6 weeks your elderflower tincture will be done and all you need to do is to pour the content over a strainer to finally get to the tincture.
- Discard the flowers and pour the tincture into glass bottles (ideally dark glass ones) and label them.
- Use within 1-2 years.

When to use elderflower tincture

1. To boost your immune system

2. When you have a cold, to reduce congestion
3. When you have a runny nose (whether it's a cold or allergy)
4. When you feel tired
5. To calm down the cough and soothe the chest
6. When you have a mild fever (elderflower helps the body to sweat).

Wild Ginger

Heal-all. Root traditionally used to treat colds and cough; antiseptic and tonic. Also used in compounding traditional medicine to treat scarlet fever, nervousness, sore throat, vomiting, headaches, and earaches as well as asthma and convulsions.

Ginseng

Ginseng has been used for over 5,000 years throughout the world. Native Americans considered it sacred, and warriors sometimes carried it for good luck. As a medicine, they used it to treat headaches, cramps, fever, vomiting, coughing, cuts, shortness of breath and female infertility. The herb was thought to have aphrodisiac effects for both sexes, and one tribe called it the "root of man."

Ginseng tea :

- 1 teaspoon of powdered root
- a cup of boiling water.

Let stand for 10 or 15 minutes, then strain and drink as soon as possible.

Raw ginseng isn't always easy to find, but health food stores and herb shops usually carry ginseng extracts.

(Note: Don't exceed. Taking too much may cause headaches, hyperactivity, nervousness and insomnia.)

Goldenrod

Native to North America, goldenrod was well known and often used by Native Americans. They used this herb to treat infections of the urinary tract and upper respiratory tract. In early spring, the meadows and plains throughout the greater mid-west are in full golden-yellow bloom.

First, goldenrod is not the weed that causes autumn allergies, but informants say goldenrod floral tea (fresh or dried) may protect a person from allergens (hypoallergenic).

Dried leaves and flowers can be applied to wounds (styptic). Diuretic whole-plant tea is a kidney tonic. The aerial parts infused were used to treat snakebite.

The herbs in this formula soothe inflamed urinary mucosal membranes through their demulcent, astringent, and anti-inflammatory actions. They are also antimicrobial as well as diuretic—they help flush out bacteria by promoting urination.

Goldenrod Tea:

- 1 Tablespoon goldenrod flower and leaf (Solidago spp.)
- 1 Tablespoon marshmallow root (Althaea officinalis)
- 2 Tablespoons corn silk (Zea mays)
- 1½ Tablespoons uva-ursi leaf (Arctostaphylos uva-ursi)

It's important to drink the tea at room temperature, to increase the herb's diuretic effect. It is also cautious to take an immune-stimulating tincture—in addition to the tea—to enhance the body's innate immune efforts in fighting the bacterial infection. Good immune-stimulating herbs include echinacea (Echinacea purpurea), spilanthes (Acmella oleracea), and usnea (Usnea spp.) Additionally, you can drink unsweetened cranberry and blueberry juice along with the tea. Avoid sugar and natural sweeteners until the infection clears.

Fresh Goldenrod Tea with Lemon & Honey

- 1/2 cup chopped fresh goldenrod leaves, flowers and buds
- cups boiling water
- 1/2 lemon, juiced honey to taste

Add the fresh chopped herbs to a pot, teapot, or glass canning jar. Pour boiling water over the herbs and let steep for 30 minutes. Add fresh lemon juice and honey to taste.

Goldenrod Tincture:

For sinus allergy treatment year-round.

- Chop fresh goldenrod flowers, roots, leaves, and stems and put them into a jar.
- Cover with booze of choice and cap the jar.
- Label the jar with the date and contents.

Put the jar in a cabinet somewhere out of the light, and shake it every now and again. Let it sit for about 6 weeks, and then strain and bottle.

Goldenrod-Infused Oil:

- Fill a jar 1/4 to 1/2 of the way with dried Goldenrod flowers.
- Add an oil (of sunflower, sweet almond or olive) over the flowers until the jar is full.
- You can infuse the oil the solar or the slow way

Goldenseal

Air-dried rhizomes and root fibers were used to treat diarrhea. Cherokees used root decoction as a cancer treatment and as a tonic and wash for inflammations, infections, and wounds. Goldenseal was also used as an appetite stimulant and to treat dyspepsia.

The dried root was chewed to treat whooping cough. A decoction was used for earaches. An aqueous decoction of the root was filtered through animal skin or cloth and applied as eyewash.

The root steeped in whiskey was taken as heart tonic. Tuberculosis, scrofula, liver problems, and gall problems were all traditionally treated with the root extraction.

Goldenseal - is anti-microbial, anti-biotic, anti-inflammatory and astringent. It has a long tradition in Native American culture. It's action is boosted by the addition of Marigold, especially effective as a skin healer.

Goldenseal root infusion :

- one cup boiling water
- 1/2 teaspoon powdered goldenseal
- Blend and let stand for 10 minutes.

Suggested Uses: Goldenseal is historically most associated with the mucous membranes with which it has an affinity. It was valued as a cooling, bitter tonic and used in small quantities to promote the overall strengthening of tissues. It was also combined with other herbs in various recipes.

With almond oil and the antibacterial properties of beeswax, Goldenseal salve is a must have in your herbal apothecary.

Goldenseal salve:

- 50g Organic Raw Almon Oil
- 20ml Marigold Infused Oil
- 20ml Sunflower Oil
- 25ml Goldenseal Tincture
- 20g Grated Beeswax
- 1/4 Tsp Vitamin E

Weigh out Almond Oil, add Marigold Infused Oil (20ml = 20g), Sunflower Oil and Goldenseal Tincture.

Place the bowl bain-marie style over a pan of boiling water. Turn the heat to lowest possible simmer. Allow alcohol and water from the tincture to evaporate and the Goldenseal to bond with the molecules of the fat. Stir well and allow up to 30 mins until a liquid consistency is reached.

1 Add Grated Beeswax and stir in
2 Remove from the heat and Stir in 1/4 teaspoon of Vitamin E (liquid)
3 Stir in quickly before it starts to set

4 Pour into a clean jam jar and leave to set

Gooseberry

Currants and gooseberries have longbeen used medicinally by indigenous people of North America. To soothe inflamed throats, the Comanche people used berry tea as a gargle.

A decoction from the root was made by the Potawatomi tribe, which was good eyewash to extract foreign particles or soothe irritated eyes. The Muscogee (Creek) tribe drank a powerful tea produced from the root bark toremove intestinal worms. To soothe painful and inflamed skin tissue, gooseberry juice was often applied to the skin as a wash.

Gooseberries are low in calories and fat but rich in dietary fiber, copper, manganese, potassium, and vitamins C, B5, and B6 and polyphenols, such asanthocyanin.

To use it as a pancreas tonic and as an adjuvant for liver function and for the balance of blood cholesterol it is possible to use 1 tablespoon of dried gooseberry powder to drink dissolved in water.

Against gout and for arthritis problems you can make a decoction of Gooseberry fruits and if you add honey to the herbal tea it can also alleviateiron deficiency and anemia problems.

BOOK 11 The Native American AncientRemedies Ancient Traditions and Secrets ofHerbal Medicine Part II

Gravel Root

Root decoction was used as a diuretic to treat congestive heart failure(dropsy).

The tea was used to treat asthma. Native Americans used both to treat menstrual disorders and dysmenorrhea and as a restorative for women after pregnancy. E. purpureum was used by the Cherokees to treat rheumatism andarthritis and as a diuretic. An infusion of the root is considered a laxative.

The Potawatomi used the fresh leaves as a poultice for wounds.The Navajos used the root as an antidote to poisoning.

Gravelrrot should preferably be harvested at the beginning of flowering whenthe buds are opening (early fall.) Each part of the plant is medically active and is usually taken as a tea.

Gravel Root tea :

Add one to two teaspoons of dried herb to cup of boiling water, let steep for10 to 15 minutes. Strain, and drink as often as every half hour for a cold orflu.

Use gravelroot in moderation because in large amounts it can be toxic.

Hawthorn

Hawthorn is an important plant for the heart Although Native Americans

used hawthorn to treat swelling, dysentery and internal bleeding, todayscientific research has highlighted its main beneficial properties for cardiovascular conditions.

Since the leaves, flowers and berries of hawthorn are all medically active, you can use any or all of them to make a tea. The berries are the most readilyavailable parts, so tea is usually made with the whole berries or using a hawthorn extract.

Hawthorn berry Tea:

Pour one cup of boiling water over two teaspoons of berries.

Let sit for 20 minutes, then strain and serve. You can drink the tea even threetimes a day.

Heart conditions are always serious, however, so it is essential to follow adoctor's advice before using any herbal treatment at home.

Heal-All

Documented as used by the Chinese for more than 2,200 years, self-heal wasused for liver complaints and improving the function of the liver. The wholeplant was used in infusion to stimulate the liver and gallbladder and to promote healing. It is considered alterative; that is, capable of changing the course of a chronic disease.

Horsetail

Mexican Americans use the dried aerial plant parts of horsetail in infusion or decoction to treat painful urination. Equisetonin and bioflavonoids in the plant may account for its diuretic effect. Native Americans used a poultice of the stem to treat rashes of the armpit and groin. An infusion of the stem was used by the Blackfoot Indians as a diuretic. Cherokees used the aerial-part infusion to treat coughs in their horses. An infusion of the plant was used to treat dropsy, backaches, cuts, and sores. Baths of the herb were reported to treat syphilis and gonorrhea. This is one of the First Peoples' most widely used herbs. Horsetail contains small amounts of nicotine.

Most herbalists recommend using horsetail to make a tea.

Horsetail tea :

- Add five teaspoons of dried herb (any part of the plant)
- a teaspoonful of honey
- a quart of boiling water

Reduce the heat and let simmer for 20 minutes. Strain the tea, let it cool, and take 3 cups a day for 1 month. Best paired with: dandelion, nettle

It's best to harvest horsetail in the fall when the silicon content is highest.

Horsetail is notorious for the great amount of silica in each cup of tea. This makes this herbal infusion helpful when it comes to building up bone strength, helping to fix calcium to the bones and fight osteoporosis.

Taking horsetail is said to help strengthen blood vessels, reducing the risk of hemorrhaging. This tea is able then to stimulate blood flow while at the same time it may help restore health to varicose veins.

It is often recommended as a treatment for broken bones, helping repair the bone.

The amount of calcium and silicon in this herb are also great elements to help repair brittle nails, strengthening them all the while keeping them safe from fungal or any other type of infection.

Drinking this tea could help improve tissue repair, regenerating connective tissues and collagen fibers. It may speed up recovery time helping to promote strength and elasticity.

When you have a bad cold, bronchitis or even tuberculosis, consider drinkinghorsetail tea. This herbal infusion may help you fight these afflictions, but also heal and build up the strength of your pulmonary system, boosting your defenses.

This herbal tea may help to heal weakened lungs, repairing lung tissue and boosting defenses against future ailments. It acts as an expectorant, clearingthe passageways of phlegm or harmful toxins that are causing disease.

WARNING: Do not take horsetail tea or tincture

If you have a history of kidney problems (kidney stones or kidney failure) ordiabetes, as it may alter blood sugar levels drastically ;

If you have heart problems and high blood pressure makes for a bad combination with horsetail tea. This tea may cause arrhythmia, and alsoseriously interfere with your medication.

If you are prone to thiamin (vitamin B1) deficiency, as it may causeadditional depletion;

If you are taking prescription medication, make sure to talk to your doctorbefore taking this herbal tea medicinally. It may inadvertently enhance the effects of the medication and cause more harm than good.

If you are taking other diuretics, it is best to avoid horsetail tea as it may result if dehydration or low potassium levels. This could be quite harmful,causing as first symptoms, muscle aches weakness and chronic fatigue.

Hops

Female flower clusters, typically known as strobili or seed cones, have long been known as a flavoring and stabilizing agent in beer. They are native to allof Europe and Asia. They have also been used for a variety of ailments in traditional herbalism, as a digestive aid, to relieve pain, and as an aid to facilitate sleep, relieve anxiety, restlessness, and calm muscles.

Used either alone or frequently in combination with other herbs. Inside a pillow, a bag packed with hops has often been used in folk medicine, wherethe herb's aromatic properties can help a person fall asleep.

The Mohegan tribe is known for a sedative remedy made from hops that was applied to toothaches; the Dakota people used the tea to relieve stomach pain,and the Menominee tribe treated a similar species of hops as a general panacea.

Hops tea:

To make hop tea, simply pour two cups boiling water over 5-10 hop flowercones.

The more hops you add the stronger, and more bitter, it will be.

Adding other herbs like chamomile or peppermint will help with the flavor ifneeded.

Indian Tobacco

The plant root is used to cure leg ulcers, abscesses, and bronchodilators for asthma and whooping cough. It reduces nicotine withdrawal effects.

Tobacco has been used by American Indian nations for centuries as a medicine with cultural and spiritual importance. Traditional tobacco preparation and use varies across Tribes and regions, with Alaska Natives not commonly using traditional tobacco. These variances are due to the many different teachings among Tribes of North America. In some cultures, the roles of growing, harvesting, and preparing traditional tobacco are held by specific groups of people who use traditional ways to prepare tobacco for a specific use. One common teaching involves the importance of having good attitudes and thoughts while working with traditional tobacco.

Traditional tobacco is a medicine, which can be used in a prescribed way to promote physical, spiritual, emotional, and community well-being. It may be used as an offering to the Creator or to another person, place, or being. A gift of traditional tobacco is a sign of respect and may be offered when asking for help, guidance, or protection. Traditional tobacco is sometimes used directly for healing in traditional medicine. It may be burned in a fire or smoked in a pipe, yet the smoke is generally not inhaled.

Ceremonial use :

In almost all facets of their lives, Native people of the Great Lakes had reason to solicit the spirits for acts of kindness or to give thanks for past favors.

Dry tobacco was placed at the base of a tree or shrub from which medicine was gathered, and a pinch was thrown in the water before each day of wildrice gathering to assure calm weather and a bountiful harvest.

Before setting out in a canoe, a safe return was assured by offering tobacco on the water. On journeys or hunts, Indian men paused for a smoke and left a pinch of tobacco as an offering when they encountered certain features of the landscape, including waterfalls, misshapen trees, oddly shaped rocks, and lakes or islands said to harbor spirits.

When storms approached, families protected themselves by placing a small amount of tobacco on a nearby rock or stump. Tobacco was placed at graves as an offering to the departed spirit. Requests to elders to relate oral traditions or other special knowledge were accompanied with a gift of tobacco.

Before all religious ceremonies, tobacco was offered to the spirits.

Juniper

Juniper berries were so widely used by Native Americans for healing that the tree itself became known as "the medicine tree." They used juniper berry tea as a diuretic for people with bladder infections.

The tea was also used to relieve stomach ailments and as an antiseptic to clean wounds. They boiled the berries to produce steam, which was thought to relieve congestion.

An oil made from the branches and berries of the juniper tree was used to massage joints and muscles. Moreover, the ointment was an effective insect repellent.

Juniper Berry Tea:

To make a juniper berry tea, soften two teaspoons of fresh berries by soaking them in water for a few hours. Then add them to a pint of boiling water and let them cook for 30 minutes. Let the tea cool and drink as needed.

WARNING: Juniper berries are toxic if taken in large quantities or used for long periods of time. They should not be used during pregnancy, by those with kidney problems or by anyone allergic to pollen.

Lady's Slipper

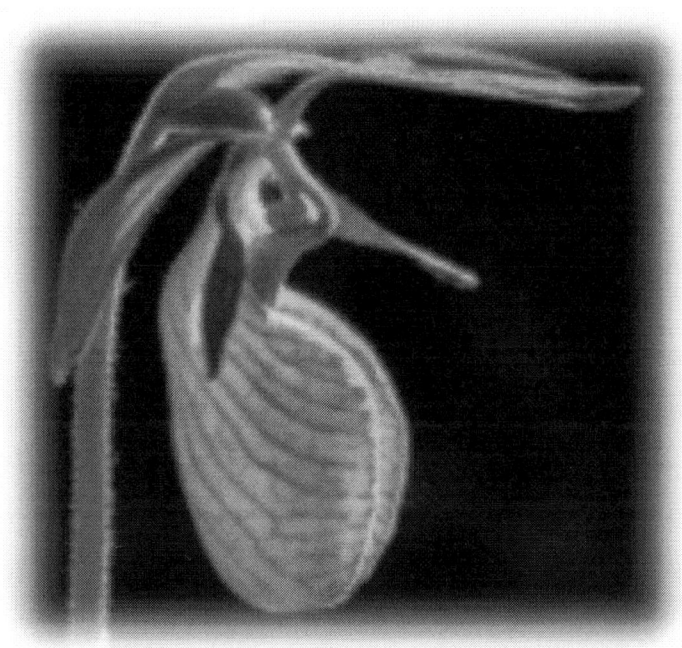

The lady's slipper flower is so beautiful, Native American women often wore it in their hair. However, the herb was valued less for its beauty than for its medicinal brawn. Native American healers used lady's slipper to treat painful menstruation, difficult childbirth, hysteria, chorea (uncontrollable spasmodic movements), and insomnia.

Lady's slipper tea to relieve insomnia:

Add two teaspoons of dried root to a cup of boiling water. Let steep 10 to 15 minutes, strain, and drink as often as necessary.

Lavander

Lavender plants are not native to the Americas; they were brought over by Europeans, probably in the 1800s. References to "lavender" in Native American folklore and ethnographies usually refer to desert lavender, a flowering shrub with some physical similarities to lavender, but which actually has nothing to do with lavender. Desert lavender, also known as lavender bushmint, grows in parts of Arizona, southern California, and northern Mexico, and has long been used as a medicinal herb by Native American tribes living there. It has been used by Native Americans to treat this and other female inflammatory conditions.

Desert Lavender infusions and tinctures reduce hyper secretions in the

stomach, and were used to treat inflammatory conditions of the upper digestive tract, such as gastric and peptic ulcers, and acid reflux.

Lavender Honey

Here below is a recipe for lavender honey, a natural healing remedy; it was in fact used to help the healing of wounds by means of compresses and external applications on the skin which allowed a better healing.

Lavender honey is also useful against insect stings as it is a very effective pain reliever and anti-itch.

In cooking, lavender honey can be tasted naturally and it must never be cooked because it would lose its excellent qualities.

It is often combined with fruit and cheese, in particular with Sardinian and Sicilian pecorino and Montasio, all having an intense flavor. You can prepare it with Lavandula angustifolia or latifolia.

Listed below, the ingredients that you would require for preparing this Native American herbal recipe:

- Fresh or Dried buds of lavender flower
- Local honey, raw

Instructions for preparing this Native American herbal recipe. You need to follow these instructions in the given order:

Fill the jar (either half or quarter) with the flower buds. Next, fill it with honey. The air bubbles should be removed by poking with a knife or chopstick. Then mix well.

Allow the mixture to infuse for a week or month, depends on the preferred strength. You need to taste it occasionally till it's suited perfectly to tastebuds.

Licorice

Native American tribes used licorice root to soothe coughs and sore throats, especially so they wouldn't be heard by game when they had to hunt.

Licorice has many healing properties.

For conditions such as arthritis, colds or chronic fatigue, licorice is usually used as a tea. You can also use the tea externally to treat skin problems.

Benefits of Licorice

- Antioxidant and anti-inflammatory.
- Antimicrobial.
- Counteracts gastroesophageal reflux, heartburn and stomach pain.
- Counteracts peptic ulcers.
- Reduces the risk of cancer. Relieves respiratory disorders.
- Improves blood sugar levels. Counteracts menopausal symptoms.
- Improves skin health by fighting acne and eczema.

Licorice Tea:

Add a teaspoonful of dried, powdered licorice root, or a teaspoonful of licorice syrup, to a cup of boiling water. When using licorice root, let stand for about 10 minutes, then strain and serve.

With licorice syrup, you can drink the tea as soon as it's mixed and has cooled to a comfortable temperature.

For a licorice antiseptic, it's best to make a very concentrated liquid.

Add a pound of fresh licorice root to three pints of water and boil until the liquid is reduced by about one third.

Rather than using fresh or dried root, some herbalists recommend making a licorice syrup, which can be stored in a covered container in the refrigerator.

Licorice Syrup:

Fill a baking dish with fresh or dried licorice root, cover with water, and simmer in the oven or on the stove top for three to four hours.

Discard the roots, strain the remaining liquid, add two teaspoons of honey for every cup of liquid, and store in a sterilized container with a tight-fitting lid.

The syrup can be used to make licorice tea, or taken undiluted, one or two teaspoonsful at a time, to relieve a sore throat, cough, or upper respiratory congestion associated with colds or flu.

Because the compounds in licorice can cause water retention, the herb should not be used by pregnant women or by anyone with heart problems, kidney complications, or high blood pressure. Licorice may cause side effects such as lethargy, headaches, or a rise in blood pressure.

Lemon Balm

A Cherokee elder called the balm "bee," or wa du li si. The herb is used for ointments; the leaves to make cold drinks or hot tea.

It is used to relieve menstrual cycle symptoms such as cramps, headaches and/or anxiety.

The balsamic period of the plant is said to be just before flowering and therefore the best time to harvest it. It was also used in one of several formulas to calm the spirit of a person who was said to be "acting strangely".

Cold and Fever Tonic

- tbsp spearmint leaves
- 1 tbsp yarrow flowers
- 1 tbsp elderflowers
- 1 tbsp lemon balm leaves

In 2 cups of boiled water, steep the above herbs for 15 minutes, covered. Strain and serve warm or cool. Drink a half cup at a time, beginning at the onset of symptoms and repeated every few hours until symptoms subside.

Safe for children and adults.

Relaxation Tonic

- 1 tbsp hops
- 2 tbsp chamomile flowers
- 2 tbsp lemon balm
- 1 tbsp spearmint leaves
- 1 tsp lavender leaves, chopped (or flowers)

Steep in 2 cups of boiled water, covered. Strain after 10-15 minutes anddrink half a cup to 1 cup to relax. Effective in case of anxiety due to overthinking.

Magnolia

The magnolia in bloom is a tree of rare beauty and fragrance. But its seductive charm is not its only merit: the magnolia is also a powerful medicine. History is full of reports of successful treatments with this aromatictree. According to one colonial historian, a Swedish colonist with ulcerated leg sores healed quickly after being bumped by a Native American who anointed the sores with a mixture of magnolia ashes and pig fat.

Other reports tell of Native Americans boiling branches from the magnoliatree to make a tea, which they used to treat colds, fevers, dysentery, musclecramps and intestinal worms.

The most medically effective part of the magnolia tree is the bark, which iscommonly made into a tea. The solitary, fragrant flowers resemble water lilies because of the spiral arrangement of their elements.

Internal use:

In case of abdominal swelling, stomach pains, diarrhea and vomiting associated with difficult digestion, asthma, cough with abundant mucus(bark); shortness of breath related to gastric indisposition (flowers).

Magnolia Bark Tea:

Add two teaspoons of shredded bark, fresh or dried, to a pint of boilingwater.

Simmer for 30 minutes, then add water to make 16 ounces. Strain the tea andtake by the tablespoon as needed.

When using magnolia externally, double the amount of bark used in therecipe.

Mayapple

Minute doses of mayapple were used by Native Americans to treat a variety of illnesses. It treated verrucae (warts produced by papillomavirus). The whole May Apple plant, apart from the ripe fruit, is toxic. The herb producesnausea and vomiting, and even inflammation of the stomach and intestines, which has been known to prove fatal. The root is toxic and was used to kill worm infestations. Root powder was applied externally on difficult-to-heal sores.

It is said that a potent extract from mayapple was used by Native Americans to commit suicide. In the mid-twentieth century, mayapple resin was injectedinto venereal warts as a treatment.

Maple

Maple syrup is a sweet liquid obtained from the sap of two varieties of maple: Acer saccharum (sugar maple) and Acer saccharum nigrum (black maple). There are in fact different varieties of maple cultivated all over theworld, however syrup is mainly obtained from the sap of some species of maple of Canadian origin (mainly spread in Quebec).

Native people since ancient times used to extract the sap of these trees inorder to obtain crystals for the sweetening of foods.

Sap of maple is extracted in spring (March-April) and then boiled in order tomake syrup. The price of the product is pretty high but also justified by the fact that for a liter of product are needed 40 liters of sap.

The extraction of sap does not seem to be a process that makes the tree suffer.

Maple syrup is rich in properties and substances beneficial for our body. It contains mineral salts such as potassium, calcium and iron as well as vitaminsand malic acid.

It is therefore remineralizing and energizing and also depurative and draining.Excellent food to provide a certain amount of antioxidants that help fight cellular aging and the skin health.

Maple syrup helps the digestive and intestinal system, it has low calories andit is also an ally for weight loss, because it reactivates fat thermogenesis (it has fat burning properties). It is a natural product also appreciated for its average glycemic index, which is lower in comparison with other sweeteners.Iroquois compounded the leaves in water and drank the drug as a blood purifier. Bark infusion was used as an antiseptic eyewash. And the inner bark was decocted as a cough remedy and expectorant. A maple bark bath helps against fever, chills and tropical illnesses. With fresh leaves it is possible to prepare a natural remedy against inflammations, swollen feet, insect bites and fevers.

Maple conveys calmness, durability and energy. It is the tree of consciousness, it allows you to clarify your thoughts and gives you the abilityto find an order in your daily life.

The medicinal properties of the maple leaf is sedative and tonic. It is an excellent remedy for the liver as well the spleen. It does not only treat theseorgans but it will bring about a tranquil nature to them as well.

Maple tea:

Put one teaspoonful of the powdered leaves or the bark to one cup of boilingwater to make tea.

Take up to three cups of tea per day for ailments and it is more effective whenmaple leaves tea is taken on empty stomach.

Maple Sap:

Maple sap (also called maple water) comes from our native Sugar Maple *(Acer saccharum)* and contains many trace minerals including Potassium, Magnesium, Iron, Copper, Zinc, Manganese and Calcium, antioxidants, polyphenols, electrolytes, over 50 different micronutrients, and some sourceseven say prebiotics. It has all the nutritional benefits of maple syrup, but without the high sugar content.

Sap runs the most in the spring, as the trees are waking-up, and is the substance that is collected and then boiled down to make maple syrup.

Marshmallow

Extracts of marshmallow root contain starch, pectins, mucilage, sugars, fats and tannins. In particular, mucilages give the plant emollient, soothing and protective properties of mucosa membranes.

For this reason, it is indicated in the treatment of all forms of inflammation.

The decongestant and antiseptic activity of the plant on the soft tissues of ourorganism, makes it an effective remedy in the treatment of respiratory tract disorders, such as cough and cold; in case of sore throat and irritations of themouth such as abscesses, stomatitis and gingivitis.

It also has therapeutic applications in the digestive system, in case of irritations and infections of the intestinal mucosa, caused by irritable bowel syndrome or external viruses (enteritis, colic, diarrhea, constipation); lesions of the gastric or duodenal mucosa such as ulcers; and in case of inflammationof the bladder and kidneys, due to stones or cystitis. Moreover, the mucilage of marshmallow has shown a strong hypoglycemic activity useful in case of hyperglycemia and diabetes.

Marshmallow is also used in case of renal insufficiency in dogs and cats.

Marshmellow Cold Infusion:

1. Fill a jar 1/4 of the way with marshmallow root, then fill the jar withlukewarm water and cover with a lid.
2. Let sit for a minimum of 4 hours or overnight. The water should changecolor to a soft yellow.
3. Strain off the roots. The resulting liquid should be thick and viscous.

Uses:

As mouth wash for painful mouth conditions. Mouth ulcers, canker sores, cuts on the inside of the cheeks, inflamed gums and even sore throats are soothed with a marshmallow rinse. Simply swish the cold infused tea aroundin your mouth to coat the affected tissues.

As heartburn home remedy and ulcers, and inflamed intestines. Besides beingable to soothe inflammation, marshmallow root is also a vulnerary, healing wounds within the digestive tract. Herbalist Paul Bergner calls this a bandaid for the stomach. Of course, addressing the root cause of these issuesis recommended for long term care. It's a great heartburn home remedy.

As Skin Wash Marshmallow root is an amazing topical treatment for woundsand burns. In the past it was called mortification root because of its ability toprevent gangrene.

Marshmallow Root Tea:

- o cups water
- 1 tablespoon cut and sifted marshmallow root

Bring water and marshmallow to a boil, then cover and simmer on low for20 minutes. Remove from heat, strain with a mesh strainer or cheesecloth,and sweeten if desired before serving.

Marshmallow Root Poultice

Make a paste using powdered marshmallow root and very hot water. Apply tothe area once it has cooled a little and cover with a cloth or bandage.

Milkweed

The latex juice from the milkweed stems, plant tops, and the stem has been used for medicinal purposes by many native tribes. The Miwok people used Milkweed latex to cure warts. A decoction of the dried plant tops was made by the Cheyenne and used as an eyewash to treat snow blindness. Pleurisy root, also dubbed as butterfly milkweed (Asclepias tuberosa), was made intoa cough remedy and was ultimately used by the people of Cherokee, Delaware, and Mohegan.

Milkweed Tea:

Boil four ounces of fresh root in three quarts of water until the liquid is

reduced to a quart.

Strain, let cool, and drink as needed.

To remove warts, break the stems to extract the milky juice and apply it directlyto the wart once a day.

Mullein

Tea for upper respiratory-tract conditions, coughs, congestion, and infections. Used for treating bronchitis and tracheitis. Leaf and flower infusion used to reduce and thin mucus formation. Induces coughing up of phlegm (expectorant). Often combined with other expectorants: thyme (Thymus vulgaris) and coltsfoot (Tussilago farfara), for example.

Native Americans made a necklace of the roots to be worn by teething babies. Decoction of leaves used for colds, and raw crushed leaf poultice overwounds and painful swellings. Mucilaginous leaves also rubbed over rashes. Said to be helpful reducing pain from stinging nettle. Dried leaves smoked to stop hiccups and to induce coughing (expectorant).

Although mullein flowers are the most medicinally useful, the leaves and roots also have medicinal powers. For an effective cough remedy and decongestant, herbalist Ana Nez Heatherley recommends using mullein as atea.

Mullein Tea:

Add an ounce of fresh, broken mullein leaves to two cups of boiling water. Let steep 10 to 15 minutes, strain, and take as needed. Some people add honey to the tea, which improves the taste.

WARNING: The seeds of the mullein plant are toxic and shouldn't beused. Mullein also should not be used in any form by people on anticoagulant medication or those who are pregnant.

Nettle

Native Americans made a necklace of the roots to be worn by teething babies. Decoction of leaves used for colds, and raw crushed leaf poultice overwounds and painful swellings. Mucilaginous leaves also rubbed over rashes. Said to be helpful reducing pain from stinging nettle. Dried leaves smoked to stop hiccups and to induce coughing (expectorant).

Nettle leaves are ingredients with a long medicinal and herbal tradition. Probably, the predominant use of nettle is for the topical treatment of rheumatoid arthritis (in Germany). Nettle has also been widely used in traditional Austrian medicine for internal use (fresh or dried leaves) for the treatment of kidney and urinary tract disorders, the gastrointestinal tract, thelocomotor system, the skin, the cardiovascular system, bleeding, influenza, rheumatism, and gout.

Nettle is used in specific shampoos to control dandruff and (it is said) for shiny hair. This is also why some farmers supplement their cattle feed with nettles. Nettle root extract has been extensively studied as a treatment aimedat reducing the symptoms of benign prostatic hyperplasia (BPH).

Tea for upper respiratory-tract conditions, coughs, congestion, and infections. Used for treating bronchitis and tracheitis. Leaf and flower infusion used to reduce and thin mucus formation. Induces coughing up of phlegm (expectorant). Often combined with other expectorants: thyme (Thymus vulgaris) and coltsfoot (Tussilago farfara), for example.

For internal conditions, nettle is best taken as a tea.

Nettle Tea:

Add one to two teaspoons of the herb to a cup of boiling water, let stand for10 minutes, then strain and drink as needed.

For arthritis, don gloves to protect your hands and lightly bat the plant against the affected areas.

Oak

A symbol of strength and power, the oak tree was used by Native Americans to keep themselves powerful, or at least healthy. The Houmas tribe would pound the roots of the tree and mix them with alcohol for a pain-relieving poultice for joints. The Ojibwa boiled the bark as a remedy for diarrhea. Other tribes used oak bark tea as an expectorant. Some used enemas made from the tea to relieve the pain and itching of hemorrhoids.

The medicinal properties of oak are particularly concentrated in the bark. The most potent bark is harvested in mid to late spring.

Oak Tea:

To make a tea, add a teaspoonful of fresh or dried bark to a cup of boiling water.

Let stand for 10 to 15 minutes, strain, and drink up to three times a day.

Oats

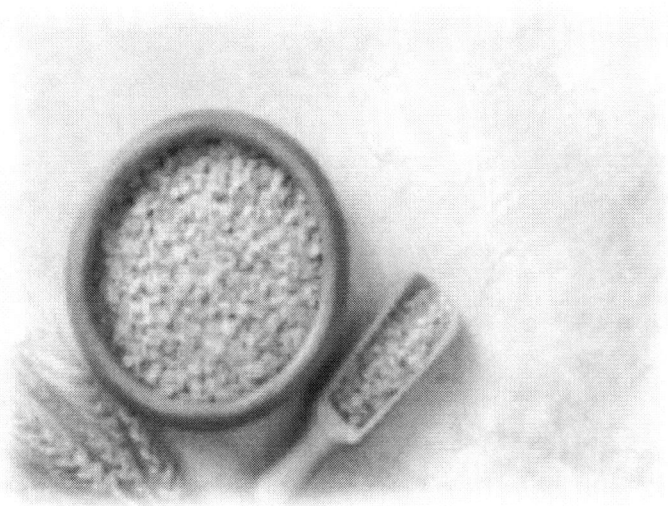

Best known today as a healthful breakfast food, rich in B vitamins, phosphorus, iron, and dietary fiber and minerals, oats were once considered as much a medicine as a meal.

Native Americans used teas made from oats to treat diarrhea. Oats were also considered a relief for anxiety and depression. Poultices made from oats were used to help heal skin conditions such as cold sores, eczema, boils, and hives.

It isn't just the oat seed that is used in herbal medicine either. The grass stalk or 'oatstraw' from the whole plant is harvested when still green and the oats are as yet unripe and 'milky' (when pressing a fingernail into a seed releases a milky liquid). These stalks and unripe seeds are then dried or tinctured to use in herbal brews.

Dried oatstraw makes a beautiful earthy base for herbal tea mixes.

Even though all parts of the oat plant are medicinally active, it's the grainthat's most used, often in skin-soothing baths.

In his book The Green Pharmacy, herbal authority James A. Duke, Ph.D.,recommends adding several handfuls of oatmeal to a warm bath to help relieve dry, itchy skin and to reduce the irritation of hives.

Oat tea:

Use the dried oat tops or straw to make a nourishing tea blend. Add one big handful (½ – ¾ cup) to a glass quart jar.

Pour boiled water over the herb, cover, and let steep overnight to extract asmuch of the medicinal and nutritive qualities as possible.

Oats are a food-grade herb that can be taken consistently over long periodsof time. Drink 1 – 2 quarts of overnight-steeped oat infusion per day.

Winter-saviour facemask

- 1 tablespoon Oatmeal (blast in a processor to make it fine if you can) 1tsp honey
- 1 heaped teaspoon of soothing dried herbs (try rose, chamomile, lavender or calendula)
- 250mls of boiling water
2. Make an infusion with your chosen herb by placing the herb in a cup and covering with 250mls boiling water. Cover the cup and allow to steep for 10 minutes. Afterwards, strain the herb away and retain the leftover infusion.
3. Place 1tbsp of oatmeal (for best results, and ease of application, use regular oatmeal ground fine in a processor) in a bowl. Mix in 1 tbsp of the warm infusion. Mix and cover, allow to steep for a couple of minutes. Uncover the oats and stir in 1 teaspoon of honey (or leave outfor a vegan facemask).
4. Once at a cool enough temperature, smooth the oat mixture over yourface and neck area and leave for 5-10 minutes.
5. Take a cloth dampened in the rest of the cooled herbal infusion and re-moisten the mask all-over and then gently wipe away. Wash your face again with water if required. Pat your face dry and add a natural moisturiser to your skin.

Oregon Grape

Mahonia aquifolium is a particularly beautiful plant, that creates an atmosphere of refined elegance in the garden. Mahonia aquifolium is characterized by its abundant spring flowering.

In this period of the year the plant is flooded with delicate golden flowers.

Roots are used to fight psoriasis, acne, eczemas. Together with the shoots they are used to purify the blood. Indigenous tribes of America used the Oregon grape for several illnesses, including fever, stomachaches, liver problems, jaundice, arthritis, diarrhea, among other illnesses.

Oregon grape is best prepared as a tea.

Oregon Grape Tea :

1. Add half an ounce of dried root to a quart of boiling water and let steep for 10 to 15 minutes.
2. Strain, let cool, and drink up to three cups a day.

This preparation also can be applied to the skin to treat psoriasis and acne.

Osha Root

Native Americans used oshà root to treat fever, cough and sore throat, gastrointestinal problems and wounds.

In Mexico, the Tarahumara tribe used L. porteri during ritual ceremonies for protecting people against negative energies and spirits; pieces of the root are burned on the hot rocks during sweatlodge as part of Native American ceremonial smudging. The Zuni people chewed it during healing rituals.

A decoction (essentially a long, slow simmer) will extract the medicinal properties of the root into a flavorful, dark tea, which can be sipped purely, or mixed into any variety of tea-lattes or broths.

Osha Root Decoction:

1. Simply add a handful of dried roots to several cups of water and bring to a boil.
2. Reduce to a gentle simmer and allow to reduce for at least thirty minutes though five to six hours is preferable as the longer the roots simmer, the stronger, and more beneficial the decoction.
3. When finished, the water will be a translucent, grey-brown tint, reflective of the root's color, and rich in beneficial plant-properties.

Pasque Flower

In homeopathic medicine, pulsatilla is indicated in cases of depression, cystitis, gastric disorders, otitis and sleep disorders. Used historically by the Blackfoot tribe to induce uterine contractions leading to abortion. Also believed to speed difficult childbirth. The Dakotas call it hokshi-chekpa wahcha (twin flower). The Lakotas call it hoksi' cekpa (child's navel).

Blackfeet call it napi (old man). Omaha and Ponca call it te-zhinga-makan (little buffalo medicine).

It was one of the sacred power medicines of the Omahas and Poncas and esteemed very highly. Among the latter two tribes, the right to use the pasqueflower was limited to the medicine men of the Te-sinde gens.

WARNING: The plant is slightly toxic; the toxins are dissipated by heat or by drying the plant. Pulsatilla is a toxic plant. Improper use can lead to diarrhea, vomiting and convulsions, hypotension and coma.

Magical Uses: The plant is used in spells for health, protection and healing. According to folklore, the flowers, when picked in early spring and wrappedin a red cloth, can prevent disease when carried on the person. The flowers can be used in all healing rituals, and red anemones can be grown in the garden to protect both home and garden.

An infused oil made from the flowers can be used to dress candles used in airmagic, as the plant has a strong connection with the element Air.

Passionflower

Fresh or dried aerial parts or whole driedherb used in infusion as mild sedative. Also used to treat nervousness and insomnia—a sleep aid. Antispasmodic effect of infusion considered a gastrointestinal aid. People used the infusion of crushed root for treating earache. They also pounded root, and applied the mass as a poultice on inflamed contusions, boils, and cuts. The root water of the plant was mixed with lye-treated corn and used to wean babies. The tisane was considered a blood purifier for many tribes. Pioneers used the whole plant with Epsom salts as a sedative bath. Root tea and aerial-parts tea used for treating hemorrhoids.

Modern research seems to support this perspective. In this clinical trial, anextract containing passionflower, valerian root and hops had a beneficial effect on both sleep quality and duration.

Nervines are often used along with adaptogens during challenging times to increase our resilience during acute or long-term stress.

The indole alkaloids in passionflower may have a positive effect on neurotransmitters other than GABA – dopamine, serotonin and noradrenaline to be specific – that are tied to our overall mood.

Passionflower tea:

Place 1-2 teaspoons dried herb in a cup. Pour 8 ounces of boiling water over the herb, cover the cup with a small plate or lid, and allow the infusion to steep for 20-30 minutes. Strain out the herbs and drink 4 oz. up to four times per day.

Passionflower with valerian root blend:

Bring 1 1/3 cups water to a light simmer (not a boil) and add 1 teaspoon valerian root.

Cover and simmer on low for 20-40 minutes, then remove from heat. Add the passionflower, cover, and allow to steep for an additional 20-30 minutes, Strain out the herbs, then serve.

Peppermint

Peppermint has many therapeutic properties:

- Carminative action: mint acts by relaxing the esophageal sphincter, reducing the volume of intestinal gases.
- Decongestant and balsamic action: mint has a refreshing, decongestant and fluidifying action on respiratory apparatus secretions, therefore it is used to treat cold, fever and cough. Aromatic action: mint is used in cooking and also for the production of beverages and liquors
- Anesthetic action: on mucous membranes and skin it causes an initial vasoconstriction followed by a vasodilation, in this way there is a local anesthetic action.
- Analgesic action: mint extract is an important remedy against headaches and migraines of tension type, with a significant reduction of pain.
- Applied on the forehead and temples, a solution of menthol, relieves all the symptoms of migraine such as nausea, vomiting and intolerance to light and noises.
- Antiseptic action: mint has strong antiseptic, antiparasitic and germicidal properties thanks to its polyphenol content.
- Cosmetic action: in cosmetics, mint has a refreshing, toning and purifying action.
- Purifying action

Peppermint was one of native american's most beloved medicines, used to help digestion, increase appetite, reduce fever, relieve stomach pain, soothe menstrual cramps, treat colds and stop colic in children. Peppermint poultices were applied to reduce swelling and soothe painful joints. Dried peppermint leaf powders were sometimes sniffed to treat headaches and improve concentration.

Soothing peppermint tea has long been a part of the kitchen, and medicinalcultures are certainly familiar with its properties.

Thus, this herb is well known for its ability to soothe the digestive tract and reduce the severity and duration of stomach pains. *Ways of using peppermintare nearly as numerous as the conditions it can treat.*

- Against flatulence: Suck on a sugar cube to which you've added two or three drops of peppermint oil.
- To relieve abdominal pain: Drink a cup of warm milk flavored with fresh peppermint leaves.
- To facilitate sleep in case of insomnia: Drink a cup of peppermint tea, made by adding a teaspoonful of fresh or dried peppermint to a cup of boiling water and allowing it to steep for 10 minutes.
- To cure colds or flu: Drink a cup of peppermint tea that includes a teaspoonful of fresh or dried chamomile.
- To relieve headaches: Crush freshly gathered peppermint leaves and apply them as a poultice to your forehead.
- To relieve toothache: Apply a few drops of peppermint oil to the sore tooth.
- To soothe inflammation and sore throat: Gargle with lukewarm peppermint tea.
- For insect bites or stings: Crush a fresh peppermint leaf and apply the poultice.
- To improve breath: Chew on a cluster of fresh peppermint leaves and stems.

Peppermint Summer Tea:

It is an amazing and excellent recipe for a hot summer day. We have listed below the ingredients that you would require forpreparing this Native American herbal recipe:

- Half cup or one cup dried or fresh peppermint leaves.
- Half gallon of tap water.

Given below are the detailed instructions for preparing this Native American herbal recipe. You need to follow these instructions in the given orde:

1. Put peppermint & water in half a gallon of a glass jar.
2. Put in a sunny area for two to eight hours.
3. Move to the fridge and let it cool. Enjoy it as a cold drink.

Persimmon

Persimmon fruit symbolizes autumn, season "of passage" often responsible for tiredness and psychophysical stress; thanks to its interesting nutritional values and related properties, persimmon represents an excellent way to startautumn in the best way.

First of all persimmons are considered very energetic: in this regard they aresuitable for children, elderly people and sport lovers. Moreover, the fruits have laxative, diuretic and hepatoprotective properties.

Before the first frost, the Cherokee people gathered the fruits and turned theminto an astringent herbal syrup to cure diarrhea. The Choctaw sun-dried the fruit and, for the same reason, baked it into bread. The Catawba tribe developed a fruit poultice to cure warts and a decoction from the bark of the tree to use as a mouthwash for thrush (a type of fungal infection). To ease heartburn, the Rappahannock Indians used to chew the bark.

With plenty of hot spices, this naturally warming and anti-inflammatoryinfusion is just the thing to sooth an ailing stomach or ward off a chill.

- cups/64 oz filtered water
- One 3 inch piece peeled and thinly sliced fresh ginger
- One 3 inch piece peeled and thinly sliced fresh turmeric root 1 teaspoon fresh good quality peppercorns
- good quality cinnamon sticks, preferably celyon cinnamon
- 2 small or 1 large fuyu persimmon, thinly sliced (save a few slices for serving)
- Sweetener of choice (ex. honey or stevia) to taste

1 Place the water, ginger, turmeric, peppercorns, cinnamon sticks and persimmon slices in a large saucepan and bring to a boil. Lower heat,and simmer on low for 20 to 30 minutes.

2 Strain tea through a fine mesh strainer (or pour through a coffee filter tocatch sediment).

3 Pour into cups or bowls. The softened persimmons may also be added oradd a few fresh slices for garnish and serve adding preferred sweetener to taste.

4 Alternatively, you can cool the tea to room temperature and refrigeratefor a couple of days and reheat as desired.

Pine

Pine is a plant that performs an antiseptic action for the uterine, respiratoryand liver tracts;

it's expectorant-fluidifying of bronchial secretions and antirheumatic.

These properties of pine are especially useful in colds, bronchitis, tracheitis, pneumonia, asthma; influenza; chronic cystitis, prostatitis, leucorrhoea and cholecystitis.

The chemical constituents of pine, however, are:

- Oleoresin, from which the essence of turpentine is obtained by distillation
- Essential oil, rich in monoterpenes Coniferoside
- Bitter substances

Pine was one of the Native Americans' most important medicines.

They made chewing gum from pine resin, which they found soothing for sore throats.

Pine needles were crushed and made into a paste for an aromatic headache poultice. The bark was also used as a poultice for such things as wounds, burns, ulcers, and hemorrhoids.

Salves made from pine resin were used to treat sore muscles and joints, and pine tea was a popular remedy for colds, coughs, and upper respiratory congestion. In some cases, the needles were ignited because Native Americans believed that breathing pine fumes could relieve backache.

Scots Pine buds can be used for the treatment of respiratory diseases, against fever, cold and bronchitis. Moreover, they are useful for calming coughs, eliminating mucus and phlegm, but also as a disinfectant for the urinary apparatus (also because of their diuretic action) and as an anti-rheumatic agent.

The buds of pine can be used to make decoctions, useful for disinfecting the skin, and as an air freshener, whereas the leaves of pine have a purifying action, useful for lungs, kidneys and bladder. Pine essential oil is also used in natural cosmetics to produce soaps and detergents that have purifying, deodorizing, stimulating and energizing properties against fatigue.

The essential oil can also be purchased pure and used through inhalers against cold and bronchitis, given its balsamic, sedative, and anti-inflammatory properties.

Besides the needles, an essential oil of lower quality is also obtained from the bark, which is used to make natural cosmetic bath products. Instead, from the resin we obtain the essence of turpentine.

In case of cough, sinusitis and cold, you can make an infusion with a cup of hot water and a spoon of needles. After 10 minutes of infusion it is possible to filter, add 20 drops of pine glyceric macerate and consume up to 2 cups per day.

Against rheumatism, instead, it is possible to massage a mixture of sweet almond oil and 1-2 drops of Pine essential oil on the interested parts.

Pine Tea :

Pour a cup of boiling water onto half a teaspoonful of dried needles and young buds, which are best collected in the spring.

Let stand for 10 to 15 minutes, strain, and drink as needed, usually up to three times a day.

To use pine as an inhalant :

Put two or three handfuls of fresh needles, buds, and twigs in a large saucepan, cover with water, and bring to a boil. Reduce the heat and simmer for five minutes. Remove from heat, then inhale the steam for 15 minutes by leaning over the pot, using a towel over your head to trap the steam.

For a relaxing, skin-friendly bath :

Soak three handfuls of fresh pine twigs in approximately two pints of water for 30 minutes. Then bring the mixture to a boil and simmer for 10 minutes. Strain the liquid and add it to your bathwater.

Plantain

When plantain was first brought to North America by the Europeans in the late 1600s, it spread so rapidly that Native Americans called it "white man's foot."

However, plantain became early a Native American medicine. As a tea, it was used to treat diarrhea, kidney and bladder problems, bed-wetting in children, low back pain, arthritis, excessive menstrual flow, and respiratory problems such as coughs, asthma, and bronchitis.

The plant was used also externally as a lotion or poultice to cure burns, wounds, snake bites, stings from poisonous insects, poison ivy, eczema, andhemorrhoids. Some tribes chewed plantain root to relieve toothaches.

Both the seeds and leaves of plantain have medicinal value. Juice squeezed from the fresh leaves can be applied directly to burns, cuts, insect bites, andpoison ivy rashes. A tea of the dried leaves can also be used externally.

Plantain tea:

To make a tea, add two teaspoons of herb to a cup of boiling water and allowto steep for 10 minutes, then strain and drink as needed.

Weight-loss and cholesterol-lowering preparation from the seeds:

pour a cup of boiling water over a teaspoonful of the seeds. Allow the mixtureto cool, then drink it down, seeds and all. It's best to take this remedy about 30 minutes before eating.

Evening Primrose

Evening Primrose, the edible nocturnal wildflower. Native Americans usedwarm root poultice to treat hemorrhoids. Roots were chewed to increase strength and endurance. Whole plant was soaked and used as a poultice on bruises and sores.

An oil infusion of the flower used twice daily, helps improve skin health incase of acne, eczema, psoriasis, split ends and signs of ageing.

Evening Primrose Oil Infusion :

1. Look for Evening Primrose and try to avoid her if she is by any roads ortrails. You don't want any toxins being infused. Only collect a small amount and make sure you only take up to one-third of any patch.
2. Once you've harvested, dehydrate the flowers. Removing moisture is keyto a successful oil infusion. You can do this by drying in a paper bag fora few days, placing over cheesecloth or mesh in a warm place for a couple of days or for an instant fix, you can buy a dehydrator. This will allow you to remove any excess water from the flower overnight.
3. Place in a small jar and fill to the very top with any oil. Typically olive oil, grapeseed, apricot and almond oils are used. I've used jojoba oil asit sinks easily into the skin.
4. Screw the lid on tightly and place in a warm environment away from direct sunlight. On top of the fridge works well. After eight weeks, youcan strain and apply when you need an extra magical healing touch.

Prickly Pear Cactus

This plant has the significance of being a vegetable, fruit, and herb, scientifically known as

Opuntia Engelmanni, which has been used both for food and medicine. It is also known by many common names, including Texas Prickly Pear, Cow's Tongue Cactus, Desert Prickly Pear, among others, and is native to Mexico; in fact, this plant lives luxuriantly in the Andean Cordillera.

The fruit is oval shaped and has a variable color among green, yellow, orange, red and purple. The fruit pulp is totally edible but rich in seeds and must be peeled carefully to remove the exocarp which is covered with small thorns. (In case the peel is not completely and carefully removed, the glochids (the smallest thorns, similar to hair) could be ingested causing many discomforts to the throat, lips and tongue. Some populations of Native Americans, such as the "Tequesta", rolled the fruits in the sand until glochids were completely removed; alternatively, it is possible to burn them on a live fire, however avoiding to "cook" the pulp as well).. The younger pads were used by Native Americans for food, and mature pads were used as a poultice for cuts, burns, boils, bleeding slows, enlarged prostate, and as an antiseptic. Teas have been prepared to cure tuberculosis, urinary tract infections and the immune system. Cholesterol reduction and the treatment of diet-related cardiovascular disease and adult-onset diabetes may also be treated effectively with this plant.

Prickly Pear Syrup:

Clean fruits of glochids and remove seedy/pulpy center. Put flesh into large pot, mash it, and bring to a low boil. Strain through cheesecloth to separate seeds. Put seeds to the side and add sweetener to make syrup to your liking. Bring to a boil and place in clean glass jars. Refrigerate or boil in open-water bath.

Purslane

Purslane is one of those herbs that's as valuable as a vegetable as it is as a medicine. Eaten cooked or raw, purslane is a superb source of the antioxidant vitamins A, C, and E. It also contains :

Riboflavin, Calcium, Phosphorus, Iron, Magnesium.

Purslane also is the richest known plant source of omega-3 fatty acids. These fatty acids, which are mainly found in fish oils, may help reduce the risk of heart disease by lowering cholesterol and blood pressure and by reducing the tendency of the blood to form clots in the arteries.

Research has also shown that omega-3 fatty acids may boost immunity and help ease the pain of arthritis. Because purslane contains abundant amounts of magnesium, it's sometimes recommended for combating chronic fatigue and headaches. It also contains lithium, a mood-stabilizing compound that can help ease depression.

Native Americans probably ate purslane, but they were more interested in its medicinal applications. Juice from the plant's leaves was found to soothe burns, insect bites and stings, and earaches. A tea made from the leaves was thought to relieve diarrhea, stomachache, and urinary tract infections—and because purslane contains a lot of vitamin C, it could be used to treat and prevent scurvy.

The leaves, stems, and flowers of purslane can be eaten raw as salad ingredients, or steamed or boiled as a vegetable similar in taste to asparagus. The plant's seeds can be ground and added to flour or other foods as a nutritional boost.

For medicinal use, the leaves can be broken and their juice applied directly to burns or insect bites and stings.

To use purslane internally, boil the entire plant for 15 to 20 minutes.

Strain the water, let cool, and drink as a tea. Some herbalists recommend this remedy for soothing stomach pain, diarrhea, and painful urination, although in cases of bladder infection, don't overlook your doctor's advice, which may include a prescription for antibiotics. Purslane can also be used as a diuretic to help rid the body of excess water.

As a skin aid, purslane has the advantage of being a lot cheaper than fancier commercial preparations.

To prepare a skin cleanser and astringent, place a cup of chopped purslane leaves and stems between two pieces of double-layered cheesecloth. Put the bundle in a bowl and mash thoroughly with a potato masher or pestle. Once the herb has been well crushed, add a cup of cool water to the bowl and continue mashing the purslane until all the juices have been extracted.

Apply the mixture to your face and leave it on for about five minutes, then rinse thoroughly. Purslane will clean, tighten, and refresh the skin, and can help smooth fine lines and superficial wrinkles.

The preparation will keep for up to five days, as long as you store it in the refrigerator in a tightly sealed container.

Raspberry

Perhaps more than any other herb, the raspberry proves that Native Americans could see what modern scientists sometimes fail to see.

Today, raspberry is officially recognized only as a flavoring ingredient.

However, Native Americans knew it well. They used the leaves to treat nausea, intestinal problems and eye inflammation.

Both the leaves and berries of the raspberry plant have medicinal properties, but the leaves were traditionally used most often.

Raspberry Tea:

Add two teaspoons of dried leaves to a cup of boiling water. Let stand for 10 to 15 minutes, strain, and drink as needed.

You can also use this tea as a gargle for a sore throat and as a milddisinfectant for cuts and other skin irritations.

Rabbit Tobacco

Also recognized as Sweet Everlasting, Cherokee Tobacco, Indian Posey, Cudweed, Poverty Weed, Fussy Gussy, and Sweet White Balsam, it is formally called Gnaphalium obtusifolium. In pastures, woodland, prairies,and thickets in the eastern states, east of Colorado, it grows almost everywhere.

It has long been used by Native Americans for a number of medicinal purposes using the stem, leaves, and flowers for treating asthma, diarrhea, cough, colds, flu, bronchitis, pneumonia, as an insect repellant, sleep aid, andmany other purposes.

It was mostly smoked by both Native Americans and early settlers in place oftobacco and did not contain nicotine. The smoke was thought to have held formany Indians a mystical or magical influence.

The Cheyenne also dropped leaves on hot coals, and it was known to havebeen used by the Cherokee in sweat baths. The Creek used it as a cold remedy, as a poultice for mumps in which it was applied to the throat, and asa sedative.

The Montagnais make a decoction of the plant for cough and tuberculosis.Furthermore, the Koasati for fever and the Menominee for headache, and dried leaves were steamed in the form of anodyne for "foolishness."

Some tribes also believed the smoke had a vital power that could awaken theunconscious or paralyzed. It was used on bruises and skin and mouth sores when a poultice was made.

The Cherokee also developed an herb salve made of rabbit tobacco blendedwith lard and applied on the chest to alleviate congestion and encourage sweating.

The plant's juice had both a reputation as an aphrodisiac and an anti-venerealpotion. It induces sleep, helps migraines, sinus problems, cough, asthma, stomach problems, is a mild sedative of the nerve, and increases appetite.

Rabbit Tobacco tea:

With flowers or leaves.

It is such a richly scented herb that it doesn't take much to make a nice cup offlavorful tea.

Use a small pinch of herbs- maybe 6-8 large leaves.

Pour boiling water over theleaves in the strainer and filter after 10-15 minutes.

Ragleaf Bahia

This flowering plant belongs to the daisy family and is also widely known as yellow ragleaf or yellow ragweed. It is known officially as Bahia Dissecta and was also referred to by the

Navajo tribe as Twisted Medicine. It was usedby many tribes as a contraceptive in teas. It is indigenous to the southwesternUnited States as far north as Wyoming and also northern Mexico.

Red Clover

Red clover (Trifolium pratense) is a wild flowering plant belonging to the same family as peas and beans. It is widely used in traditional medicine as aremedy for menopausal symptoms, asthma, whooping cough, arthritis and even cancer.

However, health experts are suspicious of its supposed benefits due to the lack of scientific evidence. Floral tea was traditionally used as a panacea, acure-all. Decoction or tea were used as an external wash on burns, wounds,and insect bites.

How to make a Red Clover Decoction:

1. Place 3 tablespoons of dried herbs into a small sauce pan.
2. Cover the herbs with a quart of cold water.
3. Slowly heat the water to a simmer and cover.
4. Allow to gently simmer for 20 to 45 minutes.
5. Strain into a quart jar, but do not discard the herbs. Some water willhave evaporated, so your strained liquid will not fill the jar.
6. Pour additional hot (but not boiling) water over the herbs in the straineruntil your jar is full.
7. Once your decoction is finished simmering, you can infuse more delicateleafy herbs or flowers into the hot water that cannot stand up to the lengthy simmer time, straining the mixture again after another 10 to 15 minutes.

Rosemary

Many Native American tribes knew Rosemary to be a holy herb, and with good reason: it is simply one of the most powerful natural plants for relievingjoint and muscle pain. Rosemary will also help strengthen the immune system, the nervous system, digestion, and circulatory system.

For decades, Rosemary has been used for medical purposes as a source ofcalcium, iron and vitamins A, C, and B-6.

It's an aromatic evergreen shrub belonging to the family of Lamiaceae and tothe genus Salvia. There are many varieties of rosemary, including white flower rosemary.

It is mainly used as an aromatic herb in cooking, but it is also one of the mostknown medicinal plants all over the world, for its precious beneficial properties.

In case of spices or aromatic herbs, keep in mind that their intake through thediet is really minimal, therefore, in order to benefit from their properties in the best way, it could be useful to take an herbal supplement, like essential oil.

Rosemary's essential oil has considerable advantages for the health. Let's see some of them:

- It improves concentration, memory and, in general, brain function. Promotes blood vessel dilation and circulation.
- Reduces inflammation and joint pain.
- It has antioxidant and anticancer properties. Promotes digestion and liver function.
- Counteracts hair loss and promotes hair growth. Reduces stress.
- Cognitive stimulant that can help to enhance the efficiency and performance of memory.

Contraindications of rosemary:

Consumption of rosemary as a medicinal plant does not have particular contraindications, however, before using essential oil or supplements, it is advisable to consult the doctor in case of pregnancy, lactation, hypertension or use of anticoagulant drugs.

Cooking Uses

This aromatic plant is irreplaceable in cooking, especially in the Mediterranean diet. It is indispensable on meat, fish, in the preparation of sauces and marinades.

Rosemary leaves, fresh or dried, are added to many dishes such as roasted meat, gravies, potato dishes and rustic pies, or on bread and buns.

Moreover, sprigs of rosemary are used together with garlic to aromatize olive oil and vinegar with excellent results. Its use makes foods not only tastier, but also more digestible.

Even rosemary flowers are edible and are often used for aromatizing and garnishing salads.

Rosemary tea

It is very simple and easy to make rosemary tea at home. You only require two ingredients, water and rosemary to make rosemary tea:

- Bring to a boil ten ounces of water (295 ml).
- Insert one tsp of loose rosemary leaves into the hot water.
- Then put the leaves in a tea infuser. Allow them to steep for five to ten minutes. This all depends on how tasteful you like your tea.
- Using a mesh strainer with small holes, strain the rosemary leaves from the hot water or remove them from the tea infuser. Used rosemary leaves should be discarded.
- Pour in a cup of your rosemary tea and enjoy. A sweetener, like sugar, honey, or agave syrup, can be added if you prefer.

Your mood and brain, and eye health can benefit from drinking the tea or even simply inhaling its aroma. The oxidative disruption that may lead to multiple chronic disorders can also be avoided.

It's necessary, though, to be mindful of its possible interactions with certain drugs. Using only two ingredients, rosemary tea can comfortably be made at home, and it fits perfectly into an overall safe and nutritious diet.

Sage Shrub

Native Americans considered this herb sacred and saw it as a symbol of immortality. This may perhaps even explain the herb's Latin name, *salvare*, which means "to save."

Native Americans used sage leaves to make a tea for treating fevers, headaches, arthritis, and diarrhea. As a gargle, the tea was used to soothe sorethroats, sores in the mouth, and infected gums. A tea made by boiling the roots was used to relieve menstrual pain and to help reduce the symptoms of menopause. This powerful warrior plant is used for smudging and sweeping to rid the victim of bad airs and evil spirits.

Leaves are used as a tea to treat infections or ease childbirth or as a wash for sore eyes. Leaves are soaked in water and applied as a poultice over wounds.

The tea is used to treat stomachache. Tree limbs are used as switches in sweatbaths.

The infusion was used to treat sore throats, coughs, colds, and bronchitis.

A decoction or infusion was used as a wash for sores, cuts, and pimples. The aromatic decoction of steaming herb was inhaled for respiratory ailments and headaches. The decoction was said to be internally anti-diarrheal and externally antirheumatic. This panacea drug was also drunk to relieve constipation.

Sage Tea :

Add two or three teaspoons of dried sage leaves to a cup of boiling water. Let stand for 15 minutes, then strain and drink as needed.

The tea can also be used as a gargle for mouth sores, gum infections, or a

sore throat.

Sage and Honey Cough Syrup:

- One cup or two of sage leaves, organic and fresh One cup or extra of honey (raw), local preferred
- One clean glass container or jar which can be tightly sealed & can contain at least twelve ounces

Given below are the detailed instructions for preparing this Native American herbal recipe. You need to follow these instructions in the given order.

Wash & dry the sage properly.

The leaves should be trimmed from the stems.

Put sage leaves into the glass jar. Then pour honey over the sage leaves. Itwould take some while for honey to move between the leave and soak themthoroughly.

Take a spoon and mix properly. Mix it daily. Allow it to sit for a week. Pull out the leaves and squeeze to take out all honey. You can also decant or leave it here & spoon it out as required into a container.

WARNING: Nursing mothers and pregnant women shouldn't use sage. Those with epilepsy also should avoid it because large amounts could trigger a seizure. In exceptionally large doses, sage may increasethe risk of convulsions, even in people without epilepsy.

St. John's Wort

Native American used Saint John's Wort to treat wounds, for its antibiotical and antibacterial properties, in addition toits skin regeneration effect.

It is widely used today in herbal medicine as a psychoactive antidepressant,for menopausal symptoms, attention-deficit hyperactivity disorder (ADHD)and somatic symptom disorder. Topical use of St. John's Wort is promoted for various skin conditions, including wounds, bruises, and muscle pain.

The flowers are used to make liquid extracts, pills, and teas.

Often blooming around the summer solstice, St. John's wort has a poetic andcomplex relationship with the sun. It has excellent anti-inflammatory and vulnerary effects. There are many applications for use with St. John's wort. Itcan be used as a tincture, infusion, oil, salve, or liniment.

The sun-shiny yellow flower about 3 feet in height, holds the energy of the sun and summer season. St. John's Day, which falls annually on June 24th, istypically the beginning of its blooming season. Energetically, St. John's wort is known as being a slightly warming and drying herb. It is also astringent, bitter, and sweet.

St. John's Wort Infused Oil

When making a St. John's wort infused oil you need to use the fresh or freshly wilted plant.

You can make a potent St. John's wort infused oil by using the young flower buds before they have opened. If you don't have access to a lot of St. John's wort, then you can also use the flowering tops including the uppermost leaves. To make the infused oil, I pick the buds from the plant and put them in a half-pint canning jar. I lightly pack the buds in the jar, filling it almost to the top.

Fill the jar with oil. For the facial serum recipe, I prefer to use jojoba oil because it is nourishing for the skin and it has a light, non-greasy feel. You can use any carrier oil of your choosing.

Once you have the fresh St. John's wort and the oil in the jar, stir it well and cover it with a tight fitting lid. While the flower buds are infusing, I place the jar in the sun.

After several weeks, once the oil has turned to a brilliant dark red, strain off the flowers. The resulting oil can be used as is, or in the decadent recipe below.

Also note that although the oil is often infused in the sun, once the herb has been strained off, it is best to keep it in a dark, cool location.

Here are the essential oils and extract that we will be adding to the facial serum:

Lavender (Lavandula angustifolia)

One of my favorite essential oils because of its lovely scent, lavender is also a wonderful choice for protecting and healing the skin. It has a long history of use for healing burns as well as infections.

Rosemary (Rosmarinus officinalis) Antioxidant Extract

Rosemary antioxidant extract contains rosmarinic and carnosic acids, both extensively studied for their antioxidant qualities. It is often used in cosmetics to increase the shelf life of natural products. You can find rosemary antioxidant extract at herbal apothecaries.

St. John's Wort Tincture

St. John's wort tincture has many uses. It can be added to the above oil recipe to create a liniment and used topically, or it can be taken internally, in a small bit of water, to support nervous tension, stress, and overall mood.

190-proof alcohol

1 pint-sized canning jar with lid Fresh St. John's wort aerial parts

- Collect enough plant material to fill a sterilized glass jar halfway. Pour enough alcohol

- to cover herb and fill the jar.
- Shake the mixture daily for 4 weeks.
- Strain the herb, reserving the liquid. Compost the herbs and bottle the tincture in a labeled amber-colored glass bottle.
- Keep the final tincture in a cool and dark place. Take 15-20 drops of tincture three times a day.

To help call in the sunshine during the long winter months, prepare St. John's wort preparations during the summer in an effort to support your future self. As an herb with many actions, it can be of great use for varying acute and chronic conditions and health presentations. From burns and scrapes to darkening mood, St. John's wort preparations are profound staples to keep in your herbal toolkit.

St. John's Wort Face Serum

This face serum combines several sources of oils, extracts, and essential oils to create a deeply nourishing and restorative oil for the skin. I use it both morning and night on my face, neck, and shoulders. This blend is also ideal for healing scars.

- 2 ounces fresh infused St. John's wort oil (see above for instructions)
- 1 teaspoon rosemary antioxidant extract
- 20 drops lavender essential oil (optional)

Add all the ingredients to a glass measuring cup with a pouring spout. Stir well.

Pour the mixture into a 2-ounce glass jar. Cap with a lid. I prefer using a treatment pump bottle so I can easily dispense the oil. You could also put it in a traditional tincture bottle with a dropper, or any other small decorative bottle that seals well.

Yield: This recipe yields approximately 2 ounces of oil. With daily application it should last about 3 months.

WARNING: By internal use, St. John's wort can weaken the effects of many medicines, including crucially important medicines

Sassafras

Few plants were regarded as highly or used as widely by Native Americans as the sassafras tree.

Native Americans used sassafras roots to make poultices for wounds and skin infections. Both the roots and berries were widely used to make teas for treating nausea, fevers, fatigue, gas pains, menstrual pain, scarlet fever, and even syphilis.

Used externally, a decoction made from sassafras root has been shown to be a helpful antiseptic. Many herbalists recommend this decoction to ease poison ivy rashes and to kill lice.

A preparation made from the gummy core of sassafras branches wasreportedly used by Native Americans to soothe tired eyes.

To relieve rashes or disinfect superficial cuts or scrapes

Sassafras lotion :

Add two ounces of fresh sassafras leaves to a pint of boiling water and letsimmer for 15 minutes to an hour.

After the mixture has cooled, apply it to the affected areas as a wet compress.

WARNING: Sassafras essential oil should no longer be used, either orally or for external use, due to the presence of safrole (one tablespoon ofoil can kill humans), which is toxic to the liver and heart.

Squaw Weed

As the name suggests, squaw weed, also called "life root," was used primarily to female problems. The Catawba of the Southeast, for example, used a squaw weed tea to ease the pain of childbirth and to relieve symptomsof difficult menstruation. The herb was used by other tribes to stop internal bleeding and was also thought to be a stimulant.

Squaw weed is best taken as a tea, using a teaspoonful of dried herb (root orleaves) in a cup of boiling water.

Allow the tea to steep 10 to 15 minutes, strain, and drink three to four times aday.

WARNING: Don't drink squaw weed tea more than four times a day because it can be toxic in large amounts.

Saw Palmetto

This small palm, known as Serenoa Repens in scientific terms, grows in the southeastern parts of North America. Known for its rebalancing action on thehormonal system, it is useful against alopecia and prostate problems. Let's discover it better. The fruits of serenoa have a rebalancing action on the hormonal system, mainly male, and are used in the treatment of prostate disorders and alopecia (androgynous baldness), which afflict a great number of men. The active principles contained in the plant are sterols, free fatty acids, carotenoids, essential oils and polysaccharides. The action of the phytocomplex depends on the combination of an antagonistic effect on sex hormones, with anti-inflammatory and diuretic effects.

Serenoa is successfully used in the treatment of diseases of the male urogenital apparatus, in benign prostatic hypertrophy (BHP) at the first stage

Native Americans used saw palmettos for a variety of purposes, includingfood; the leaves were used to weave baskets and ceremonial dance fans.

Serenoa was used as well as pounded into flour for traditional medicinal purposes. It has been used for diarrhea, stomach pain, digestive support, prostate health, coughing, breathing, inflammation, sexual vigor, congestion and increased appetite.

Whole berries have a milder effect than extracts, and make a mild diuretic tea that eliminates infectious bacteria in cases of prostate infection.

Saw palmetto Decoction:

Crush the berries to extract the herbal properties.

Use 1 teaspoon to each cup of water. Bring to a boil over low heat and simmer for 10 min. Drink warm.

Seneca Snakeroot

The Ojibwa call Seneca snakeroot *bi'jikiwuk'*. The name translates, literally, as "buffalo medicine". When made into medicine among the Ojibwa, Seneca snakeroot is usually combined with one to seven other herbs, the resulting combination also called *bi'jikiwuk*.

Seneca snakeroot is considered to be the principal herb, without which the preparation would not be efficacious. *Bi'jikiwuk'* was the principal war medicine carried by the Ojibwa. It was said to make men strong and to be a powerful healing medicine.

An Ojibwa warrior's custom was to chew it and spray it from the lips on his body and equipment.

The herb was considered to be effective in counteracting negative influences directed toward a person. It was taken four times daily all throughout life and was considered to enhance and increase the vitality and personal power of the person taking it.

Seneca Snakeroot tincture:

1:5 in 60% alcohol. Doses of 1.2 ml three times daily.

Seneca Snakeroot Decotion:

½ teaspoon of the dried root in a cup of water and simmer for 5-10 minutes. A common dose is one cup three times a day.

WARNING: The herb should be avoided during pregnancy and while nursing and it should not be given to children. People with ulcers or duodenal ulcer should not use it.

There is a possibility that senega can interact with some medication such as anticoagulants, antidiabetic agents, and antidepressants, therefore anyone taking such drugs should consult a professional healthcare provider prior to use.

Skullcap

Skullcap, or Scutellaria is native to North America, but some varieties are also found in Europe and Asia. Also recognized as Hoodwort, Blue Skullcap, Virginian Skullcap and Crazy Dog, it has beneficial effects on the reproductive system.

Various parts of the plant, including leaves and roots, were used in traditional Chinese medicine and by Native Americans for centuries. It was historically cultivated and used for menstrual cycles by Native American women. The plant generates soothing effects, which can lift the mood, producing a mild "high".

When flowering, the plant develops numerous tubular flowers, blue in color. Some variants may take on different shades. Among Native Americans, the plant has played an important role as a natural healing product.

The herb has been used by several tribes in purification ceremonies.

The Iroquois used a root infusion to keep the throat clean, while some plants were used by other tribes as bitter tonics for the kidneys. Its effectiveness against stress relief, help for the nervous system, insomnia, tension, and restlessness have also been found. It is an effective medicinal plant, anti- inflammatory, abortifacient, used as a sedative to treat epilepsy, hysteria, and anxiety, infections of the throat, headache, discomfort, anxiety, seizures, and more.

The Skullcap should not be taken by pregnant women.

Skullcap is a tonic for our nervous system. It can calm anxiety and irritability and also lift our spirits.

How to make a skullcap tincture:

- Take a ½ pint jar, ½ cup of dried skullcap leaves, and 100-proof vodka to fill your jar
- Fill the jar ½ way with dried skullcap leaves. Pour 100-proof vodka over the leaves until the jar is full. Stir and cap your tincture in progress. Label the jar "Skullcap (Scutellaria lateriflora) tincture," with the date 6 weeks from now to decant it.
- Open and stir your skullcap tincture every day for the first week. Allow the skullcap tincture to sit and infuse for 5 more weeks.
- Shaking the jar or stirring it every few days is a great idea. Keep the tincture out on the counter so you'll be reminded to do so.
- However, make sure it is kept out of direct sunlight.
- Strain the skullcap tincture into cheesecloth that is set into a strainer. Then, compost the leaves. You can clean out the jar you were brewing it in, and pour your finished tincture in the same jar for storage. Store out of direct sunlight. LABEL your jar "Skullcap (Scutellaria lateriflora) dried in 50% alc." Pour some into a tincture bottle for ease of use. You can also use any bottle or jar and administer with a teaspoon.
- Reach for your tincture if you're going through a particularly stressful time in your life, you may want to take a dropperful of tincture 3 or 4 times a day at mealtimes and

just before bed.

How to Make Skullcap Tea From Dried Skullcap Leaves

- 1 cup of dried organic scullcap leaves
- 2 cups of hot water
- A sealable container to store tea for future use

First bring water to a boil, then add the leaves and let steep for five minutes. Place a ceramic bowl in sink and place a colander on top to extract the leaves from the liquid. Save leaves for future use by storing inglass Tupperware container.

Slippery Elm

The Slippery Elm formally called Ulmus Rubra, is a genus of elm native to eastern North America, from east to southern Quebec, south to northern Florida, and west to eastern Texas, from southeast North Dakota. The tree had many typical Native American uses, including inner bark fiber for yarn, bowstrings, cords, clothes, and more. For various purposes, the wood was used, and for medicinal purposes, the bark along with leaves in washes and teas.

The characteristic properties of slippery elm:depurative,

- astringent,
- sudorific,
- disinflammatory of mucous membranes
- healing properties

The parts used to obtain natural remedies such as herbal teas, mothertinctures, buds and other extracts are principally bark and leaves.

The main active principles are tannic substances, phlobafenes, and phytospherin, minerals such as potassium and silica as well as bitterprinciples.

Mucilage, for example, is rich in special tannins and is contained inparticular in roots.

These special mucilages are capable of adhering like a film on the intestinalwalls protecting and regenerating them, for this reason elm is a very useful remedy for gastrointestinal problems.

It also helps to dissolve and expel mucus and toxins by purifying the surface of many organs thus promoting the development of their functionsin the best way.

Dosage is usually dependent on weight.

If making SE tea at home (see below) use about 2–3 teaspoons of powderper one-cup serving. You can consume the tea 1–2 times daily.

There are many ways you can incorporate slippery elm into your diet.

Slippery Elm Tea

- 1 tablespoon slippery elm bark powder
- 1 cup boiling water
- 1 teaspoon local honey (optional)
- ounces almond or coconut milk 1/2 teaspoon of cacao
- Sprinkle of cinnamon

1 Add boiling water to cup.

2 Add the slippery elm bark powder and stir well.

3 Then add the honey, almond or coconut milk.

4 Stir again.

5 Top of with a sprinkle of cinnamon.

Spruce

In long, freezing winters, Native Americans knew that tea made from spruceneedles helped people remain well.

Spruce needles have long been used by indigenous tribes for relieving coughsand sore throats. They also contain plenty of chlorophyll, which helps growing and healing tissues, controlling cravings, as well as transporting oxygen to cells. In Quebec City, Settlers started to suffer from scurvy in the 1500s (caused by a vitamin C deficiency). The Iroquois Indians shared with them this effective solution. In addition to curing them of scurvy, drinking spruce tea and spruce beer, dubbed Newfoundland spruce beer, became an essential preventive measure.

You can eat spruce needles just as they are or add them to smoothies and salad, or to season soups and other dishes used as rosemary. Dried needles canbe used for tea.

Stoneseed

Also, commonly known as Gromwell, this plant genus belonging to the family Boraginaceae is technically known as Lithospermum Officinale. For along time, the mature seeds have been ground into a powder and used as a sedative to treat bladder stones, arthritis.

Some Native Americans have used the roots as a contraceptive, such as the Shoshoni., syrup from the root and stem decoctions were also used in treatingeruptive diseases such as smallpox, measles and itching.

Stoneseed is currently being studied by pharmaceutical companies interestedin methods of fertility control.

A handful of the dried root, chipped, boiled in water and drunk daily as a teafor 6 month results effective for birth control.

Valerian

All parts of the plant (leaves, flowers, stems, seeds, and roots) have been used for their sedative and mild psychoactive effects. This species is commonly used as a painkiller and mild sedative in the same manner as opium among the Indians of northern Mexico.

Native Americans were well aware of valerian's relaxing effects—on the body as well as the mind. The roots were eaten either dried or raw to treat muscular cramping, intestinal colic, and the pains of menstruation. Some tribes ground valerian's carrot-like roots into a flour, which they mixed into bread or mush.

Valerian is one of the most widely used herbs in the world today.

Valerian root tea: add one to two teaspoons of dried herb to a cup of boiling water.

Let it steep 10 to 15 minutes, then strain and drink as needed.

Cats are strongly attracted to the aroma of valerian, so don't be surprised if your cat tries to dip his whiskers into your cup. Be sure to store the herb well sealed.

Unfortunately, rodents are also attracted by the smell.

Violet

Valued for more than its pretty face, the wild violet became a medicinal mainstay for many Native American tribes.

The Ojibwa used a decoction made from the roots of the white violet for treating bladder pain and one using the roots of the yellow violet for sore throats.

The Potawatomi used the roots of the yellow violet as a tonic for heart problems. Other tribes used various species of violet for diarrhea, fever, gas, indigestion, bronchitis, headaches, and poor circulation.

Scientists have found that most species of violet, in addition to being great sources of vitamins A and C, contain chemical similar to the active ingredientin aspirin.

Violet, mainly known as an ornamental garden plant, is used in the field of herbal medicine and perfumery for the particular healing properties it has onthe skin. From the processing of this plant is obtained a hydroalcoholic extract largely used in cosmetics and skin care treatments.

Violet extract can purify the skin and help it in case of issues such as acne,eczema, herpes and psoriasis. It can be used on its own or added to other ingredients with similar virtues to create powerful and natural home remedies.

Violet can be used both for internal use (through infusions) and for externaluse (through masks, toners and creams). By applying a violet tonic to the skin, it is possible to eliminate impurities and give the skin a relaxed, elastic and shiny appearance.

Violet milk gently cleanses makeup residue and is suitable for even the mostsensitive and irritated skin.

Violet also proves to be particularly useful in rebalancing the skin's sebaceous production. It is particularly indicated for oily skins and hashealing and anti-inflammatory properties.

Violet creams moisturize the skin and help at the same time to prevent theappearance of wrinkles and stretch marks.

Violet also has analgesic and expectorant properties.

All parts of the violet are medicinally active and can be used fresh or dried.

Violet Tea:

Boil any part of the plant for about 15 minutes, using a teaspoonful of herb ina cup of water.

You can make the tea into a syrup with further boiling to reduce the liquidand adding a little bit of honey.

Native Americans sometimes used violet poultices, which they applied to thehead as a treatment for headaches.

Watercress

Native Americans used watercress as a food source, eating it raw or cooked.It has a peppery flavor and sometimes is eaten in salads or as a garnish and potherb.

Watercress is rich in beneficial properties; its main characteristic is to stimulate general nutritional processes in the body and activate secretions ofcertain organs.

The plant is a source of vitamins in high concentrations, especially vitamins C, A, B, PP, E and mineral salts essential for the health of the body. In particular, vitamins A and C help keep the skin smooth and hydrated, and theassociation with manganese, magnesium and calcium supports bone formation.

Thanks to its high content of iron, folic acid and vitamin B6, watercress is recommended for anemic, asthenic and weak people. The precious minerals contained, phosphorus, copper, zinc, manganese, iodine and calcium, give the plant antibiotic properties: it blocks the proliferation of germs and bacteria, prevents colds and acts favorably on the pulmonary system.

In addition, because of its expectorant and detoxifying action, it is particularly suitable for smokers.

Watercress leaves contain glucosinolates, which help the liver in its detoxification process; moreover, they are powerful natural pesticides, which protect the plant from fungi and worms, whereas on the human body they have an anti-cancer effect: they contrast the formation of cancer cells.

Watercress, as well as other vegetal species belonging to the same family, has antioxidant properties (protects the body from many chronic degenerative conditions) and diuretic properties (contrasts water retention and hypertension). The plant is also used to stimulate and firm the gums, rubbing them with fresh leaves; moreover, thanks to the content of iron, zinc and vitamin A, it strengthens hair and nails. Its sulfur active principles have the function of activating the peripheral blood circulation, with a direct action on hair bulbs and scalp.

Watercress Tea:

Add a teaspoonful of dried or fresh herb to a cup of boiling water.

Let stand for about 10 minutes, then strain and drink as needed. The same tea can also be used as a skin wash for rashes, eczema, or acne.

For a more astringent facial tonic, crush the leaves to extract the juice and apply it to your skin. Some herbalists recommend mixing watercress juice with a little vinegar and applying it to the forehead to get a quick jolt of energy.

Wild watercress should be thoroughly washed because it may harbor parasites.

In large amounts, it may irritate the kidneys, so you don't want to use it everyday.

Witch Hazel

Witch hazel was used by the Cherokee, Chippewa, Iroquois, Mohegan, Menominee, and Potawatomi peoples living in the range of the plant east of the Mississippi. They used the leaf tea externally to treat muscle aches, athlete's foot, wounds, burns, and various skin afflictions.

Tea was consumed for coughs, asthma, colds, sore throats, dysentery, and diarrhea. Twigs and inner bark are still used in infusion to treat colds, pain, sores, fevers, sore throat, and tuberculosis.

An infusion of twigs was used to treat dysentery and diarrhea.

A decoction of new-growth tips and shoots from the base of the plant was used as a blood purifier or spring tonic. Young end tips were used in decoction to treat colds and coughs. Root and twig decoctions were considered a cure-all for just about any ailment: bruises, edema, cholera, and arthritis.

Today, witch hazel is still the key ingredient in a popular cleansing product for hemorrhoids. Witch hazel is an astringent, which means it causes blood vessels to constrict. This may be an effective way to stop hemorrhoids from bleeding and to reduce painful swelling.

How to infuse Witch Hazel

1. Place the dried herb(s) in a clean, sealable glass jar and cover completely with witch hazel extract. Make sure extract covers the herbs by at least 1-2 inches.
2. Cap tightly with a nonmetallic lid, or if using a metal lid, put a piece of waxed paper or parchment between the jar and lid before sealing.
3. Shake to blend and set aside for a few minutes. Check back after a bit, and top with more witch hazel extract as necessary to keep herbs fully covered.
4. Place in a cool, dark place.
5. Allow to infuse for two weeks, shaking the jar daily. You will notice that the witch hazel will quickly take on the scent and color of the herbs. Add more witch hazel as necessary to keep herbs fully covered.
6. Once finished, strain the herbs out using cheesecloth. Squeeze to get every drop of goodness. Discard herbs.
7. Pour infused witch hazel into a clean, sealable jar.
8. Because witch hazel is not recommended for internal use, clearly label the jar so there are no mistakes.
9. Depending on which botanicals you used, shelf life can vary significantly, from several weeks to several months. For best results, store in the refrigerator.

White Pine

Eastern white pine is native to North America and grows from Newfoundland to Manitoba and eastern Canada. The resin and needles were considered for their medicinal effects. As a soothing ointment, the resin, which has certain antiseptic qualities, was spread on wounds and boiled to make a tonic drink.

Rich in vitamin C, the needles provided a tea that helped prevent and treat scurvy.

Pine had good sales potential and possessed some antiseptic properties: the strong odor reached blocked sinuses.

In addition to the apparent one of providing wood, eastern white pine also had many non-medicinal applications. First Nations used the resin to seal the seams of canoes; pine resins later became the basis of consumer goods such as pitch and turpentine. Eastern white pine is harvested primarily for its lumber and pulp.

Oils used for medicinal purposes are a byproduct.

The needles, inner bark and resin have been used by civilizations around the world for similar ailments. Internally, for coughs, colds, asthma, and diseases of the urinary tract and sinus, pine is a typical treatment.

Topically, pine is used in arthritic ailments to combat skin diseases and to decrease joint inflammation. Some twenty species of pine have been used similarly as a medicine by native communities across the continent, including the Chippewa, Cherokee, Iroquois, Apache, Hopi and numerous other groups.

Medicinal Use of Pine Needles

The fresh needles and buds collected in the springtime are called "pine tops." They are boiled in water, and for fevers, coughs, and colds, the tea is consumed. The needles are also used for their diuretic features, helping to improve urination.

Pine-top tea, particularly given the abundance of pines in the area, is one of the most valuable historical medicines of the rural south-eastern United States. Famed Alabama herbalist Tommie Bass uses the needles in a steam inhalation to break up the lungs' tenacious phlegm.

For this reason, you may mix pine tops with sprigs of fresh thyme and bee balm. Pine induces relaxation by its relaxing expectorant, antimicrobial, & anti-inflammatory characteristics in sinus and lung congestion. Vitamin C is also in the fresh, younger needles.

Try mixing peppermint and catnip as a tea with pine needles, which can be sipped to soothe cold symptoms during the day. For the entire household, this mixture is a healthy cure.

Pine needles, in the form of infusion, syrup or tablets, have a diuretic action but above all a balsamic action; this last action, together with the expectorant one, is mainly carried out by the essential oil, rich in monoterpenes, obtained by steam distillation.

For external use, terpenes have muscular decontracting and anti-rheumatic activity.

Powerful Pine Tea

- 1-quart water
- A fistful of pine needle tops (about five to seven branch tips; fresh or dried)
- One and a half tbsp dried peppermint
- One tbsp dried catnip

For twenty minutes, boil the pine needle tops in water. Turn the heat off, and the peppermint and catnip are inserted. Cover and allow to steep for an extra twenty minutes. If needed, strain and add honey. While hot, sip on the tea, reheating each cup during the day as needed. Adults can consume three cups a day. The dosages for children should be lowered proportionally.

Pine Bark

The inner bark contains more resin than the needles and is more astringent.It has traditionally been used for muscular aches and pains as an antimicrobial wash and poultice and infused into bathwater. It is sometimesboiled in water and consumed for coughs and colds as a cure. The knotty pine wood of many pine types is mixed into wine in Traditional Chinese Medicine and then used topically for joint pain.

Pine Resin

There are numerous local first-aid applications of the resin, also called pitch. It is used as an antimicrobial dressing for wounds and to extract splinters. Pine resin has been used internally as a strong expectorant in minute quantities. You can use pine pitch to pull out splinters, glass, and thecontaminants left from toxic bug bites prepared as a salve. Pine resin salve is effective in reducing muscle aches and inflammation of the joints.

Pine Pitch Band-Aids: Forest First-Aid

Take a semi-hard but pliable piece of pitch and form it over the affected region into a flat bandage. While also being anti-inflammatory and antimicrobial, this basic first-aid has excellent drawing ability. Cover it andleave it on overnight with a Band-Aid or clean bandage

Pine Pitch Salve

- One-part clean pine pitch
- Two parts extra-virgin olive oil
- Grated beeswax beads

Melt the olive oil pitch using a double boiler (1-part pitch to 2 parts oliveoil, by volume) until it is completely melted (it's okay if a little resin stayssolid).

Add the grated beeswax (one-part beeswax per four parts of the combined pitch and liquid oil). Before inserting lids, pour into jars and leave to cool.

Wormwood

Tewa nation people chewed and swallowed juice to relieve gas and upsetstomach. Leaf infusion also used to treat fever and chills.

The herb has traditionally been used as a smudging agent. The green plant iscut and gathered together in a bundle and wrapped with small string and allowed to dry. The end is lit and used as a "smudge wand" in ceremonial smudging. The plant is also used, dry or moistened, in the sweat lodge. The plant is placed on the hot stones in the center of the lodge and the resulting vapor inhaled.

You can prepare wormwood as tea or tincture. The best way for you to experience the wormwood benefits covered above is to start with dried wormwood. You can find wormwood essential oil, but wormwood oil is oftentoo strong for most wormwood tea or wormwood tincture preparations. So you should not ingest pure essential oils of wormwood. In fact, this is true for most essential oils.

Wormwood essential oil may contain unsafe levels of thujone. You can safely consume tea or tinctures, however, as they contain only a trace amount of thujone.

Wormwood tea ("artemisia tea") is a great natural remedy for digestive issues, low energy, or as a cleanse. If you think you have been exposed to a parasite, you can also use strong wormwood tea to kill any parasites in your system.

To make wormwood tea:

Combine 1/2 to one (1) teaspoon of dried wormwood herb per 6-8 ounces of water and steep for 5 to 10 minutes.

As a rule of thumb take only such a small amount of wormwood herb as fits between three fingertips (max 1 gram) and start with a short steeping time (1 minute and increase up to 5-10 minutes maximum) to avoid that the tea becomes too bitter.

You can drink a freshly prepared cup of warm wormwood tea a maximum three times a day – half an hour before meals if you lack or to regulate appetite, half an hour after meals if you have digestive problems. The daily dosage is a maximum of three grams of wormwood herb.

The medicinal plant must be avoided during pregnancy and lactation as well as in the case of gastrointestinal ulcers.

To make warmwood tincture: You can use the tea recipe to make a water-based tincture. Just steep the tea for 15-20 minutes to make a stronger solution. Store in a glass jar or tincture bottle, in a cool, dark place. For a stronger, alcohol-based version, prepare the following:

In sealable glass jar, combine 8 ounces of 80-100 proof grain alcohol (vodka) with 1 cup of whole fresh wormwood plant or dried wormwood. Cover and store in a cool, dry place for 4 to 6 weeks. Strain all plant matter out of the solution and store in tincture bottles.

Yarrow

Yarrow is ranked as one of the most important herbs used by Native Americans.

Whole plant (aerial parts) infused and used to treat acute infections: colds, fever, flu, and as a diuretic.

Whole plant infusion is used to control coughing. Wash (infusion) of the whole plant is also used for bites, stings, snakebites.

Root decoction may be used as a wash for pimples.

Leaves are infused and consumed as tea to induce sleep, as an antidiarrheic, and to reduce fever (febrifuge).

The leaf infusion is also a poison ivy treatment.

The leaves dried, crushed, and snorted are snuff for headaches, placed in thenasal cavities they also stop nose-bleedings.

Fresh or dry leaves are used as a poultice over wounds, or as a fomentation orpoultice over breast (nipple) abscesses.

Bella Coola people chewed leaves and applied them as a poultice to treat burns and boils, used leaves and flowers in decoction for headaches or forchest pains, and poultice of flowers (masticated) to reduce edema.

Finally, leaves mixed with animal fat may be used used as a poultice on thechest and back to treat bronchitis.

How to Make Yarrow Tea:

Add 1 teaspoon of dried yarrow flower to one cup of boiling water. Coverand steep for 30 minutes, then strain and serve.

How to make Yarrow salve:

- 1,5 to 2 cups of Olive Oil
- Yarrow Stalks~ 2 cups of Yarrow Leaves and Flowers 1/4 cup of Beeswax Pellets

1 Infuse your carrier oil with yarrow using the slow, solar infusionprocess, or heat infusion.

2 In a double boiler on the stove, slowly melt 2 tbsp of beeswax and 1/2 cupof yarrow-infused oil.

3 Once melted, remove from heat and pour into a small mason jar.

Yellow Dock

Most Native American tribes mashed the root and applied it to the skin to treat arthritis. Cherokee used the root juice for treating diarrhea. One unusualuse was rubbing the throat with a crushed leaf to treat sore throat. Cooked seeds were eaten to stem diarrhea. Dried and powdered root used to stop bleeding (styptic). Pioneers considered the plant an excellent blood purifier, aspring tonic for whatever ails you.

How to make a Yellow Doc Detox Tea:

- 1 tbsp yellow dock root
- 1 tbsp oatstraw
- 1 tbsp rosehips (deseeded)
- 1 tbsp hibiscus (crumbled)
- 1 tbsp tulsi (aka holy basil)
- ½-1 tsp licorice root powder (depending on how sweet you like your tea)
- 2 cups just-boiled water.

Pour water over the herbs, cover and allow to steep for about 20 minutes.Strain and sip throughout the day.

Yellow Root

Officially named Xanthorhiza Simplicissima, from Maine south to northernFlorida and west to Ohio and eastern Texas, this woody-stemmed plant is native to the eastern United States.

Although Yellow Root is poisonous in large quantities, for treatment of mouth disorders, stomach ulcers, stomach ache, Native Americans made a teaand used it externally on skin conditions, sores and swelling. It has also been shown to be effective for reducing blood pressure and the liver's well-being.

Yellow Root Tea Recipe

- Take 1 gram of finely chopped yellow root. Boil 500 ml of water in the saucepan.
- Once the water comes to boiling point, add the 1 gram of chopped yellow root to water.
- Reduce the heat and simmer for about 20 minutes.
- Check whether the water has gained a bright yellow color hue.
- If the required yellow hue is achieved after 20 minutes, turn off the stove.
- Strain the mixture and make sure that no particles of the root are present in the strained tea.
- Allow the Yellow Root tea to cool and serve.

Yew

As a means of contraceptive, women of the Okanagan tribe and other northwestern coastal tribes consumed yew berries. To cure tuberculosis,arthritis and kidney failure, the Quinault people cooked the bark as a decoction and consumed it in very small quantities. The Cowlitz Indiansdeveloped a needle poultice and applied it to wounds topically.

WARNING: *However, the leaves are toxic, and not to be consumedorally.*

Zizia Aurea

Native Americans used the pulverized root to treat sharp pains; a tea was made from the leaves and flowers to treat ""female disorders""; poulticed rootwere used on inflammations and sores.

A tea made from the root is febrifuge. The root is also believed to bevulnerary and hypnotic.

The flowers, with the main stem removed, are a welcome addition to a tossedgreen salad. They are also a delicious cooked vegetable.

Book 12 The Native American AncientRemedies Some Other Specific Remedies

Handed Down by the Natives

May the sun bring you new energy during the day,

May the moon gently regenerate you at night,

May the rain wash away your worries,

May the wind blow new strength into your being,

so, you can walk through the world and know

its beauty every day of your life.

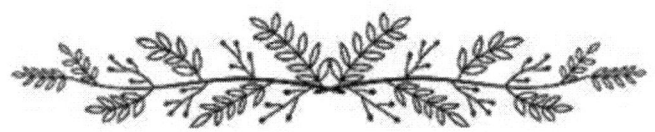

(Native American Apache Blessing)

Analgesic Tea

Ingredients:

- 25 drops black cohosh tincture
- 90 drops wild cherry bark tincture
- 90 drops mullein tincture 1 cup warm water

1 Combine the above herbs in a glass container and cover with the water.

2 Take one-third of the mixture three times daily.

Warming Compress for Back Pain

Makes 1 compress. This simple application provides immediate relief.

Ingredients:

- 16 fluid ounces water
- ½ cup dried ginger (see Tip)
- ¼ cup Epsom salts

1 In a small pot with a tight-fitting lid over high heat, combine all the ingredients. Cover and bring to a boil. Reduce the heat and simmer for 5 minutes. Meanwhile, fill a hot water bottle.

2 Soak a cloth in the hot tea, holding it by a dry spot and letting it cool in the air until hot but comfortable to the touch.

3 Lie down and place the wet cloth over your back. Cover with a dry clothand lay the hot water bottle on top. Get comfortable and let it soak in for10 to 20 minutes. You should feel warmth, relaxation, and relief from pain.

4 Repeat as often as desired.

TIP: Have pain, but no dried ginger? If all you have on hand is fresh ginger from the grocery store, you can use that, too—sliced, chopped, orgrated.

Soothing Back Pain Tea

This tea can help relieve pain caused by nerve irritation. teaspoon chopped valerian root

- teaspoons white willow bark
- 2 cups cold water

1 Combine the herbs in a pan and cover with the water.
2 Soak overnight; strain.
3 Take up to one cup a day, a tablespoon at a time.

Tummy Tea

We have listed below the ingredients that you would require for preparingthis Native American herbal recipe:

Ingredients:

- Dried chamomile flowers
- Dried lemon balms leaf
- Dried catnip leaf

Given below are the detailed instructions for preparing this Native American herbal recipe. You need to follow these instructions in the givenorder.

1 Combine equal parts of lemon balm, chamomile and catnip thoroughlyin a jar. Then cap & label.
2 Then To brew tea, put one tablespoon of the tea blend into eight ouncesof water boiled. Then allow it to steep for three to four minutes.
3 You can add sweeteners as per your taste, or you may not. Finallyenjoy.
4 Keep in mind one thing that chamomile will get bitter if it is steeped fora long time.

Anti-stress Tonic Tea

Oats are my go-to herb for feeling calmer and more nourished. They blend beautifully with other gentle, soothing herbs to support the nervous system.Use the recipe below as a starting point, and switch out the linden for otherherbs such as lemon balm, violet and/or chamomile as you wish.

Ingredients:

- 1 cup Oat tops
- ½ cup Linden
- 1-2 tablespoons Lavander

Mix together all the herbs. Add ¼ cup of this blend to a glass quart jar. Cover with boiled water, cap, and let steep overnight, or at least 6 hours. Strain and drink at room temperature, or gently re-heat.

Aches and Pain Blend

Ingredients:

- 1/4 cup of Comfrey Dry Leaves
- 1/4 cup of Calendula Flowers Dried
- 1/4 Cup of Rosemary Leaves Dried
- 1/4 cup of dry buds of Lavender
- 1/2-1 cup of magnesium or Himalayan pink salt

INSTRUCTIONS AND USAGE:

1. Add all the ingredients to a big canning jar, then mix (hands work) thoroughly.
2. In 1 quart of boiling water, utilizing a 1/4 to 1/2 cup herb mix. Steep for 15 mins.
3. Soak the kitchen towel in infusion as a compress and put over the sprain/strain. Twenty minutes to rest and swap out and keep things warm.
4. When soaked-add infusion either to a foot bath or, if necessary, full.
5. Repeat throughout the day several times.

Cough Formula

Ingredients:

- cup of honey (alternatives are molasses and brown sugar)
- 1/2 cup water Glass containers with lids (as many as you need for the different cough mixtures)

To make cough syrup base

1. Boil the water in a pan
2. Warm the honey in a pan
3. Combine the two to make the base

You can play around with the amounts. Make sure it isn't too runny, as you'll be adding more liquid when you make the cough mixtures.

Burns Healing Internal Formula

By use of vulnerary herbs for extreme burns can aid speed healing and decrease scarring. Symphytum officinale is a long-standing curing agent, so Calendula officinalis facilitates dermal circulation and strengthens connective tissue development in the basement membrane.

The study is minimal; however, it is suspected that Calendula officinalis promotes wound healing by facilitating glycoprotein & collagen production,hastening regeneration of dermis. *Hypericum perforatum* tends to decrease pain and repair nerve ends that are damaged. *Centella asiatica* has been shown to be useful in supporting post-burn epithelial regeneration.

You may prepare this formula as a tincture or even a tea.

Centella Asiatica Symphytum Officinale

Calendula Officinalis

Hypericum Perforatum

Blend in similar proportions. For a week or more, take 1 tsp of the blended tincture six times every day. Using 1/2 ounce of each herb to create the mix toprepare it as a drink. Each cup of hot water and strain, steep 1 tbsp of the herbmixture. If necessary, drink five to six cups a day, and proceed for one week or two.

BOOK 13
The Native AmericanPractices
Sacred Rituals and Ceremonies to beconnected with Nature and all its Elements and Creatures

Chapter 1:
Native AmericanRituals and Ceremonies

The Life Vision

The vision that underlies the Native American way of life on all physical andspiritual planes, and of all their practices and healing methods is very simple.To live a healthy life, people must live in harmonic relationship with Nature.

In their culture, each person is seen as a traveller along the circle of life and his journey must be of respect and harmony towards people, animals and nature. General harmony contributes to the maintenance of health and balance, while its lack leads to imbalance and illness. According to this view,medicine focuses on a healing path of the soul rather than on the care of the body, affecting not only the body but also the mind and spirit.

The primary task of healers is to preserve inner balance. They are forbiddento market healing, which does not involve a fixed cost per service, but a giftthat is synonymous with gratitude on the part of the patient who has made arequest for help. The harmony between patient and healer is also necessary for an effective healing. Without the patient's consent, healing can be ineffective or even harmful to both the patient and the doctor.

The interpreter of the body-mind-experience sphere of the patient is represented by the figure of the counselor, a spiritual guide who helps hispatients to seek the symbolic meaning of the pathology and their life.

Moreover, the North American natives use sacred ceremonies of communities accompanied by prayers, songs and music to honor and communicate with both living people and spirits or to invoke healing and eliminate illness and unhappiness.

To fight diseases, among natives there are"men of medicine" specialized inthe use of herbs with healing properties.

Conclusions: In comparison with western medicine which put the origin of the disease on a predominantly biological basis, the North American nativesmedicine includes multiple factors and also emotional, social and spiritual aspects.

The growing interest in traditional healing practices even among non-nativeshas led to the development of alternative approaches based on the integrationof Western medical practice to the psychological and spiritual care of the natives.

The commonalities between the various Native American traditions correspond to the commonalities of shamanic practices around the world.

Some common traits of shamanism in general and in the different Native American populations are:

A cosmic vision of the world that can be outlined in:

World Above, Father Sky, Heart of Heaven, Paradise World Below, Mother Earth, Heart of the Earth Middle World, the world of ordinary reality

The perception of a reality that is not visible with normal senses The presence of disembodied beings called spirits

The possibility to move with the consciousness across other worlds and dimension

The possibility to move even only with the consciousness in this reality The ability to alter consciousness to access the invisible worlds

The possibility to connect with benevolent spirits, allies, in the invisible

worlds who can be of help in the explorations of these worlds. The material world is considered permeable to the spiritual world, there is no division. The presence of spirits can be perceived even under normal conditions.

The presence of a regulating and creative principle, which permeates everything, from rocks to seas, from plants to clouds, from sun to moon, etc. According to the different tribes, it assumes a different name, for the Lakota it is Wakan Tanka (the great mystery), Algonquin People, the most populous group living in Canada, call it Cree, and in the northern part of the USA, and for the Ojibway and Iroquois, it is Manitou.

The importance of Ancestors, who in some cultures become real spiritual beings who help their people, such as the Kachinas in the Hopi tradition. In the Hopi tradition the Kachinas are not only Ancestors but also spirits of animals, plants, minerals, stars and natural forces.

Among the Hopi, for example, when you speak to an animal you can speak to the animal itself or to its spirit. In this case it is necessary to be very careful about what is said. In some ceremonies they wear a mask of a certain animal. The one who wears the mask must be worthy and has to follow particular rules and behaviours, otherwise it could break the cycle and the harmony between man and this animal or even with the whole universe.

An ancient Cherokee legend has it that the Creator gave Mother Earth all the animals and plants.

These could communicate with each other by speaking the common language of peace, harmony and friendship. At that time, people hunted only what they needed and did not forget to express their respect and gratitude. As the centuries passed, they began to multiply and plan for the future, cultivating the land and building fences and borders.

Humans forced animals into smaller and smaller spaces and invented tools that gave them an unfair advantage. Soon realizing their superiority, they began to trample ants, worms and other small creatures. At first, without thinking about it and later with contempt. They began to hunt the larger animals for meat and skins. They also killed for fun or simply to show their superiority, forgetting that they were children of the same Creator.

The natives of North America have always had a special relationship with nature. Nature and all creatures are blood brothers because they are children of the Great Spirit.

Only in the relationship with nature, the human being finds himself. If one expresses benevolence towards the earth, it will express it towards us; on the contrary, lack of respect for the environment leads to lack of respect for people. The feeling of brotherhood with all the creatures of the Earth is a concrete principle from which consequences arise: if the heart of man separates from nature it becomes cruel and evil.

The identity of a human being can be appreciated on the basis of his active behavior towards everything around him. The Great Mother Earth is a divinity conceived as feminine and primordial: for this reason, she is seen as a Mother who gives her body for the nourishment of her children.

For the natives, the ecological balance and the preservation of natural resources are the guarantee of their existence, it represents the very foundation of their identity; moreover, the Earth has no economic value for them.

The relationship that natives have with Mother Earth is total and involves all the senses of man both on a physical and spiritual level. The concepts of spirituality and religion are deeply correlated to the concept of nature. For the native's nature represents the stage where the kingdom of spirits and the human world meet.

The title "medicine person" is bestowed upon a man or woman by the community as a sign of courage and selfless devotion to the community. In addition, becoming a traditional healer is very hard work: it requires years of rigorous training, tests and demonstrations of endurance, courage, patience, generosity and generally strong character.

Generally, the training of the medicine man is entrusted to a senior member of the community, who in turn is a medicine man. However, the person being trained must possess specific aptitudes, including humor, which is an essential trait. Elders would never teach people who take themselves too seriously, nor would they train a lazy person.

Some healers are associated with specific animals, natural elements, and powers that they invoke and are attuned to. In the healing practice common to many Native North American healers, both healer and patient may ask friends, family and members of their community to participate in the healing by praying, singing or performing ceremonial actions.

The importance of the concept of community for the Lakota tribe of natives has been described extensively in the book "The Medicine Men" by psychiatrist and medical anthropologist Lewis H. Thomas: Rituals facilitate a benevolent participation of the community to the pain and the problem, while encouraging the individual with a therapeutic influence.

Among the Native American peoples, of the Siouan linguistic group, the Sioux are the best known. The Sioux Nation is divided into three main ethnic groups, the Dakota, the Nakota and the westernmost tribe, the Lakota.

Before the arrival of the white man on Turtle Island - America's native name - the life of indigenous peoples was marked by rituals. So, it was for the Lakota as well. Every moment of their social life, as well as their individual life, was regulated by some main rituals and by many minor ones.

With the persecution and genocide perpetrated, first by the conquerors, then by various waves of migration of white Europeans, many of their rituals, besides being forbidden and declared illegal, fell into oblivion. Only a few elders continued to practice them clandestinely. It was these elders who preserved and handed down the rites, customs and traditions to the generations who, finding their identity, wanted to live following the ancient rules.

In the last decades, after the reawakening of the native pride and conscience, following hard legal battles, but also fought with weapons, at the cost of the life of many martyrs, especially after having obtained the right to practice their religion, the respect and the interest towards the ancient spiritual practices has been reborn.

The main rituals can be divided chronologically into three groups. The ancient ones, which date back to the mists of time, before the arrival of White Bison Woman, those that she herself taught and the more recent ones, received in vision by some Medicine Men (Wichasha Wakan).

Tradition has it that Whopi, White Buffalo Woman, as she predicted will return among the Lakota, at the end of time. According to some legends, she is back on Earth, in the company of a woman: she walks the streets of Turtle Island, preparing people to face the last and most difficult period for humanity.

The most ancient rituals are the Inipi (the Sweating Hut), the Yuwipi (the Rite of the Sacred Stone) and the Hanblecheya (the Quest for Vision).

Lakota Worldview and Spirituality

Both the worldview and the profound spirituality of the Lakota can be summed up in a single phrase: Mitakuye Oyasin, everything is my kin. These two words, in the Lakota language, teach the unique origin of beings and things, their interconnectedness and interdependence, on all levels of Creation, on the spiritual as well as on the material plane, Manifest World and Unmanifest World.

Everything comes from Wakan Tanka, the Great Spirit: the Macrocosm and the Microcosm, Light and Darkness, Male and Female.

Dualities and dichotomies are the basis of life, in all forms. All levels of Creation were formed in the four successive periods. During the first period, Wakan Tanka emanated four Higher Spirits. In the second, these four in turn created the four Associated Spirits. In the third, these created the four Lower Spirits.

All these Spiritual Entities, together, are called the Sixteen Great Mysteries that preside over the Creation of eight other Supernatural Spirits.

Ancient Medicine and the Use of Plants and Herbs

Plant medicine is probably the oldest and most widespread healing tradition on the planet. According to Native North Americans the active ingredient, though important, is not everything. Tradition teaches that plants are endowed with intelligence, energy and a spirit of their own, but their power to heal, reduce pain and cure disease must be awakened and activated through ceremonial actions, such as prayers and offerings. Native North American culture makes use of certain plants, known in Western medicine for their healing abilities by virtue of specific active ingredients.

For example, many native tribes chew willow bark, or make a tea from it, to treat headaches or fevers, but also as a wash to flush out a swelling. In Western therapy, this places its biological rationale in the action of salicylates known for their antipyretic and anti-inflammatory activity. Other tribes chew the root of echinacea purpurea, a known immunostimulant, to treat colds and sore throats. Some native California tribes used Tassolo, a known antiblastic, isolated from the bark of the yew tree, as a decoction to purify the blood and a panacea for all ills. Healers considered the whole plant to be an active principle, rather than the single chemical component extracted or isolated.

Whole plants, compared to extracted active ingredients, generally have less side effects and less toxicity, because unlike drugs they reach the circulatorystream more slowly and with reduced concentrations.

Even the appearance or even the name of some plants is important and functional to treat a disease or a specific injury to a part of the body. The aspect of a plant is considered a divine sign suggesting its use: the "Black-eyed Susan" (Ahwi Akata, in Cherokee) in relation to its aspect is used as ananti-inflammatory for weak or reddened eyes.

Still, many tribes consider the famous American ginseng as a powerful general tonic, as its root resembles a human being. The color of a plant can bejust as important. The "Yellow Root" (Xanthorrhiza simplicissima) can treat nausea or vomiting, while the red-colored "Blood Root" (Sanguinaria canadensis) is widely used for blood flow disorders4.As described above, a plant's energy is activated and enhanced when individuals are gathered and connected to each other within a ceremony.

Some plants, such as those that have hallucinogenic properties, are dangerousto use outside of ceremonies. For example: Peyote and Datura Stramonium, which are sacramental herbs that must be harvested and ingested only after ceremonies, due to their powerful effects. The plants are effective even without an offering of gratitude, however in this way they only treat the symptoms without reaching the emotions and the spirit of the cured person inwhich reside the deepest causes of the illness.

The Ceremonies

Rituals are a crucial aspect of traditional Aboriginal healing and are foundedon the principle of interconnection between body and soul.

To honour and communicate with both the living persons and the deities, inthe tradition of the Native North Americans, ceremonies are performed, characterized by a series of actions, accompanied by prayers, songs and music often played on the drum and can have different durations from a fewminutes to several years.

The ceremonies can be personal, inspired by visions and dreams, or they can be tribal traditions, transmitted from generation to generation. They may be performed individually or, more commonly, by the entire tribe or community,and are conducted by a ceremonial leader.

Ceremonies are mostly performed in sacred places, although they can takeplace anywhere it's needed: in homes or outdoors, such as in the desert.

Generally, they include some activities that aim to restore or maintain abalance between man and nature.

The philosophy of the ceremonies is based on the mutual influence betweenthe action of man and nature. Prayers, drums, songs, poems, legends and the use of various ceremonial instruments are part of it.

Traditional healing rituals are considered sacred wherever they take place andare performed only by native healers and local spiritual facilitators. Non- natives may participate by invitation only.

The Sweat Lodge

The sweat lodge ceremony takes its name from the artificial structure in which it takes place and is perhaps the oldest of the North American Nativeceremonies. In the Lakota language, the Sweat Lodge is called Inipi, word that means "huts of the breath of life," or Oinikagapi, "place where life is renewed." In the tradition of the Sweating Hut, people sweat out illness, unhappiness, negativity, and invite spirits with prayer and song. The SweatLodge is generally a temporary structure, characterized by a dome made of branches with a pit filled with hot stones in the center.

Originally, the hut was covered with bison skins, but now tarpaulins, large fabrics and blankets are used. Inside, in the center, there is a hole called the "Cradle of Rock" where the incandescent stones, the Tunka Yatapika, are placed during the ritual. The opening of the Inipi is turned towards the West,where, besides the Altar and the Sacred Path seven steps long, there is the Fire Without End, the Peta Ohiankesni, over which the stones are red-hot.

The door is low, one must bow to enter and once inside, one always proceedson all fours and in a clockwise direction. The one who leads sits next to the door, to the west.

A dozen participants at a time sit around the pit to purify themselves withheat and steam. The red-hot pit symbolizes the center of the universe, theabode of the Great Spirit and his power.

When the ceremonialist carries the hot stones to the pit he walks on a kind of"umbilical cord," symbolically tracing the path of life from Creator to Creation. Participants humbly enter the Hut and look for a place to sit cross- legged around the fireplace.

They are naked and covered with a towel or a bathing suit, ready to face lifewithout masks and renouncing the identity that distinguishes them in the outside world. The janitor uses a pitchfork, or if he follows the old tradition using deer antlers, he carries the red-hot stones to the entrance to bring theminto the hut. The doctor, already sitting inside, checks the placement of the red-hot stones and may use a small horn to help place them in the pit.

The first four stones symbolize the four directions of the circle of life; the next three represent heaven, earth, and the center of the universe. The onlysource of light inside the hut is provided by the faint glow of the red-hot stones. Participants take turns pouring ladles of water and incenses on therocks, creating intense heat inside. This expands all the senses and opens them up to the natural elements.

Afterwards, the ceremonial leader then asks each person to pray aloud, oneafter another. In many tribes, a dip in cold water follows the warmth of the hut. Fire, water or their combination are used for purification throughout North America.

Natural hot springs and steam caves also have a sacred connotation as theyare filled with the breath of Mother Earth and are universally considered avenues of access to the spirit.

This ceremony represents a physical and spiritual purification and is an opportunity to commune with the forces of nature: earth, water, fire and airand the Great Spirit who created them. When people are in the sweat lodge,they are said to be in the hands of the gods.

With this practice participants "sweat away" illness, negativity, and all formsof physical, emotional, mental, or spiritual obstruction making room for Truth. The sweat lodge is also a powerful purification after a painful experience such as the death of a loved one and to renew our faith in the Spirit in times of difficulty.

In addition, this ceremony is a powerful place to pray: a person can participate in the ceremony in order to pray for a specific purpose, for example: the welfare of children, protection from misfortune, peace in the country or the world, or victory during times of war. Finally, the sweat lodgeis also considered a healing intervention in itself.

Negative energies (including spells), fears, insecurities, alienation, and apathy exude and dissipate in the steam. The intensity of the sweat helps participants express their prayers in a direct and powerful way, while the prayers of othersenter more deeply into the soul. It is reasonable to assume that the heat itself has a direct effect on the participants' bodies. In fact, it can act as a sterilization process by killing bacteria, viruses, and other organisms that thrive at body temperature. In addition, heat simulates fever, the body's physiological reaction to a state of discomfort, dilates blood vessels and stimulates circulation, increases heart rate.

Yuwipi - The Rite of the Sacred Stone

The origin of the Rite of the Sacred Stone dates back to ancient times, beforethe arrival of Whopi, the White Bison Woman. This complex ceremony is also much discussed because of some "paranormal" phenomena that can occur during its performance. Yuwipi is celebrated by the Yuwipi Man - The Dreamer of Stones - a shaman specialized in finding lost beings and things. He operates with the help of the most ancient deity of the Lakota, Tunka. His intervention, during this ritual, is invoked for a peculiarity: he is omniscient. He is the most ancient Being on Earth.

According to the legend, Tunka fell from Heaven, in the form of a Rock, before our globe was inhabited by other living beings. He is privy to all secrets, and can give indications as to where and how to find lost people andlost objects. Tunka is the innermost imperishable essence of the Creator, uncreated, without beginning or end.

Everything has a birth and a death, but Tunka was never born and will never die. Tunka is the Spirit that fell from the sky. He is a rock. He knows all the secrets. He finds what has been lost."

(R. Erdoes - Crying for a Dream - Ed. Xenia)

In the Lakota language there are two masculine terms to indicate the rock: inyan (stone) and tunka (rock). Tunkashila, Grandfather, is another way to invoke Wakan Tanka. Whoever wishes to know something about a missing person or wants to find a lost object must ask for the intervention of the Yuwipi Man.

His request must be formal, accompanied by a Sacred Pipe and the precise verbal commitment, to provide for the preparation of the banquet that follows the ritual.

In a room, or tepee, the participants and the requestor sit in a circle. The shaman is wrapped, from head to toe, in a blanket bearing the design of a star. He is then tied with ropes or strips of skin, so as to look like a large cocoon, and then laid, face down, on the ground, in the center of the circle.

The lights are turned off and in complete darkness lights are seen flashing, resplendent stones fly, sounds, chants and noises are heard. At the end of the ceremony, the lights come back on and the shaman is completely free from his cocoon and his bonds. Finally, he is ready to report the information he received from Tunka during his shamanic journey. The whole thing ends with the meat banquet.

Hanblecheya – Vision Quest

This individual ritual is practiced for different purposes.

The first Vision Quest normally faced boys at the threshold of puberty, as a transition from childhood to adulthood, to find their identity, name and direction in life. It often preceded a hunting or war enterprise. Even today a Hanblecheya is undertaken to ask for a clarifying vision for the future life, to obtain new spiritual powers, in view of important changes or before facing very difficult trials, such as, for example, the Sun Dance or the Dance of the Spirits.

The aspirant goes to a holy man or to one who is authorized to conduct a Vision Quest, makes his request and indicates the period he wishes to remain in solitary prayer. The Hanblecheya may last from one to four full days and nights. Throughout the period, the aspirant takes in neither food nor water.

Before undertaking this ritual, the aspirant purifies himself by participating in four Inipi. He chooses his place, prepares 405 tobacco offerings, tied on a single thread, which will serve as the enclosure of his sacred circle where he will remain for as long as he indicates. On the day of the beginning of the Hanblecheya, the aspirant goes to the sweat lodge and receives further instructions, prays for the success of the undertaking and is given water to drink for the last time. At the end of the second door he goes out and from that moment on he does not speak or look at anything or anybody: he does not belong to the physical world anymore, he enters himself and turns totally to the Spirit World. He is accompanied to the place chosen by him and is entrusted to the Great Spirit.

He is left alone for the period of time indicated by him.

At the end of the time he is taken back, enters the Inipi and at that point he can begin to speak and tell about his experience and receives water to drink. At the second opening he comes out and thus ends his Vision Quest. Outside the sweat lodge he is refreshed, thirst quenched and a small feast awaits him with an exchange of gifts.

The Sacred Pipe

The "Sacred Pipe" is part of a spiritual path used to communicate with the Great Spirit. With the pipe you mix the power of your breath with the breath of nature represented by the tobacco plant.

The Pipe is sacred only if it has been blessed by an elder and can only be given to people who have performed courageous acts and good deeds towards others. For example, raising ten orphans, volunteering in a hospice, bringing peace among people or countries, saving soldiers during an ambush or risking one's reputation to defend the truth. In short, the most important values that make a person worthy of receiving this instrument are integrity and responsibility. Not everyone can receive the Sacred Pipe, but anyone can be invited to smoke it during a Ceremony. Some pipes, however, are referred to as "War Pipes," and are smoked to propitiate success in battle.

The spirits, like humans, love tobacco, and have put it on earth to help people and communicate with each other, but also with nature and the Creator. Many native tribes believe that tobacco acts as an intermediary between the human, natural and spiritual worlds. Tobacco is a sacred herb of prayer. Its smoke is offered to the spirits to express gratitude in exchange for their protection.

The importance of tobacco is such that legend has it that Father Sky and Mother Earth planned the creation of the world while smoking tobacco. After lighting the tobacco, with the first puff, one thinks about a good purpose or making a prayer, with the second puff, one quiets the mind and rests. With the third puff, you may receive enlightenment: such as an image, a word spoken by the spirit, or an intuitive feeling. Many stops smoking altogether or begin smoking only on special occasions, when they are in a prayerful mood. Also, many regular smokers manage to get rid of their addiction because they consider the use of tobacco something sacred that brings them closer to the Great Spirit.

Native Dances

Dances have always been significant in the lives of Native Americans, both as common entertainment and as a solemn duty. Many dances played a vital role in religious rituals and other ceremonies, while others were held to ensure the success of hunting, harvesting, thanksgiving and other celebrations.

Commonly, these Indian dances were held in a large structure or open field around a fire. The movements of the participants illustrated the purpose of the American Indian ritual dance, expressing prayer, victory, thanksgiving, mythological stories, and more. Sometimes a leader was chosen; in others, a specific individual, such as a war chief or medicine man, led the ritual dance.

Many tribes danced only to the sound of a drum and their own voices, while other native tribes, also incorporated bells and rattles into the ritual dances. Some Amrican Indian dances included solos, while others included songs with a leader and chorus. Participants could be part of the entire tribe or just specific to men, women or families.

In addition to public dances, there were private and semi-public dances for healing, prayer, initiation, storytelling, and courtship.

Dancing, cultural and ritual dances, continue to be an important part of Native American culture. Dances are regionally or tribally specific and singers usually perform in their native languages. Depending on the dance, sometimes visitors are welcomed while, in other cases, the ceremonies remain private.

This list of American Indian ritual dances is far from all-inclusive, as there are literally hundreds of dances and variations throughout the Americas.

Associative Dances Dance of Fantasy The Ghost Dance Snake Dance

The Rain Dance

Stomp Dance Sun Dance Dance of War Pumpkin Dance Grass Dance Hoop Dance

Associative dances

There are several semi-religious festivals or ceremonies, with a large number of participants, that are handed down from one tribe to another. One of the best-known examples is the Omaha or grass dance, also practiced by the Arapaho, Pawnee, Omaha, Dakota, Crow, Gros Ventre, Assiniboin, and Blackfoot tribes.

Its symbols are traced to the Pawnee, who taught the dance to the Dakota Sioux around 1870. The Sioux, in turn, shared it with the Arapaho and Gros Ventre, who taught it to the Blackfoot. Later, the Blackfoot brought the Omaha dance to the Flathead and Kootenai tribes to the west.

Meetings of these native tribes were held at night, in large circular wooden buildings built for that purpose. Some of the dancers wore large feathered headdresses called "raven belts" and a special headdress made of hair.

Members of some of these tribes, were often known for helping the poor and practicing acts of self-denial.

Other dances, such as Creek dancing, pumpkin dancing, and horse dancing, are known to belong to other tribes and villages. However, from tribe to tribe, each has its own distinct ceremonies and songs, to which additions are made from year to year.

Fantasy Dance

The Fantasy Dance was created by members of the Ponca tribe in the 1920's and 1930's to preserve their culture and religion. During that time, Native American ritual dances, were outlawed by the United States and Canadian governments. Traditional dances became secret to avoid problems with the government.

However, this dance, loosely based on traditional war dance, was considered appropriate for visitors to "Wild West" shows. The Ponca tribe soon built its own dance arena at White Eagle, Oklahoma.

Other tribes continued the practice and created new dances that could be legally danced in public. In the 1930s, the Kiowa and Comanche created new dance styles for this dance without backstory.

In the late 1930's, women also began to perform the fantasy dance.

The dance is fast, colorful, and very energetic, often including tricks and extremely athletic movements. The dance costume includes brightly colored feather headdresses and belts, beaded bodices, leggings, shawls and moccasins. Dresses are also decorated with fringe, feathers, embroidery or ribbon and other rich designs and materials. Beaded cuffs, chokers, earrings, bracelets and eagle feathers are also worn.

Ghost Dance - A Promise of Fulfillment

The Ghost Dance (Natdia) is a spiritual movement that originated in the late 1880's when conditions were bad for Native Americans and they needed something to give them hope. This movement originated with a Paiute Indian named Wovoka, who proclaimed himself to be the messiah come to earth to prepare the Indians for their salvation.

Snake Dance

The most widespread Hopi ritual is the Snake Dance, held annually in late August, during which performers dance with live snakes in their mouths. The dance is thought to have originated as a water ceremony because snakes were the traditional guardians of the springs. Today, it is primarily a rain ceremony, serving to honor Hopi ancestors. The tribe considers the snakes to be their "brothers" and rely on them to bring their prayers for rain to the gods and spirits of their ancestors.

The Snake Dance requires two weeks of ritual preparation, during which the snakes are collected and watched over by children, until the time of the dance. On the last day of the 16-day celebration, the Snake Dance is performed.

Due to the local population's percentage of snakes, most are rattlesnakes, but all types of snakes are freely included.

Before the dance begins, participants take an emetic (probably sedative herb) and dance with the snakes in their mouths. There is usually a priest "of the Antelope" who helps with the dance, sometimes stroking the snakes with a feather.

The dance includes swaying, rattling, a guttural chant and a tour across the square with the snakes.

After the dance, the snakes are released in the four directions to carry the dancers' prayers to nature spirits and ancestors. Although part of the Snake Dance is performed for the tribe, this is only one part of a long ceremony, most of which is conducted privately in kivas.

Although the dance was once open to the public, it is now only open to tribal members due to the disrespectful way tourists take photos and the lack of respect for Hopi traditions and ceremonial practices.

Rain Dance

The rain ceremonial dance is performed by many agricultural populations, especially in the Southwest, where summers can be extremely dry. The ceremony was performed to ask the spirits or gods, to send rain for the tribes' crops. The dance usually takes place during the spring planting season and before the crops are harvested. However, it was also performed at times when rain was desperately needed.

One aspect that makes the rain dance unique from some other ceremonial dances is that both men and women participate in the ceremony. The dance varies from tribe to tribe, each with their own unique rituals and costumes. Some tribes wear large headdresses while others wear masks. Accessories often include body paint, beads, animal skins, horse and goat hair, feathers, embroidered aprons, and leather, silver, and turquoise jewelry.

Feathers and the color blue are often found in clothing and accessories, symbolizing wind and rain, respectively. These special robes and accessories, which were worn during the rain dance, were generally not worn at other times of the year, but rather were kept for this specific ceremony, as is still the case today.

The dance steps usually involve moving in a zigzag pattern, as opposed to other ceremonial dances that involve standing in a circle, perhaps jumping in place.

Stories of the origins of ceremonial dances have been passed down orally from generation to generation. When Native Americans were relocated in the 19th century, the U.S. government banned some tribal ceremonial dances. In some regions, tribal members would tell federal authorities that they were performing a "rain dance" rather than reveal the fact that they were actuallyperforming one of the banned ceremonies.

Although the rain dance was most often performed by tribes in the Southwestsuch as the Puebloan, Hopi, Zuni, and Apache, other tribes also celebrated the rain dance, including the Cherokee in the southeastern United States.

Many tribes continue to celebrate this ceremony today.

Stomp Dance

The stomp dance, is followed by various tribes of the Eastern Woodlands, including Muscogee Creek, Yuchi, Cherokee, Chickasaw, Choctaw, Caddo, Delaware, Miami, Ottawa, Peoria, Shawnee, Seminole, Natchez and Seneca-Cayuga, the Stomp Dance is a ceremony that contains both social and religious significance.

The term "Stomp Dance" is an English term, referring to the "shuffle and stomp" movements of the dance. In Muskogee's native language, the dance iscalled Opvnkv Haco, which can mean "drunken," "crazy" or "inspired" dance, referring to the healing effect the dance has on participants.

These dances are generally performed several times during the summermonths to ensure the well-being of the community.

Performed by men and women, these events may include about 30 or moreperformances, each sung by a different leader and may also include other dances such as the Duck Dance, Friendship Dance or Bean Dance.

When a leader begins, they circle the sacred fire and are followed in a singleline by those who wish to participate. Leading the dancers counterclockwisearound the fire, participants chant, shake rattles, and dance with a stomping, pounding step. Men and women alternate positions behind the leader, organizing themselves by age and ability, with younger and less experienced dancers at the end of the line.

The "pounded" dance typically begins after dark and continues until dawn thenext day. Participants who have a religious commitment will begin the fast after midnight and are required to stay up all night. The "medicine" taken by participants consists of roots and plants collected and ceremonially preparedby a Healer shaman. The dance continues until the sun rises, at which point the event is over.

Sun Dance

The Sun Dance is primarily practiced by tribes found in the Great Plains andRocky Mountain areas. This annual ceremony, is usually performed on the summer solstice, with preparations beginning up to a year before the ceremony.

Although the dance is practiced differently, by different tribes, the Eagle serves as a central symbol in the dance, helping to bring the body and spirit together in harmony, just as the buffalo, because of its essential role in food,becomes a symbol of the clothing and shelter built by the American Indians of the Plains.

Apache Sun Dance

Many ceremonies have features in common, such as specific dances and songs passed down through many generations, the use of the traditional drum, pipe prayers, offerings, fasting, and in some cases ceremonial piercing of the skin, which is done by making two cuts in the chest below the largest muscles, into which pieces of bone are introduced and to which leather laces are attached.

Although not all sun dance ceremonies include ritually pierced dancers, the object of the sun dance is to offer personal sacrifices as a prayer for the benefit of one's family and community. The pain endured until the dancer passes out are the personal sacrifice each participant gives to the tribe.

In the late 1800s, the United States government attempted to suppress the SunDance. The Cheyenne ceremony became secret, only to resurface in the 20th century.

In August 1890, the Kiowa Sun Dance was discontinued, by order of the U.S. Army. However, in September of that year the first Spirit Dance was held, and for many years it took the place of the Sun Dance.

The last Ponca Sun Dance was held in 1908. The government's policy of suppression, ended with the issuance of the Indian Religious Circular of 1934 for Indian culture, and from then on, the sun dances continued to be held uninterruptedly, it can be said really in the sunlight.

War Dance

Many tribes would practice a war dance the night before an attack, to observecertain religious rituals to ensure the success of the operation. Warriors would participate in the war dance, thinking about the suffering they might suffer if they were captured, filling their minds with urges for success to prepare for battle.

Although war dances vary from tribe to tribe, there are commonalities amongmany of them, including singing, often extending over a full day and night, interspersed with prayers, use of sacred objects or bundles, and occasional dancing. Sweat lodge rituals or other purification ceremonies were also oftenpracticed, incense was burned, faces were painted, and a pipe was often passed among the participants.

Generally, the only musical instruments used in these ceremonies were rattles, drums, and whistles. In the Pacific Northwest, the Pueblos of the Southwest, and the Iroquois of the Wooded Lands, participants were often dressed and masked to represent the various deities or supernatural creaturesthat acted out parts of the ritual.

The name of war dance, vary among Indian communities, with the fantasy dance incorporating the war dance rituals of the Kiowa, Cheyenne, Arapaho, Comanche and Kiowa - Apache tribes.

For the Shoshone and Arapaho tribes, the wolf is symbolically linked to a warrior and the ritual is called a "wolf dance." The Omaha dance of the Lakota Sioux is named after the Omaha tribe, who taught the dance to the Lakota, and the war dance is known to the Paiute tribe of Utah as the FancyBustle, referring to a part of the dancers' costume.

Pumpkin Dance

Believed to have originated with the Kiowa tribe, the pumpkin dance is oftenheld to coincide with a Pow-Wow, although it consists of unique dance techniques and history.

Kiowa legend says that while a man was alone on a journey, he heard an unusual song coming from the other side of a hill. Upon investigating, hediscovered that the song came from a red wolf dancing on its hind legs.

After listening to more songs throughout the night, the next morning the wolftold him to take the songs and dance back to the Kiowa people. "The howl" atthe end of each pumpkin dance song is a tribute to the red wolf. The pumpkindance, in the Kiowa language is called "Ti-ah pi-ah" which means "ready to go, ready to die".

The Comanche and Cheyenne also have legends about the pumpkin dance.The ceremony soon spread to other tribes and societies.

The dance is performed by men but women can participate by dancing in place behind the men and outside the circular arena. The drum may be placedon the side or in the center of the circle and the dancers perform around the perimeter of the area, usually dancing in place.

The dance is simple, with participants lifting their heels with the beat of the drum and shaking their rattles. The dress is also not elaborate, with belts being worn by the dancers, either around the waist or draped around the neck, reaching to the ground. Despite the bans mentioned above, several tribes haveresurrected the dance today. Some pumpkin societies do not distinguish race as a criterion for joining, allowing even non-Native Americans to be includedin their pumpkin societies. However, the Kiowa only allow members who arehalf blood or more. Today during Pow-Wows, the gourd dance generally occurs before the Great Entry. The rattles used in Pow-Wows are not made from a gourd, but rather a tin or silver cylinder filled with beads on a beaded handle.

Grass Dance

The grass dance, is one of the oldest and most widely used dances in NativeAmerican culture, it was the job of the grass dancers, to flatten the grass in the arena before other important celebrations. However, the name "grass" does not come from stomping the ground but, rather, from the old custom oftying braids of sweet grass to the dancer's belts, which produced a swaying effect.

Traditionally only a male dance, it is thought that the tradition of this dance,began with the Indians of the northern plains, particularly the Omaha-Ponca and Dakota Sioux. An ancient legend has it that it was created by a boy from the northern plains who was handicapped and wished to dance.

After consulting a medicine man, he was instructed to seek inspiration on the prairie. Following the advice, he went alone to the plains where he had a vision of himself dancing in the style of swaying grasses. When he returned to the camp, he shared his vision and told himself that he was eventually able to use his legs, performing the first grass dance.

In addition to its practical purpose, another goal of the dance is to honor and respect the ancestors and to gain spiritual strength from their mother earth. A popular dance today in which men and women participate, the dance is full of color and movement.

The dancers resemble a swaying multicolored mass of yarn or fringe that represents grass.

As the dancers move in fluid, bending positions following the rhythm of the music, their positions replicate the movement of the grass blowing in the wind breeze. Today's dance is largely inter-tribal, thanks to its longevity, in part, to a modernization of ceremonies fostered by the oppression of the early twentieth century. Special blessings are bestowed not only on dancers but also on observers.

Hoop Dance

Going back for centuries, the Hoop Dance is a narrative dance that includes the use of 1 to 40 hoops to create static and dynamic shapes. These formations represent the movements of various animals and other narrative elements.

In its earliest form, the dance is believed to have been part of a healing ceremony designed to restore balance and harmony in the world. With no beginning or end, the circle represents the infinite circle of life. Circles, usually made of reeds or wood, are used to create symbolic shapes, including butterflies, turtles, eagles, flowers, and snakes.

There are several accounts of how the circle dance came about. Some say the Creator gave a set of wooden hoops and the "dance" to a dying man from the northern plains who wanted a gift to leave behind. Another story in the Southwest says the hoops are developed by cliff dwellers so that children would learn dexterity.

A more important legend that has the Circle Dance, originating in the Anishinaabe culture, tells of the time when an otherworldly spirit came into the world to live among the people. The boy showed no interest in typical boy activities, such as running and hunting, preferring to be alone and watch animals. This forced his father to avoid him, leading the boy to be recognized by the name Pukawiss: the disowned or unwanted.

However, the boy continued to observe the movements of eagles, bears, snakes, and birds, and before long he was moving like an eagle in flight, hopping through the grass like a rabbit, thus creating the Circle Dance to teach other Indians about the ways animals move and live. Before long, Pukawiss became so popular that every village wanted to learn the dance.

Today, the Hoop Dance remains popular. It is generally performed by a solodancer, who begins with a single circle, evoking the circle of life. Additionalcircles are added, representing other elements of life, including humans, animals, wind, water, and seasons. The dance incorporates very rapid movements in which the circles are made to interlock and extend from the body, forming appendages such as wings and tails.

Practiced by a number of tribes today, this dance has evolved over the years,becoming faster and incorporating many non-traditional influences. It has also become a highly competitive event, with the first World Hoop Dance Competition held at the New Mexico State Fair in 1991. Today, the most popular competition is held annually at the Heard Museum in Phoenix, Arizona.

The Medicine Wheel for Self-understanding

The main purpose of the medicine wheel is to be a multidimensional symbolic tool for making connections with Cosmic Powers and natural energies in order to create balance between the individual and Nature. Itworks on all levels and can be used to achieve several specific goals.

Below, we will go into the main purpose of the medicine wheel, which is to understand oneself through a process of harmonization with natural energies.

As a shape, it is represented by a cross inside a circle. The circle represents the totality of the space of the entire universe, as well as our personal spaceboth inside and outside. It is a universal mandala, a source of benefit for all humanity, not only for the Native Americans who honored and preserved it.

The medicine wheel is a catalyst capable of producing change, as well asintegrating segments and aspects into a coordinated unity.

Therefore, it combines the components of the human being that are mistakenly considered separate (body, mind, soul, spirit), to make them workin unison, and pursues the goal of bringing us into harmonious relationship with other beings and with the entire universe.

Our responsibility as human beings is to understand that life on the outsidecorresponds with life on the inside, and consequently, to transform the outside, we must transform the inside.

The purpose of the medicine wheel is to generate change within the individual, so that harmonious changes can take place in his or her externalreality.

We are first and foremost responsible for ourselves as individuals.

If it is built outdoors, eight stones delimit the circumference indicating the cardinal and non-cardinal points, symbolizing the universal forces and the individual, arranged in a balanced way, testifying to the Cosmic Law of harmony and theeighths. Inside, eight other stones create a smaller circle, representing the sources of inner forces.

This symbol is constructed in such a way as to indicate an approach to life inharmony with the spirit, an approach that implies a willingness to participateand cooperate on all levels of being and in all planes of existence.

It serves to promote balance, harmony, and beauty within the environment inwhich we find ourselves, and to use the energy to express ourselves.

Harmony is a force that places the development of the individual in balancewith that of the whole.

The four cardinal points are four powerful forces, Cosmic Intelligences whose presence influences all animate beings, as well as the environment andthe earth's atmosphere.

These intelligences belong to a dimension that transcends physical and mental reality. They generate movement, and influence the nature of eventsthat are about to manifest. In some cultures they were even worshiped as gods.

Some indigenous tribes of America referred to them as "Guardian Spirits," for their role as guardians of the universe. They were considered benevolententities, despite being endowed with extraordinary powers. To represent them, and to offer at the same time symbolic connectors, totems were used. The totem of the North is the Buffalo, an animal that provided the natives with everything they needed to survive, a symbol of compact strength.

The totem of the West is the Grizzly, emblem of inner strength and introspection. The totem of the East is the Eagle, the bird which is consideredable to fly closer to the Sun, symbol of light.

The totem of the south is the Rat, a tiny animal associated to fast growth, which reminds man of the importance of not judging strength according tophysical size.

Everything that, through a mystical, magical or metaphysical system, is associated to a cardinal force, connects it to an expression of energy andinfluences its action. Sooner or later, each individual experiences the consequences of this association. The cardinal point, therefore, acquiresconsiderable relevance, as well as the motive and the intention.

BOOK 14 The Native AmericanPractices Part II

Sacred Rituals and Ceremonies to beconnected with Nature and all its Elements and Creatures

Connection with Cardinal Points

If we harmonize and cooperate with the Forces of Nature, our surroundings will support and sustain us. If, on the contrary, we interfere with Nature, or let ourselves be guided by selfishness, source of chaos and dishonesty, we contribute to the imbalance of the environment, with disastrous consequences. So how can we connect to the cardinal points, and recognize their powers?

North, on the Medicine Wheel, is placed at the top of the circle. The perspective is that of an observer viewing the North Star from the earth.

East is on the right, West on the left, and South at the bottom.

It is possible to perceive the energy of each of the cardinal points and receive personal teaching by connecting to them through the following practices:

Connection to the North Force

On a full moon night go outside, locate the North Star, and line up with its direction so that you face North.

Focus on the North Star and bring your attention to the imperceptible movement of the entire galaxy around that seemingly tiny pivot.

Connect to the Northern Force. You can do this by simply expressing a firm intention to will it, with confident expectation. Among the qualities of this force is the expression of renewal. This connection will activate in you the ability to be reborn, to start from scratch, leaving the past behind and regenerating yourself completely.

Be receptive, keep your mind open and your body relaxed, ready to accept the information that comes. Be open to receive any sensation. Let the Northern Force energize you. Allow this energy to remove blocks and conditioning that have limited you in the past, and have prevented you from seeing reality for what it is. Allow the quality of clarity brought by the North to be integrated into you.

When you feel that you have finished, give thanks and write down all the information and feelings that you have received from the experience and any lessons learned.

Connection to the West Force

For this practice you need to be outdoors at the time when you can observe the Sunset.

Facing West, watch the Sun as it sets behind the horizon, relax, allow the warm, embracing red light and golden colors to permeate you, and connect with the Force of the West.

The West possesses, among others, the quality of transformation. Be touched by the Force that brings change, which will allow you to transform into a new and more complete version of yourself.

Try to get in touch with the sensations and experience the change without the filter of the rational mind, letting yourself be guided by perception.

You can ask the Force of the West to give you a teaching about transformation and remain receptive waiting for the answer, which may come to you through an intuition, an image, a word or a physical sensation. In the meantime, when the Sun has fully set and night has replaced day, you can return to your home and transcribe the messages and teachings you have received from the experience.

Connection to the East Force

Get up before dawn and get outdoors, in a quiet place and in touch with Nature. Face East, standing up, and stay listening to the night's stillness.

Let the silence envelop you and pay attention to the noises. Just before the sun rises, you will hear the songs of birds announcing the arrival of the newday. As soon as the horizon begins to brighten, connect with the Eastern Force, and let the vitality of the dawn and the rising Sun fill you. Feel the force rising within you and illuminating the dark areas of your life.

One of the qualities of the Eastern Force is illumination.

Pray to her to enlighten you with teaching in the form of intuition, image, word or sensation so that you can expand your awareness. At the end, transcribe your experience and the information you received, remembering tosay thankyou.

Connection to the South Force

Head to an open space surrounded by Nature around noon. Place yourself in a southerly direction, the point where the Sun is at noon. With relaxed attention, raise your left arm, as if to touch the Sun with your hand. A gentle movement is all that is needed, so no effortor tension is required.

Simply connect to the Southern Force, so that you feel its energy and luminosity. As you inhale, notice the inner warmth and flow of energy from the outside to the inside of you. Continue to breathe for a few minutes in thisposition, then lower your arm and bring it back along your side.

One of the characteristics of the South is adaptability. Ask the Southern Forceto help you glide more smoothly through the path of life, to adapt with ease to different circumstances. Ask it to give you the flexibility to flow through changes with ease, and to suggest how to develop intuition.

At the end, put in writing the feelings and messages you have received.

The forces of these Guardian Spirits respond according to the motive and intention with which they are summoned, and according to the vision of thenatives, each of them generates a movement within each quadrant of the Medicine Wheel, and has an influence on the development of our entire being.

Among them, the Force of the West also activates the intelligence of the physical body, allowing it to interact with the substances that form our bodystructure.

The Northern Force enlightens and purifies the mental aspect.

The Southern Force strengthens and invigorates the intuitive "Self".

The Eastern Force brings flashes of inspiration from the most intimate andtrue "Self", that is, from the most conscious and noble part of our being.

The Four Forces and Colors

In the medicine wheel, each of the four forces is associated with a color.

North - WhiteWest - Black East - YellowSouth - Red

Color is a vibratory expression of the intrinsic qualities of each force, and ittoo has an impact on the human energy system.

The Spirits of the directions are intangible creative forces, inaccessible to thehuman intellect with which shamans can make contact. Below are the essential characteristics of the Spirits of Directions, the totems associated with them, and the areas of influence on human beings

Force of the North

Color: White

Totem: Buffalo Keyquality: Intelligence

Influence: Purity and Intensity Main human aspect: Mind Strength of:

Regenerationacceleration purity

clarity

Force of the West

Color: Black

Totem: Grizzly bear Core Quality: Resistance Influence: stability

Main human aspect: physical bodyStrength of:

consolidation foundation introspection transformation

Force of the East

Color: Yellow

Totem: Eagle

Key quality: foresight Influence: spirituality Core human aspect: SpiritStrength of:

awakening enlightenment

dispelling darkness and ignorance

rebirth

Force of the south

Color: Red

Totem: Mouse

Key quality: closenessInfluence: vitality

Main human aspect: emotionsStrength of:

receptivity

feeling intuition discoverygrowth

Wakan Tanka

The movement indicated by the Medicine Wheel, which goes counterclockwise from the North to the West, crosses the East and proceedsclockwise to the South, is spiral in nature.

Represented on a two-dimensional circle, it results in an S-shaped figure, a symbol for Native Americans of Wakan Tanka, the Great Spirit in Manifestation. It is represented as it rises from the Mind of the Great Spirit inthe North, and then heads West, manifesting itself by means of physical form,to reach the East.

Here it is activated by Spirit and moves south, where it lives as a child of Nature, and thus gives to the Spirit the opportunity to experience expressionin matter.

This symbol also indicates the movement of energy into form, and of form into energy. Combining the North polarity with the South polarity, the shapeS becomes a new symbol, a figure of eight, the twin circle of movement between two polarities: the physical and the spiritual, the visible and the invisible, mind and matter, feminine and masculine, in an eternal continuity of existence.

The Four Elements

The elements, Energetic Beings responsible for the substance and structure ofmatter, thanks to which energies can take a form and physically manifest themselves, are transformational processes endowed with spacific qualities, and with their own intelligence, since their motion is guided by the Spirit.

Each Element has a direct influence on the physical, mental and spiritualprocesses of human beings. To be in harmony with them, it is therefore essential to understand them.

Trying to manipulate or control them would have negative consequences.According to Western mystical traditions, there are four Elements:

Water

Air Earth Fire

They were considered fundamental components of everything that exists inphysical reality. They are metaphysical principles that determine the manifestation of matter.

In any case the Elements represent movements of energy, indicators of atransformation and transmutation of energy.

Sometimes they were represented with a cross included in a circle, as symbolof balance and stability.

Every Element was associated with a Cardinal Point, as an indication of a mode of action related to a Cardinal Force, more than a special arrangementin itself.

The association of Air with North, Water with South, Fire with East andEarth with West, represents a balanced and harmonic approach.

Every Element is Spirit.

The four Elements contributed from the origins to shape the substance and the structure of planet Earth, from the moment when it started to manifest itself, and are still involved in the organization and constitution process of everything is about of taking a form.

Every Element has its own qualities and characteristics.

Fire is creative, expansive, explosive, transformative, vigorous Water is fluid, adaptable, subject to contraction and dispersion Air is boundless, endless, fast, unpredictable

Earth is stable, patient, nurturing, tenacious

Every Element is predominant in each of the four bodies of the human being:

The Earth Element predominates in the physical body The Water Element predominates in the energy body

Element Air predominates in the mental body The Fire Element predominates in the Soul

Each Element governs an aspect of Life:

Earth is the substance of Life Water is the flow or river of Life Air is the breath of Life

Fire is the spark of Life

The Spirits of the Elements, arranged in classes possess spatial expressions of Self: the Elementals. These can be seen as the builders who operate on an unconscious level, putting into practice the project of the Elements, which operate on a level that transcends consciousness.

Elementals don't have a physical body, but can appear to man in the form of images.

The Elements are creative and constructive intelligences emanating from the Great Spirit, operating in a dynamic relationship in Nature, each expressing a quality of movement.

The Animal Totems

In Native American traditions, each Element was associated with an Animal Totem, which, in addition to allowing for a deeper understanding of its fundamental properties, also served as a connector.

For Native Americans, Fire was associated with the Eagle and the Sparrowhawk, both because they flew very high, metaphorically close to the Sun, and because in their mythology, they were associated with Thunder and Lightning. The Sparrowhawk, symbolizes understanding and immediacy, like the sudden flash of lightning, and the power of transformation. Therefore, the Fire Element, the Sparrowhawk andthe Eagle, are bearers of inspiration, generators of enthusiasm, source of purification and invigoration.

The Frog represents the Water Element, because of itsadaptability and ability to adjust to environmental changes, from water to land. The Water Element, therefore, is a Spirit that has qualities of adaptability, flexibility, sensitivity.

The Turtle is the Totem Animal associated with the Element of Earth for its characteristics of solidity and inertia. Like its animaltotem, the Earth Element is distinguished by qualities of endurance and tenacity.

Air is associated with the Butterfly, because of the constant changes in movement typical of this insect. The Air Element has theability to constantly change movement and modify the environment accordingly.

Totems are tangible means of connection with intangible forces, very effective in offering immediate access to the intrinsic characteristics of thecorresponding element.

The association of an animal Totem to an Element allows to enter more easilyin contact with it and to integrate its essential qualities.

Connection with the Four Elements

At this point, we can find out how to connect to the four Elements. We will begin with Air, as it, on the Medicine Wheel, is associated with the North andthe qualities of clarity and renewal, that we want to integrate internally.

On the Medicine Wheel the North is the place of Renewal, because the Strength of the North is that ability to start something from scratch, which comes from being able to see clearly what was not understood or perceived inthe past. Air is an Element in constant activity and movement, it is unpredictable, unexpected, stimulating and revitalizing. For these qualities it is associated to thought and mind.

To realize the following experience, it is necessary to return to a place undisturbed and known, with notebook, pen, rattle and a bag for the offering

Connection with the Air Element

Upon reaching your chosen location, walkaround shaking the rattle and let it lead you to a point where you can connect to the Air. In the meantime, try to collect an object connected with an animal from the North. A bird feather, a tuft of fox hair, or a tuft of horsehair will do.This will help you discover what you need among the gifts the Universe has to offer, accompanying you like an assistant.

The goal to keep in mind is to renew your Life and begin a new and exciting phase that will lead to transformation and fulfillment.

Interrupt the rattle music, sit with the symbolic object clutched in your left hand, above your navel. Hold your right hand over your left hand. In this way connect the object with the center of your energy system and your connection to the Whole.

Ask that you be granted the wisdom to understand the nature of Receiving, which on the Medicine Wheel corresponds to the North. Receiving is not to be confused with getting or taking. Stand by for a response in an attitude of attentiveness and observation. The answer may come to you from the flight of birds in the sky, the wind or the clouds. Then note the teaching you have received.

Now connect more intensely with the Air element, feel the Freedom. Remember that the contact is between your Spirit and the Spirit of the Element and the reason is Love and Harmony.

Allow your senses to experience being Air, feel its delicate touch through the breeze, consider its incredible Strength. Listen to the sound of Air in the Wind. Smell its freshness. Absorb it. Let it invigorate you, let it stimulate you.

Now ask the Air Spirit to teach you about the idea of yourself, and to clarify thoughts about yourself that are not authentic, because they come from a part of you that is not your real and authentic "I". These are thoughts that have prevented you from realizing your potential and that have held you back, because they have weakened and reduced your self-esteem, minimized your value and deprived you of inner strength.

When you have identified the limiting mental conditioning, you can get rid of the old idea of yourself, and give your life a renewal boost. Relaxed but alert, observe what the Air is trying to reveal to you. What is he telling you?

Listen to the murmur of the wind. Watch how the air moves. From which cardinal point does it come? In which direction? What is it trying to show you through these nonverbal signals?

Reflect carefully and transcribe your experience in your notebook. Then scatter your offering to the wind and give it to the Northern Force in gratitude for the revelations you have received.

Turning your gaze toward the horizon in a northerly direction, ask yourself, "How can I be greater than what I think I am?"

Take note of the response, then spread an offering around again to thank the Air Element and the Northern Spirit.

Now, on the Medicine Wheel, move to the West, to activate the power of transformation, that is, to change what is into what can be. This is the process of developing potentialities through Becoming.

The West is associated with the physical body, the material aspects of life, the Mineral Kingdom, and the conservation of Energy. On the Medicine Wheel it is the place of Introspection, where the Force from within is found.

In the West we connect to the Element Earth, and the qualities of stability, solidity, nourishment and power of manifestation.

For the following experience, go back to your place, in Nature, with notebook, pen, rattle, and a pocket for offering.

Connection with the Earth Element

While you are looking for a place to sit in the trees, gently shake the rattle. Find a stone to hold in your hand. Choosethe one you feel attracted to and ask it to be your assistant.

If you sense that the answer is affirmative, take it with you, in your left hand, while with the right hand you will continue to shake the rattle.

Otherwise, leave the stone where you found it, and go on searching, until theone you'll find will give you a positive answer.

The stone will be your assistant in your journey towards West.

Let the attractive power of a place to conduce you behind or near to a tree. Don't search for it, but let it call you.

When you feel you have found the right place, play the rattle while circling the area, to get in tune with it. Then stop and sit on the ground, facing west, with the stone clutched in your hand.

Establish contact with the Spirit of the Earth Element. Simply formulate theintention. Remember the reasons for the connection: Love and Harmony.

They occur between your Spirit and the Earth Spirit, without the interferenceof the mind. In the beginning you can involve your senses.

What feelings are you experiencing? What feelings are you experiencing, to be like the Earth? What impressions do you have? What does the Earth sound, taste, or smell like?

Write down what you experience.

Observe the stone in your hand. The importance of the West is in the act of Preservation, in guarding the essential, in changing only what is needed for our development. Ask to be shown what, of what you have preserved in your life, hinders you in the path of growth and progress. Identify what keeps you in inertia and what causes the same problem to keep recurring.

It's something you hold onto that keeps you from being free.

Look at the stone, observe its shape carefully and ask it to help you understand what you need to change in order to be free to become who you really are.

Observe the marks, the traces, the conformation. What message do they convey to you? What do they remind you of?

Relate them to you and your life circumstances. Write down the impressions in your notebook. Hold the stone at navel level, with your right hand resting on your left, close your eyes and observe the image of these circumstances inside your mind, as if it were an almost solid energy with a weight that has crushed you downwards. Allow that energy to pass through the stone, to be absorbed and retained. Observe the load leaving you and the feeling of release and relief.

Now bury the stone near where you are sitting so that the Earth can absorb, disperse, or recycle the negative energy.

You are now ready to receive the teaching from the Earth.

Sitting facing west, with your back against a tree, and your legs apart, feet in line with your shoulders, focus on the space of earth between them and ask the Earth Element to communicate to you what you need to learn now.

Remember that your goal is Love and Harmony and your intention is to learn to be more secure and stable inwardly. How can the qualities of this Element help you?

Write down the message you receive and reflect on its meaning.

Next, look at the horizon to the west and formulate the following question four times:

How can I manifest the best version of myself? Write down the answer.

Finally, spread an offering around again to thank the Earth Element and the West Spirit, and play a rattle around the place where you communicated with them.

The following phase of our practice with the Medicine Wheel consists in the movement toward the Center, before reaching the East, because the Center is the point of harmony and balance of Energies.

The connection with the Center can also be made in a quiet place at home, after performing a purification practice.

Before engaging in any activity, you should remove any negative vibrations from the area in which you will be working and from yourself, in the same way that you wash your hands before cooking or eating. Native Americans used sage suffixes to purify the air and the human aura. The act of purification with slowly burning sage was called smudging.

With a bunch of sage, you form a stick and light one end of it. To the sage you can add glyceria or lavender, provided with similar properties.

The smoke released should be dispersed in the environment and pushed towards yourself, towards the chest, on the head and all over the body, including the feet, so as to envelop the entire energy body. Breathe deeply three times in order to inhale it.

For the connection with the Center, choose a time when you can remain quiet and undisturbed in your place, at home. Obtain a candle, incense and a mixture of dried sage and mint, an earthenware bowl, a small fan, a roll of paper, and long matches.

Remember the rattle, notebook and pen. Keep the smudge handy.

Connection with the Center

Light incense or smudge and cleanse the room and yourself, focusing on why you are having this experience of Love and Harmony.

Finally, extinguish the incense and light the candel. Sitting comfortably on the floor or in a chair, play the rattle around you and focus on your goal of contact with the Center. After placing the rattle on the floor, stare into the flame, the symbol of inner light.

The Center is the place of harmonious being, of the Medicine Wheel, where all energies are channeled, where balance can be created and where communication with the Source can take place, for it is the nucleus from which we originated as individuals Authentic individuality is a harmonious fusion with the Whole, not a separation from the Whole, and implies the union of the Self with the entirety of being.

Meditate for a few moments on the flame and the source of inner Light. Bring to light a problem, situation or recurring condition in your life that causes imbalance and that you want to resolve. Once identified, consider its source. Does it stem from some connection, or expectation, or action or omission?

Identify a key word to describe it and write it down on a page torn from your notebook.

You are in the process of freeing yourself from that condition, seeing it in a different light as you surrender it to your inner light. Ask yourself what the condition that afflicts you wants to teach you, what venture it proposes, and allow your inner light to perceive it as an open window to new opportunities.

Wright down the teaching you have received.

This will allow you to free yourself from the resentments, fears, or guilt associated with that condition. Forgive anyone who has caused you pain orsorrow, including yourself.

Offer the written page to the candle flame, and let it all fade away.

Finally, while staring into the flame, repeat the following question four times:When I am at the Center of Myself, am I the creator of my own reality?

The next experience will allow to communicate with the Fire Element, placed in the East on the Medicine wheel. The strength of the East is enlightenment that is the ability to perceive reality from a higher perspective, because the East is the point from which the Sun and Light rise.

East is connected with the Spirit.

Choose an outdoor location where there is a hill or slope from which you cansee the view below. Go there on a sunny day with your notebook, pen, and rattle.

Connection with the Fire Element

Chose a place from which you can observe from above, gently move the rattle, with the intention of connectingwith the Fire Element, and harmonizing your life as best you can with Spirit.

With your eyes on the horizon to the East, ask the Spirit of the East to enlighten you about an aspect of your life that is unclear to you or a situationin which you can find no way out.

Be vigilant and attentive, without clinging to prejudices, for the teaching will come unexpectedly, like a flash of lightning. Take note of what happens.

Turn toward the Sun, and connect with the Fire Element through the Sun. Inhale the solar energy, feel its radiance and expansiveness. Feel the rays on your face, be aware of the clarity it offers you, so you can see what is distant.

Smell the aroma that the warmth of the sun gives off from the surroundingnature. Feel the taste of it. Perceive the Transforming Force of the Sun, of Fire. It's time to ask the Fire Element to enlighten you, to be able to make decisions in harmony with the Spirit and not with the Ego, so that Life cancome into balance with the aims of the Soul.

Write everything down in the notebook and reflect very carefully. Consider that you too are a Sun at the center of your universe of consciousness, in theprocess of understanding its true nature.

It's time to ask the Fire Element to enlighten you, to be able to make decisions in harmony with the Spirit and not with the Ego, so that Life can come into balance with the aims of the Soul.

Write everything down in the notebook and reflect very carefully. Consider that you too are a Sun at the center of your universe of consciousness, in theprocess of understanding its true nature. Four times ask yourself:

Why haven't I discovered who I want to be yet? Write the answer in your notebook.

Offer something of your own, such as some saliva. Thank the East Force and the Fire Element with the rattle before leaving. Over the next few days, meditate on the teaching you received.

Connecting with the Force of the South, you can acquire the disposition to learn, that is, a mind open to accepting new ideas, with an innocent openness to new experiences, as if they were an adventure to be discovered. The South on the Medicine Wheel is referred to as the place of Staying Close. For this experience go near the Water, with the rattle, the notebook, the pen and the offering bag.

Connection with the Water Element

Go to a place near water, from which you can face south. Formulate an intention to have an open mind that allows you to understand a truth about yourself by shaking the rattle and invoking the Southern Force.

On the Medicine Wheel, the element of Water is connected to the Southern Force, and affects the Energetic Body and emotions, is associated with the Vegetal Realm, and is related to the act of Giving.

Sit in front of the Water and focus on the flow, watch the movement carefully and try to tune in to it. Listen to its sound, notice how it adapts to the ground, feel its rhythm. Touch the Water, if you can, and feel its fluidity. Observe the pleasure of being in contact with this Element.

Now ask the Water Spirit: How can I best express what I am and give it away? Ask Him to learn how to harmonize and balance your emotions. Let Water communicate its message to you, and write it down in your notebook.

Observe your image reflected on the surface of the Water. Ask four times: Who am I, changing the intonation each time you repeat the question.

Write down the answer and meditate on it.

To thank her, scatter the offering by shaking the rattle, before leaving. After the communication with all the cardinal points, it is good to return to the Center. For the last practice of the sequence, you can stay at home, in your sacred space, devoting an hour to it.

Take a candle, smudge, matches, rattle, notebook and pen.

Connecting with the Inner Center

Place the candle and smudge in front of you, on a table or on the floor. Light the candle to begin your practice. Smudge the room and your person and shake the rattle around you. The inside of the candle flame represents your Spirit, the Luminous Center of your inner self, the Essence enclosed in the Heart of your Inner Flame. The awareness of Spirit extends beyond rationality. Meditate for a moment on this understanding. Then reconsider all the teachings you have received during your practice with the Medicine Wheel and the experiences you have had.

On your journey you started in the North, then headed West, crossed the Center to head East and finally South, tracing the symbol of Wakan-Tanka. Finally reconnecting with your inner Center, you traced a pattern in the shapeof an 8, the symbol of infinity and infinite possibilities.

Now you can continue on your life path open to these new infinitepossibilities that will arise!

BOOK 15
Native American Remedies Common Diseases and Herbal Solutions

Entering the Realm of Herbal Remedies

When you enter the realm of medicinal herbs and plants as remedies, you need to be conscious of their power. Don't gather wild herbs if you are not sure about what you're doing; it can be extremely dangerous for your health.

Natural is not equal to beneficial as absolute; you need to know how to select the right herbs and herbal combos for your health needs.

Follow three simple principles to identify and meet your specific herbal and nutritional needs:

Identify the condition or disorder that is affecting you, then identify areas of your health state and specific needs that require additional support.

Choose the most appropriate and adequate system of care for your needs, following this guide or the advice of an expert herbalist, including herbs, enzymes, vitamins, minerals and phytochemicals.

As always, if you have particular conditions, such as chronic diseases, heart disease or diabetes, or if you are taking medications of any kind, or if you are pregnant, consult a specialist who can recommend you the most suitable treatment.

Herbs and other supplements can alter the absorption of synthetic drugs. Sometimes they can improve the effectiveness of medications, but in other cases they can also interfere with the action of a particular drug.

This book and the formulations provided herein are not intended to replace the services of a holistic physician or well-trained health care professional.

Abscess and Gingivitis

An abscess is a local accumulation of pus. It canarise almost anywhere on the skin or in the body and gums of the mouth.

Abscesses can be very painful and are characterized by inflammation, swelling, heat and often fever.

Abscesses are caused by bacterial infections or parasites, often treated withantibiotics. But herbs are an effective and safe alternative without the side effects of antibiotics.

Relevant tissue states: heat (inflammation), dampness

Relevant actions of herbs: anti-inflammatory, antimicrobial, antibacterial, astringent

HERBAL ALLIES	REMEDIES
Calendula flower	
Chamomile flower	
Echinacea	
Goldenrod leaf and flower	
Licorice root	Herbal mouthwash
Oregon grape root	
Plantain leaf	
Rose	Topical Wash
Sage leaf	
Thyme leaf	
Ova-ursi leaf	
White Oak	
Aloe	

Aging

The aging process, characterized by wrinkles, joint pain, fatigue and hair loss or graying, is accelerated by food shortage, lack of exercise, excessive exposure to sun (ultraviolet rays) and unhealthy habits and lifestyle. These and other factors increase free radical activity.

Free radicals are highly unstable molecules that damage the DNA and interfere with the cell's health.

Various herbs have antioxidant properties, which effectively reduce free radicals.

HERBAL ALLIES	REMEDIES
Gingo Biloba	
Ginger	
Pasley	
Black currants	
Edelberries	Antioxidant tea
Horse Tail	
Aloe	Memory tea
Saint John's Wort	
Evening primrose	

HERBAL ALLIES	REMEDIES
Agrimony	
Heal-all leaf and flower	
Barberry root	
Calendula flower	Flower decoction
Goldenrod leaf and flower	
Goldenseal	Allergy relief tea
Marygold	
Milk thistle seed	Nettle tea
Mullein leaf	
Nettle leaf	
Oregon grape root	
Plantain leaf	
Yerba sante	

Allergies

An allergy is an abnormal and exaggerated immune system response induced by contact, inhalation and/or exposure to normally harmless foreign substances called allergens. Allergies occur when the body's immune system malfunctions, going into "overdrive" to protect the body from one of these substances.

The tissues involved in this reaction are mainly the nasal mucous membranes, the eyes, the bronchi and the skin; these become hyperactive and, under certain external conditions such as the presence of pollutants, become even more sensitive. Common symptoms include nasal congestion, coughing, watery eyes, sneezing, fatigue and headaches. Some allergies can cause hives or an itchy rash.

The best way to treat an allergy is to avoid the offending substance. When this is not possible, herbs can help control the inflammation, excessive tearing, nasal discharge and coughing that occur with some allergies. The most common allergens are the pollens of herbaceous plants and trees, especially those produced by grasses, olive, beech, birch, hazel, cypress, paretaria, mugwort, ragweed and plantain; in this case, in order to detect these allergies, it is necessary to know the specific pollen calendar from region to region.

Other common allergens are: dust mites, or rather their excrement released into the air, foods, drugs, pets, substances transmitted through insect bites and stings, household chemicals, spores produced by molds in humid environments

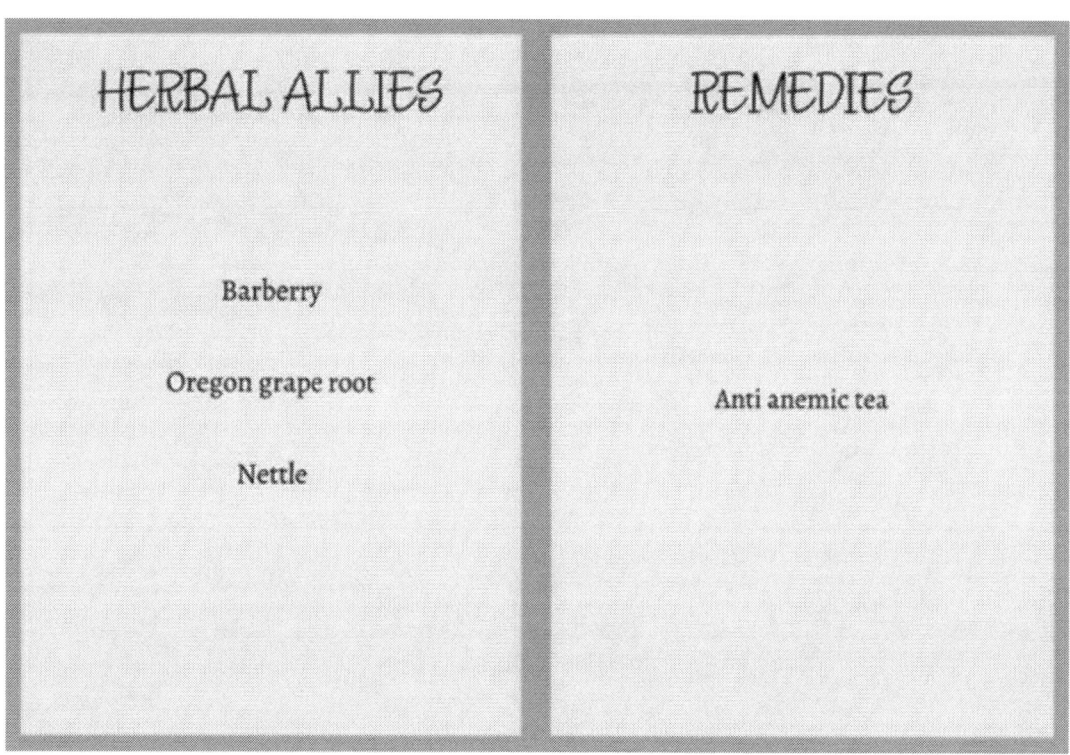

Anemia

Iron deficiency anemia is the most common type of anemia. It is also called sideropenic anemia (from Latin sìderos = iron and penìa = poverty) or martialanemia. This is a condition in which there are not adequate levels of iron in the body and this compromises the transport of oxygen through the blood causing, among other things, fatigue and shortness of breath.

Iron is a mineral that is essential for certain biological functions, includingthe formation of hemoglobin. When there is a lack of iron, caused by poordietary intake, problems in absorption, blood loss, the production of hemoglobin is insufficient and this leads to poor circulation of oxygen through the body. It affects all age groups, mainly children, adolescents, women of childbearing age, pregnant and lactating women.

Arthritis

The term "arthritis" refers to a chronic inflammatory condition that can involve one or more joints, both large and small joints, frequently accompanied by swelling, redness, fever, pain, increased joint stiffness andconsequent functional loss.

There is often a tendency to confuse arthrosis and arthritis, two diseases that are very different, despite of some common features. The confusion probably derives from a terminological problem: arthrosis is also called osteoarthritis, according to a definition derived directly from the English osteoarthritis.

What do arthritis and osteoarthritis have in common? They are both rheumatic diseases and both attack the joints, bringing pain that makes it difficult to move the limbs.

What are the differences? Osteoarthritis is a degenerative disease that results from wear and tear of the joint cartilage. The pain caused by arthrosis is due to the abnormal proximity and direct contact of the joint heads.

Generally, osteoarthritis affects the largest or most heavily loaded joints such as the hip, knee, foot, shoulder, and hands. Painful symptoms occur upon use of the joint and diminish after rest.

Arthritis is a chronic autoimmune inflammatory disease. It is not related to specific factors and can occur in people of all ages. It typically develops in the joints of the wrists, hands, ankles, and feet bilaterally. The main symptoms of arthritis are swelling, joint stiffness and pain that occurs at anytime.

There are a hundred forms of arthritis that all fall under the broader category of rheumatic diseases, each with specific causes and characteristics.

The following treatments are effective for both osteoarthritis and rheumatoid arthritis.

(see the table at next page)

Herbal Allies for Arthritis

HERBAL ALLIES	REMEDIES
Balsam bilberry	
Black cohosh	
Currant	
Cascara sagrada	
Cayenne	Quick analgesic tea
Chamomile	
Devil's claw	Bedtime tea
Feverfew	
Mullein	Arthritis ointment
Nettle	
Wild cherry	
White willow bark	
Yucca	

Asthma

Asthma is a chronic inflammatory disease of the airways, characterized by obstruction, generally reversible, of the bronchi.

Obstruction of the bronchial tree is caused by inflammation of the lower airways and its consequences: due to the inflammatory process, the bronchi contract, fill with fluid and produce an excess of mucus, overall reducing the spaces available for the free circulation of air.

As a result, bronchial asthma causes shortness or difficulty breathing, cough, whistling or wheezing breath, sense of pressure in the chest.

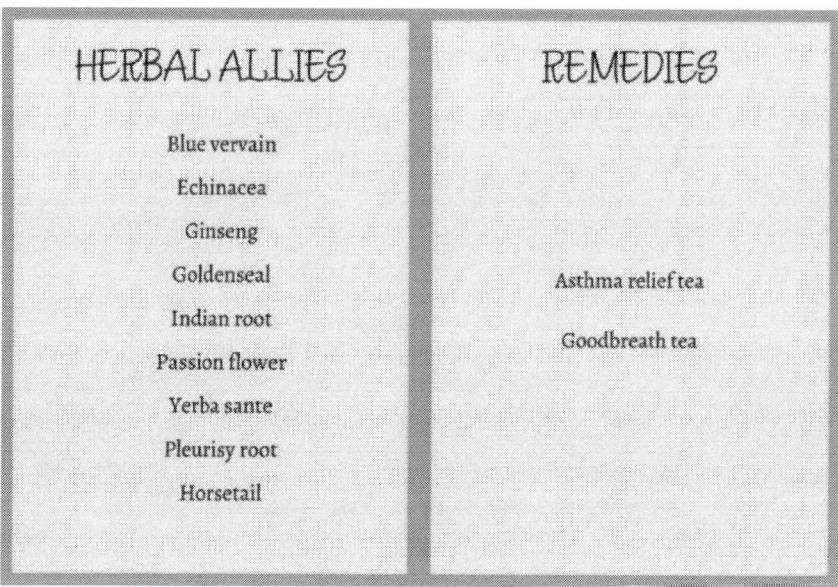

HERBAL ALLIES	REMEDIES
Blue vervain	
Echinacea	
Ginseng	
Goldenseal	Asthma relief tea
Indian root	Goodbreath tea
Passion flower	
Yerba sante	
Pleurisy root	
Horsetail	

Bedsores

Bedsores are real skin ulcers, which heal with great difficulty and which not only affect the superficial layers of the skin, but also go deeper. They are not, therefore, wounds like any other: they do not heal on their own and, indeed, it is often necessary to resort to specific therapies to promote healing.

Bedsores affect people who are bedridden or seated for long periods of time and who, therefore, are immobile. This can happen either due to degenerative diseases, such as multiple sclerosis, or due to temporary conditions, such as casts and broken bones.

When you remain in a static position for too long, you continue to put pressure on certain parts of your body, which causes blood flow to proceed improperly. Over time, blood vessels may become clogged and form clots that will then lead to tissue death and the creation of pressure sores.

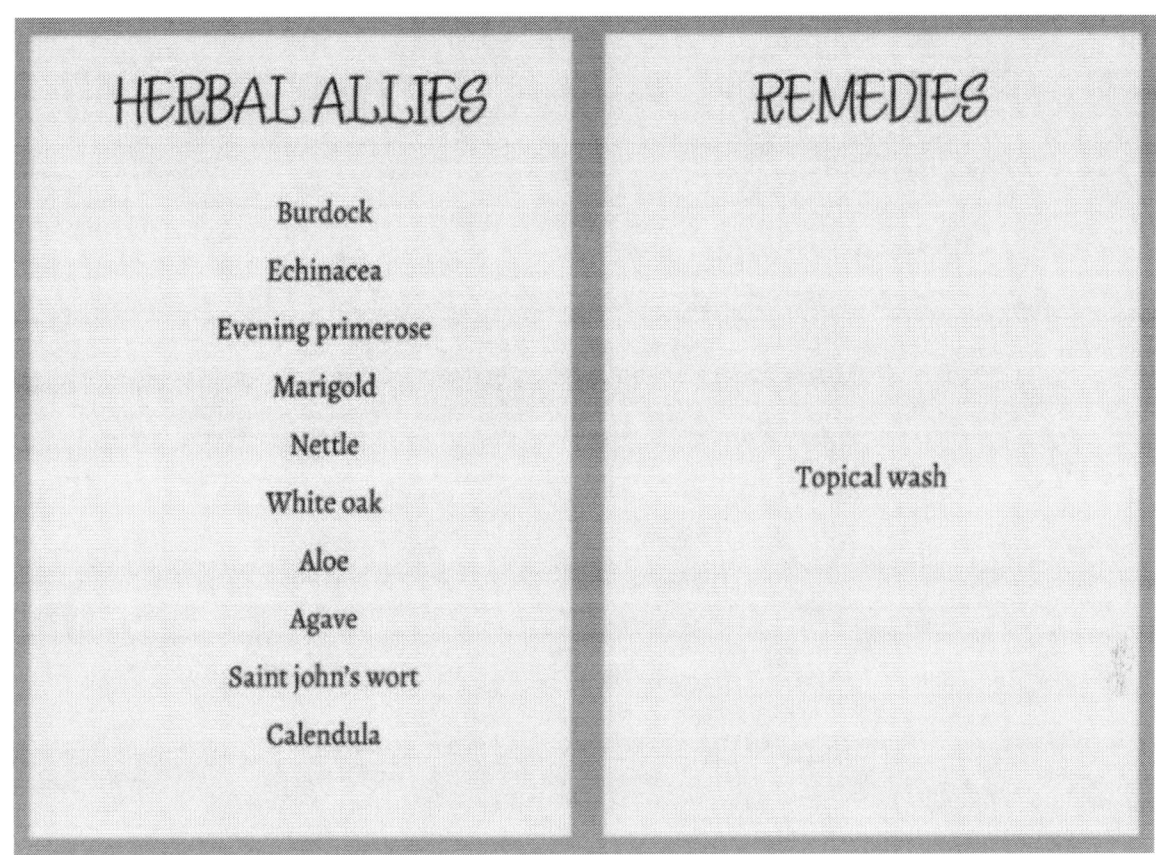

In the initial stages of formation, the skin of the affected area will simply be reddened, but over time blisters will form and, then, real open wounds, which can range in color from purple to brown.

Bites and Stings

Most of us have been bitten or stung by mosquitoes, bees, wasps, ants, spiders, ticks, or even more exotic creatures like snakes or jellyfish. We call it a "bite," but most insects and other creatures puncture the skin rather than take a bite. The signs of an insect bite represent the result of injecting venom or other substances into the skin; the severity of the reaction and the appearance of symptoms depend on the individual's sensitivity to those substances. Most stings can cause pain, itching, burning, swelling and other mild side effects, which tend to disappear within two days. Typically, these local skin reactions can be managed and treated without medical intervention.

Whether it's mosquitoes, black flies or fire ants, most insect bites are fairly simple: We just need to reduce the inflammation. Bee and wasp stings are a bit more intense: In this case, our goal is to extract the venom if possible, reduce inflammation and help the immune system deal with the venom that has entered the body. Beware of anaphylaxis! If a person who is stung or bitten has difficulty breathing, seek help immediately

HERBAL ALLIES

Chamomile
Echinacea
Seneca shakeroot
Black currant
Ginger
Ginko biloba
Aloe
Licorice
White willow
Calendula
Plantain leaf
Rose
Yarrow leaf and flower

REMEDIES

Bite relief spray

Topical wash

Skin soothing ointment

HERBAL ALLIES

Angelica
Barberry
Boneset
Cascara sagrada
Aloe
Cayenne
Chicory
Dandelion root
Ginger
Oregon grape
Sunflower

REMEDIES

Bowel-stimulating tincture

Bowel-soothing tea

Digestive tea

Hydrating infusion

HERBAL ALLIES	REMEDIES
Black cohosh Angelica Black elder Chamomile Echinacea Elder Ginger Garlic Licorice Peppermint Pine Queen of the meadow Sage leaf Slippery elm Seneca shakeroot	Fire cider Bronchitis relief tincture Throat soothing tea

Bronchitis

Bronchitis is simply the inflammation of the mucosa that internally lines thebronchi, the most important airway in the passage of air to the lungs.

The causes that can generate this pathological condition are essentially of twotypes: a toxic cause, in which a substance foreign to the body comes into contact with the bronchial mucosa causing irritation, or an infectious cause, in which this process is caused by a bacterium or a virus. Depending on its course, bronchitis can be acute or chronic.

Acute bronchitis usually occurs after a respiratory infection of viral origin, has a sudden onset and, if properly treated, heals without leaving after-effectsor residues.

Chronic bronchitis, on the other hand, is the result of prolonged exposure over time to agents that have damaged the bronchi, with little or no chance ofrecovery.

When the chronic inflammatory state continues for weeks, months or years,the mucous membrane of the bronchi thickens, causing a narrowing of the bronchial lumen and increasing difficulty in breathing: the patient breathes with difficulty

Burns and Sunburns

Since man has learned to "tame" the fire, small burns and scalds have becomeone of the most common injuries suffered in the home, work and recreationalenvironment. BurnsIt has happened to everyone, at least once, to inadvertently touch an object too hot or to get the classic burn for staying too long in the sun without adequate protection.

A burn is, by definition, a more or less extensive injury to the skin, and sometimes the underlying tissues, caused by a thermal, physical or chemical agent. Numerous and heterogeneous are therefore the possible causes, as wellas different is the extent of the damage caused by them.

Burns can be caused by heat, chemicals, electricity or radiant agents (the sunor any other source of UVA). They can be first, second or third degree depending on the severity. For mild burns it is possible to intervene with natural remedies. Apply any of the herbal allies in a wash, compress, poultice, or infused honey. Don't use oily preparations on burns, because they trap the heat in the tissue.

Do not underestimate the power of a marshmallow root poultice! Simply saturate a handful of marshmallow root with enough cold water to make a gloopy mass and apply it to the burn. Cover with gauze and leave in place for20 minutes. Repeat frequently.

Relevant tissue states: heat

Relevant herbal actions: anti-inflammatory, antimicrobial, antiseptic,vulnerary

(see the table at next page)

Herbal Allies for Burns and Sunburns

HERBAL ALLIES	REMEDIES
Sunflower	
Echinacea	
Aloe	
Wild indigo root	Sunburn spray
Goldenrod	
Peppermint leaf	Burn salve
Plantain leaf	
Rose petals	Immunity booster
Hyssop	
Sant john's wort flower	

Canker Sores

Canker sores are small lesions of the skin that mainly affect the female sex. Although they are very annoying and, in some cases, may represent the alarmbell of other diseases, canker sores can be healed within ten days and should not cause great concern.

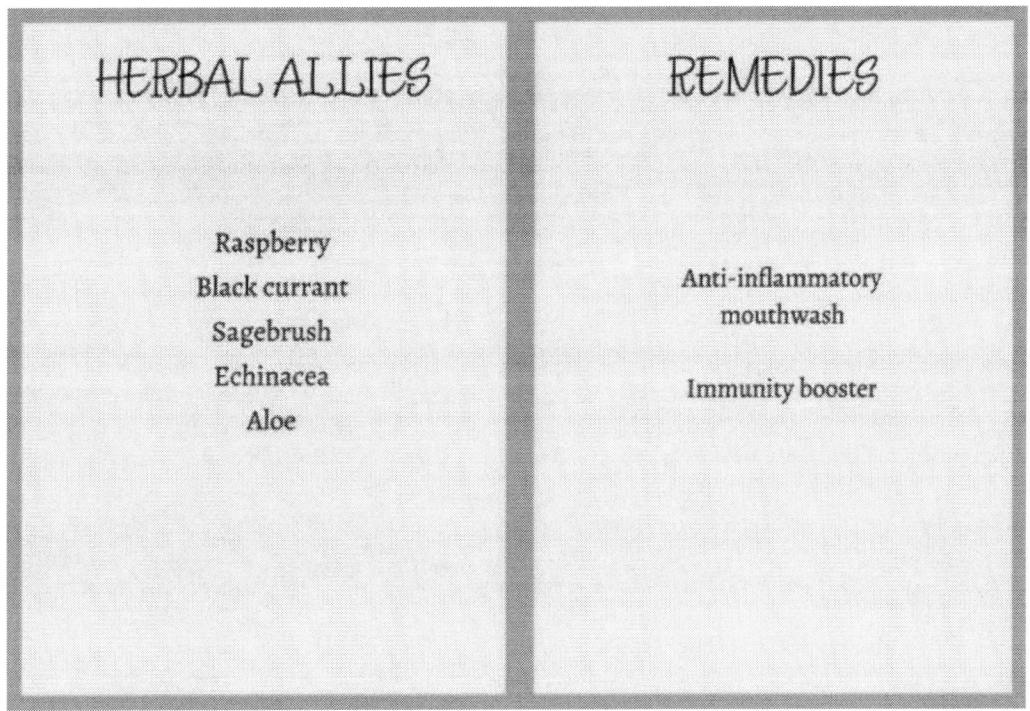

Canker sores form inside the mouth, on the soft tissues of the oral mucosa and therefore on the palate, cheeks, tongue or at the base of the gums. To theeye they are similar to small excoriations of a few millimeters, round and whitish in color. They can be very painful, preventing us from eating or speaking. Canker sores can be brought on by stress, viral infections, poor dental hygiene, and nutrient deficiencies. Injuries (such as certain dental procedures) can also cause canker sores to develop.

Cold Sores

Cold sores (or herpes labialis) is an infectious disease characterized by theappearance of numerous blisters around the lips or other areas of the face,such as the cheeks and nose

The causative agent is the herpes simplex virus, which is contracted through saliva, kissing or, more generally, through direct contact with infected people. After the regression of the first infection, the herpes labialis virus hasthe peculiar characteristic of going to take refuge, through the nerves of the skin, in the neuronal ganglia closest to the site of infection. In this place, the pathogen enters into latency, that is not only survives the immune system, butis not even eliminated through the use of drugs. Even after a long time, lip herpes can reoccur: the virus takes advantage of states of "weakness" in the body (drops in immune defenses, periods of stress, general fatigue, etc.), thenreactivates and causes the classic lip lesions.

HERBAL ALLIES	REMEDIES
Chamomile flower	
Yerba mansa	
White oak	
Thyme leaf	Colde sore infusion
Golden seal	Cold sore balm
Saint john's wort leaf and flower	Cold sore tea
Calendula flower	Cold sore cataplasm
Echinacea	
Aloe	
Plantain leaf	

Relevant tissue states: heat (inflammation)

Relevant herbal actions: immune stimulant, lymphatic, vulnerary

Constipation

HERBAL ALLIES	REMEDIES
Angelica	
Barberry	
Boneset	
Cascara sagrada	Bowel-stimulating tincture
Aloe	Bowel-soothing tea
Cayenne	Digestive tea
Chicory	Hydrating infusion
Dandelion root	
Ginger	
Oregon grape	
Sunflower	

Intestinal constipation (also known as constipation or constipation) describes a gastrointestinal disorder marked by difficulty evacuating stool, often accompanied by other related symptoms, such as headache, intestinal meteorism and flatulence, and a bloated belly. It is, however, a condition that can affect your daily life and may affect your psychophysical well-being, if not addressed in the most appropriate way.

Each of us can suffer or have suffered from constipation, but usually it is a temporary and not serious condition, linked, for example, to an unbalanced diet in that period.

The severity of constipation is related, however, to the continuation of this symptom, so as to configure a chronic condition. It is a chronic condition when the difficulty in emptying the intestine through the stool occurs often. It is called chronic constipation when the physiological frequency is 3 times a week or less.

Before resorting to the help of laxatives, both in temporary and chronic cases, it is good to try to modify one's lifestyle habits and also try with the adoption of good practices. This allows to contrast the symptomatology without resorting to medicines.

Sometimes, constipation is simply a sign of dehydration—drink some water! If it's a chronic issue, it may be an indication of a food allergy or simply a sign that you're not getting sufficient fiber in your diet. A good, thick, cold infusion of marshmallow solves both problems: It rehydrates better than water alone, and it includes a lot of polysaccharides and fibers that help move stool along.

Relevant tissue states: cold (stagnation), dryness, tension

Relevant herbal actions: bitter, carminative, demulcent, hepatic, laxative

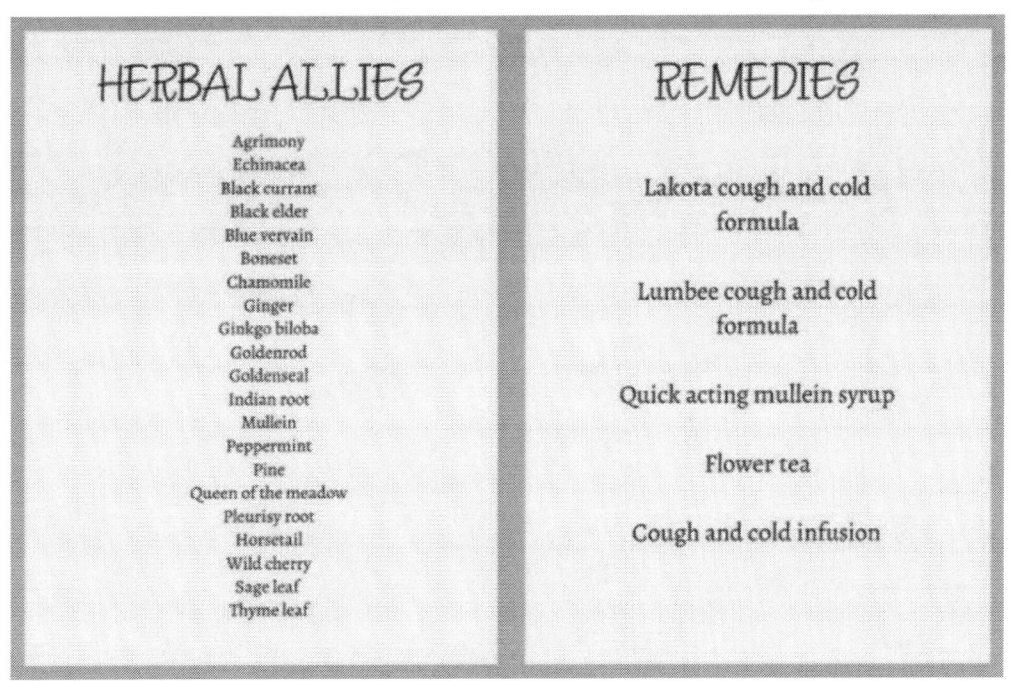

HERBAL ALLIES	REMEDIES
Agrimony	
Echinacea	
Black currant	Lakota cough and cold formula
Black elder	
Blue vervain	
Boneset	
Chamomile	Lumbee cough and cold formula
Ginger	
Ginkgo biloba	
Goldenrod	
Goldenseal	Quick acting mullein syrup
Indian root	
Mullein	
Peppermint	Flower tea
Pine	
Queen of the meadow	
Pleurisy root	Cough and cold infusion
Horsetail	
Wild cherry	
Sage leaf	
Thyme leaf	

Colds

A cold is an acute infection of viral origin, usually nonfebrile, that causes symptoms affecting the upper airways, such as a runny nose, cough, and sorethroat. The disorder occurs after a 24-72-hour incubation period and, in mostcases, self-limits within 10 days.

The cold typically begins with a "scraping sensation in the throat" or pharyngodynia, sneezing, rhinorrhea, nasal congestion, and general malaise.Nasal secretions are initially clear, watery and profuse, then become mucoidand purulent, thick, whitish or yellowish.

In about 50% of cases, colds are caused by a rhinovirus, most easily transmitted through interhuman contact, although spread can also occur through large aerosols. Other infections can be caused by coronavirus, influenza and parainfluenza viruses, enterovirus, adenovirus, respiratorysyncytial virus, and metapneumovirus.

Relevant tissue states: heat (irritation) or cold (depressed vitality), drynessor dampness

Relevant herbal actions: antitussive, astringent, decongestant, demulcent, diaphoretic, expectorant, pulmonary tonic.

Cramps

HERBAL ALLIES	REMEDIES
Black cohosh	
Ginseng	
Ginger	Warming ointment
Wintergreen	
Yerba mansa	Muscle rub
Goldenrod leaf and flower	
Meadowsweet flower	Muscle relaxing tea
Wild lettuce	
Yarrow leaf and flower	

Cramps are involuntary and sudden contractions of striated muscles. Their onset is characterized by very intense painful twinges, which often immobilize the affected part.

The muscle affected by a cramp appears hard to the touch, but does not have edema or bruising. Cramps occur most frequently in the thigh, calf and foot.

These contractions are transient and generally last a few minutes.

When they occur during the night rest, muscle cramps can lead to frequent awakenings, disturbing sleep.

At the origin of this symptom there can be various causes. Often, cramps are the result of excessive dehydration, intense stress, physical fatigue or holding a position for a long period of time.

Relevant tissue states: heat (inflammation), tension

Relevant herbal actions: anodyne, nervous tropho-restorative, relaxant, rubefacient

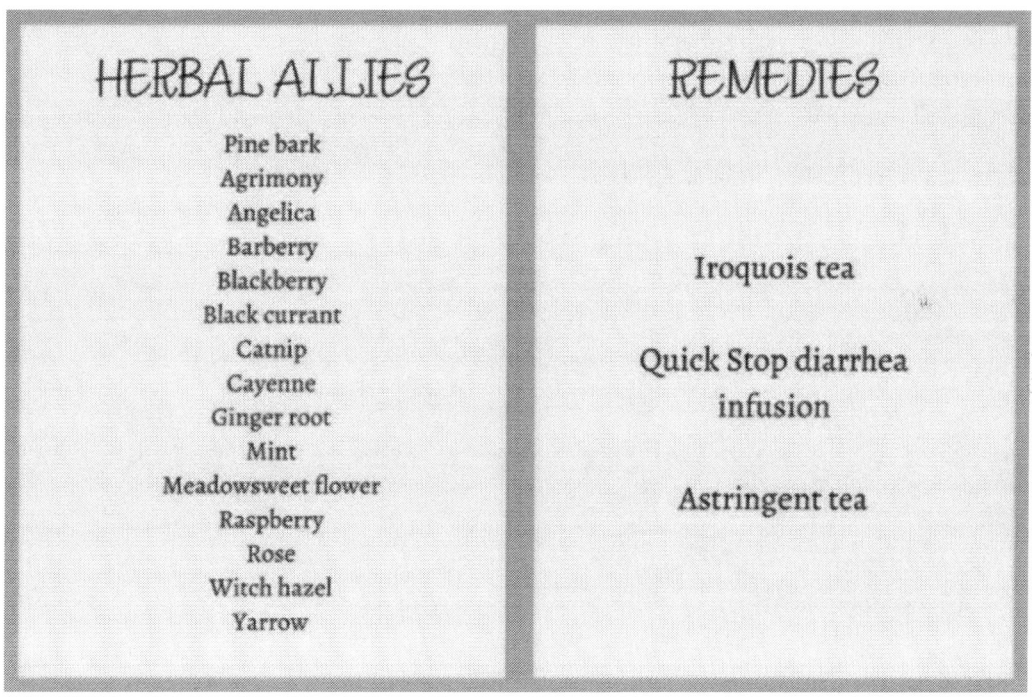

Diarrhea

Diarrhea is a defecation disorder characterized by the rapid emission of abundant and poorly formed stools.

Both of these conditions must be present at the same time: at least three evacuations per day, alterations in the quantity or quality of manure (presence of poorly formed stools: liquid or semi-liquid)

Diarrhea is not a real disease but an aspecific symptom, common to many diseases (mostly gastrointestinal) or non-pathological conditions (trivial foodintolerances, stress, etc..). Often diarrhea is accompanied by the continuous urge to evacuate, even in the absence of fecal material (rectal tenesmus). Wetalk instead of dysentery when the diarrhea is complicated to the point of causing an important evacuation of liquids with characteristics no longer fecal (presence of water, mucus, pus, proteins, electrolytes, fats and blood).

Relevant tissue states: laxity (barrier compromise), dampness

Relevant herbal actions: astringent, demulcent

Fatigue

Fatigue is more than just being tired. Instead, fatigue is a prolonged or excessive reduction in the capacity to function, beyond what normal effort would cause. Those who push themselves to the point of physical exhaustionare certainly familiar with fatigue.

However, fatigue can be a symptom of more than just overexertion; it is a symptom of a number of conditions including anemia, circulatory problems (such as angina pectoris, atherosclerosis and high blood pressure), chronic fatigue syndrome, diabetes, hepatitis, inflammatory bowel disease, multiple sclerosis and respiratory conditions including pneumonia and pleurisy.

Relevant tissue states: cold (depletion, depression, exhaustion)

Relevant herbal actions: adaptogen, exhilarant, stimulant

HERBAL ALLIES	REMEDIES
Cat's claw	
Angelica	
Blackberry	Energy tea
Ginkgo biloba	
Ginger root	Uplifting infusion
Licorice root	
Mirabilis	Revitalizing tea
Pulsatilla	
Raspberry	
Saint john's worth	

Headache

The common headache, which physicians identify with the term cephalalgia, is defined by them as pain localized within the head or upper neck.

Headaches are caused by the alteration of physiological mechanisms and processes that activate and/or involve structures sensitive to the pain stimulus, located in certain areas of the head and neck: periosteum of the skull, muscles, nerves, arteries and veins, subcutaneous tissues, eyes, ears, sinuses and mucous membranes. It remains unclear, however, why these painsignals are initially activated. Primary headaches are almost never caused by a single cause: in most cases, they are the result of the interaction between genetic predisposition, endogenous causes (internal to the body) and triggering factors (i.e. the stimuli that trigger the alterations). In other cases, headaches may be the result of a trauma to the head or, rarely, a sign of a more serious medical condition.

Relevant tissue states: heat or cold, damp or dry, tense or lax

Relevant herbal actions: anodyne, anti-inflammatory, astringent, circulatory stimulant, relaxant

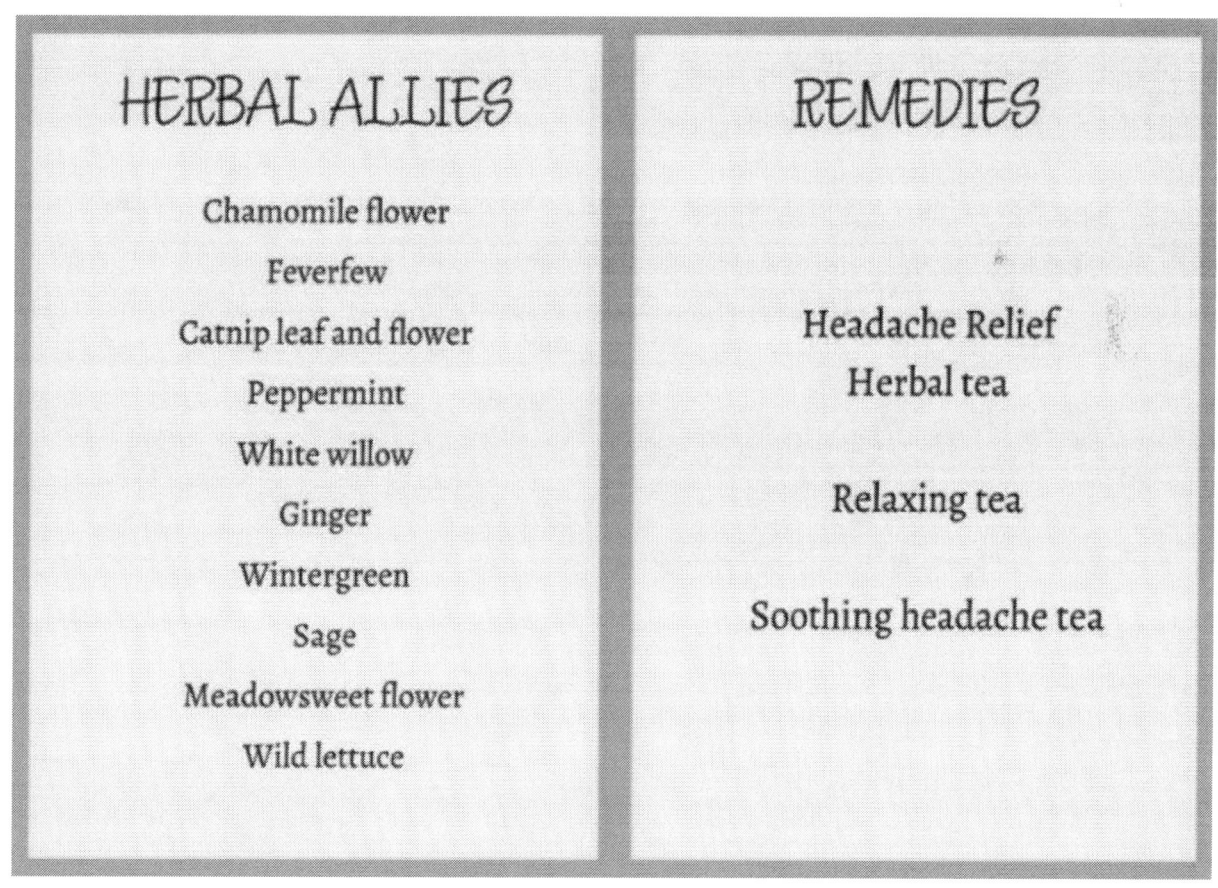

HERBAL ALLIES	REMEDIES
Chamomile flower	
Feverfew	
Catnip leaf and flower	Headache Relief
Peppermint	Herbal tea
White willow	
Ginger	Relaxing tea
Wintergreen	
Sage	Soothing headache tea
Meadowsweet flower	
Wild lettuce	

Reflux/Heartburn

Gastroesophageal reflux is a disorder characterized by the rising of the acidcontent of the stomach into the esophagus. Heartburn, acidity and regurgitation: these are the typical symptoms of gastroesophageal reflux.

Gastroesophageal reflux can be a passing disorder, but it can also become areal disease, subject to serious complications. In milder forms, it can be successfully treated by simply changing diet and lifestyle. In more serious cases, instead, these rules must be integrated by a specific pharmacologicaltreatment.

Relevant tissue states: heat (inflammation), laxity

Relevant herbal actions: bitter, carminative, demulcent, vulnerary

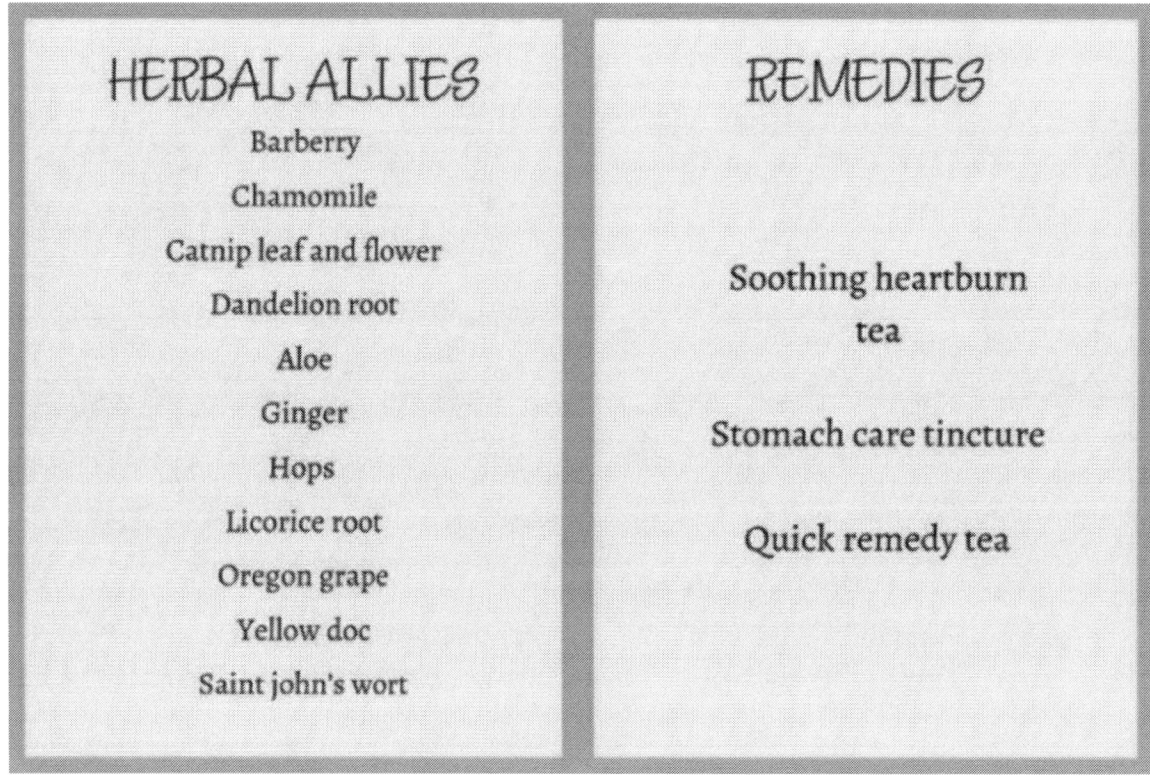

HERBAL ALLIES	REMEDIES
Barberry	
Chamomile	
Catnip leaf and flower	
Dandelion root	Soothing heartburn tea
Aloe	
Ginger	Stomach care tincture
Hops	
Licorice root	Quick remedy tea
Oregon grape	
Yellow doc	
Saint john's wort	

Hypertension

Arterial hypertension is a state, constant and not occasional, in which blood pressure at rest is higher than the physiological standards considered normal.

Hypertension is one of the most common diseases in industrialized countries;in fact, it affects about 20% of the adult population and represents one of the major clinical problems of modern times.

Hypertension is also known as the "silent killer", because it does not involveany symptoms and acts in the shadows, degenerating into severe complications, sometimes fatal. When this occurs, the stage is set for blood clots, clogged arteries, strokes, and heart attacks.

Relevant tissue states: heat, tension

Relevant herbal actions: hypotensive, nervine, relaxant, sedative

HERBAL ALLIES	REMEDIES
Black cohosh Currant Dandelion Garlic Ginger Ginkgo biloba Ginseng Goldenseal Raspberry Rose Slippery elm Yarrow	Happy heart tea Heart herbal tea Healthy arteries tea freeflow tea

Indigestion/Dyspepsia

HERBAL ALLIES	REMEDIES
Angelica Barberry Catnip Chamomile Dandelion root Echinacea Ginger Licorice root Oregon grape Peppermint Sage	Enzymes activator Carminative tincture Digestive tea

Indigestion can have many causes, but the vast majority of stomachaches aredue to trivial reasons, such as a large meal or one eaten too quickly.

Indigestion is a general term for a number of complaints that occur after a meal and can be burning, heaviness, nausea, widespread pain in the abdomensense of bloating, meteorism, and so on.

Indigestion, also called dyspepsia, is a set of symptoms that can be triggeredby many different factors.

It is generally distinguished into three types: Occasional dyspepsia, when it occurs only once in a while, recurrent or chronic dyspepsia when it occurs forseveral consecutive days or with a high frequency, functional dyspepsia whenit is chronic, but without specific causes, and the discomfort related to poor digestion occurs either immediately after a meal or one or two hours after eating.

Relevant tissue states: cold (stagnation), tension

Relevant herbal actions: bitter, carminative, relaxant

Insomnia

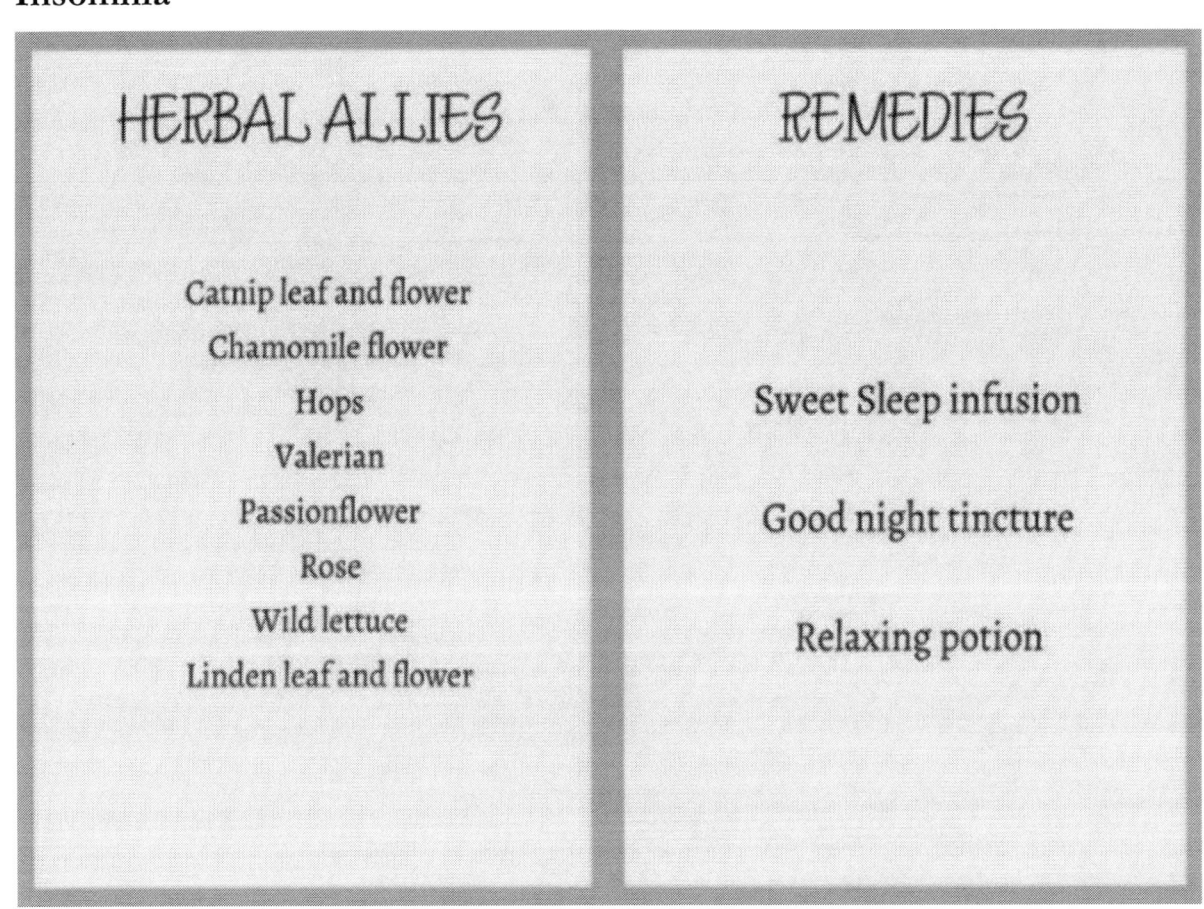

HERBAL ALLIES

Catnip leaf and flower
Chamomile flower
Hops
Valerian
Passionflower
Rose
Wild lettuce
Linden leaf and flower

REMEDIES

Sweet Sleep infusion

Good night tincture

Relaxing potion

Insomnia is any difficulty in sleeping. Some people find it difficult to fall asleep, while others can fall the term insomnia derives from Latin insomnia and literally means "lack of dreams". In common language it indicates a lackof sleep or poor relief from sleep at night, this means that an individual is sleepless not only if he sleeps a few hours but if these few hours do not get adequate relief to maintain its social function and work during the day.

Insomnia is often the consequence of various psychological or physical pathological conditions, or the result of bad habits regarding diet, physical activity and the pace of life in general. Irritability, daytime drowsiness, andmemory impairment often affect those suffering from insomnia.

Relevant tissue states: heat (agitation), tension

Relevant herbal actions: hypnotic, relaxant, sedative

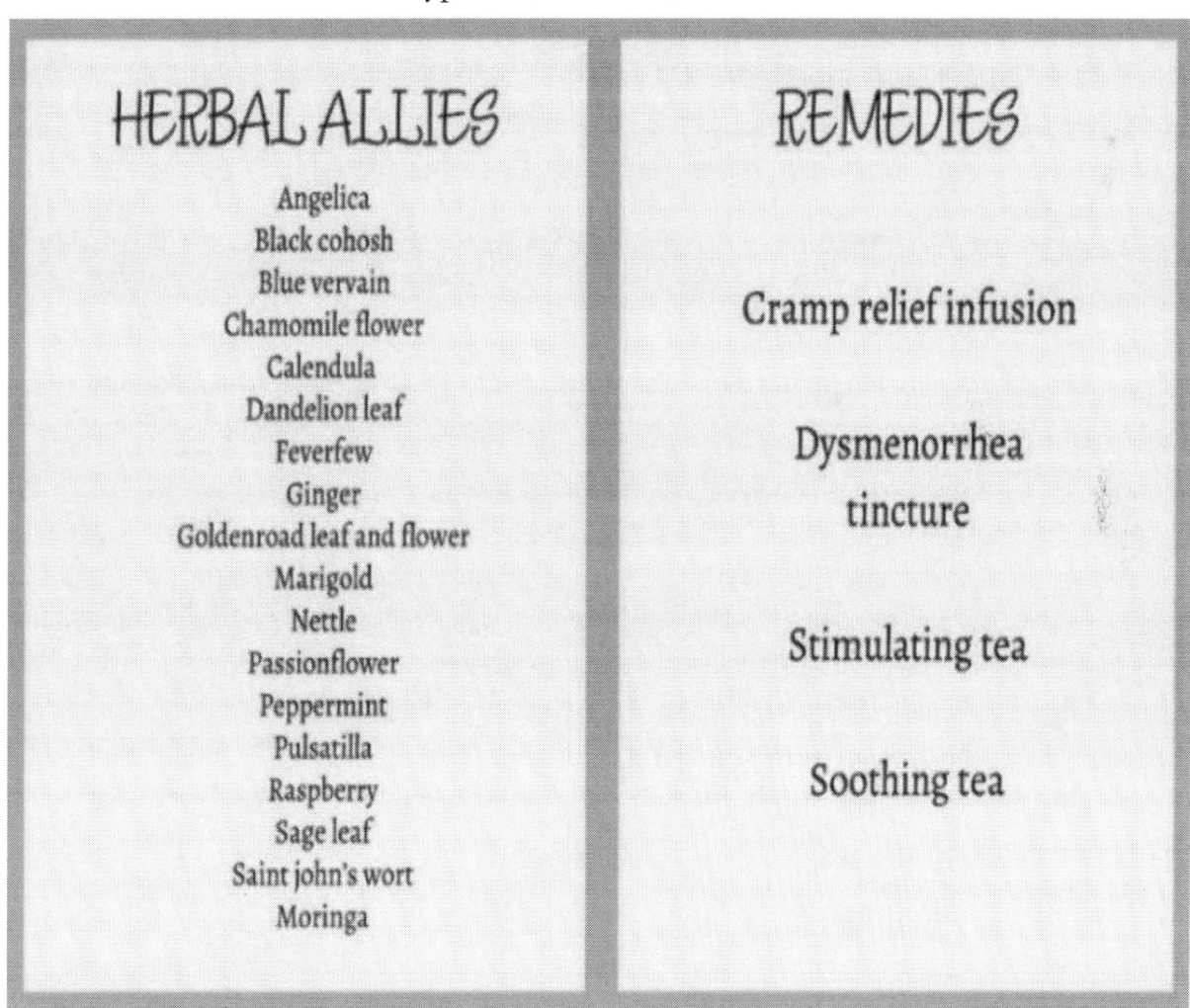

HERBAL ALLIES

- Angelica
- Black cohosh
- Blue vervain
- Chamomile flower
- Calendula
- Dandelion leaf
- Feverfew
- Ginger
- Goldenroad leaf and flower
- Marigold
- Nettle
- Passionflower
- Peppermint
- Pulsatilla
- Raspberry
- Sage leaf
- Saint john's wort
- Moringa

REMEDIES

- Cramp relief infusion
- Dysmenorrhea tincture
- Stimulating tea
- Soothing tea

Menstrual Cycle Irregularities

We talk about menstrual cycle alterations when menstruation does not occur every 28 days. This regularity is more common in the middle of the fertileage of a woman, between 20 and 45 years.

Before the age of 20, irregularities are quite common because "we are in thepresence of a uterine engine and hormonal set-up that are starting to work," explains Dr. Vitobello.

After age 45, on the other hand, "we approach the end of menstrual life andfertile age, and we are faced with a uterine engine at the end of its life cycleand an altered hormonal set-up."

Overheavy bleeding generally comes from hormones not clearing efficiently at the liver, though it may also be connected with the development of fibroidsor polyps. If heavy bleeding persists, seek medical attention.

Dysmenorrhea, or menstrual pain, which usually begins just beforemenstruation, may occur in the lower abdomen or the lower back.

Other accompanying symptoms may include nausea, vomiting, headache, and either constipation or diarrhea. This condition affects more than half of all women.

Relevant herbal actions: astringent, carminative, circulatory stimulant, emmenagogue, nutritive, rubefacient

Nausea and Vomiting

Nausea is a symptom of discomfort in the upper part of the stomach; this mayspread to the chest or the back of the throat and is often associated with a sense of vomiting.

The causes of nausea are numerous. Mainly, the origin of this symptom maybe problems affecting: the abdominal or pelvic organs, the central nervous system or the balance centers of the inner ear.

Nausea shouldn't be underestimated when it is associated with: a head trauma, headache, severe abdominal pain. Only an adequate diagnosis allowsto establish the correct treatment; treatment that depends on the severity of the symptoms and the triggering causes.

It can also occur because of motion sickness, headache, or pregnancy. Sometimes unpleasant smells or tastes, and even emotional anxiety, can bringon nausea.

Relevant tissue states: heat (agitation), tension (spasm)

Relevant herbal actions: antiemetic, carminative, relaxant (see the table atnext page)

Herbal Allies for Nausea and Vomiting

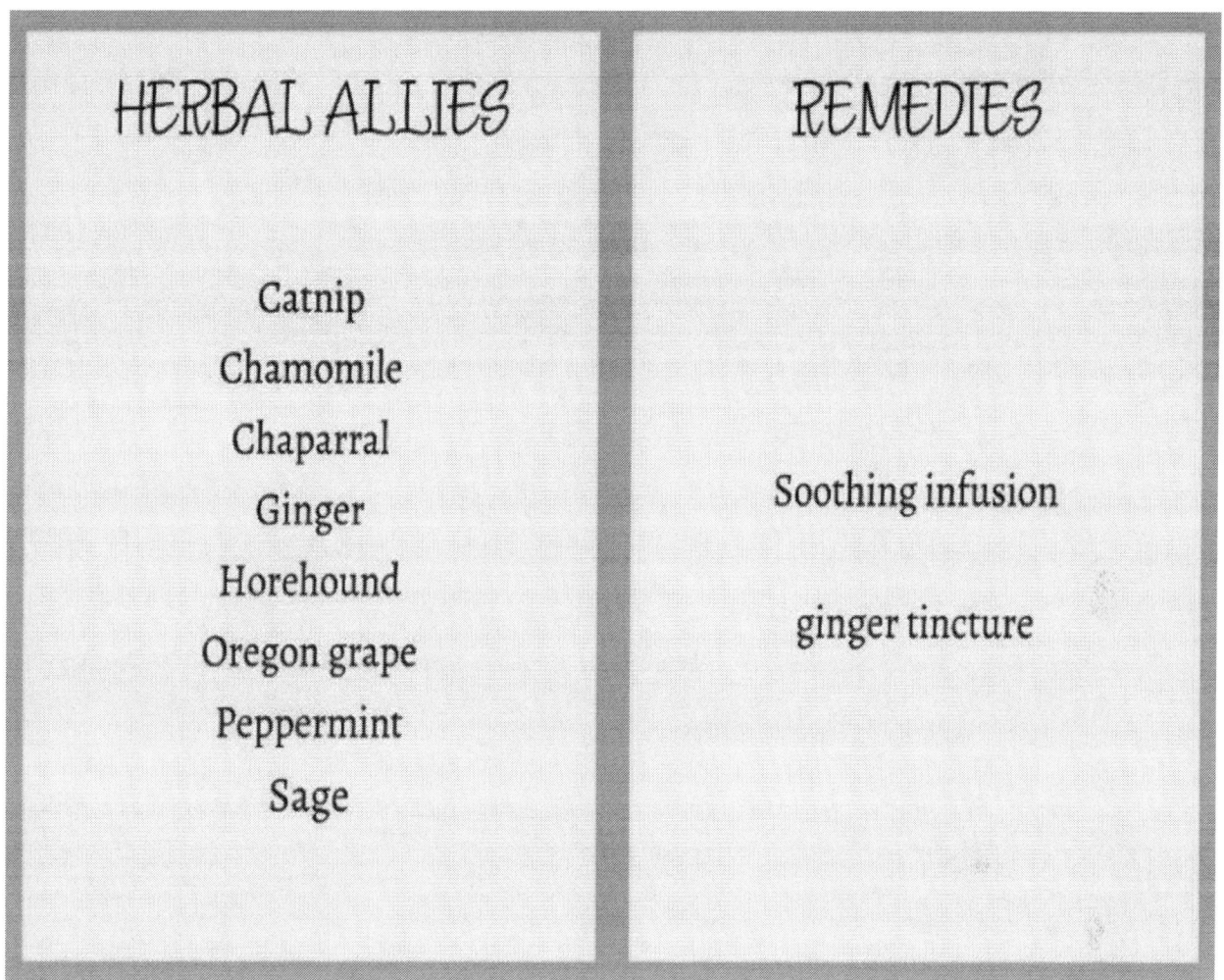

Rash

Skin rashes are visible alterations of the skin, which can occur as a result of infections, allergies, primary skin diseases, autoimmune diseases, the state of pregnancy, excessive exposure to sunlight, diabetes mellitus, skin tumors, vasculitis, adverse reactions to vaccines.

Phenomena limited to certain anatomical areas or to the whole body, rashes can be associated with: pain, swelling, itching, presence of vesicles or blisters, papules, ulcers, pustules, scales, furuncles, spots more or less close together, heat and changes in skin coloration. The treatment of rashes is based on the treatment of the triggering causes, knowledge of which requires a rather accurate diagnostic procedure.

Relevant tissue states: heat (inflammation), dryness or dampness, laxity

Relevant herbal actions: anti-inflammatory, astringent, demulcent

HERBAL ALLIES

Calendula
Echinacea
Aloe
Evening primrose
Goldenseal
Licorice root
Oregon grape
Plantain leaf
Rose
Slippery elm
Saint john's wort leaf and flower
Uva-ursi leaf
White oak
Yarrow
Yellow doc

REMEDIES

Rash lotion

Soothing salve

Soothing tea

HERBAL ALLIES

Bayberry
Black elder
Calendula flower
Echinacea
Garlic
Ginger
Ginkgo biloba
Ginseng
Goldenseal
Goldenrod
Licorice
Pine
Rose
Slippery elm
Valerian
White willow
Wild indigo
Witch hazel
Sage leaf
Thyme leaf
Uva ursi leaf

REMEDIES

Balsamic steam bath

Sinus relief infusion

Breath life tea

Sinusitis

Sinusitis is an inflammation of the sinuses, the cavities found in the bones surrounding the nose. It usually originates from a cold or allergic rhinitis, but an infection in the teeth or an abnormal conformation of the nose, such as deviation of the nasal septum, can also cause it.

Typical symptoms of sinusitis are: nasal congestion (feeling of a stuffy nose), pain in the face, under or behind the eyes, frontal headache (pain localized to the forehead), discharge from the nose for several days (7 to 10). These symptoms may be associated with: lacrimation, halitosis (bad breath), hyposmia or anosmia (difficulty or inability to smell), oily cough, fever, when the infection spreads beyond the sinuses.

Mucus buildup and the resulting pressure on the sinuses are the main cause of the pain that characterizes sinusitis.

Relevant tissue states: heat (inflammation), laxity (mucous membranes)

Relevant herbal actions: antifungal, anti-inflammatory, antimicrobial, astringent, decongestant, demulcent

Sore Throat

The throat is a fairly delicate area of our body and when it is affected it is almost always due to an upper respiratory tract infection, whether bacterial or viral.

The viral cause is the most common and follows a seasonal pattern, and winter is the season during which we get sick more easily. Closed and unventilated environments, little attention in touching eyes, nose and mouth are an assist to the virus that is highly contagious and spreads by air, but is also able to resist on surfaces.

Different is the bacterial load, which remains unchanged even in the warm months. For this reason, it is possible to suffer from a sore throat even in the summer months. In these cases, the bacterium responsible for the sore throat usually belongs to the streptococci family.

Dry and reddened throat, burning sensation and difficulty in swallowing are the classic symptoms of sore throat, whose inflammation concerns the first tract of the respiratory tract, the pharynx, which is called pharyngitis.

Relevant tissue states: heat (inflammation), dryness or dampness

Relevant herbal actions: anti-inflammatory, antimicrobial, astringent, demulcent, mucous membrane tonic (see the table at next page)

Herbal Allies for Sore Throat

HERBAL ALLIES	REMEDIES
Balsam fir Bayberry Black elder Blue vervain Cayenne Echinacea Ginger Goldenrod Indian root Licorice root Sage leaf Seneca snakerooot Slippery elm Sumac Wild cherry Witch Hazel	Throat soothing gargle Troath soothing tea Immunostimulating tea

Sprains and Strains

A sprain affects a joint and represents the temporary and reversible loss of congruity of the bony segments that constitute it. It may be accompanied by injury to the passive restraining structures, joint capsule and ligaments, or extend to tendon and bone structures. Such a traumatic condition is usually caused by sudden and extreme movement beyond the normal range of motionof the joint.

A strain is defined as a painful condition caused by inflammation, overuse (orunbalanced), and overstretching (or tearing) of one or more of these components: muscles, tendons, and joints.

Relevant tissue states: heat (inflammation), tension and/or laxity

HERBAL ALLIES	REMEDIES
Bilberry Black cohosh Currant Ginkgo biloba Goldenrod leaf and flower Horsetail Licorice root Meadowsweet flower Peppermint e.oil Raspberry Saint john's wort Valerian White willow Wintergreen	Injury salve Pain relief tea

Relevant herbal actions: anti-inflammatory, circulatory stimulant, connective tissue lubricant, lymphatic, nerve tropho-restorative, vulnerary

Stress

Stress can be defined as a response of the organism to events and demands placed on it. It is accompanied by physiological, biochemical, cognitive and behavioral changes. Not all events are perceived as stressors and in equal measure by all individuals.

The English term "stress" (close to the Latin "strictus") means "effort, tension, pressure" but also "push", is therefore characterized by a double meaning. In fact, what we commonly call "stress", with a negative meaning, refers to the concept of distress, a negative and problematic form of stress that involves anxiety, tension and worry.

Negative, uncontrollable, unpredictable, ambiguous, and threatening events tend to be the best candidates for the onset of (di)stress. The Covid-19 pandemic in this respect fully meets the criteria of a negative stressful event. On the other hand, a fair amount of stress can be beneficial as it can push, motivate and guide people to achieve their goals. This type of stress is referred to as eustress because of its beneficial stimulatory characteristics.

Depending on the duration of the stressor event, we can talk about: acute stress, if the event-stimulus occurs in a timely manner for a limited time, chronic stress, if the event-stimulus persists for a prolonged period of time, chronic intermittent stress, if the event-stimulus occurs regularly, making predictable over time. The best tool to fight off the effects of stress is a well-balanced diet and lifestyle.

Relevant tissue states: heat (agitation), tension

Relevant herbal actions: adaptogen, nervine, relaxant, sedative

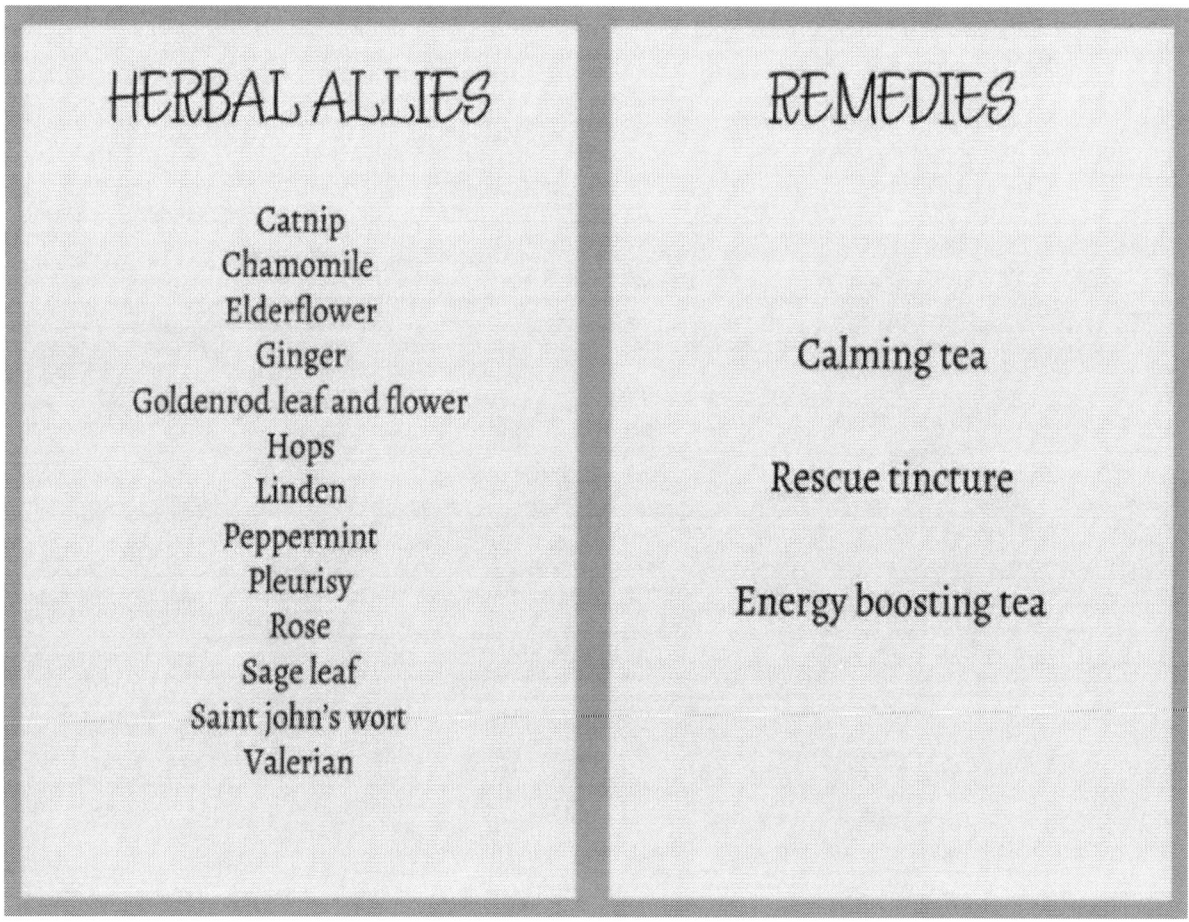

Herbal Allies for Stress

Wounds

A wound is an injury to the superficial layer of the skin, sometimes with associated blood loss.

There are abrasions (superficial lesions of the skin caused by a trauma that strikes the surface of the body, without blood loss), excoriations (superficial lesions of the skin with blood loss), puncture wounds (caused by sharp objects), cutting wounds (caused by sharp objects, with regular edges), lacerated wounds (caused by sharp objects, with irregular edges, sometimes unstuck) and lacerocontact wounds (caused by sharp objects, with irregular edges and with underlying contusion).

When there is no blood loss (as in abrasions) healing usually occurs spontaneously within a few days. It will be sufficient to disinfect the part. Incase there is a slight leakage of blood (as in excoriations) it will be good to

wash and disinfect the wound with care and protect it with a plaster.

Depending on the course, wounds are distinguished in acute wounds andchronic wounds.

Relevant tissue states: heat (inflammation)

Relevant herbal actions: antimicrobial, astringent, emollient, lymphatic, vulnerary (see the table at next page)

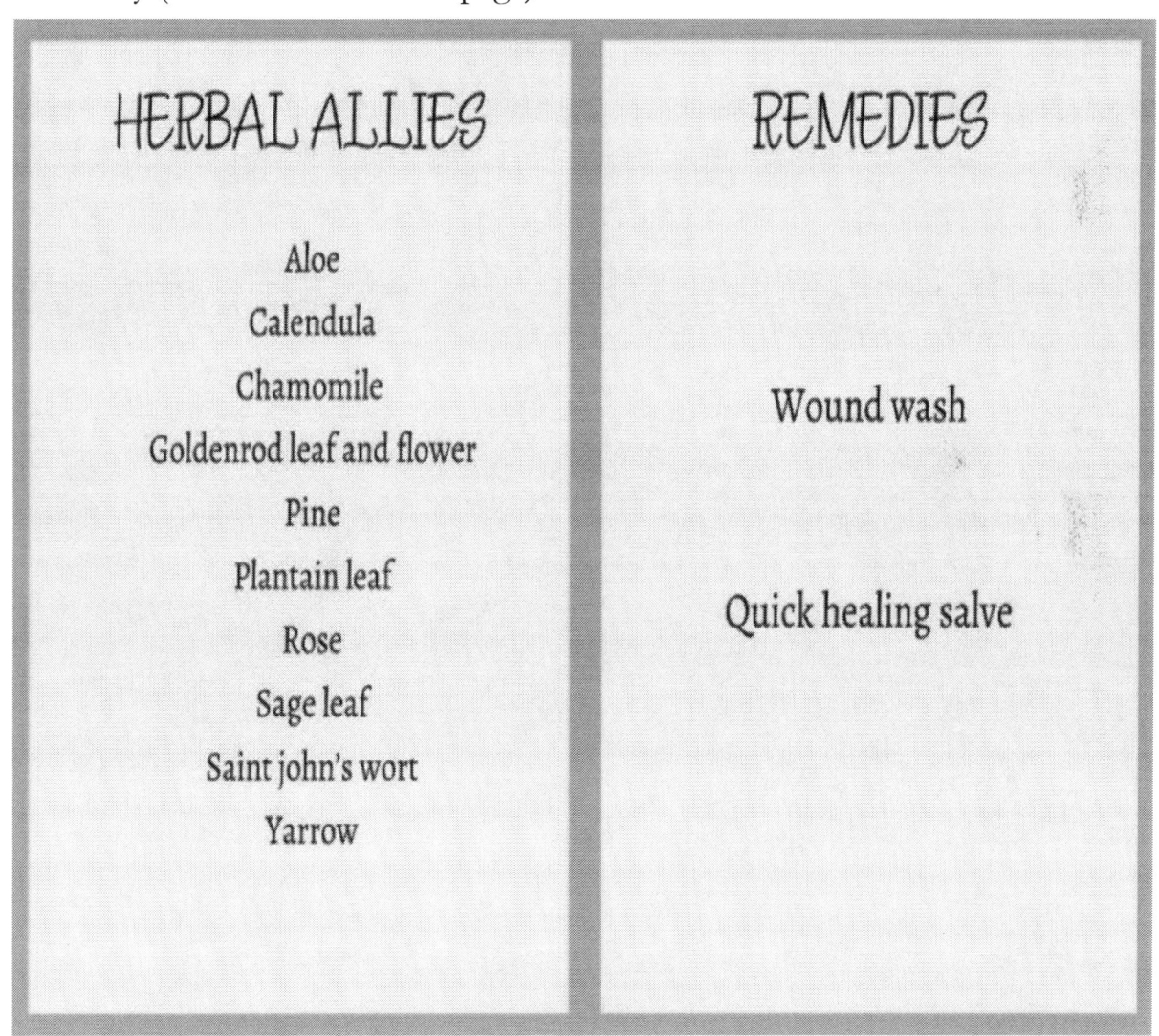

HERBAL ALLIES	REMEDIES
Aloe Calendula Chamomile Goldenrod leaf and flower Pine Plantain leaf Rose Sage leaf Saint john's wort Yarrow	Wound wash Quick healing salve

Herbal Allies for Wounds

CONCLUSION

Get Your Bonus Now:

Made in United States
Orlando, FL
29 November 2023

39745867R10191